MW01004017

Characteristics of Games

Characteristics of Games

George Skaff Elias, Richard Garfield, and K. Robert Gutschera

foreword by Eric Zimmerman

drawings by Peter Whitley

The MIT Press
Cambridge, Massachusetts
London, England

For information about special quantity discounts, please email special_sales@mitpress.mit.edu

This book was set in Stone Sans and Stone Serif by Toppan Best-set Premedia Limited. Printed and bound in the United States of America.

Library of Congress Cataloging-in-Publication Data

Elias, George Skaff.
Characteristics of games / George Skaff Elias, Richard Garfield, and K. Robert Gutschera ; foreword by Eric Zimmerman ; drawings by Peter Whitley.
p. cm.
Includes bibliographical references and index.
ISBN 978-0-262-01713-8 (hardcover : alk. paper)
1. Games—Design and construction. 2. Games—Rules. 3. Game theory. I. Garfield, Richard. II. Gutschera, Karl Robert, 1964– III. Title.
GV1230.E38 2012
793—dc23

2011031296

10 9 8 7 6 5 4 3 2

To Sadie, Ike, and Lucy, to Terry and Schuyler, and to Karl and Deborah Gutschera
And to the memory of Martin Gardner

Contents

Foreword

When Richard, Robert, and Skaff approached me about writing the foreword for their book and I cracked the first pages of the manuscript, I must admit I was taken by surprise. The book they had written goes against the grain.

Unlike the spate of publications about games hitting shelves over the last few years, *Characteristics of Games* is not brimming with promises about how games are going to change the world. This book is not going to tell you how games are going to revolutionize education, business, society, or other aspects of Life as We Know It.

There is nothing wrong with those kinds of books. But they often miss the trees for the forest. In promising a grand purpose and glorious future for games, they generally neglect to look closely at games themselves.

Characteristics of Games is different. It is a meticulous book about the design of games by some of the legendary craftsmen of the form. It is an investigation into the *details* of games—the nuts-and-bolts minutiae of how games actually work.

As book readers go, I swing both ways. I can enjoy riding high on the hype about games—because, truth be told, I *do* believe that games represent the most vital and vibrant form of culture today, and that they have the power to transform our society in ways we can scarcely imagine.

But getting there isn't going to happen by reading books about how great they are. It is going to happen through the rigorous work of brilliant designers and theoreticians, slowly unlocking the great secrets of games. The book you hold in your hands charts just this kind of journey; *Characteristics of Games* may say less, but do more.

Games have a very long history—from their roots in the play of higher mammals, to ancient sports and games of millennia past, up through today's complex boardgames and videogames. Although we find ourselves in a time when games seem newly relevant, the truth is that games are nothing new. As a wellspring of pleasure, games are a cultural universal: our species, it seems, has always liked to play them.

But despite their seductive appeal, the nerdy little secret of games is that they are intensely mathematical. Games as a form of culture have a unique relationship to math—to systems, structures, and numbers. And so it's no surprise that *Characteristics of Games*, as a detailed study of the form, is intensely analytical.

The question is, can systems be dramatic? Can math be breathtaking? Can numbers move your soul? If you study, or play, or make games with any kind of depth—whether your game is poker, basketball, *Scrabble*, *Tetris*, or *Halo*—you already know the answer.

So let this be a warning: playing a game may be an exercise in pleasure, but this book is not easy reading. It is difficult fun, stuffed with hard-won insights that are not laid out on a silver platter for easy consumption. But if you take the time, this book will open your eyes to the beauty of games.

The authors command a formidable expertise in the way games work, and a charming fearlessness for taking on what seem like fools' errands. They tackle the minefield of measuring the amount of skill and luck in a game: how would you compare, for example, chess versus poker versus roulette—not just in general terms but in specific numerical ratings? Or another: charting the density of choices in a game over time, to understand how climax and denouement take shape in the system of a boardgame, or a real-time strategy game, or an MMO. And they actually make graphs.

Analytical? Certainly. But don't let their logical style fool you. There is a passion beating beneath these chapters. Its relentless rigor is its strength, breaking through the numerical surfaces of games to the universes of pleasure swimming underneath.

You may still be asking yourself about the relevance of a book like *Characteristics of Games*. It may have insight, but is it useful beyond communities of expert players, hardcore fans, critics, scholars, or game designers?

To answer, let me take another example: a fundamental phenomenon of games that the authors call the catch-up. It represents a deep paradox of play: to stay engaged, game players need to feel that the possibility exists for them to win, even up until the very end of a game (would you really keep on playing if you knew you were going to lose?). But at the same time players can't feel that only the end of the game matters—they need to sense that their actions have meaning from the very start, that all of their choices accumulate in a way that brings them logically and steadily to a knowable conclusion.

Does this impossible idea—that a game must keep hope alive for a reversal of fortune, even while reassuring players that everything they do has a place in a fixed progression—have relevance outside of game design? Absolutely. This little drama of free will and fate plays out in every game, but it also rears its head in questions of economics and the psychology of choice, in designing behaviors across massive online social networks, and in classic philosophical problems of ethics and responsibility—such as motivating voters to participate in a democracy. Every game is a context for reflection, a laboratory for thinking about thinking.

So, yes, games are relevant to life outside the game—nearly infinitely so. But games shouldn't be thought of as valuable because they are relevant to other fields of research. Above and beyond any definable utility, games are valuable because they are a fundamental form of human expression. Like making music or telling stories, playing games is an activity that connects us more deeply to who we are.

So believe the hype about games, but understand that realizing their potential means setting aside grand visions and glittering surfaces. Instead, just play—spectate, participate, analyze, modify, design. This book is here to help you do just that: play more deeply.

And it's damn hard to argue against putting more play into the world.

Eric Zimmerman

Preface

This book is meant for anyone interested in games: designers, reviewers, critics, and players. We hope that anyone who looks at games and wonders how to make them better, or wants to understand more clearly how they work, will get something out of it. Our own background is that of game players and game designers rather than academicians or reviewers, and that is the approach we take here. It is not a "how-to" book on game design, though, but a way of looking critically at games and talking intelligently about them. In short, one can think of *Characteristics of Games* as a framework for game analysis from the point of view of a game designer.

From our point of view, games include boardgames, card games, sports, computer games, and many other kinds of games—we mean to be inclusive. We think these different genres of games have many things to teach each other. For example, card games provide many good examples of the power of standards, sports are strong at supporting spectation as well as direct participation, and boardgames have wrestled extensively with the issues arising from multiple independent players.

A word of warning, though: some topics that might seem central to someone whose main interest is in computer games, say, or in sports, might receive a less thorough treatment than they would in a book entirely about that subject. For example, single-player games are central to computer gaming, but are rather a special case when viewed from the vantage point of gaming as a whole—we discuss them, but not nearly in the depth a book about computer gaming would.[1] We hope the gain from our broader point of view makes up for this inevitable loss of detail.

Given our intended scope, we choose examples from a great many different genres as we discuss various issues. We try to pick well-known games within these genres

1. Similar remarks apply regarding the briefness of our treatment of story in games and of griefing, both of which are especially prominent in computer games.

whenever possible, so as to lighten the burden on the reader. Also, in appendix C we have a list of games referred to in the text, with brief descriptions of each. The reader with a broad experience of games, and a broad view of what gaming is, will be more likely to find our book congenial reading.

Other than presupposing an interest in games, and at least some familiarity with them, this book has no formal prerequisites. There are occasional mathematical digressions for which a familiarity with high school algebra would be helpful, but these can by and large be skipped with no loss of continuity. In particular, this book is by no means a book about mathematical game theory, although we do give brief surveys of its two main branches (with references for the interested reader) in the first two appendixes.

The different chapters are largely independent, and readers are encouraged to read start to finish or as their interests take them. It is perhaps worth beginning with chapter 1 ("Basics") because some terminology is introduced there that's used throughout the book. Determined readers can ignore this advice, though, and look up any unfamiliar terms as they go.

This book is based on a course, also titled *Characteristics of Games,* taught by the authors at the University of Washington from 2006 to 2009.

About the Exercises

Exercises are included throughout the book. Depending on the class's background, some exercises may need modifying, most commonly by replacing a game in the exercise that the students don't know with a game that they do. Some exercises may require a little research for students lacking certain bits of background information (e.g., the three-act narrative structure is mentioned in one exercise), but in most cases simple web searches should suffice to fill any holes. For some simpler games mentioned frequently in the exercises (such as werewolf and *Survivor*), it may be useful to have the students play (or watch) the game during class or as an assignment. Gaining familiarity with other games (e.g., bridge or go) will take more effort, but it can be well worth it for the serious student of games. In general, though, we have avoided exercises that require familiarity with specific complex games, especially ones many students may not play.

A few exercises (especially those in chapter 5, "Indeterminacy") require some mathematical skills, but nothing beyond some algebra and some basic probability. Instructors may assign these exercises to students with the appropriate background; in a longer course it may even be practical to teach some of the relevant mathematics—all of which will in any case be useful to anyone serious about games. In a course where further mathematical analysis of games is desired, the references in appendixes A and

B may prove helpful (we particularly recommend Bewersdorff's excellent survey of the mathematics of games).

Many of the exercises make good in-class discussion topics as well, and instructors are encouraged to spend some class time in this manner. And, of course, the exercises here should be supplemented by larger projects, such as designing a complete game (paper games are sometimes more suitable than electronic ones for this purpose), giving detailed critiques of existing games, and so on.

Acknowledgments

The authors would like to thank Julie Villegas and especially Wanda Gregory at the University of Washington for helping us start the course on which this book is based. Thanks also to our teaching assistant Jonathon Loucks, and to all of our students for serving as willing, and even enthusiastic, guinea pigs.

Timothy Chow and David Reiley gave many helpful comments, as did the three anonymous reviewers. We would also like to thank Hilary Ross and Adam Dixon at Wizards of the Coast for their help.

Many thanks to the gang at the Pit, who, while not directly involved in the book, formed the best working environment a game designer could hope to inhabit.

The third author would like to thank Bill Rose, Jason Robar, and David Brevik for being generous with time for the course and the book, and Eleanor Rieffel for advice and support with the wild world of academic publishing. Thanks also to the Chit-Chat Café and the Honey Bear Bakery. And last of all, but also first of all, thanks to Sandy, Scotte, Jan, Sean, Eric, Judy, Sarah, Daryl, Dan, and all the rest of the original gaming group.

Introduction

Figure I.1
©iStockphoto.com/Baris Simsek

Figure I.2
©iStockphoto.com/Pamela Moore

Figure I.3
©iStockphoto.com/Jess Wiberg

Relatively little scholarly work has been written about games compared with the amount produced on other cultural phenomena of similar size such as films.

Historically most of the material on games, such as Huizinga's *Homo Ludens* or Caillois's *Man, Play, and Games*, has focused on the place of games in society, and thus on historical, sociological, and cultural issues. Less attention has been paid to the games themselves, as games: what it is like to play them, what features differentiate one game from another, or what features make one game a more or less enjoyable experience for its players. Other books, such as Bell's *Board and Table Games from Many Civilizations*, Murray's *A History of Board-Games Other Than Chess*, or Parlett's various books on boardgames and card games, are primarily catalogs of game rules or historical treatments—excellent references, but without much analysis of games as a whole. Later academic work, such as that of Avedon and Sutton-Smith in the 1960s and 1970s, continued to focus largely on historical and cultural issues.

Today most of the published material on games comes from the computer gaming industry, in the form of books with titles like *Secrets of Game Programming in C++*. These books tend to focus on practical advice relevant to computer gaming, concerning issues such as programming or project management (important exceptions include

Crawford's various books and Schell's *The Art of Game Design*, which focus on the process of game design itself), rather than the more general approach we hope to pursue. There are also a growing number of academic titles, often collections of essays, such as Cassell and Jenkins's *From Barbie to Mortal Kombat* or Wolf and Perron's *The Video Game Theory Reader*. These books tend to have a somewhat different approach from ours, though, with more sociological and cultural issues and less gameplay-specific analysis; they also tend to focus on computer games. One notable exception is Salen and Zimmerman's *Rules of Play*, which has a great deal of gameplay discussion and devotes considerable space to boardgames and card games.

Our intention is to focus more on issues intrinsic to the games themselves, the kinds of topics that game players or game designers often discuss but rarely write down.[1] Again, to take film as an example, when students come to the university to study film, they arrive having a rough familiarity with a large number of basic narrative concepts: character, plot, theme, irony, foreshadowing, and a host of others.[2] Every subject has its own collection of basic concepts, but those belonging to games have been largely neglected until recently, and much past study of games has attempted to adopt the concepts belonging more properly to other disciplines. There is, of course, a place for the interdisciplinary approach, but it's no substitute for developing the basic concepts peculiar to the discipline under discussion. That development for games is now beginning, and our hope is to assist in the process with this book. We hope it will help lead to a better understanding of games as games, and pave the way for more advanced work to follow.

Since so little has been done (at least in any structured way), this work will necessarily take a fairly high-level view. Many of the topics we cover could be books of their own. We hope to provide an overall framework and some basic discussion of a number of topics, but we do not by any means have the last word in any of these areas. To use the film analogy again, this is not an advanced work of film criticism; rather, it's an attempt to explain in a basic way character, plot, foreshadowing, and similar concepts. Although we can't hope to cover everything in as much depth as we'd like, we have attempted to include all the topics we see as most important.

General Approach

Although we are attempting to develop a vocabulary for games, we are not interested in defining terms per se, but rather in choosing some topics for discussion and beginning the discussion on those topics. Our approach is not primarily academic—all three

1. Some discussion can be found on the Internet, though—see, for example http://www.sirlin.net, http://www.boardgamegeek.com, or http://www.costik.com/weblog/.

2. These particular concepts are of limited use when studying games; see section 7.2 on conceit and motif.

of us are game designers first and academicians second, and that is the approach we are taking. What we are writing here is very much a continuation of the kinds of discussions we as game designers have had with each other and with other designers and thoughtful players of games.

In general, we tend to be descriptive rather than prescriptive—we are trying to start a conversation about games, not write a how-to guide (although we believe a better understanding of games should lead to better games, so we hope this book will prove useful to game designers in that sense). Games are a big field, and different people like different kinds of games, which is a fine thing. Still, though, we have our own preferences and biases, and when we feel one approach is better than another we'll say so. Usually, though, we prefer to talk about how this or that game feature makes a game more suitable for this or that audience.

Characteristics

Our discussion is centered around the concept of the *characteristics* of games: general groups of features that give a high-level description of the sort of game it is. These are the sorts of features another player might ask a friend about (or that the back of the box might mention, if it's a boardgame)[3] before agreeing to play a game: How many players does it take? How long does it take to play? Is there a lot of luck in the game? Typically answers to questions like these are a lot more useful than a description of the rules of the game.

There are some questions along these lines that are harder to phrase, and that only fairly advanced players are likely to ask (although many players will notice them when things go amiss): How possible is it for a losing player to catch up? Do you spend a lot of time waiting for your turn to come? Are there a lot of difficult or boring calculations you're forced to make if you want to be at all competitive? What information in the game is hidden from the players? Is there danger of a player who is out of contention determining, on a whim, which other player will win the game?

Sometimes answers to these questions appear in disguise. For example, if someone asks "what kind of game is it?" and is told "it's a card game," she is getting, in one fell swoop, a host of information about how long the game is likely to last, how much luck there may be, and various other game characteristics. (And indeed, if the game turned out to be played with small thin pieces of cardboard but otherwise had nothing in common with any card game, the questioner would surely feel misled.)

We're primarily interested in "player-centric" questions like these, rather than in issues of sociology, history, or aesthetics—although such issues come up in our discussions, and we address them to some extent.

3. Oddly enough, computer games tend to be much worse at giving this kind of basic information to potential customers.

Our list of characteristics is not meant to be final or definitive. Not all characteristics will be relevant to all games, and we don't claim the list is exhaustive. Some characteristics could perhaps be split into two, or different ones combined—the characteristics are in no way "official" but simply our way of structuring a discussion about games.

Exercise I.1: In about fifty words, describe a game to a friend of yours in an attempt to convince your friend to play.

Computer Games and Deliberate Design

For us, computer games are just one more kind of game. As a genre, computer games have their own issues and problems, but so do boardgames, or card games, or sports. As stated above, we're happy to draw on all these genres for topics for discussion and for specific examples.

However, computer games are different from other game genres in one very important way: they are almost all deliberately designed. There are card games and boardgames that have been designed by specific people, but always against a backdrop of well-known "classic" games that have evolved over time.

One can think of the distinction between designed games and evolved games as parallel to that between modern novels, with specific authors, and ancient oral poetry or folktales. Perhaps an even better parallel is the distinction between modern architecture and traditional architecture: as Christopher Alexander discusses in *Notes on the Synthesis of Form*,[4] even very intelligent people can have trouble designing complex systems as good as ones that have evolved gradually over time.

Our feeling is that these classic games and sports, which have evolved through an unselfconscious process, are an especially good source of examples for the modern-day deliberate game designer. Many problems that crop up repeatedly in deliberately designed games have been "evolved out" of classic games. Indeed, for many characteristics one can go to modern games for examples of problems, and classic games for examples of solutions—not because ancient people were geniuses, but because the classic games that survive today have undergone a long process of evolution and of weeding out.

On Definitions, of "Game" and Other Things

It is common to begin a treatise on games with a definition of games. Our feeling is that such an approach is of limited use.

4. See especially chapters 4 and 5.

Words (and the concepts they represent) as people actually use them do not possess necessary and sufficient conditions that define their boundaries.[5] There are no precise definitions of complex concepts like "game," no definitions that will include all things that people accept as games and exclude all things that people reject. Instead, as Wittgenstein pointed out, a category like "game" includes a great many different things that have a family resemblance rather than exact boundaries:

> There is the tendency to look for something in common to all the entities which we commonly subsume under a general term. We are inclined to think that there must be something in common to all games, say, and that this common property is the justification for applying the general term "game" to the various games; whereas games form a *family* the members of which have family likenesses. Some of them have the same nose, others the same eyebrows and others again the same way of walking; and these likenesses overlap.[6]

Some members of the family of games can be thought of as "especially good examples of games," like chess or hearts. Some other games are still clearly games, but less central: perhaps *Settlers of Catan* or the word game ghost. Other things are so marginal that one doesn't often use the word *game* to describe them: a footrace or a crossword puzzle. Yet people typically refer to, say, *Mario Kart* or *Bejeweled* as games. Are they so different? Perhaps people call them games just because they're on a computer. But you can do a crossword puzzle on a computer—does it then become a game?

5. For a survey of this line of thinking about conceptual and linguistic categories, see George Lakoff's *Women, Fire, and Dangerous Things,* especially chap. 2, "From Wittgenstein to Rosch."

6. *The Blue Book,* 17. Another related passage, from *Philosophical Investigations,* is worth quoting at length:

> 66. Consider for example the proceedings that we call "games." I mean board-games, card-games, ball-games, Olympic games, and so on. What is common to them all?—Don't say: "There *must* be something common, or they would not be called 'games'"—but *look and see* whether there is anything common on all.—For if you look at them you will not see something that is common to all, but similarities, relationships, and a whole series of them at that. To repeat: don't think, but look!—Look for example at board-games, with their multifarious relationships. Now pass to card-games; here your find many correspondences with the first group, but many common features drop out, and others appear. When we pass next to ball-games, much that is common is retained, but much is lost.—Are they all "amusing"? Compare chess with noughts and crosses. Or is there always winning and losing, or competition between players? Think of patience. In ball-games there is winning and losing; but when a child throws his ball at the wall and catches it again, this feature has disappeared. Look at the parts played by skill and luck; and at the difference between skill in chess and skill in tennis. Think now of games like ring-a-ring-a-roses; here is the element of amusement, but how many other characteristic features have disappeared! And we can go through the many, many other groups of games in the same way; can see how similarities crop up and disappear.
>
> And the result of this examination is: we see a complicated network of similarities overlapping and crisscrossing: sometimes overall similarities, sometimes similarities of detail.
>
> 67. I can think of no better expression to characterize these similarities than "family resemblances"; for the various resemblances between members of a family: build, features, color of eyes, gait, temperament, etc., etc. overlap and criss-cross in the same way.—And I shall say: "games" form a family.

Even a good definition of game, like Salen and Zimmerman's carefully constructed "A game is a system in which players engage in an artificial conflict, defined by rules, that results in a quantifiable outcome," necessarily suffers from these difficulties of definition. As Salen and Zimmerman themselves point out, things like crossword puzzles, which people generally do not call "games," do meet the definition, and things like *Dungeons & Dragons*, which people do call a "game," arguably do not. Or consider the stock market—is it a game under this definition? Perhaps one should take *artificial* to mean, among other things, that the game is being done "for fun" in some sense, not as part of a serious purpose such as making a living. This approach would exclude the stock market, at least for most people. But then is professional baseball not a game, while amateur baseball is? None of these are faults with this particular definition so much as they are limits to the definitional enterprise.

Asking "Is X a game?" (or worse yet, "Is X *really* a game?") is not a useful question when done with the idea that there is a "right answer" one must find, although it can be useful as a mental exercise. Searching for a definition that exactly separates games from nongames is, for our purposes at least, not helpful, and finding such a definition is ultimately not possible. The subject matter of our book is games in the common sense of the word, and we take our examples largely from boardgames, card games, computer games, and sports (both sports that tend to have the word *game* attached to them and sports that do not), but we will take examples from other activities when it seems enlightening to do so, without worrying too much about whether they are "really" games. In particular, we utterly reject the point of view that some games are worse than others because they are "not really games": games can be better or worse than others for all kinds of reasons, but adherence to some definition of what is a "real game" is not one of them.

In other words, for us a "game" is whatever is labeled a game in common parlance. Our subject matter is these games and whatever other activities are close enough to them to be fruitfully joined to them in discussion. We exclude the games without formal rules that very small children play (e.g., "playing house" or swinging);[7] we include most sports, even those such as footraces where the label "game" is not generally used, and we include activities like crossword puzzles that we find not fundamentally different from, say, card solitaire or *Minesweeper*. These inclusions and exclusions are not meant to be a formal definition of game, but merely a description of the subject matter we discuss.[8]

Our skeptical point of view on definitions carries over into other discussions of category as well. In general, we are not greatly concerned with questions of the type

7. See Caillois's *Man, Play, and Games*, 168, for a discussion of games with and without rules.

8. What Wittgenstein calls an "ostensive definition" (see, e.g., *Philosophical Investigations*, chaps. 27–30): pointing to the thing you mean as a way of defining it.

"Is X in category A or category B?" When we give definitions of concepts, it's in order to be able to discuss them, and we accept that there will be borderline cases, cases that may or may not fall inside the definition. Such borderline cases are often interesting to discuss, but deciding on which side of the border they fall is moot. So, for example, the question "Is *Risk* a political game?" is not really the right question—the correct question (for which the aforementioned is often a shorthand) is more along the lines of "How political is *Risk*?" or "What can you say about politics in *Risk*?"

If one were to explore the meaning of the word *game*, a better approach than trying to find necessary and sufficient conditions might be to list various properties that push an activity in the direction of being gamelike—in other words, to find some of the family resemblances. For example, many games involve making tactical decisions (chess, football, and gin do; *Candyland* or a footrace do not). Many games are played on a board (chess and *Candyland* are; gin, football, and a footrace are not). Typically people refer to football, chess, and *Candyland* as games, but not a footrace—arguably because the former do have "enough" of the family properties of games, but a footrace does not. Even with this approach, though, one shouldn't expect an exact procedure for determining what is and isn't a "game." In any case, this enterprise may well teach one more about linguistics than about games, and it is not something we will undertake here.[9]

If *game* is a difficult term to come to grips with, *art* is even tougher. The classic question of "Are games art?" is not one we intend to address. For us, it seems to be more a question about words (and particularly about the meaning of the word *art*) than a question about games. We are doubtful whether the question can be answered even in principle. In any case, it is a question very different from the ones that will concern us here.

Formal Definitions: Orthogame and Agential

Although trying to find exact boundaries for existing English categories is not useful, occasionally defining new words is useful. If there's no good word for something already, sometimes one must make something up. We have no objection to definitions in this sense (this is defining in the sense that mathematicians do it: declaring what a word means for purposes of a subsequent discussion, rather than trying to find the "true definition" of some preexisting word).

In general, we prefer to use existing terms where possible, but there are a few terms that we haven't found available.

9. For readers interested in the various attempts to define the term *game*, there is an excellent survey of a number of different definitions that have been offered over the years in Salen and Zimmerman's *Rules of Play*, 71–83.

The first is *orthogame*,[10] which we define as a game for two or more players, with rules that result in a ranking or weighting of the players, and done for entertainment. Explicit winners or losers, scores, or time to completion all count as rankings or weightings—the point is there is something explicit to tell you how well you've performed.

This definition is meant to exclude games like *Dungeons & Dragons* or *World of Warcraft*, where there is not an explicit win condition, and players may have many different goals.[11] Also excluded, due to the "done for entertainment" clause, are professional military simulations and other "serious games."[12] In general, our focus is on orthogames, but we will occasionally discuss nonorthogames as well (games that violate the ranking/weighting condition frequently, games that violate the entertainment condition rarely).

Many characteristics of a game depend on its audience as much as on the game itself. A game might be played quickly or slowly, as a two-player game or as a multiplayer game, casually or seriously, all depending on the pool of players. We'll say a characteristic is *systemic* if it depends mainly on the game as a system (e.g., on the rules) and *agential* if it depends primarily on the player base. (We derive the latter term from the use one sees occasionally of the term *agent* to mean a player in a game; one can think of *agential* as a more euphonic version of "player-ential.") Although our default set of players is "all the players in the world," we'll sometimes discuss a specific subset, such as "players in Africa" or "middle-aged women with disposable incomes of over $50,000 a year." Often we'll compare two different subsets, like hardcore players versus casual players, or wealthy players versus poorer ones.

One can think of a game's characteristics as depending on the combination of the game itself and the people who play it. Since player populations are changing all the time, the game's characteristics can change without any systemic feature of the game changing.

The terms agential and systemic are very much relative: hardly any property is purely one or the other. For example, there are certainly systemic reasons that a game of chess takes longer to play than a game of tic-tac-toe, but there are agential consid-

10. *Ortho-* from the Greek word meaning "straight" or "correct," the idea being that orthogames are the most "normal" or "usual" kind of game.

11. Although RPGs and MMOs have plenty of numbers in them, no one number is completely authoritative in the sense that you "win the game" if you have the highest score in that number. One player might be glad to have reached a certain level, another player might be happy to have a large amount of gold, and yet another player might care most about the items she has and how powerful they are.

12. Although some issues we discuss in this book will be relevant to simulations and "serious games," our focus is on games played for fun. We don't generally concern ourselves with features that might be needed to increase the educational value or simulational accuracy of a game.

erations in the length of playtime as well—some playgroups consistently finish games of chess very quickly, other groups will regularly take hours. The fact that horse racing has a lot of rich people involved in it is an agential property, but there are systemic reasons supporting it (you need a horse to play, and poor people in the West may find it hard to keep horses).[13]

So claims such as "this characteristic is agential" should be read as "this characteristic has a lot of agential properties, which we'll now discuss." The point is not to classify all characteristics as either agential or systemic, but rather, for each characteristic, to look at its agential and systemic properties. Characteristics are more or less agential or systemic, not all one or all the other. In particular, beware of the frame of mind where everything seems systemic ("after all, everything stems ultimately from the properties of the game system, right?") or everything seems agential ("it all depends on how people choose to react to it, after all"). While there's some theoretical truth to each of these points of view, neither is much use for analyzing games and drawing distinctions between them.

Minor Conventions in the Text

We sometimes use "he" and sometimes "she" when referring to people (typically players of games). Often we use both as a way of differentiating two different players. Nothing is meant by any particular gender assignment beyond the fact that "he" and "she" are not the same person.

Our statements (if they are correct at all) are more often generally true as opposed to being true without exceptions. In a field as large and varied as gaming, there will be exceptions to almost every rule. We may point out some of these exceptions if they seem interesting or enlightening, but often we leave it to the reader to discover them. It is very tedious always to repeat phrases such as "generally," "for the most part," and "with very few exceptions," so while we will resort to them occasionally for emphasis, the absence of such phrases should not be taken to mean that we are claiming a statement holds in every single case.

We follow the American English convention in using *soccer* for European football and *football* for the rugbylike game played primarily in the United States and Canada.

When we discuss specific game examples, it is usually the case that the analysis applies to other games of that genre (e.g., we may use *Starcraft* as a stand-in for RTS games generally, or hearts as a stand-in for trick-taking card games). We do this because concrete examples are easier and more enjoyable to follow than very abstract statements about categories. In most cases, a moment's thought should make it clear how

13. In some parts of the Third World, many people have horses, and sports involving horses there are not the exclusive province of the wealthy.

much the remarks about that game extend to others—when it is problematic, we will try to call it out.

Of course, when we criticize a game on some narrow grounds, that doesn't mean we think it is a bad game. (In general, we choose games we like as examples.) In any case, we are not intending to rate or evaluate games as good or bad—we are interested in using the examples to illustrate the general principle. Also, a game can be lacking in an area without it being the case that "fixing" that lack would improve it—for example, chess has weak "atoms" (satisfying chunks of play shorter than a full game), but trying to introduce stronger atoms to chess would not necessarily improve the game. In other words, certain weaknesses may need to be accepted to get other strengths.

In general, we take the point of view that players are trying to win, and that part of the designer's task is to make the game enjoyable under the stresses of players' attempts to win. So when we speak of heuristics, balance, strategic collapse, politics, and so on, the background assumption is that most often, players will want to win and will engage in behaviors that help them do so. This is not to deny that players have many other motivations as well (killing time, socializing, aesthetic enjoyment of the game materials, and countless others). But even players who are playing to satisfy other motivations usually still try to win, and games shouldn't provide a bad experience when they do. Also, note for some games, especially orthogames, such as chess, "winning" is fairly clearly defined, and for others it's vaguer, or there are multiple different ideas of winning in the heads of different players, or even in the head of the same player (examples include paper RPGs, MMOs, and sandbox games like *SimCity*).

1 Basics

We begin our survey of game characteristics with three so basic that they influence all the others. The first two, length of playtime and number of players, are familiar to everyone. Anyone, when asking a friend about a game, might well ask how long it takes to play and how many players it requires. Most boardgames give this information on the back of the box. But even though this information is basic and seemingly simple, there is actually quite a bit of complexity hidden here, and we try to unpack some of it.

Our third basic characteristic, heuristics, may seem more esoteric. But by "heuristics" we simply mean the rules of thumb by which players play games ("develop your pieces" in chess or "never draw to an inside straight" in poker). When players discuss among themselves a game they know, it is these heuristics that they talk about. Given our goal of analyzing games from the point of view of thoughtful players, it's only natural that game heuristics should be a basic characteristic for us.

1.1 Characteristic: Length of Playtime

It is easy for hardcore players (including most game reviewers and game designers) to underestimate the importance of game length and the cost a long playtime imposes on players, especially more casual ones. But game length is probably one of the most important characteristics people use when deciding whether to play a game: picture someone saying to a friend "want to come over and play a game?" The answer is very likely to depend on how long that game takes to play. And if the game is going to be played in some specific time slot—over lunch, say—the players will want to pick a game that can be played comfortably in that amount of time.

Note that the amount of time a game takes to play is not just a property of the game itself, but of the community that plays it—that is, length of play is agential. The African game of mancala (actually a family of related games, such as kalah and oware) is played with great rapidity in Africa, although Europeans and Americans who play it are liable

Figure 1.1
©iStockphoto.com/Lev Mel

to do so at a slower speed.[1] Chess in the West is often played relatively slowly, with games that last over an hour not being uncommon, but Eastern versions of chess, no less complex in terms of their rules, are generally played at the speed of casual checkers in the West (perhaps because the game go has taken up the "serious" gaming niche in the East that chess occupies in the West). The advent of the chess clock has meant that chess has to some extent become two different games: "normal" chess, where the total clock time is around two hours per player, and speed chess, where the total clock time can be five minutes per player. These two games have (slightly) different rules, different rating systems, and somewhat different player bases. This splitting of the audience is merely a more formal version of a phenomenon common in many turn-based games: casual players like to play quickly, more serious players prefer to spend more time on their moves, and thus informal conventions arise within different play groups as to how long a game is "supposed" to take to complete.

As the length of time to play a game changes, it can affect many other characteristics of the game: skill, randomness, costs and rewards for playing, how pleasing the game is to watch, and so on.

Units of Gameplay Length

To discuss length of playtime in more detail, it is useful to break down units of play into various pieces of (usually) increasing length:

1. Parlett, *The Oxford History of Board Games*, 217.

Atom The smallest complete unit of play, in the sense that the players feel they've "really played" some of the game (e.g., two possessions in football, or one level in *Donkey Kong*)
Game What is conventionally thought of as the length of the game—a "standard" full round of play (most typically starting from a standard beginning state and ending with the determination of a winner)
Session A single continuous period of play (e.g., an evening of play)
Campaign A series of games or sessions that are all linked in some way (the weekly poker game at Randy's place, a *match*, or an ongoing paper role-playing game)
Match A series of individual games commonly agreed on as the correct amount of play in order to arrive at a satisfactory determination of the victor. For many games this is merely "best two out of three" or similar grouping.

Depending on the game, some of these categories will make more or less sense. The categories are also sometimes subjective (especially the atom).

For example, take poker. Here, the atom is probably a single hand. The game may last until a player cashes out or gets knocked out. A session would be an evening of play, and a campaign would be an ongoing game featuring the same players. For tennis, an atom might be a couple of games or even a set, a game would be a standard tennis match, and a session might be several matches in a row, or perhaps a tournament. A campaign might be a professional tennis season, or an ongoing series of games between two friends who compare their progress. With *Donkey Kong*, an atom might be a single level, a game would begin when you put in your token and end when you ran out of lives, and a session would be the amount of time you spent in the arcade playing *Donkey Kong* that day. There might be no campaign involved, but if you went to the same arcade regularly, trying to improve your position on the high-score board, then there would be. Note that the campaign ties in very much with the "metagame"; see section 7.1 on that topic.

Typically the game is the most clearly defined unit of play, but there are exceptions even to that. Poker was already mentioned; *World of Warcraft* is another example. Some playgroups might play bridge hand after hand, without necessarily keeping game score. If a game has separate stages, like bridge, a game probably needs to include each of the stages to be considered a game: you could argue that bidding to a contract is an atom, and playing the hand is an atom, but either one alone can hardly be a game. You would need to bid and then play a contract at the very least to call it a game, even informally. Of course, to have an official game of bridge you'll need to play several hands so as to reach the required point total.

Not all games have matches, but many do. The most common form is simply to play a fixed number of games, with the winner of the majority being the winner of the match (extra games that won't affect the match outcome typically are not played, so for example a best three out of five match will end as soon as one player wins three games). Often matches are used as a sort of "extended game": if the game length is short, playing best three out of five is a way to play a longer game. Playing more games makes it more likely that the better player wins the overall match, and when determining the best player is an important goal, matches can become very long—championship chess and go matches, for example, can consist of many games played over a period of weeks or even months.[2]

So a match can be shorter or longer than a session. Multiple matches may take place inside a session, for example when playing a trading card game, or a match may be longer than a session as in the playoffs in many sports. The length of a match often varies with a particular subset of its player base. The interaction between players' skill and the game's inherent randomness sets the tone for what feels like a satisfying amount of play in terms of deciding a winner. Sometimes this lines up with a single game, but it often requires more play at higher levels of competition.

Note that although a game is generally shorter than a session, that is often not the case. A particularly long game (a complex hex wargame might be a paper example) could be broken up into several sessions. This is very common, even standard, with single-player computer games, due to the ability to save games in midstream. Even paper-based RPGs are rarely completed in a session.

An atom practically has to be shorter than a session: since the atom is the shortest satisfying unit of play, and a session is the amount of time you actually play, an atom longer than a session is not a pleasing experience. In fact, you really need the session length to be a multiple of the atomic length—that is, you want to end the session by completing an atom (if not an entire game). The shorter the atomic length, the easier it is to achieve that, and incidentally to be tempted into playing just a bit more ("let's play one more hand" in a card game is a lot more common than "let's go on one more raid" in an MMO). Computer games with save points that you can't reach before your session ends are one example of failure in this regard. Even if you can save anywhere, though, players will prefer to save at a point where they have reached a "logical stopping point" (finished a turn, killed a boss, completed a quest)—that is, finished an atom. In general, "good" atoms are ones that are fairly short, and fairly distinct, so that players can stop when they like and still feel they have had a satisfying experience.[3]

2. Japan's greatest go player, Honinbo Shusaku, had a best-of-thirty-game match with Ota Yuzo that lasted almost a year, although it only went for twenty-three games (Power, *Invincible: The Games of Shusaku*, chap. 7).
3. Of course, there are many excellent games that don't have "good atoms." It's just that, all else being equal, having short, distinct atoms is a strength for a game. This goes back to our caveat in the introduction about good games not needing to have every good thing—we'll stop repeating this, but we hope the reader will continue to bear it in mind.

There are many pressures keeping atom length long, however. Players may tend to feel a greater sense of accomplishment in longer tasks. Very often there is something like a downtime between atoms, whether that is shuffling, switching offense and defense in certain sports, or merely waiting for a computer game to save or a level to load. In each of these cases, more atoms inside a given session length leads to more downtime for the player. Also of note is that in simulation games a short atom may simply be unacceptable for appropriate suspension of disbelief.

With all of these issues, the agential nature of session length should be kept in mind. An atom length longer than the session length for a certain group of players is very likely to result in having those players cease playing the game. Thus large raids in the average MMO taking longer than an hour effectively exclude players who can only play on their lunch break. MMOs with long raids must then provide shorter atomic lengths in other areas of content to keep those customers, such as quests or grinding.

The different levels of atom, game, match, session, and campaign are of course interrelated. Longer atoms means longer games, or else fewer atoms per game. Long games make it harder to have multiple games per session. Tournaments (which can be thought of as extra-long sessions having some elements of a campaign) can be held in a day if the game length is short, but will be much harder to run if the game length is longer. If tournaments take too long to run effectively, they may not exist and instead something like a sports season—which is essentially a tournament spread out over many months—will become the standard campaign for that game.[4]

Some Examples

Let's go through a number of game genres with these concepts in mind.

Party Games

Games like *Pictionary* or charades tend to have very short atomic lengths. In the case of charades, the atom is probably more important than the game: it is very natural for people to play for however long they would like to play. Arguably there is no "game" as such, but really just atoms and sessions (in this sense, charades is similar to poker). If there is an identifiable game, it may be as simple as an agreement among the players to play a certain number of atoms (or for a certain number of minutes) and then declare a winner.

4. Sports have seasons instead of tournaments for reasons other than game length, such as the difficulty of arranging games between large teams and the limited possibility of playing multiple games back to back when physical exertion is involved. Tennis, though, just manages to have tournaments, and golf manages relatively easily because the players don't play head to head in pairs but rather all play simultaneously.

With for-purchase games, there's usually some well-defined game that comes built in (in the case of *Pictionary*, reaching the end of the board's track), but it often feels somewhat artificially imposed on top of a charades-like fundamental layer.

Campaigns do not tend to be part of party games except in a very informal way. This informal sense of campaign (memories of who did well in past games among a given group, for example) can be very important to the players, but every game that's played repeatedly among a given group of players shares this feature, so it is not a feature of any particular game.

Complex Paper Wargames (e.g., Third Reich*)*

When the game is long enough, it goes over several sessions. The atomic unit (a turn for each player is a reasonable choice of atom) is already as long as many other games. There is no real need for a campaign, because the game itself fulfills many of the needs players might have for a campaign in a game of less epic scope.

Paper RPGs (e.g., Dungeons & Dragons*)*

Here the atoms are less clear, due to the variety of gameplay; a round of combat or an encounter might be reasonable choices. The game (as a unit of length of play) hardly exists at all, since there's no winner or loser declared and no specified ending condition.[5] The focus is on the session and on the campaign.

Single-Player Computer RPGs (e.g., Diablo II*)*

The total number of hours a player might spend could be similar to those spent in a complete paper RPG campaign, but because there's an ending condition we think of *Diablo II* as having a very long game length, not as a campaign with no real game like *Dungeons & Dragons*. Due to the save-game feature, the atoms are more flexible (and thus sessions easier to end at an appropriate time). However, a natural atomic ending is finding a new teleporter, as any *Diablo* player who has stayed up later than planned looking for the next teleport pad knows. For some players, *Diablo* doesn't really have a campaign, for reasons similar to that of *Third Reich*: just the game itself is long enough. For others, experimentation with different characters might be considered a kind of campaign.

MMRPGs (e.g., World of Warcraft*)*

A game like *WoW* is an interesting hybrid of the previous two cases. The atoms are varied in length. Longer atoms, like going on a raid, are reminiscent of paper RPGs. Shorter atoms, like checking the auction house or gathering some herbs, might be

5. One might pick the adventure as the game. Note in this case the game length would be greater than the session length.

closer to *Diablo*. (Also, in *Diablo*, it's possible to interrupt an atom by saving in the middle of it, whereas in *WoW*, like a paper RPG, it is not possible to do so without the agreement of the other players.) In that it has no game but only a campaign, *WoW* is much more like a paper RPG than like a single-player computer RPG.

Classic Card Games

To take just two examples, recall that in poker an atom was a hand. The short length means you can play quite a few atoms in a session. What might otherwise be an informal campaign (like those of party games) is made more formal by means of a long-term tracking tool: money. It's quite natural for people to think about whether they are up or down over the course of several sessions, if they don't track it explicitly.

For rubber bridge, there's an atom—the hand—but also an explicit game made up of around two to five hands. Some playgroups ignore the explicit game and just play a series of hands in each play session. Most playgroups just have informal campaigns, but there are also leagues, and the recording of masterpoints gives an explicit campaign structure (here, the length of the campaign is one's entire bridge-playing career). Note that in duplicate bridge, a single hand may be considered a more satisfying atom than in rubber bridge, because a team's quality of achievement is more measurable on a single hand, and because each hand is more independent.

Chess

Here the game can be fairly long, but there is no atom shorter than the game (one could argue a turn for each player is an atom, but this would be extremely unsatisfying). This makes chess less satisfying as a game to squeeze into a few empty moments. The game length is close to a good session length. Thus sessions are less flexible (there's no short atom to let you end when you want, so you need to complete the game) but satisfying if you can find the time (you get to complete a game, and you've played a decent length of time when you've finished that game). Campaigns are broadly similar to bridge (none/informal, leagues or clubs, and lifetime ratings).

Monopoly

This game shares with chess a somewhat long playtime with no reasonable subset of the game being satisfying as an atom. Socially *Monopoly* has more in common with party games, so its campaign structure tends like theirs to be informal.

Sports

Football, baseball, and basketball are all broadly similar in terms of game length and in terms of campaign structure (leagues, often informal, at the very casual level, with seasons at the level of school or professional sports). The interesting difference is in terms of atoms: for basketball, the atom is very short, perhaps a possession or two for each side. The football atom is probably a possession for each side, which is a lot longer. In baseball, it is at least an inning for each side and very likely multiple innings so each player has a guaranteed chance to bat.

Hockey and soccer are similar to basketball in having short atoms, but the atoms are less sharply defined. The fluidity of these games means they are closer to continuous than atomic, compared with a game like basketball where there are more distinct drives in which the teams alternate possession. Football's atoms are a bit more distinct than basketball's, and baseball's much more so.

Injury time in soccer (where the referee adds a certain amount of time to the game to make up for missed time due to injuries, substitutions, and the like) can be thought of as a way of ensuring the game ends on an atom. Injury time means the game ends at the sole discretion of the referee, who is likely to end it when an action has been completed, rather than, say, at the moment a shot is headed toward the goal. A similar aim is achieved by the basketball rule allowing a shot to count if the buzzer sounds while it is in midair.

First-Person Shooters (e.g., Quake*)*

In an FPS, the typical atom might be the time it takes for a kill (either you are killed and then respawn, or you kill someone and then go look for another target). All the advantages of short atomic length, such as quick satisfying play experiences and the ability to fit play into your real-life schedule easily, exist for an FPS. Like poker, an FPS is often played as a session of atoms strung together, with no actual game per se. Formal campaigns are possible but rare. In fact, the game length structure of an FPS—at the atomic, game, session, and campaign levels—is very similar to that of poker,

From Stickball to Basketball

In the early twentieth century, children played stickball. Now the street game of choice is probably basketball. Basketball's success as a game of street culture has often been attributed to its lighter requirements in terms of space (versus baseball) and equipment (versus football). But another possible factor is basketball's shorter atomic length. Given a limited period of time, such as a lunch break or recess, it is possible to play a satisfactory amount of basketball but harder to play a satisfactory amount of football or baseball. Even a longer period of time, if it is of uncertain length (as is often the case in pickup games), benefits from having a short atomic length. Basketball's shorter atomic length may not be the main reason for its relative increase in popularity, but it does seem like a prerequisite given the modern pressures on children's leisure time.

something that might be hard to notice if one were not looking at this characteristic specifically.

Real-Time Strategy Games (e.g., Starcraft*)*

Because RTS games, like chess, progress through an early game, middle game, and endgame, their atomic structure is less distinct. One could declare an atom to be a few minutes of play, or a single battle (or round of base building), but there's no really clear atom. Probably it's better to just think of the atomic length as being equal to the game length. A session may be a single game over lunch, but it's often an afternoon or evening of several games.

Campaigns come in two different forms: in its single-player mode, an RTS usually has an actual series of linked scenarios that form a campaign. That campaign usually comes with a storyline or with a metagame of some sort (e.g., a conquer-the-world *Risk*-type map).

A multiplayer campaign (in our sense of the word *campaign*) is occasionally a "season" along the lines of a sports season, but more commonly it is centered around a leaderboard or a ratings system.

Platformers (e.g., Super Mario Bros.*)*

The original arcade platformers (e.g., *Donkey Kong*) had single screens as atoms. This evolved into "worlds" or "levels" as atoms in console platformers. As these atoms became longer, it became more annoying to replay them every time one wanted to play the game again, so save points were introduced: one could save the game at the end of a level and then resume play from that point. As game length continued to increase, at some point a level seemed more like a game than an atom, and a game seemed more like a campaign. Arguably, a complex modern console platformer has atoms something like "a few minutes of play," a game is completion of one level, and a campaign is the completion of the entire (purchased) game.

This trend is fairly common with deliberately designed games: a game may begin with a short game length and short atoms, but over time designers attempt to satisfy their more serious fans by adding content, which tends to make the atoms and the games longer.[6] Note that as the games get longer, they essentially become campaigns, which may not always be a good thing—it may make short satisfying play experiences less available to the players, and it can drive out the possibility of other campaign structures. Since many players like shorter games, the longer games may appeal to a narrower audience, opening up a space for newer shorter games: think of the relatively broad appeal of the old NES games, the often longer and more complex games on the

6. Other factors, such as the reduction of downtime, may push game length in the other direction.

Playstation 3 or Xbox 360, and then again of casual web games or Wii games. (Of course, complexity is a factor as well as play length, but the two are correlated, and more or less the same remarks apply.)

Atoms and Points

Many games with "good" atoms (short atoms with clear and satisfying boundaries) are point-based. At the end of each atom, points are recorded, and the winner of the game is the one with the most points at the end. Such a structure allows players to play a more or less complete minigame in each atom, so that atoms are satisfying. Games that benefit from this kind of structure include poker and most sports games. Games like chess or an RTS, which have a binary victory condition (kill or be killed), tend not to have such satisfying atoms shorter than the game itself. Note that if the atom is short enough and the game long enough, so that many atoms will be played in a single game, it's common for binary victory conditions to become points—for example, kills in an FPS. There are exceptions, of course, to the rule that points make for good atoms: the game go is point-based, but because points can only be calculated effectively at the end of the game, they don't serve as a basis for an atomic structure, and go winds up being more or less like chess in terms of its atomic structure.

To summarize, game length has a great influence on how players interact with a game and, indeed, on whether they choose to interact with it at all. When looking at game length, it helps to look at the length of the game's atoms, the game itself, the session, and the campaign.

In general, players will be happiest to end their session by completing an atom, if not a full game. This makes games with short and satisfying atoms easier for players to fit into their lives. Sometimes keeping the atom or game length short can conflict with other goals the game might have, such as complexity or development through the course of a game. Very often, though, a game designer can support those other goals and still support short atom and game lengths (save-game features are a very simple example of this).

In particular, there's nothing wrong with having a very short game. If players want a longer game experience with a short game, they can simply play again. If players want a short experience in a long game, it's much harder for them to find a satisfactory solution. Games with short play lengths or short atoms, such as poker and basketball, do not seem to suffer for it.

Exercise 1.1: Name some computer games whose atom length is longer than their session length. Name a sport whose game length is longer than its session length.

Exercise 1.2: What are some potential *drawbacks* of short atoms?

Exercise 1.3: Different sessions of the same MMO can have quite different lengths. What are some common session lengths for MMO play? What real-world circumstances cause them? How do MMOs satisfy these different desired session lengths in terms of their atomic lengths (i.e., what about MMO atoms makes them fit, or fail to fit, in various session lengths)?

1.2 Characteristic: Number of Players

How many players a game has seems like a simple enough question, but there is a bit to untangle. In many ways, the number of sides is even more important than the number of players: football, for example, is a two-sided game and thus takes on many aspects of a two-player game, even though it has many players. In particular, there are some issues (such as politics and kingmaking) that only arise in games with three or more sides.

When we speak of a "multiplayer" game, we mean a game that has at least three sides (and hence at least three players) unless we say otherwise. In particular, we don't use the term *multiplayer* for two-player games; this is standard usage for all games other than computer games (where multiplayer is sometimes taken to mean three or more players, but sometimes taken to mean two or more, in contrast to single-player games).

Figure 1.2
©iStockphoto.com/Ed Hidden

In this section, we'll categorize the number of players a game can have, and discuss a few examples. Later chapters will discuss issues arising from the number of players in more detail.

Categorization by Number of Players

Zero-player Some "games" can be observed, but there are no players who influence the outcome. These are games only by common parlance. John Conway's game of Life is one example. Another is Progress Quest, a parody computer RPG in which the player does nothing but observe his character leveling up and gathering treasure by fighting monsters automatically. Closer to a "real" game, but still not very close, is "raindrop races": a bored person on a rainy day chooses two raindrops on a windowpane and sees which one makes it to the bottom first. The anthropomorphization of the raindrop contestants makes this very much like a real game from the spectator's point of view, but there are no (conscious) players.[7]

One-player It is useful to break one-player games into two categories, namely,

"Pure" one-player Games where the player plays more against "the system" than against an imaginary opponent. Crossword puzzles, *Tetris*, card solitaire, *Zork* or *Myst*, and *Asteroids* all fall into this category. Arguably even going out for a run (especially if you are timing yourself) would fit. In addition to having only one human player, these games have no playerlike elements in the game that behave like the player (e.g., when you play *Tetris*, there is no computer player arranging blocks in the same way you are).

One human, simulated opponents ("one and a half player") This category exists almost exclusively in the computer world.[8] A human plays one side of the game; the computer AI plays other simulated opponents. The simulated opponents may follow essentially the same rules a human would (e.g., playing *Starcraft* against the AI) or may have their own rules (e.g., playing *Diablo* against the AI-controlled monsters). Almost any computer game that has a multiplayer version falls into this category in its single-player version. Other examples include *Civilization*, any first-person shooter, and *Mortal Kombat*. Platformers fall somewhere between this category and the pure one-player category, depending on how active the enemies are (trying to jump onto a certain platform is a one-player experience; fighting a boss is a simulated two-player experience).

One may think of such games as a kind of Turing test—if you can write a good AI, you've passed a Turing test in a limited domain, in that the (human) player experience

7. Unless you have unusual ideas about raindrops. This game goes back at least to A. A. Milne's "Waiting at the Window" from *When We Were Very Young*, and probably back to the invention of window glass.

8. For an exception, consider a single person playing blackjack against the house.

may be quite similar to the experience that player would have against another human, at least in terms of gameplay.[9] With poker bots, this is literally true: go online, and you don't always know if you're playing against humans or bots.

To some extent, any one-player game can be thought of as a one and a half player game depending on how much you wish to anthropomorphize your opponent. Thinking of the computer as resembling a human opponent seems quite natural in a one-versus-one RTS battle against a computer AI, fairly natural with a computer RPG, but a bit strange when playing *Tetris* or (card) solitaire. There is in effect something of a continuum from one-player games to one and a half player games to two-player games where the gap is bridged by computer AIs who may or may not play by the same rules as humans and whose existence may or may not even be known to their human opponent.

Two-player This is the core category in the sense that two-player games feel like the "best" examples of games (in the same way that the sparrow feels like a particularly good example of a bird).[10] There are countless examples, such as chess, gin, *Battleship*, *Scrabble*, tennis, most trading card games, most miniatures games and wargames, and *Starcraft*. Note that many of these examples have multiplayer variants. Some games that are commonly multiplayer can also be played two-player, such as basketball or *Quake*.

Two-sided team games These are games where there are two sides or teams. Each side plays (or tries to play) as a single entity, and each side wins or loses as a unit. Examples include football, team shooters (e.g., *Counterstrike*), bridge, Mafia/werewolf, and *Axis & Allies*.

In general, two-sided team games have more in common with two-player games than they do with true multiplayer games. In particular, the political issues unique to multiplayer games, such as kingmaking, do not appear. If one imagines a team as a kind of complex player, two-sided games just reduce to two-player ones. The one difference is in the interteam dynamics—that is, how a single player interacts with her teammates and contributes to the team effort.

One-sided team games A game can have a single side playing against an AI (or against the rules of the game); this is simply the team analog of a single-player game, in the

9. Perhaps unfortunately, computer games don't always simulate humans very well. For example, RTS AI opponents often have a superhuman ability to click quickly and target units—that is, they have superhuman micromanagement, but then they have very limited ability to act strategically. The experience of playing against an AI might be more fun (and more useful in terms of improving one's game) if the AI played in a manner a human might hope to attain. Of course, such an AI would be harder to write. Most AI designers feel their job is done when the AI can (depending on setting) beat most human players, regardless of how the AI does it.

10. As compared to, say, a kiwi or an ostrich. See Lakoff, *Women, Fire, and Dangerous Things*, 41.

same way two-sided team games are similar to two-player games. One-sided team games are commonly referred to as "cooperative games." Examples include *Gauntlet*, Knizia's *Lord of the Rings* boardgame, fighting a raid boss in *World of Warcraft*, or playing *Starcraft* as a group against the AI. Although it may vary based on a particular group's style of play, this is the most common way to think of paper role-playing games like *Dungeons & Dragons* as well. The distinction between "one-player" and "one and a half player" applies here as well.

Multiplayer This category includes games where there are several players or sides (at least three), each pursuing his or her objectives.[11] Examples are golf, a marathon, poker, *Trivial Pursuit*, *Scrabble* (again), first-person shooters, (free-for-all) *Starcraft*, *Candyland*, *Risk*, and *Clue*.

Note very few high-interaction sports or high-interaction classic games fall into this category.[12] Traditionally, these genres have only achieved a true multiplayer state at the cost of very low player interactivity. We'll discuss this more in the next chapter, but for now we'll just note that high interactivity and the ability to have multiple players (both desirable things in and of themselves) are very difficult to combine well.

Massively Multiplayer This category encompasses games where the number of people a given player interacts with is much smaller than the number of people playing. *World of Warcraft*, *Everquest*, *Killer* and other live-action assassin games, and pari-mutuel betting are examples. The stock market or war might count as examples, but the stakes are high enough that people generally do not classify them as games.

Given these categories, it's not hard to come up with other possibilities. An RTS game might have three humans and three AI opponents, either as teams or in a free-for-all. There are multisided team games, such as *Dark Age of Camelot* PvP or a team bicycle race.

Games that allow a varying number of players often have a "sweet spot"—the number of players where the game is best. For example, hearts is probably best with four players. Pari-mutuel betting just needs to be "large enough," but there's no upper limit: ten thousand players or a million players both look the same to an individual player. Most people would consider the sweet spot for Texas Hold 'Em to be eight or nine players. With *World of Warcraft*, the sweet spot is probably in the 1,500–2,500 range; fewer than that and the server seems empty, more than that and not only is

11. One-sided and two-sided team games are also multiplayer in the literal sense of having multiple players, but, as mentioned above, we prefer to discuss them separately since the issues tend to be different.

12. Classic multiplayer games that do have significant interaction limit it carefully. In Chinese checkers, players help their opponents but can't directly harm them. In poker, players bet against each other but can't directly affect each other's hands. See section 2.2, on interactivity.

lag an issue, but the crowding limits comfortable access to mobs, questgivers, vendors, and so on.

Sweet spots are usually agential. *Scrabble* provides an excellent example where for a certain competitive section of the audience the two-player game is the clear sweet spot. A more social or casual group of *Scrabble* players will often prefer a full game of four.

Single-Player Games

Before computers, single-player games were relatively uncommon. When people think of traditional games, they tend to think of two-player games like chess, or games for even more players like hearts. There are some exceptions to this rule. Certain sports such as racing or weightlifting can be done alone as well as in groups, although doing so may be considered practicing or training rather than "really" doing the activity. Puzzles of various kinds (crossword puzzles, jigsaw puzzles, sliding block puzzles) are meant for one person. Interestingly, though, the noun *game* and the verb *play* aren't generally used for these activities—you don't call weightlifting a game, or play a crossword puzzle—perhaps indicating these activities feel less like "normal" games to most people. Other notable examples of single-player games include card solitaire (typically considered a game, perhaps because the platform, a deck of cards, is so strongly associated with other activities labeled games) and slot machines (in fact, many gambling games are single-player, with slots being perhaps the most extreme example). Overall, though, the activities earlier generations imagined on hearing the word *game* involved two or more players.

Exercise 1.4: Why do you think we use the verb *play* and the term *game* with blackjack, the slots, or other gambling games, when we don't use it with things like crossword puzzles?

Perhaps one reason for the historical scarcity of single-player games is simply that nonelectronic single-player games are hard to make. Uncertainty in outcome[13] is at the heart of games, and a human opponent provides much uncertainty. In fact, if the game is fair and the opponent is equally skilled, then one's chances of winning (in a two-player game) are 50/50—maximal uncertainty.

Without a human opponent, uncertainty needs to come from somewhere else. Sometimes, as in card solitaire, the game rules plus a built-in randomizing mechanism provide enough uncertainty. Sometimes, as in crossword puzzles, the uncertainty comes from hidden information or human ignorance, although in that case the game's content may be exhausted—having done the crossword puzzle once, you won't want to do it again. To keep playing, you'll need fresh content. (And indeed, one can think

13. See section 5.1, on randomness.

of the rules for some layout-heavy card solitaire games as a sort of automatic randomized puzzle generator.) Thus single-player games are more prone to exhaustion (i.e., have less replayability) than multiplayer games. This is not to say that individual single-player games can't be very replayable, just that on average multiplayer games tend to be better for repeat play—and indeed many electronic games are designed with a single-player core meant to be played by all, and a multiplayer mode meant to give a high degree of replayability for those who want more.

However, computer games are very often played alone. Indeed, before computer networking was common, PC games were almost always single-player. Even arcade games, which tend to be played in social spaces, almost always have a single-player mode, and many have only that mode, with social play consisting simply of score comparison.

Some computer games (e.g., *Myst*) take the same approach as crossword puzzles. Some (e.g., *Minesweeper* or *Tetris*) are like card solitaire—generating a randomized puzzle. However, computer games have a third option: create a simulated opponent. Doing this in a paper game is awkward at best (a few wargames do it, with exact instructions for playing the other side). But in a computer game the level of complexity a simulated opponent requires can be hidden from the player, and highly complex opponents can be created. Even fairly simple opponents, like the ghosts in *Pac-Man*, can provide a lot of uncertainty (although good players will eventually learn the patterns involved if there's no randomness in the system—in a sense, *Pac-Man* changes from a game to a puzzle as you get better at it). Even if a computer game opts for the handcrafted content-providing ("puzzle") approach, or the randomized scenario-generating approach, the computer's ability to store information and execute algorithms helps to provide more complex content with a lower burden on the player. (The occasional downside is that hiding the details of how the system works from the player can make it harder for the player to understand what's going on and how she should play the game—that is, it makes it harder for her to climb the heuristic tree.)

The risk of low replayability may be their natural disadvantage, but single-player games have some big natural advantages as well. The greatest of these is the ease of getting a game started—if you want to play, a single-player game lets you start right away without having to find anyone else. Also, people like winning (although they may get bored if you let them win all the time), and with a single-player game a player can win more than half the time, something impossible on average with a two-player game. If a designer thinks people would be happiest winning about 70 percent of the time, she can make a game where that's what happens (or make a game with multiple difficulty levels, which amounts to making several games, with players choosing how often they'd like to win by choosing among them). Single-player games also benefit from having player performance that is more *comparable*: if we each play games of chess or *Quake*, and I win mine but you lose yours, it doesn't mean much[14] about our relative skills—too much depends on the quality of our opponents. But we can compare our scores in *Tetris*, or you can boast that your guild has defeated Onyxia (a boss monster in *World of Warcraft*) before mine, and the comparison means something.

Note that all the pros and cons of single-player games are really about single-*sided* games: games where there is only one side, one team, trying to achieve victory. If that team has a single player, the game is a single-player game; if that team has multiple players, then it's a cooperative game. The one exception to this generalization (of single-player attributes applying to single-sided games) is, of course, that the ease of getting a game together really does stem from there being exactly one player of the game.

It is also perhaps worth repeating that many single-player (or single-sided) games, especially digital games, have an opponent that is simulated in enough detail that much of the logic and analysis from two-player games still applies—what we've been calling one and a half player games. In other words, a game that technically has just a single human player might best be analyzed as a two-player game: playing chess against a computer is much like playing chess against another person, at least from the point of view of game mechanics (less so psychologically).

Changing Categories

Many games can be played in different forms (e.g., two-player or multiplayer) or have variants that allow you to play with a different number of players. Such flexibility is very powerful, but the game dynamics often change so much that it's arguable whether it's even the same game.

The power of changing the number of players comes in part because it allows players who like the game to play in different circumstances. Whether there are one, two, or a larger number of people together who'd like to play a game, the game that can support varying numbers of players is more likely to get chosen. Also, since the different options do vary so widely, fans of the game have the chance to have very different experiences with their favorite game.

When the number of players in a game changes,[15] the game dynamics can become very different. Even a game like *Scrabble*, which on the surface seems fairly similar as a two-player game and as a four-player game, can change a great deal. In particular, the ability to restrict your opponent's play, and to modify the board in hopes of

14. In the absence of a rating system such as Elo ratings.

15. Changes categories as described above—that is, changing from, say, four-on-four teams to five-on-five is a relatively minor affair in comparison.

improving your next play, both change significantly.[16] Other games, like team basketball versus one-on-one, change so much that one might not even consider them the same game. Above all, taking a two-player (or one and a half player) game and turning it into a game with three or more players can result in a great many unintended consequences; we'll have much more to say about this topic when we further discuss multiplayer games below.

Sometimes it's easier to create variants involving different numbers of players from games that have a large number of complex parts, like *Magic: The Gathering* or *World of Warcraft*.[17] With such games, a designer has so many pieces to work from that there are many ways of creating variants.[18] Games with complex emergent behavior coming from simple rules, like chess or go, often fare less well under this treatment, but there are plenty of exceptions like basketball or first-person shooters.

Some variants are easy to create: two-player games can often be converted into two-sided team games by allowing multiple players to share a side. A two-sided team game such as Werewolf or *World of Warcraft* battlegrounds can be made into a multiplayer nonteam game by assigning one point to each person on the winning team, randomizing the teams every round, and declaring the person with the highest point total at the end of the session the overall winner.[19]

Two common ways of creating multiplayer games are by having several players simultaneously play one-player games more or less independently, or by adding more players to a two-player game. We term these *races* and *brawls* respectively, and discuss them at length in the next chapter.

For games that do allow varying numbers of players, which variant is preferred is necessarily (being a player preference) agential, but systemic influences are important.

In face-to-face play, two-player variants (or one-player variants, if they exist) often have the edge over multiplayer variants simply because of the ease of assembling a smaller number of players. With computer games, even those for which the 2+ player

16. Roughly speaking, in a game's two-player form the payoff to setting up a board position or damaging your opponent (both presumably at some cost to yourself) will be higher, and in a multiplayer format it will be lower (but the cost to yourself may be the same). Sometimes this effect is strong enough to push these strategies out of the pool of strategies that good players will use.

17. *World of Warcraft* contains subgames in each of our categories except, ironically, pure multiplayer.

18. However, there will be play balance challenges in games where the players can pick from among the parts, and balancing in all of the environments simultaneously will be especially tricky (see Gutschera's "Costing and Balancing Game Objects").

19. In most established team games, players come to know and enjoy playing with the same teammates regularly, and such a system would probably be rejected. So although simple and elegant, this method is not always applicable.

versions are considered the "standard," the majority of play may occur in the single-player campaign; this is common for RTS games. It's much easier to assemble one player (yourself) for a computer game than it is to go online to play. Once you do go online, though, getting several players together isn't that much harder than finding a single opponent, so multiplayer variants are quite common. But hardcore players, if the multiplayer variants are highly political, may wind up preferring the two-player version (see section 2.3, on politics).

Exercise 1.5: What is the minimum number of players in a game of werewolf? (*Hint*: How low can you go before the game is predetermined?) Maximum? Sweet spot? Why is this the sweet spot? What is the number of sides in werewolf?

Exercise 1.6: Name some games you've played with a variable number of players. Name some two-sided games you've played with a variable number of players.

Exercise 1.7: Can you name a party game with a fixed number of players?

1.3 Characteristic: Heuristics

Many games, in order to satisfy players, need to allow players to gain mastery in the game over time.[20] Players typically gain skill by developing heuristics: rules of thumb that help them play the game.[21] Some of these rules might be quite concrete ("never draw to an inside straight" in poker) and some might be fairly vague ("develop your pieces" in chess).

Discussions among players after a game are often about heuristics—what moves were most effective, what decisions could have been made differently, what the correct winning strategies are. "Monday morning quarterbacking" and other postgame analysis from spectators also tend to be about heuristics. And if someone asks "how do you play that game?" and they already know something about the rules, chances are they are looking, not for even more detailed rules, but for some basic heuristics. So although they may not use the term *heuristics*, players of games are very much concerned about heuristics, and discuss them all the time.

As an extreme example of the lack of heuristics, consider a game we'll call "Guess the Digit." Each round, we have a computer pick a random number between a million and a billion. We then each try to guess that digit of pi; whoever comes closest wins. This is a deterministic game (once the computer has picked the digit), but there are no apparent heuristics, so the game is essentially random for its players. Most people

20. A purely random "game," like a slot machine, would be a counterexample.

21. Again, there are exceptions, such as purely physical games like a footrace, where heuristics are of minimal importance and physical improvement is the focus. In a sprint, "run as fast as you can" is pretty much the only heuristic.

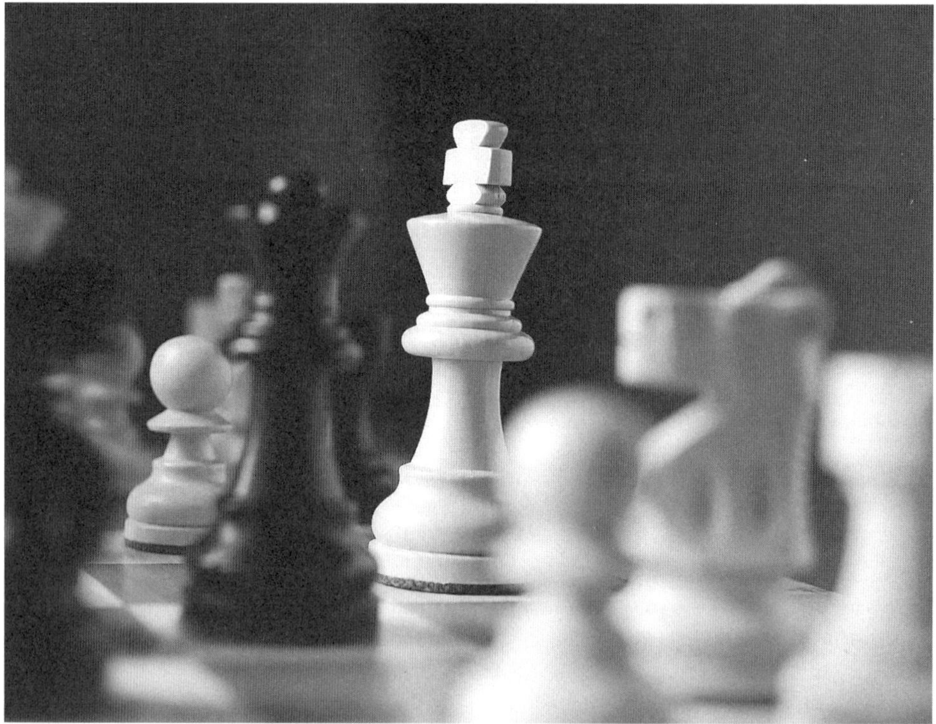

Figure 1.3

would have little interest in playing this game—anyone who wanted to play a purely random game would probably prefer rolling dice or flipping coins. Perhaps if one knew enough about the distribution of the digits of pi, there might be some useful heuristics, and the game might become more interesting. But as it is, it's not much of a game, due to its lack of heuristics of any kind.

It's useful to distinguish two kinds of heuristics:

Positional heuristics These are heuristics that evaluate the *state* of the game—that is, tell you who's winning. Examples include seeing how many people are ahead of you (and by what distance) in a race, or counting the point values of the pieces on each side in chess.

Directional heuristics These are heuristics that tell you what *strategy*[22] you should follow. Examples include rules like "run as fast as you can once you see the finish line" or "try to control the center squares."

22. Or tactics. No distinction between the two is intended here; the point is merely to emphasize "a choice that you as a player might make" over the evaluation of the state of the game itself.

For those familiar with boardgame-playing AIs, these can be thought of as board evaluation algorithms and move generation algorithms respectively.

Playing well in a game involves using these two kinds of heuristics in conjunction. The two kinds of heuristics are of course related—for example, one simple directional heuristic is "make moves that, when I apply my positional heuristics, look good."[23] Note in particular that if you have no useful positional heuristics (i.e., you can't tell which game states are good for you and which are bad), it's hard to develop any directional heuristics at all. On the flip side, "I'm winning if I've achieved a lot of my directional heuristic goals" is a possible state heuristic.

Although in general positional and directional heuristics support each other, exceptions are possible. Consider the following two games, "Money in the Bag" and "Money on the Table." In Money in the Bag, each player has access to two buttons, a red one and a blue one. Pressing the red button gives a player one dollar 80 percent of the time; blue gives one dollar only 20 percent of the time. Any money a player receives goes into a bag, and the contents of the bag are only revealed at the end of the game. Each player receives ten presses. This game has powerful directional heuristics—"always press the red button!" is a perfect guide to play. But there are no state heuristics: which player is ahead is an utter mystery until the end of the game.

In Money on the Table, there is no bag; any money gained is placed on the table in front of the respective players. However, one button gives a dollar 51 percent of the time, the other only 50 percent of the time, and players don't know which is which. This game has very clear state heuristics (the amount of money on the table), but essentially no directional heuristics (players won't be able to deduce which button is which).[24]

Besides heuristics, depending on the game, a greater or lesser amount of specific physical skills (running fast, aiming at onscreen targets using a mouse) may also be involved, as may a certain amount of reading out moves (if he goes there, and I go there, and then he goes there, what do I do then?).[25]

Our focus, though, is not on how to win games. Why, then, are we concerned with heuristics? The answer is that for players to have fun, they need to have (not necessarily conscious) heuristics. Human beings playing games need to know if they are winning or losing, and they need to know what they want to do next. We say a game has "good heuristics" if there are heuristics available to the players that let them do

23. This heuristic is the basis for the standard search tree used in so many boardgame AIs.
24. The general version of this problem—where a player has a number of buttons to press, those buttons yield different unknown returns, and a player wishes to maximize her returns under repeat play—is known as the "bandit problem" (as in "one-armed bandit," a nickname for slot machines) and is the subject of much study in statistics.
25. These topics are discussed respectively in "Skills Players Need" in section 6.1 and in "Calculations" in section 6.5.

these things. Note this is very much dependent on the player base as well as the structure of the game itself.

The phrase "good heuristics" is quite general, and it's important to ask "good in what sense?" Heuristics can be:

Clear vs. muddy How easy is it to understand and use the heuristics?
Rich vs. sparse How many heuristics does the game have? Do they cover most of the situations that arise in actual play?
Satisfying vs. unsatisfying Do players find the heuristics enjoyable to execute, or do they seem more like work than fun (highly agential, of course)?
Powerful vs. weak Do the heuristics provide a great deal of help in winning, or do they just nudge the heuristic user's chances up a bit?

In general, when we use the phrase "good heuristics" we mean good for the game, in the sense that their presence makes the game more enjoyable. That includes being clear, rich, and satisfying, but it doesn't necessarily mean being powerful. Players who want to win will naturally seek out the most powerful heuristics they can, and in that sense they might think of powerful heuristics as "a good thing," but having extremely powerful heuristics may not be good for a game. Indeed, if the heuristics are too powerful (as in Nim or tic-tac-toe, where the heuristics tell you everything you need to win), they will be bad for players' enjoyment of the game. We discuss this topic further below.

Climbing the Heuristics Tree

A great deal of enjoyment in a game,[26] especially for more serious players, comes from the process of "climbing the heuristics tree": learning successively better and more sophisticated heuristics for a given game. For a more "serious" game, say chess, this process of learning is arguably the main appeal of the game. Of course, this learning and skill-gaining process is inextricably intertwined with the process of winning more often, at least against an imaginary fixed opponent. In practice, one often tends to find opponents of one's own level, and thus win roughly the same ratio of games, so the improvement may come from being able to beat better and better opponents.

For sports, and for computer games that rely heavily on reflexes, the heuristics are only part of the process of improvement, and specific physical skills are a large part of one's ability at the game. In a sprint, say, it's almost entirely physical skill, but of course there are many sports where heuristics play a larger part. Sometimes the heuristics are not so much at the individual-player level, but at the level of the coach or team manager. Even if the heuristic operates at an individual level, it often must be

26. Or indeed in almost any human endeavor—hardly surprising given that games are to some extent abstract and purified models of everyday human existence.

thought of in advance, trained repeatedly, and then performed automatically during an actual match (think, say, of fencing).

But for games without physical skill, which includes many computer games and almost all boardgames and card games, one's improvement at the game is based on one's improvement in heuristics.

Heuristics at Different Skill Levels

Like most game characteristics, the heuristics of a game will be perceived differently by players of different levels of skill. In go, the heuristics are very unclear to a beginning player: they cannot tell who is winning, and they are often at a loss for what to do. In fact, beginners often have difficulty telling if the game is over or not![27] Chess has excellent heuristics for absolute beginners (checkmate the other player's king, or failing that take his better pieces) and for advanced beginners (make advantageous trades according to the point value system, develop your pieces, control the center). But intermediate players may reach a state where they feel they are simply avoiding moves that are obviously bad, waiting for their opponent to err—the intermediate-level heuristics for chess are not as friendly. Indeed, chess is sometimes described as the game where the winner is the person who makes the second-to-last mistake. Intermediate go players have a much easier time finding profitable moves, since many moves will increase one's score at least somewhat.[28]

In some games, there are heuristics of sufficient quality that, once known, players can play perfectly (the game is "solved"). Tic-tac-toe is one such game (although arguably this is more a matter of reading out the game tree than heuristics per se). A better example is Nim. Note that for Nim, there are not many good heuristics for levels of skill below the complete solution. Thus Nim isn't really a very fun game—it has an excellent one-time metagame for the mathematically inclined (figure out how to solve

27. Technically, a game of go is over when both players pass. However, this should only occur when neither player can make a move that would affect the score, and beginners cannot tell when the game has reached such a state.

28. Part of what's going on here is that in some games, one finds situations where it seems that no move at all is better than any of the choices one can make—what in chess is called "Zugzwang" (the chess term is in fact drawn more narrowly, but the underlying idea is close enough that the term is worth stealing for this more general concept). In chess, it's quite common to find situations where most moves worsen one's position. In go, it's more common that most moves improve one's position, at least a little. Zugzwang in this broad sense—of game positions where bad ("bad" in the sense of "worse than doing nothing") moves abound, and good moves are rare—is quite common in games. (For a digital example, think of the paralysis a beginning FPS player can feel moving out of a spawn point—surely, she thinks, the best choice is not to stay at the spawn point, but when all other choices lead to death, what is she to do?) Zugzwang tends to make for unsatisfying beginner heuristics.

Nim), but it is hard to play an interesting game of Nim before you figure out the solution, and impossible to play an interesting game once both players know it. In particular, it is basically impossible to know anything at all about the state of a multipile Nim game until you have entirely solved Nim.

As an aside, note that the possibility of a game having heuristics so powerful that the game is "solved" does not depend on the game being deterministic. One could construct a game "rando-Nim" where two players played Nim, and then a die was rolled to see who won (say 1–4 the winner of the Nim game, 5–6 the loser). Once the players understand Nim heuristics, this becomes a purely random game, but its strategy and its heuristics are the same as those of Nim.

What Makes for Good Heuristics?

There are a number of different axes on which one can measure the quality of a game's heuristics.[29] Ideally:

- Heuristics exist at all levels, from beginner to advanced. Players should be able to improve at the game by acquiring increasingly sophisticated heuristics.
- Some heuristics should be easy for players to discover on their own; others need to be more difficult (if they are all easy, eventually they will all be discovered and the game will be exhausted) and will typically be learned from other players.
- The set of heuristics should be powerful enough to cover most situations (so that the player is never without guidance) but not so powerful as to *completely* cover more than a few situations (lest those situations, or worse yet all situations and thus the game itself, be "solved").[30]
- The heuristics are "satisfying" in the sense that the player feels she is exercising judgment using rules of thumb, rather than executing a computer program. The Nim heuristic or a memorized chess opening is not satisfying in this sense; "develop your pieces" or "bluff occasionally, so that other players will call you when you do have the best hand" is. One common way for a heuristic to be unsatisfying is for it to be completely deterministic, eliminating judgment; another is for it to involve a great deal of calculation (see the discussion in section 6.5 on reward/effort ratio).

29. Again, this is heuristic quality in the sense of contributing to a good game, one that players will enjoy, not heuristic quality in the sense a player might mean it (how much the heuristic helps the person who uses it to win). Solvable games like tic-tac-toe or Nim have terrible heuristics in the first sense despite, or rather because of, having excellent heuristics in the second sense.

30. In chess, many endgame positions are "solved" and certain opening positions are to some extent solved. Thus perfect or near-perfect heuristics of limited scope need not be fatal. Those parts of the game are simply played through relatively quickly, and to some extent are removed from active consideration. In other words, they become busywork.

Beginner heuristics, also called "zero-level heuristics," are particularly important. Players who first learn the game need to have some idea of what they are trying to do and how they might go about it. Even heuristics that look quite ineffective from an advanced player's point of view may serve, since beginners can use them against other beginners and hope over time to improve their heuristics. But with no good zero-level heuristics, the game may be so unenjoyable the beginner simply gives up. Games with good zero-level heuristics include *Uno* (even out your suits) or even bridge (win a trick with the lowest card you can, bid what you can make[31]). Games with bad zero-level heuristics include go and some European boardgames, where there are often a plethora of options with no one obviously better than any other ("silk costs more, but gives me more victory points, compared to wheat . . . which should I pick?"). In general, any game with a large number of options, carefully balanced to preserve gameplay variety for advanced players, runs the risk of damaging its zero-level heuristics. This risk is one reason one might want bad cards in a trading card game or bad items in an RPG: they provide zero-level heuristics, choices that even beginning players can make and improve their game.

If a game does have weak beginner heuristics, more advanced players can often help beginners get started by giving them some heuristics that are not too difficult to apply but that would be difficult or impossible for the beginners to discover on their own. Chess openings are an example of this kind of transmission at a somewhat more advanced level. At a more basic level, the relative values of the pieces in chess provide a simple and powerful heuristic for beginners. Too many of these transmitted heuristics, however, can create a burden on the memory.

Heuristics and the Player Base

As players gain skill at a game, the heuristics can change. Tic-tac-toe has decent heuristics if the player base is small children, but the heuristics are not good for the adult player base. Games like chess or go evolve over time as players learn more and develop better heuristics.[32]

An interesting extreme example of heuristic dependence on the player base and development of heuristics over time is Dots and Boxes. Commonly played by schoolchildren, Dots and Boxes has slightly weak zero-level heuristics—for example, "move

31. An example of a heuristic that is terrible for intermediate and advanced players, but that might help a group of beginners get started (even a single more advanced player in the playgroup would probably prevent such a heuristic from taking hold, though). Note we are not claiming bridge is an easy game to learn (the rules are quite messy, and beginners are often taught difficult advanced heuristics like bidding systems from the start), merely that if a group of beginners all knew the rules, there would be some simple low-level heuristics they could use to play.

32. See the discussion "Skill Is Agential" in section 5.2.

randomly except don't complete the third side of a box." But it has some good, reasonably easy to discover, intermediate-level heuristics that apply to its endgame (in particular, the trick of not taking the last two boxes in a long chain, thereby forcing your opponent to begin a new chain). The beginning stages of the game seem impossible to analyze—that is, there are no obvious positional heuristics, and play tends to proceed essentially at random. However, relatively recently, advanced techniques in theoretical mathematics (namely combinatorial game theory) have allowed one to play the earlier stages in a productive way.[33] In other words, Dots and Boxes now has very interesting and powerful heuristics for a certain small player base, namely combinatorial game theorists. Schoolchildren, presumably, have chosen to continue as before.

Exercise 1.8: What are some first-order heuristics in werewolf? What gives werewolf so many basic heuristics?

Exercise 1.9: What are some heuristics that *Risk* and RTS games share? Name some other games that share these heuristics.

Exercise 1.10: What are some heuristics that bridge and hearts share?

Exercise 1.11: Name some games (besides go) with poor first-order heuristics. Why are they so poor?

33. See the references in appendix B, and in particular Berlekamp's *The Dots and Boxes Game*; Berlekamp, Conway, and Guy's *Winning Ways for Your Mathematical Plays*, vol. 2; and Albert, Nowakowski, and Wolfe's *Lessons in Play*.

2 Multiplayer Games

When a game has multiple players, many phenomena arise that are absent in two-player games. We discuss a number of them in this section. Most of them are, properly speaking, phenomena of multi*sided* games: when a game has three or more sides, one side can be eliminated but the remaining sides continue to play, or perhaps two sides collude against the third (an example of politics), or perhaps the losing side picks which of the two frontrunners actually wins (kingmaking). It's easiest, though, to think of these phenomena in games where there is just one player per side, and hence we normally speak (somewhat imprecisely) simply of "multiplayer" games.

Multiplayer games can allow a widely varying amount of interaction among the players. This amount of interaction will lead to critical differences in many aspects of play.

Some multiplayer (multisided) games can be categorized as races. Races are generally games built up from one-player games. Other games are best categorized as brawls, which are at their core irreducibly two-player games with extra players added.[1] Many of the multiplayer characteristics of a game will come out of this distinction. In particular, races tend to have logical elimination (defined below) and low amounts of interactivity, politics, and kingmaking; brawls tend to have high amounts of interactivity, politics, and kingmaking.

There are of course games that fall in between these two extremes. Typically they can vary between these two styles of play inside the rules, and agentially differ in how the gameplay is expressed. Purposefully constructed games can attempt to cut this line down the middle; *RoboRally* is one example. Some of the interest in playing such a game is seeing just how the play develops from session to session.

Although many multiplayer phenomena can be seen most clearly in games where there is one player per side (and three or more sides), there are, of course, many important games that *do* have multiple players on a single side. The most basic case

1. Our categorization here is similar to James Ernest's distinction between "racing games" and "fighting games" (Salen and Zimmerman, *Rules of Play*, 594).

is the two-sided team game, like soccer or bridge. In these games, issues of teamwork arise—what roles do the different team members play? How do they communicate with one another? And, as a special case, sometimes there is only a single side, and all the players are on it, winning or losing together. These are the cooperative games, such as *Hacky Sack* or (sometimes) *World of Warcraft*. They are, quite simply, the team analog of single-player games, just as two-sided team games are the team analog of two-player games.

It's worth spending a bit more time discussing races and brawls before examining the multiplayer characteristics themselves.

Races are built[2] by gluing together a number of copies of a one-player game, one for each player. Each player is pursuing her own victory condition. A footrace, *Scrabble*, and golf are all races. Although there are multiple players, one can imagine the race taking place with just one player (perhaps with some rules tweaks).

Brawls are built by taking a two-player game that is not built up from one-player games and adding more players—think, for example, of adding more players to chess. *Risk* and free-for-all *Starcraft* are examples of brawls. There are few if any examples from classic games and sports, for reasons we will discuss below. Unlike a race, it is hard even to imagine reducing a brawl to one player.

The winner of a race is typically determined by some sort of scaled performance: a point score, time, or distance. Often players cannot affect each others' progress much.

The winner of a brawl is typically determined by some variant of "last-person standing": the players knock each other out of contention. Players definitely can affect each other's progress, and indeed much of the gameplay centers around just that.

Many games do not fit this distinction well, in particular poker and many other card games. Gameplay will tend to follow not this categorization of construction, but rather other underlying characteristics such as amount and type of interactivity, type of elimination, and amount of politics. Our focus will be on these basic characteristics rather than general form.

2.1 Characteristic: Player Elimination

In a game, players can be *eliminated*: they're out of the game, but the game continues. Players can be eliminated *strictly*, in the sense that they are entirely out of the game, or *logically*, in that they have no chance of winning although they continue to play (in a sports season where the object is to make the playoffs, this is usually referred to as "mathematical elimination"). Being out of a game is generally less fun than being in it (or one would not play); being in a game but having no chance to win is often

2. "Built" in the sense of how their gameplay is logically constructed; no claims about the games' historical origins are intended.

Figure 2.1
©iStockphoto.com/Sergejs Razvodovskis

even less fun than that. So how a game handles player elimination can make a big difference to the enjoyability of the game.

One can also speak of *effective* or *perceived* elimination: where a player has a chance to win that is extremely low, but not quite zero, so that she is effectively eliminated, or she thinks of herself as all but eliminated. Such a measure is highly subjective, of course—different players in the same game, or the same player at different times, may perceive the same game state in different ways. The nature of the game itself matters a great deal as well—a player in a lottery might see himself as very much in the running with a less than 1 percent chance to win, whereas that same player might feel effectively eliminated in a chess game where he had the same chance. Players who perceive themselves to be eliminated may be unhappy to continue the game, and they may resign if the game rules (either written rules or social conventions) permit.

One-Sided Games

The situation here is basically equivalent to that of two-sided games (below). Note that computer players are generally quite bad at conceding appropriately, though. In some computer games (e.g., *Civilization*) the distance between logical elimination and strict elimination of one's computer opponent can be dismayingly great. In one-sided games where the human player perceives himself as eliminated, there is essentially no social pressure against resigning. The effective elimination problem is in some sense halved.

Two-Sided Games

The analysis of player elimination is quite different depending on the number of sides. In a two-sided game, strict elimination poses no special problems: the game is over, and someone has won. A new game can now be started if the players wish to continue playing.

One exception occurs with two-sided team games, where it's possible to be out of the game (perhaps because of injury in a sport, or the elimination of all your units in an RTS) while your team plays on. As in any case of strict elimination, the eliminated player is converted into a spectator, but in this case he is a more interested spectator, since his team is still in the game.

Logical elimination can be an issue with two-sided games, but there is an easy solution: the eliminated (i.e., losing) player can concede. If the losing player does not concede, the game is now pointless for both players, at least from the point of view of winning. So why would the losing player not concede? There are at least three possible reasons.

First, the losing player may not understand that he has lost. He might feel that he is merely behind but still with a chance to win. This is most likely to occur in games with a great deal of skill where the less skilled player is behind. (It can also occur in games with hidden information, where the losing player doesn't see the information that would let him understand he is losing.) His positional heuristics may simply be inadequate. This will be somewhat frustrating to the more skilled player, but the less skilled player feels he is playing a real game, so it's not especially frustrating to him (other than the frustration he'll feel for losing).[3]

Second, the losing player may simply be stubborn or feel that it's "right" to "finish the game." In fact, in some playgroups, this may be the preferred or expected behavior. On some level, the feeling that a hopeless game should be played to completion (or more generally, how hopeless a game has to be before conceding makes sense) is just a social convention. If both players share the same understanding, it's not often a problem; if players have differing views (especially common online), frustration can ensue. It is interesting that some classic games that often have an especially long period of effective elimination have developed extensive cultures of resignation. Chess provides the best example of this. The game has solved this problem agentially over

3. One particularly nice way to reward the better player for that player's superior positional heuristics is the doubling cube in backgammon (a remarkable device from a number of perspectives). A winning player can offer a double, and if the losing player makes the wrong decision on accepting it, the winning player will be rewarded. Use of the cube does require, however, that the players play for money, or at least for points.

time, and clear deviations from accepted resignation standards in competitive play can be the source of scandal.

Third, the losing player may understand that it is annoying to the winning player to be forced to continue playing, and deliberately draw out the game to frustrate her. This is less common in games among friends (in part because friends presumably are less likely to want to annoy each other, and in part because anyone who gets in the habit of playing this way will find whatever friends he has remaining are unlikely to want to play games with him). It is more common in tournaments. It is even more common online, where inhibitions against antisocial behavior are few, and where losing players can even hope to get a win by concession from their frustrated opponent. In RTS games, it can take the particular form of "hide the farm": a defeated player will build a small building in an out-of-the-way place in the hope that it will take the winning player a long time to find it (see the discussion of griefing in section 7.5).

In environments where losing players are likely to draw out games, it's usually best if the game mechanics allow a winning player quickly and easily to turn a logically eliminated player into a strictly eliminated one. Automatically revealing hidden buildings of an RTS player who has no army and no economy is one example of such a mechanic.

Multiplayer Games

When one player is strictly eliminated, the others typically keep playing. On the one hand, this can be seen as a bad thing: the eliminated player is no longer able to have the fun of playing the game. If the game takes a long time for the remaining players to finish, the eliminated player may well decide to go do something else and thus not be available to join the next game, leading the session to break up.

On the other hand, the alternative is often for that player to be logically eliminated, which can be worse. Race games, such as *Scrabble*, are particularly prone to this—the simplicity of the race game positional heuristic makes it easy to see that you have no chance. Playing a game when you have no chance to win is frustrating. And if you are strictly eliminated, at least you can go to the bathroom, get a snack, or simply relax for a few moments. The length of time until the next game starts is probably the largest factor in how annoying players will find it to be knocked out of a game (beyond, of course, the annoyance of losing). In poker, people sit out hands all the time and it's no big deal because the next hand starts quickly. In *Monopoly* or (multiplayer LAN) *Starcraft*, players may sit out for quite a while.[4]

In party games, where people are more focused on being together socially and relatively less focused on the game itself (and who is winning it, and by how much),

4. In online *Starcraft* play, as opposed to LAN play, a player can immediately find a new game, and the cost of elimination goes way down.

strictly eliminating a player is especially costly. So avoiding strict player elimination in party games is especially important, particularly if long wait times are involved, and logical elimination, while still bad, is perhaps not quite as bad as it would be in a more competitive game. *Monopoly* used to live in the party game space but has to some extent been supplanted by games like *Pictionary* and *Trivial Pursuit*; long wait times for eliminated players may be part of the reason.

Although being strictly eliminated is often preferable to being forced to play while logically eliminated, far better is not to be eliminated at all. Many games are designed to allow players, even ones who are clearly behind, still to have some chance to win. *Trivial Pursuit*, for example, although it is a race game, has no upper limit to how far one can progress in a single turn. Thus any player has a chance of taking the lead at any point.[5]

One variant that is occasionally used is to eliminate the winners: in card games where the object is to eliminate one's hand, such as Old Maid, people stop playing once they have won, and the potential losers continue to play. In a footrace, players drop out of the race beginning with the winner. The same considerations (e.g., keeping wait times short for those sitting out) still apply, but the annoyance of elimination is considerably lessened psychologically by the reward of winning. Ending the game with the elimination of a single loser is another possibility; see section 3.3 for further discussion.

Overall, though, a game tends to be faced with three basic options, each of which carries its own risks:

1. Strictly eliminate players.
2. Logically or effectively eliminate players.
3. Give everyone a chance to win until the very end.

The first option, common in brawls, risks making the eliminated players unhappy. The second, common in many games, risks making them unhappy (once they realize their state) and leaves them in the game where they may disrupt play for others. The third is tricky to do, and may lead to a game where only the very last portion of the game is relevant.

Playing for Points

Some games, bridge for example, track points in each subgame, so that a player cares how much he loses by. That means there is no logical elimination (or, if you prefer, that logical elimination's pernicious side effects are avoided), because it is always valu-

5. This design feature can backfire. The authors know of one family, extremely good at trivia, that bought a copy of *Trivial Pursuit*, sat down to play, and had the first team on its first turn go all the way to the end and win. They decided the game was pointless and never played again.

able for a player to eke out a few more points even if he is fated to lose that particular subgame. Without the pressures of logical elimination to drive it, strict elimination becomes unnecessary in such games as well,[6] so elimination in general is pretty much a nonissue.

Games played for money are particularly good examples of how a point system can prevent the problems of logical elimination. Money can be thought of as a point-tracking mechanism that matters even after the game is over, so that no matter how far behind you are, you still care about playing as well as you can. In poker, even if you have no chance at having the most chips at the end of the night, you still care about how you do in those last few hands.

Informally, players who are losing in games with logical elimination may play in an analogous fashion, playing to do as well as possible according to some simple positional heuristic, usually score or distance along a track. For example, in *Scrabble* a player who may have no chance of getting the most points, and thus winning the game, will probably be playing to get as many points as possible anyway. (Of course, it's hard to play this way in games without simple positional heuristics.) This way of playing allows players who are losing still to find some meaning in their choices and in their play of the game, and thus presumably to find some enjoyment despite being logically eliminated. Sometimes this behavior will be called "playing for points" (if the game has points) or "playing for second" (or third, etc.).

In a game that allows for this sort of play, it is often an unspoken social convention that players should play this way if they are logically eliminated. If a player who has no chance to win forgoes this style of play and instead chooses to focus on affecting the play of other players in an attempt to determine which other player will win the game, the group will not be pleased. Such play is called "kingmaking" and is discussed below.

Online Play

The logic of player elimination shifts somewhat with online play.

Some things get worse: many kinds of behavior that are fairly rare in face-to-face gaming become more common online. For two-player games, the additional problems are enough to take player elimination from a relative nonissue in paper gaming to a moderately serious one in computer gaming. "Hide the farm" and other failures to concede are the most obvious examples.

Some things get better: strict elimination can generally be solved by having the eliminated player immediately begin a new game. This solution comes with its own set of problems, though: repeat play with the same group of people becomes more

6. Bridge has it nevertheless, but the duration is short and it serves largely as an opportunity for one essentially random person (the dummy) to get drinks for the table.

difficult, and players who are only losing by a bit may just quit to try again, leading to some unsatisfying games. Players that perceive themselves as eliminated generally have a much stronger recourse during online play than in physical play. They can either join a new game instantly or begin griefing the other players by remaining as long as possible. In many ways the effectively eliminated player has gained power at the expense of others. This can be an especially large problem if a player's perception of his chances differ greatly from his teammates. He may leave a game still being contested, often dooming his side prematurely. Direct social pressure virtually eliminates this possibility in offline play. The anonymous nature of most online play provides challenges for designers struggling to use social structures to solve problems of effective elimination in the same way the chess community does.

Still, although the frequency of the various problems may be different, many of the fundamental issues are the same. And for some forms of online play, such as a group of friends wishing to play several games in a row, the situation can look very similar to face-to-face play.

Exercise 2.1: Describe the strict and logical elimination in werewolf. Describe the effective elimination.

Exercise 2.2: Describe the strict and logical elimination in *Survivor*. Describe the effective elimination.

Exercise 2.3: How much logical elimination is there in chess? Discuss the effective elimination in chess. How does it vary based on player skill?

Exercise 2.4: How much logical elimination is there in soccer? How much effective elimination? Why is resignation a common part of chess, but not soccer?

2.2 Characteristic: Interactivity

Games vary widely in their interactivity: the ability of players to influence the progress of players other than themselves.[7] A boxing match, or a game of chess, is highly interactive. A footrace is almost entirely noninteractive. Note that we do not use the term *interactivity* the way it is used in computer gaming, meaning something like the reciprocal action of the player and the game system on each other (see chapter 6 of Salen and Zimmerman's *Rules of Play* for extensive discussion).

7. Note that even to discuss interactivity presupposes at least some basic level of positional heuristics. You can't know if you are changing the progress of other players if there's no way to tell how other players are doing. As an example, imagine a game where each player rolls a die in secret, and then all dice are revealed, with the highest untied die roll winning. If just before dice are revealed players may force other players to reroll, is the game interactive or not? The question is moot.

Figure 2.2
©iStockphoto.com/Brane Bozic

This section introduces interactivity, and sections 2.3 and 2.4 on politics and king-making pursue the subject in more detail.

Races, Brawls, and Interactivity

In some games, each player is trying to achieve a result, and players can't influence each other (or can't do so very much). If a winner is declared in a race game, it will be based on some sort of score (often the score is time, i.e., whoever achieves a certain result first is the winner, but it may be some other score, as in golf). Classic sports races are the most common example, but many track boardgames, such as *Candy Land* or *Parcheesi*, are to some degree races. Any solitaire game with a score can be played as a race, with each person playing separately and the scores compared at the end; this is a common play pattern for arcade games. Such play patterns can serve as the basis for more interactive variants, as in the case of the card game Spit.

Even in games where players can't directly influence each other, they often can react to each other's progress by altering their strategy. A longer race, like a marathon or (in our sense of "race") a golf tournament, is more likely to give opportunities for such a reaction. The reaction may simply be one of trying harder (physically or intellectually). On a more strategic level, the reaction usually takes the form of a press-your-luck strategy: when ahead, be conservative; when behind, risk falling even further behind in an effort to win. Examples of nonsports games that are essentially races and that have a strong press-your-luck element include *Yahtzee* and *Can't Stop*.

Note that a game can be more or less of a race, just as an activity can be more or less of a game (and indeed this point of view applies to all our definitions). A sprint is very much a race, since players hardly interact at all. A marathon or a game of *Yahtzee* is essentially a race, but perhaps a less pure one since players can press their luck when behind.

Backgammon is somewhat like a race, in that both players are heading toward their own personal win condition. And after a certain point many backgammon games become a true race, with the opposing pieces having passed each other and no longer able to interact. But backgammon is somewhat like a brawl, in that the level of interaction is fairly high and players can capture each other's pieces. It is hard to think of chess as a race at all. Note that in backgammon one can imagine playing solitaire with no enemy pieces on the board, attempting to win as quickly as possible, something difficult even to imagine with chess.

Sometimes players are trying to interfere with one another directly, as in a brawl, and strong player interaction is built right into the system. Just as various game features can be added to increase interaction in a race (think for example of the shells in *Mario Kart*), limits can be added to a brawl to control its level of interaction. But in the absence of such limits, brawls will exhibit certain common features that we discuss in sections 2.3 and 2.4 on politics and kingmaking. And in the absence of added interactivity, races will not exhibit these features. So while the race or brawl core of a game may push it in a certain direction, ultimately it is the level and kind of interactivity that is telling.

Targeted Interactions

It is useful to break down the interaction between players not only by amount, but also by the degree of control over the interaction a player has. If a player has an opportunity to interact with another player, and that first player may choose which player to interact with, we refer to the interaction as *targeted*. A common example in a game with customized cards is a card that allows the user to choose another player and do something bad to him (typically take one of his assets, i.e., take one of his chips—see below). This distinction is obviously meaningless in two-player games, but it becomes very important in multisided ones, as we will soon see.

Note that despite the terminology, targeted interaction often is not negative to the player being targeted. The ability to trade with other players gives a positive game state change to the two trading. *Scrabble* provides another example, where playing long words and stretching the board might give an advantage to the current player and the one immediately following. In a three-player *Scrabble* game, depending on player skill and the board state, by deciding how defensively to play, one is effectively targeting one of the other players.

Interactivity and the Number of Players

The right way to think about interactivity depends very much on the number of players, or more precisely on the number of sides. Interactivity is at its most complex and most problematic in games with more than two sides, and, after a brief discussion of the simpler cases, that case is the one we will focus on, both in this section and the related sections to follow.

For true one-player games, there's nothing to discuss—no other players means no one to interact with.[8] For "one and a half" player games, discussions of interactivity run along the lines of such discussions for two-player games, with the imagined or computer opponent taking the place of the human one in the two-player case. A computer's behavior, of course, will often be different from a human's: computers are not good at conceding appropriately, but are otherwise unlikely to engage in griefing. The underlying level of gameplay interactivity will be about the same.

In two-sided games (of which two-player games are of course a special case), interactivity is relatively unproblematic, at least in principle. By and large, it's good for the players to be able to influence each other, because it makes the game more interesting. If the players can't influence each other at all, they might as well play solitaire against a set score, so why go to the trouble of finding an opponent for such a game? And indeed, two player races are rare.[9] The vast majority of two-sided games are highly interactive—chess, soccer, fencing, a one-on-one *Starcraft* match, and *Mortal Kombat*, to name just a few.

In multisided games, as we will see, the situation is quite different.

Exercise 2.5: Describe the degree of interactivity and targeting in werewolf player interaction.

Exercise 2.6: Describe the degree of interactivity and targeting in *Survivor* player interaction.

8. This points out again the difference between our definition of interactivity and the definition used in computer game studies. In the computer game sense of "interactivity," there is a great deal to say about single-player games; indeed they are arguably the model case for interactivity discussions. Again, we point the interested reader to Salen and Zimmerman's *Rules of Play* and the references contained therein.

9. This argument raises the question of why there are races at all, which will be discussed below.

Exercise 2.7: What is the degree of interactivity in (touring) bicycle racing? Why is this form of race no longer an individual event (the Tour de France started as an individual event)?

2.3 Characteristic: Politics

The Chip-Taking Game

Imagine a game, which we'll call the "chip-taking game," where each player starts with a pile of ten chips. Players take turns going around the table. On her turn, a player may take one chip from any player and discard it. The winner is the last person with any chips left.

Most people would not enjoy playing this game for long. There is no real skill involved, other than the skill of convincing other people not to take your chips. And even if you possess that skill, once the other players notice you have it, they will probably react by trying to eliminate you first.

Unfortunately, many multiplayer games reduce to the chip-taking game, in the sense that most of their game features are irrelevant for determining the winner, who is instead chosen ultimately in chip-taking fashion. All that's necessary is that the game be highly interactive, in the sense that players can affect the positions of other players, and also that players can target whoever they affect.[10] Players can simply choose to hurt ("take chips from") the leader using whatever means the game offers. Even if the leader is highly skilled, he is unlikely to be able to withstand the onslaught of all the other players. Once the leader is eliminated, or at least knocked back from his leading position, the players can attack some new player.

As a simple albeit artificial example, suppose we modify the chip-taking game so that on a player's turn, she chooses another player and plays a game of chess against him; if she wins he discards two chips, and if she loses he discards only one. This game has all the complexity and skill of chess, but it doesn't matter. Kasparov is no more likely to win than anyone else at this game, and probably less; the other players are likely to choose him consistently until he's eliminated.

Targeted Interaction, Politics, and Voting Games

Our previous observation can be restated: a game with a high level of targeted interaction will tend to be a chip-taking game. Note that *both* interaction (in the sense that

10. Oddly enough, poker is not a "chip-taking game" in our sense, because you don't choose your victim. You can only take chips from people who choose to go up against you, a choice based in large part on the randomness of the cards. So in a sense poker is similar to a tournament with random pairings.

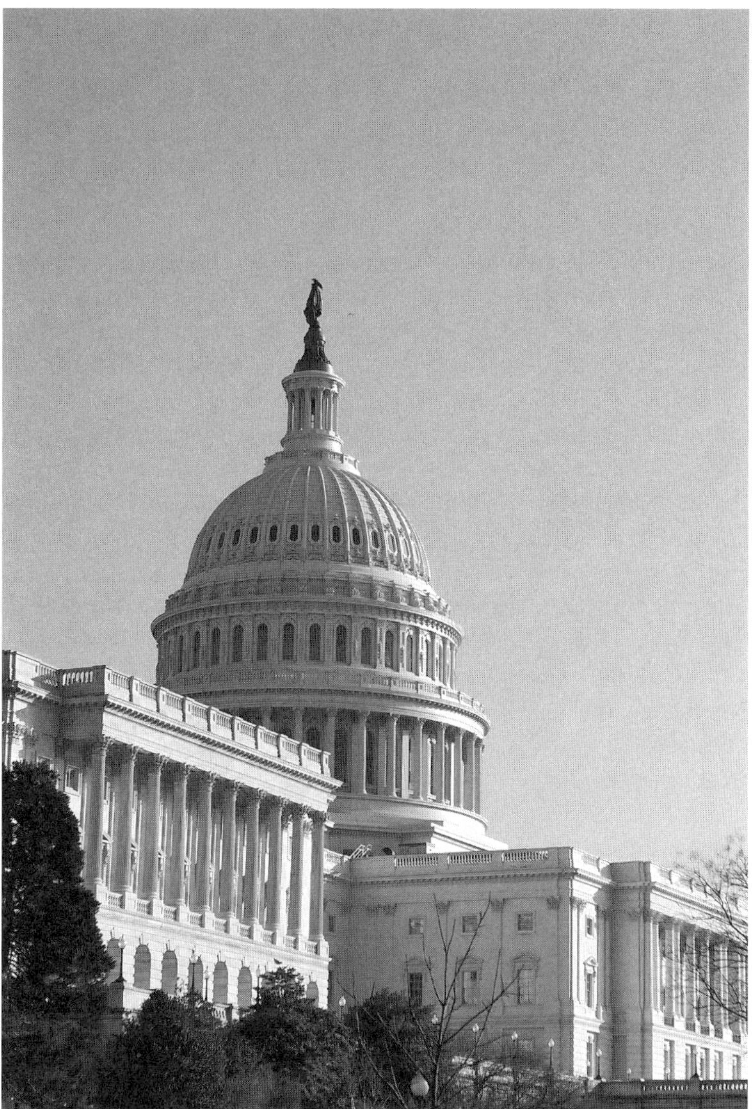

Figure 2.3
©iStockphoto.com/Shane Stezelberger

players can significantly affect other players' game state) and targeting (players can choose who they will affect) are necessary.[11]

When players can target other players in an arbitrary way that differentially affects their game states, we refer to this as *politics*. The higher the degree of interaction (ability to affect each other's game state) and the higher the ability to target specific players, the more political the game is. A game may have political mechanics inside it without its general character dominated by politics.

Some less obvious examples of political mechanics in games include the trading in *Settlers of Catan* or *Monopoly*. Here the players are not choosing someone to hurt, but rather someone to help. The politics arising from trading in these games are mitigated by the rules or by social convention and for most playgroups do not dominate the rest of the game.

Another way to describe a game with a lot of politics is as a *voting game*: the players are essentially electing a winner.[12] As a concrete model, consider the game where in every round, players literally vote for someone to be eliminated, until only two people (who are the cowinners) are left.

Calling a game political, calling it a chip-taking game, or calling it a voting game are all broadly similar. A game with few restrictions on the amount or targeting of trading falls into this category as well. *Political* is the most general term; *chip-taking* emphasizes the ability of players to damage the positions of other players by targeting; *voting* emphasizes the fact that players are choosing a winner according to their tastes rather than that the game process is choosing a winner based on some combination of that winner's skill and whatever luck may be inherent in the game.

Note that virtually no classic boardgames, card games, or sports fall into these categories; examples of highly political games are almost all from modern games. Perhaps this is because politics tends to be "evolved out" of games, or perhaps people's taste in games is changing.

Also keep in mind that all these terms, and indeed this entire section, apply only to games with three or more sides. You can't choose among opponents if you only have one opponent.

Exercise 2.8: Play "Truel" (tri-duel). In this game, three players take turns shooting a target of their choice. One player has an 80 percent hit chance, one 60 percent, one

11. Even with interaction and targeting, a game may still avoid being a chip-taking game by giving players reasons to target one player over another. More on this below.

12. Some games have explicit voting mechanics, in the sense that at certain points during the game players actually vote on something as part of the game. It is not necessary for a game to have a voting mechanic to be a voting game in our sense, although games with voting mechanics may become voting games in our sense to a greater or lesser extent if care is not taken.

40 percent.[13] A player who is hit is out, and the winner is the last person left. Rotate who gets the first shot in each game. Play thirty or so games. What are the results? Are you surprised? What explains your results?

Strategies Found in Political Games

Political games and chip-taking games lead to certain common behaviors among players, such as

- Lying low so that players do not perceive you as a threat.
- Waiting while other players fight it out and then mopping up the pieces.
- Cajoling, whining, or begging other players not to hurt you.
- Offering out-of-game benefits ("I'll get you a Coke") or making out-of-game threats ("You'll have to walk home!") to influence other players' behavior.
- Hurting the player who last hurt you ("revenge").
- Threatening revenge in an effort to get another player to choose a different victim.
- Deliberately taking an action that harms another player but also hurts your own chance of winning, due to anger or in order to establish credibility as a player who will indeed avenge hurts (the latter may be thought of as a rational attempt to win more often in repeat play).
- Taking turns hurting other players, or deciding randomly who to hurt, perhaps to be "fair" or to reduce victims' desire for revenge.
- Explaining to the victim why your choice was the rational one given the current game state (for reasons similar to taking turns above).
- Arguing that a player's choice of you as the victim is not optimal, and that their chances of winning would be higher if they chose another victim.
- Arguing that some other player should "fall on the grenade": make a sacrifice to stop the leader from winning (or getting too far ahead).
- Deliberately passing up an opportunity to stop the leader from winning when your turn comes, so that the last remaining player who has a chance to stop her is forced to "fall on the grenade."
- Kingmaking: near the end of the game, a player who has no chance to win determining which of the players still in contention actually wins (discussed in the next section).

We will sometimes refer to these sorts of behaviors as "political."[14] Note how generic these effects are, in the sense that they occur independent of the game mechanics of any particular game. If the game has targeted interaction, the above effects will occur.

13. If you can't find a ten-sided die, use a six-sided die and reroll all 6s (so the first player hits on 1–4, the second player hits on 1–3, and the third player hits on 1–2).

14. We make this somewhat inconsistent word choice partly because "the kinds of behaviors that tend to arise from strong targeted interaction" is just too long, and partly because it accords with the common usage of game players.

If the game has enough targeted interaction, the above effects will dominate the game, and in some sense all games with enough targeted interaction are the same game.[15] One's ability to win such a game will depend more on one's skill with the above behaviors than with any skills specific to that particular game's mechanics.

Problems with Politics

If political games have a problem, it is not that political interaction is inherently uninteresting—although there are some players who play games hoping to avoid that sort of thing—but that it can overwrite the rest of the game. Skill at the game doesn't necessarily increase one's chances of victory,[16] and in fact it may decrease it as one becomes more of a target for the other players.

If one considers games from the point of view of heuristics, the potential problems of political games are highlighted. Normal positional heuristics become largely irrelevant: if at any point any player can be "picked on" and eliminated by group consensus, how can one know what one's position in the game is? And if positional heuristics are irrelevant (or, more precisely, if positional heuristics relating to the mechanics of that particular game are replaced by general social heuristics involving predictions of who is likely to do what to whom), then directional heuristics (again, of other than the social kind) are likewise irrelevant.

Depending on the playgroup, climbing the heuristics tree in highly political games can be very interesting. Without a good grasp of the basic positional heuristics (those independent of politics), the effect of political interaction can be mitigated. Once a set of players has developed a good set positional heuristics independent of the politics, the game can often be reduced to a simple voting one, but that process of understanding who is in the lead and how to stop them is often an interesting one.

Games with targeted interaction are more prone to arguments. In a game without targeted interaction—a two-player game like chess, for example—there's no need to argue with someone that she is following the wrong strategy. If the other player is hurting herself, then so much the better for your chances.[17] But if someone is taking

15. The cynical (or realistic, depending on your point of view) may see some resemblance to life in general.

16. Thoughtful readers will notice a paradox: How can skill not increase one's chances of victory, since being skillful at a game means by definition that one does things that make one more likely to win it? A more precise way of stating the situation would be that skill at making game choices that increase one's progress toward the victory condition doesn't actually increase one's chances of victory, and that the true skill in the game is thus the skill of convincing players to attack players other than oneself, through means such as lying low until the last minute, looking harmless and friendly, threatening out-of-game consequences, whining, browbeating, and so on.

17. Of course, in a friendly game one might point out an error just to be helpful. And a very nasty player might try to talk someone out of a winning move (which is why it often pays not to listen to an opponent's advice in very competitive situations).

one of your chips in a game with targeted interaction, it is to your advantage to convince him to take someone else's chip. Perhaps there are good reasons for him to take someone else's chip, and you need only make him understand that—and how frustrating if he does not! But if the game is very political, and his choice is essentially arbitrary, there is still some pressure on you to convince him to make a different, but still arbitrary, choice, a situation unlikely to lead to enjoyable or productive conversation.

Players' problems with politics can also be mitigated in situations where there is some consensus that a particular move is forced due to its clearly being the best option. For instance, consider a toy game where players on their turn can either add two chips to their total or take one away from another player. The game ends when any player gets to ten chips. If players A, B, and C have two chips each, and player A decides to take a chip away from player B, you are likely to hear complaints. If instead the chip totals are respectively two, eight, and two, and player A takes a chip away from B (whose turn is next), the social situation, for most groups, will be much different.

This toy game is illustrative of a not uncommon pattern of interaction in political games, namely players try to avoid interactions that affect another player differentially until they either feel they can win despite others' political actions against them or they feel they must interact negatively with a particular player, the leader, to have any chance of winning.

To avoid misunderstanding, it should be mentioned that although political games commonly contain argument, discussion, or debate, these features are not the defining features of politics. A fast-paced game—say, a free-for-all RTS—may move too quickly to allow argument. But it still has politics because people can attack other players for arbitrary reasons: the basic ingredients of interaction and targeting are still there. And a two-sided game like werewolf/mafia has a great deal of discussion and argument, but no politics as we are defining it. With only two sides, there is no possibility of choosing an opponent, hence no scope for politics.[18]

Some Advantages of Politics

In general, we have been talking about politics as a bad thing in games, but in practice allowing room for political interaction has many excellent effects.

18. One could argue that, for example, the werewolves choose *which* member of the townsfolk they will slay. But this is more like a football player choosing who to block: there's a natural choice, namely whichever opponent is most dangerous. We don't include choices of this nature in our concept of politics. From our point of view, these choices are more analogous to a choice such as which opponent's piece to take in chess—a choice that could indeed be made arbitrarily (one doesn't like how the knight is sculpted, say) but that does not share enough of the characteristics of what we call politics to be profitably discussed with it.

One advantage of political games, or political variants of nonpolitical games (such as free-for-all *Magic* or *Starcraft*), is that they can provide opportunities for low-skilled players to participate in high-skilled games (surviving and perhaps even winning because the high-skilled players attract more attention). While some highly skilled players may object in principle to this leveling of the playfield, in practice it allows them to play more games due to an increased potential audience size. Additionally it makes those games interesting, whereas otherwise they may not be, due to the natural dampening effect on skill that political interaction can have. Finding players to play games is generally speaking the hardest part of playing the average game, and anything that can increase the potential audience size is extremely valuable to both player and publisher. This is an important effect in family games and children's games, where the set of people playing a particular game is fixed and wide skill ranges are common. *Mario Kart* and *Mario Party* find much advantage in their limited politics as a way to keep multiplayer games interesting for a single family or friend group.

Political games tend to be exciting to the very end (on the downside, depending on the game design, they may drag on too long). The lead will change many times, as each new winner is picked on in turn. Any player has a chance to win (the flipside of this is that any actions other than those near the end of the game may not matter much). One can think of "pick on the leader" as a catch-up feature. Like any catch-up feature, it can become problematic when it is too powerful (see section 4.2 on snowball and catch-up), but it can be perfectly reasonable in small doses—many multiplayer games use it to good effect.

Some people just plain enjoy the social interaction, give-and-take, alliance making and breaking, and other behaviors that are common in political games. Since complex game mechanics tend to get wiped out by politics, it's usually best to keep the game relatively simple for this audience. A good example is the boardgame *Diplomacy*: there's no need to have countless kinds of military units and detailed combat simulations with charts and die rolls. Such details would only be washed out by the negotiations, alliances, and betrayals that are the real heart of the game.

Political games can be fun to watch, even if you don't know the details of how a game is played: the ebb and flow of human social interaction is something everyone can relate to. Outrage and betrayal make for good theater as well. The TV show *Survivor* is just one example. (*Survivor* is an extreme example of kingmaking in particular: there's even an extra kingmaking step where strictly eliminated players are brought back to vote on the final winner!)

A key to understanding the place of politics in a game is understanding its audience. While classic games have evolved along with their player bases so there is a matching of political interaction with the stomach for it among the players, a new game needs to take this into account from the design. Is the game intended to be primarily for competitive players interested in differentiating their skill from one another? If so, it is probably best to keep politics to a minimum by making it two-sided, making it less interactive, giving players rewards for their absolute instead of relative finish, or hampering players' ability to target one another specifically. For a more casual intended audience, politics can be a useful way of increasing the effective critical mass for play, since more widely varying skill sets can find interesting games together. Additionally, intensity of play is not nearly as much of a prerequisite for winning in a political game.

The Difficulty of Analyzing Strategy for Targeted Interaction: The Balloon Game

Picking on the leader is not politics in the narrow sense of the term (an arbitrary decision that does not affect one's own chance of winning);[19] it's often a natural strategy of other players who are simply attempting to win themselves. But people's intuition may lead them to pick on the leader more than they should, as the following simple game shows.

Three players, A, B, and C, each have a balloon. They each simultaneously choose an opposing balloon and throw a dart at it. Anyone whose balloon is popped is out (if all three hit or all three miss, everyone goes again). If only one person is knocked out the remaining two play for the win, repeating if necessary until one of the two wins.

Suppose A has a 60 percent chance to hit his target, B a 50 percent chance, and C a 40 percent chance. The "obvious" strategy is for each person to go for the biggest target (A aims at B, B and C both aim at A). This gives B a 19 percent chance to win. If B switches to C, though, then B has a 23 percent chance to win.

Exercise 2.9: Compute the above chances.

Thus if B takes the natural "pick on the leader" strategy, he actually gets worse results. Although the balloon game may seem artificial, many multiplayer game situations are not that different in broad outline: three players, one in the lead, and both of the players who are behind attack the leader. Depending on the details of the game, that may or may not be the correct strategy.

The player who is the leader, if he understands the situation, will be especially frustrated that the other players are conspiring against him, even to the point of their own detriment. He may argue against the other players' actions, but will not necessarily be believed, for his arguments will appear self-serving (which indeed they are, although they are still correct—B is hurting both A and himself by attacking A, and C is the real beneficiary of B's incorrect choice). Such a player will probably avoid chip-taking games.

19. It is of course political in the broader sense of being a common behavior in chip-taking games.

Of some interest is the difficulty in analyzing real-world politics in a non-two-party system. This is analogous to the situation in the balloon game. The amount of power a given party in a parliament may have relative to its seats can be extremely deceptive. In the simple example of a single majority vote with parties of size 46 percent, 45 percent, and 9 percent, it is unclear which party holds the most power. *Any* two of these parties together can decide the issue, and presumably deals on future votes can be made, significantly equalizing their power despite their relative sizes.

Players with a detailed conscious understanding of political and chip-taking dynamics are rare,[20] but many skillful players have at least some intuition that politics works against them. One can see this, for example, in RTS games, where "serious" players avoid free-for-all variants and prefer one-on-one games or two-sided team games.

Exercise 2.10: What do political games do to state heuristics in general?

Exercise 2.11: How much politics is there in werewolf? Why does it feel like a political game?

Exercise 2.12: If the state heuristics in a highly interactive two-player game are poor, how might this affect the politics in a multisided version of the game?

2.4 Characteristic: Kingmaking

Often in a multiplayer game, it happens that players A and B are in contention to win, and player C has no chance. If the game has any interaction, it may be that C is in a position to determine the winner by choosing which of the two players A and B to interact with. This is commonly referred to as "kingmaking."[21] This choice is necessarily political, in that C is assumed to have no choice of winning, and thus kingmaking, like politics in general, is a property of games with three or more players (or, more precisely, three or more sides).

20. The authors hope there will be at least a few more such players because of this book!

21. The term is natural enough on its own (C is determining whether A or B will be "king"), but it's possible that it came from the Avalon Hill boardgame *Kingmaker*. In that game, based on the War of the Roses, players manipulated various heirs to the throne in an attempt to get an heir they controlled crowned king. However, a player with no viable heirs could often prevent the heir of the leading player from ascending to the throne, thereby causing the second-place player to win.

Figure 2.4

The key ingredients of kingmaking are simply targeted interaction and the existence of logically eliminated players.

Players generally, and the player who was in contention but not chosen as the winner in particular, feel kingmaking is unfair. In some sense, kingmaking is all the problems of politics writ large: at a single moment, the very winner of the game is determined by the choice of a player not in contention, and all the skill and strategy (or luck) of the other contenders is for naught. Player dislike of kingmaking is a big reason to avoid logical elimination of players, either by always giving players a chance to catch up or by ensuring they are strictly eliminated once they are logically eliminated. And player dislike of kingmaking is a big part of the reason that virtually no competitive multiplayer games are high interaction with a lot of scope for targeted interaction.

Highly political games will almost always have kingmaking. But it is possible for a game that is not otherwise a chip-taking game still to suffer from kingmaking. If a game includes many mechanisms to give players reasons to attack one player over another (e.g., resources that might be easier to seize from one potential victim than from another), a great deal of politics can be eliminated. But kingmaking may remain: once a player is out of contention, his in-game incentives to choose one victim over another largely vanish, and he makes a political decision whether he wants to or not (games played for money, or other ongoing point systems, are an exception). One example is a Swiss tournament, where a player who is out of contention can influence who makes the top eight by conceding to a player who is borderline—while a player is still in contention, she's hardly likely to concede to alter the fates of others, but after she's out of contention she may well do so.[22]

One example from "classic" sports is that of a commissioner for a league. It is quite common for a team to be logically eliminated toward the end of a season and effectively eliminated long before that. In the real world, teams are often given benefits for winning individual games beyond the benefits for winning or placing well within the season, such as revenue from increased attendance. In fantasy sports leagues, however, similar pressures are usually nonexistent, requiring a commissioner to approve all trades. Were it not for this, kingmaking could become a virtually insurmountable issue in those groups, as players who had no chance to win the season made unreasonably generous trades with friends who were in contention. In the world of physical sports, revenue pressures prevent such "giveaway" trades. In the fantasy leagues played face-to-face or among groups of friends, an agential pressure to "do your best" can inhibit them; but in online fantasy sports leagues a commissioner is needed.

Another less extreme type of kingmaking is blind kingmaking, where a player adds randomness to the choice of winner but does not preferentially choose a specific winner. Examples are poker, where a bad player in the pot will essentially give random presents to other players at the table, or *Apples to Apples*, where a player might decide to judge the winner (whose identity is unknown to the judge at the time of the decision) of a hand randomly rather than according to how well they have matched the target word. Kingmaking in many real-time computer games has a feel somewhat similar to that of blind kingmaking, because the choices happen so quickly and there often isn't time for real discussion beforehand (although somehow there always seems to be time for recrimination after the fact). Still, though, the decision was made deliberately, so negative feelings on the part of the victim can be high.

Factors Limiting Politics and Kingmaking

Politics in general, and kingmaking in particular, are common in multiplayer games because it doesn't take much for them to arise: all that is needed is the ability for players to interact, and a degree of choice as to the targets for the interaction. If these

22. In *Magic: The Gathering* tournaments, it is customary to concede to an opponent if he can make the top eight and you cannot. Although it's hardly fair to the person your opponent knocks out of the top eight, it's natural that the custom evolved, given that one can hope for reciprocity from the action at a future tournament. If the tournament is pure Swiss, kingmaking can be reduced by choosing an appropriate prize structure (giving the same prizes to people with the same records rather than to the top eight people), but if the tournament is Swiss followed by single elimination among the top eight, it's hard to avoid. This is one of the few reasons to prefer single or double elimination to Swiss.

effects are strong enough, the game may reduce to a version of the chip-taking game, which may not be what the designers or players want. Thus many multiplayer games include mechanisms to inhibit politics in some way.

Of course, as we discussed above, there are advantages to politics in games as well as disadvantages. In small doses, there may be more fun than harm, and even extremely political games have an audience. But having spent some time looking at factors that cause politics and kingmaking, it makes sense to spend a little time looking at factors that inhibit them.

One very basic way a game with many players can avoid politics is by being a two-sided team game. There are many players, but with only two sides, politics isn't a problem.[23] Sometimes it makes sense for the campaign to be about individuals competing, but for the games within the campaign still to be team-based—for example, *World of Warcraft* battlegrounds randomly assign people to teams for each game, but track success over time on an individual level.

If a game has more than two sides, then limitations to the game's politics come mainly from limitations to interactivity. Questions to ask about the game include: How strong is the interactivity—that is, how much can players affect the fates of other players? Are they limited in which other players they can select as their victims? If they are not much limited, do they at least have reasons to choose one victim over another, reasons involving in-game benefits that accrue to the choosing player?

The extreme example here is the race: no (or almost no) interactivity allowed. Races are therefore not limited to two players, and as a consequence often take advantage of this fact by adding players up to other, usually physical, limits. Highly interactive games on the other hand are almost always two-sided affairs if they have been played for many years and achieved "classic" status. In a two-player situation, there's no pressure to limit interactivity, so the greater interest in interactivity triumphs (and those who don't want interactivity will probably be drawn to one-player games). But in multiplayer games, one way to solve the problems of interactivity is to have the game be a race.

Relatively few games are pure races in the sense that there is no player interactivity at all (sprints and bicycle time trials probably come the closest).[24] Very common, though, are games where the basic structure is a race and some amount of interactivity is layered on top: in *Parcheesi* you can blockade or send pieces home, in most European

23. Politics in the sense we are discussing. In the English sense of the word, of course, there can be a lot of politics on a team, especially a team of gamers!

24. Even there, there is some interaction of the press-your-luck variety, with false starts in a sprint and cycling differently based on the time of those who have gone before you. In nonsports games, (close to) pure races are even less common, but *Candy Land* and *Trivial Pursuit* would be examples. A crossword puzzle tournament might be another.

boardgames you are accumulating points but your actions will affect the availability of various point-accumulation strategies to the other players, and in Go Fish players are racing to complete books but may steal cards from other players. The higher the level of interactivity, the less the game will feel like a race (a solitaire game where you are looking over your shoulder to see how others are doing) and the more it will partake of the phenomena we've been discussing.

If the game is at its core a brawl, it will be highly interactive. But there can be limits to which other players a given player is allowed to interact with—that is, limits to targeting. These limits can arise by means of geography: in *Risk*, you can't attack anyone you please, but only players your pieces are adjacent to. In *Quake*, you can only shoot at players in the room with you. In *Magic: The Gathering*, a standard multiplayer variant allows you only to interact with the players to your left and right.[25] And even a chess tournament can be thought of as a multiplayer game where you are allowed to interact with only one person at a time (namely your opponent for the current round), a person you do not choose. Note that a mechanism like "you can only attack those near you" is rarely chosen consciously, and is more often the result of the flavor of the game (e.g., it's natural for weapons to have a limited range). It's good to be aware of what game flavor is doing to game mechanics, though. And if a designer wants to make a game that strays from established conventions, this awareness is vital.

If players have a lot of choice as to who they can interact with, you can still control politics by giving them in-game benefits for interacting with specific other players. If a player attacks another player because she controls a lot of clay, a resource he wants, then he isn't attacking someone just because she's in the lead, or just because he doesn't like her. And she's less likely to feel picked on—after all, it's "fair" that he's attacking her, because he does want the clay.

Behaviors that involve hanging back and doing nothing are particularly pernicious, because if everyone engages in them the game grinds to a halt. In the absence of inducements to fight, hanging back can be tempting, because one can hope to mop up the weakened survivors. So it's often good to have rewards for attacking other players. In *Risk*, you attack enemy players because you want their resources. Moreover, you are encouraged to eliminate them because then you get their cards as well.[26] In

25. Other games that use a similar mechanic are the live-action game Assassin/Killer and a variant of the RTS game *Rise of Nations*. In the former case, you are assigned a specific target and there is little if any benefit to you to interact with anyone other than your target (and the person whose target you are); in the latter case, you take a high attrition damage penalty for attacking anyone other than your assigned target.

26. Rewards for eliminating players can also help shift logical elimination to strict elimination, which is typically an improvement.

free-for-all *Starcraft*, you might be inclined to hang back and let others fight; in *Warcraft III*, however, you might want to do some fighting so that your hero gains experience.

However, games with mechanisms to encourage players to attack one player rather than another may still be prone to kingmaking. A player who has no chance to win will be less likely to be influenced by whatever incentives are placed before him. So kingmaking might require separate controls, such as making sure that players who are about to lose won't be able to influence the game too much, or ways to convert logically eliminated players to strictly eliminated ones (so they won't be around for too long causing trouble), or at least a few mechanics that forcibly limit targeting.

Note that some mechanisms that limit the ability of losing players to affect the game don't affect player interaction per se, but can still help limit kingmaking. If the game is highly skill-based, that can sometimes make a difference, because it can limit the ability of a losing player (who is presumably less skilled) to harm a player in contention—think of a *Quake* deathmatch, where a low-skilled player can do little to harm a high-skilled player. Even if lack of skill is not the reason a player is losing, sometimes the very fact of being in a losing position means one has less influence—think of an RTS, where a player close to elimination usually does not have enough power to influence the outcome (an exception might be a player whose economy is completely destroyed while he still has a large army in the field: this puts him in a position analogous to the aforementioned player who is out of contention at a tournament, with no chance of winning but nevertheless an ability to influence the tournament's outcome).

Exercise 2.13: How much kingmaking is there in werewolf?

Exercise 2.14: How much kingmaking is there in *Survivor*?

Exercise 2.15: Give some examples of kingmaking in *Monopoly*.

Exercise 2.16: Give some examples of kingmaking in fantasy sports. What rules are instituted to combat this?

2.5 Characteristic: Teamwork

In games with several players, sometimes two or more of those players are on the same side—that is, they form a team. Players pursuing the same goals behave, of course, very differently from players pursuing opposing goals. In this section we discuss the dynamics among team members, with a focus on the roles of the various players (how they each contribute to the team's success) and on the communication between the team members.

Figure 2.5
©iStockphoto.com/Ana Abejon

One important special case is the cooperative game, where all the players are on the same team and succeed or fail together. We will argue that the right way to look at cooperative games is simply as a combination of single-player games and team games. Neither single-player games nor team games are especially mysterious, although of course each type has its own special issues, and so cooperative games don't have to be thought of as something mysterious either.

Roles in a Team

Players in a team game will potentially have all the desires they would in a nonteam game, such as a desire to win, or a desire to improve their skills by climbing the heuristics tree.[27] But they'll have a new goal as well: the desire to contribute to their team. A successful team game will need ways for all the players to feel they are contributing.

In part, what a player can contribute to a team's chances depends on what role the game assigns to that player. Sometimes those roles are symmetrical: in *Counterstrike*,

27. For more discussion, see section 6.2 on rewards.

every player has the same game abilities as every other. Of course, players will bring their own strengths and weaknesses to the game, but in terms of the game's mechanics, one player is like another. In *Team Fortress*, however, there are specific roles such as Medic or Scout, with different gameplay capabilities. We'll have much more to say about the symmetry, or lack thereof, in players' capabilities in section 3.5. For now, though, a brief discussion will suffice.

These roles within a team, when they exist, can be systemic, as in the *Team Fortress* example, or agential. Many team games, sports in particular, have roles (i.e., positions) that are not built into the rules, but nevertheless are so standard as to be considered very much a part of the game: in basketball, for example, the positions such as point guard or power forward have no special rules status. In soccer, the goalie has special status within the rules but all the other positions are agential.

In games with systemic roles, there may be additional agential roles layered on top of them. For instance, *World of Warcraft* classes such as Warrior, Rogue, or Druid are built into the system directly. Roles such as tank, dps (damage dealer—the term comes from "damage per second"), or healer, however, are not as directly defined. One warrior might serve as a tank; another might focus on dps. Of course, the game in general and the classes in particular were certainly designed with roles in mind, so it is arguable exactly how agential the roles are. Still, the roles definitely have a different status than the classes, and they are arguably more fundamental: it might be better to think of a *World of Warcraft* "team" as a tank, a healer, two dps'ers, and a hybrid, than to think of it as a Warrior, a Priest, a Rogue, a Mage, and a Druid.

In deliberately designed games where different roles are built in, two common strategies can help each player feel she's making a contribution. One is to *balance* the various roles, so that no one player contributes more to the team's victory than another. The other is to give each role *unique abilities*, as in an RPG where one player can heal and the others cannot. If everyone can heal a little, but some are better than others, then the roles may still be different, but the feeling a player has that her contribution is unique will be less. How different to make the roles is tricky—certain functions may be so basic to the game (e.g., dealing damage in an RPG) that it is often best to ensure everyone is good at them; others (e.g., healing) can be given out to some and not to others; and sometimes one can look for small truly unique functions and parcel them out carefully (e.g., in *World of Warcraft*, Mages get teleportation; Druids get a special swimming form).[28]

28. The situation here of a designer doling out powers to different player roles in the design is analogous to the skills one might want when putting together a good team. For example, in basketball every player needs to be able to dribble and pass well, but only certain positions need to rebound or make three-point shots well. In one case, it is a matter of the game giving abilities to certain players; in the other, of the game requiring certain abilities of the players.

If all the roles are identical (i.e., there is only one role), then potential contributions are automatically balanced—every player has the same chance to contribute. Actual contributions, of course, will vary according to player skill. Everyone on the bowling team or on a *Counterstrike* team has the same chance to contribute, but the more skilled players will tend to contribute more.[29]

If the roles vary, balance will take some work. The modern expectation is that this work will at least be attempted, and every contribution will be roughly equal (e.g., classes in an MMO or races in an RTS will be balanced). Sports, however, do not follow this logic: the quarterback contributes a disproportionately large amount to a football team, and a pitcher contributes an extremely large amount to a baseball team. And players who sit on the bench may, at least in any given game, contribute nothing at all. But even in sports, efforts are made to help give players a chance to contribute: mandatory rotation of batters in baseball, or the widening of the tennis court in doubles so that it's harder for one person to cover the whole court.

One role deserving special mention is that of leader. Team leadership may involve a formal or an informal role, though even when there is a specific team captain, that role may not be specified by the rules system. (But it's often associated with a systemic role—for example, the leader of the offense on a football team is often the player who plays the quarterback position.) The leader may be responsible for many things: helping train players before the game, making team decisions during play, or giving advice during the game. In organized sports, the leader may be someone who isn't even a player: a coach. But almost any team game has—if the team has played together more than once—at least informal leadership, typically coming from the most skilled players. In large or complex teams, there will often be multiple leaders, typically with specializations: offensive and defensive coaches in a football team, or a guildmaster, several officers, and a raid leader in an MMO guild.

Cooperative Interaction among Team Members

Team games vary widely in the amount of *cooperative interaction*[30] among the team members: the amount they can influence each other's performance. With a swim meet or a bowling league, each player is essentially playing solo, and a team score is calcu-

29. There is a subtle difference, though: in bowling, everyone *will* contribute, since the scores are averaged. It matters to the team how their weakest member performs. With *Counterstrike*, the weakest team member may be contributing nothing, or even making the team worse (say, by alerting the enemy prematurely)—this situation is discussed further below.

30. We use this somewhat awkward term to distinguish it from the type of interaction discussed in section 2.2, where players influence the performance of *opposing* players. (Simply calling it "cooperation" is problematic because it is not a feature exclusive to cooperative games, and indeed it is possible in principle for a cooperative game not to have it.)

lated by combining the individual contributions. With doubles tennis, players must decide who goes after which ball and they must avoid colliding with each other, but each player still hits the ball for himself. With football or basketball, one player throws and another player catches.

Exercise 2.17: Give some nonsports examples of various levels of cooperative interactivity.

In and of itself, cooperative interactivity is a good thing, in the sense that interacting with teammates is something many people enjoy—humans are social animals. (Of course there are definitely those for whom the low level of interaction of a bowling league is just right; solitaire would be too little and basketball would be too much—as always, knowing your audience is key.) Also, team interactions introduce all sorts of interesting heuristics (should I pass the ball now, or keep it for myself? should I heal our damage dealer or save my mana to heal our tank later?). But problems can arise when the levels of such interaction are high. The situation is loosely analogous to the one discussed in section 2.2. There, the problem was that interactivity (among opposing players) of the wrong sort led to political problems like picking on the leader and kingmaking. Here, problematic cooperative interactivity tends to take the form of socially unpleasant interactions and of role usurpation, both of which we will now discuss.

In any team game, having good teammates will help you succeed, and bad teammates will hurt your chances. The impact of your teammates on your game experience, however, will vary widely depending on how much cooperative interaction the game has. If the game has very little (e.g., a swim meet), you can still give your best performance regardless of how your teammates perform. Bad performances on their part simply lower the team's overall chance of winning. But if you interact with your teammates a lot, you will be more frustrated if they don't perform well: you might throw the ball perfectly, but they still fail to catch it. At an extreme, there are games where a bad teammate is so punishing for the group that you'd rather play a person short than have him on your team; *Defense of the Ancients* (where a teammate who dies frequently will thereby "feed" experience points to the other team, making them more powerful) is an example. Such games tend to be very hostile to beginners and low-skilled players generally, and may develop unpleasant player communities.

There is a difference in the emotional experience of being a bad player on the chess team and being a bad player on the football team. This phenomenon is partly social (different sorts of people play chess than play football), but it is partly due to game design—if I do not castle when I should, your chess game still runs smoothly, but if I drop the ball you threw, you may be outraged. And indeed, the people playing

Defense of the Ancients are probably more like the people who play chess—but they act worse to their teammates than any football player would.[31]

When a team's performance is determined by combining individual results, as with a chess team or a fencing team, even when a teammate lets you down, you still have a clear scale of your own by which to measure your performance. A player's personal achievement isn't disrupted by his teammate's poor play. The more individual achievement can be culled from team performance, the less social pressure there may be on individual team members.

Professional sports can be thought of as individual competitive games since the players are individually competing for their next contract, to the consternation of owners, coaches, and fans. In this light personal statistical achievement at the expense of the team seems very reasonable. Part of the challenge of the coach is to align player and team goals as closely as possible.

Exercise 2.18: What other factors in *Defense of the Ancients* (or another unfriendly online game of your choice) make for a difficult team environment?

Telling Teammates What to Do

In addition to interacting via the play of the game, team members may communicate directly. Games often vary as to how much communication they allow, and may have special restrictions on communication. Bridge is the classic example: direct communication is forbidden—you can't just tell your partner "I have the ace of hearts"—but signaling both in the bidding and in the play of the cards is extremely important and highly complex. Much of the interest in play is in the limitations on teammates signaling their individual hidden information. Tellingly, although hidden information is no longer an issue for one team once the dummy has been determined, information flow isn't merely restricted, it is cut off completely. If it were allowed the better player would make all the decisions on offense by simply telling her partner what to do.

The problem of one's role being entirely usurped, by having another player on your team tell you exactly what to do, is bad enough that no traditional game has it, but some deliberately designed games do suffer from it. Turn-based cooperative games are probably the most vulnerable, for reasons we'll discuss below.

In modest amounts, having someone else tell you what to do in a game is acceptable, or even good. Coaches, team captains, or simply experienced players can make a game better for team members by giving advice. Of course, not all less experienced players will follow the advice they are given. Perhaps they fail to understand it, or they cannot execute it. Or perhaps they prefer to "go rogue," trying to kill opponents rather

31. Of course, the anonymity of the Internet also has a lot to do with the unpleasant behavior. But *Defense of the Ancients* behavior is worse than most other Internet games, so again the game design is relevant.

than guard a position in an FPS or running around chasing the ball in soccer—pursuing individual glory rather than team victory. However, especially for teams of adults that play together regularly, players' desire for victory, along with peer pressure, is usually enough to induce players to follow whatever expert advice may be available.

But if communication results in the expert telling the beginner what to do to the point of the beginner being effectively removed from the game, the beginner won't have much fun. When does this effective removal happen?

Perhaps the most useful perspective is that it happens unless something prevents it—that is, the human desire to win and the greater skill of the expert will tend to push the expert into playing the game for the beginner unless there is some mechanism to stop it. Probably the most important mechanism is "skilled control": physical skill like aiming or jumping that cannot simply be told to someone. If Kasparov tells you to move your rook forward two squares, your making that move will be just as good as if Kasparov made the move himself.[32] If Michael Jordan tells you to throw the ball through the round metal hoop, there is still something for you to do. Hence chess coaches are not allowed to give suggestions to their players during a game, but basketball coaches are.

Closely related to skilled control (arguably a special case of it) are time pressure and complexity. If a great many operations have to be performed quickly, there just is not time for an expert to direct a beginner to do each one. Thus in a team RTS game, an experienced player can give advice, but the performance of the other players still very much matters. With a turn-based game such as chess, though, exact instructions can be given and carried out.

Even for turn-based team games, all is not lost. Experts can be prevented from playing the game for beginners by having rules that limit communication. Hidden information, such as cards a player holds that teammates cannot see, prevents experts from knowing enough to advise beginners (of course, simply telling your teammates what you are holding must be prevented). For games where it makes sense, role playing can help as well: the know-it-all playing the wizard may tell you the optimal strategy for your barbarian, but you may feel free to ignore him as you charge into the enemies because it is "in character."

Cooperative Games

Cooperative games are simply single-sided games with more than one player on that single side. Most if not all of the higher-level issues that arise in cooperative games can be found in some form in single-player games or in two-sided team games.

32. A classic story illustrating this point is that of the little girl who manages to defeat (or at least draw against) a chess grandmaster. She plays two of them at once, as white in one game and as black in the other. In each game she makes the move that the grandmaster makes in the other game, and thus is guaranteed to at least draw against one of her two opponents.

Limiting Experts' Ability to Play the Game for Beginners

- Skilled control
- Time pressure
- Rules limiting communication
- Hidden information
- Role playing

Cooperative games were relatively rare until recently—almost all games either had two or more sides, or were single-player games. Most examples of cooperative games come from computer gaming, with a few examples (e.g., *Pandemic* or Reiner Knizia's *Lord of the Rings*) from modern boardgames. Instances outside of these categories are few, but might include pairs figure skating, two people working on a jigsaw puzzle together, or *Hacky Sack* (perhaps also *Dungeons & Dragons*, depending on how you interpret the role of the dungeon master).

It is perhaps natural that cooperative games were rare until recently. An opponent provides so much, in terms of uncertainty of outcome and repeat play value, that having one is a big benefit to a game. If you simply cannot find one, then you will need to play a single-player game. But if you can find one or more other players, a game with opponents is probably your best bet.

All this changes with the advent of the computer. Now, the computer can be your opponent. It is still hard to get people together, but the advantages of having an opponent and the capabilities of the computer push games toward the "one and a half player" category. Add in computer networking, so that other players are now easily available, and computer games naturally evolve in two ways: those new players become your opponents (as in most precomputer games), or they become your teammates against the computer—that is, you have cooperative games. Thus the existence of both AI opponents and computer networking allows games to offer the social benefits and heuristic challenges of team play, along with the greater than 50 percent average win percentages found in single-player games.

Although cooperative games can be seen as single-sided games with teamwork, some issues do loom larger because of the combination. For example, take the issue that some team games have of expert players playing the game for beginners. In a game like bridge, if one partner begins to tell the other what to do, the opponents will object. In a cooperative boardgame like *Pandemic*, there are no opponents to object when one player directs another. Granted, the player being directed may object, but the argument is less compelling: "I'd rather play myself, thanks" as opposed to "Hey, that's cheating!"

Or take the problem of limited replayability to which single-sided games are sometimes prone. Like many single-player games, MMOs suffer from this problem, and the pressure on the content creators of the MMO is large. But the team nature of the MMO can amplify the problem, as players repeat content for the benefit of other team members. How many people would go on the same MMO raid as often as they do if not for the need to help their guildmates? Of course, on balance the additional interest generated by other players, especially teammates, more than makes up for these costs in a good MMO, but the point is that all these pros and cons can be understood as arising from issues pertaining to single-sided play, issues pertaining to team play, and the interactions between them.

Exercise 2.19: What are some roles in soccer? Which roles are supported by the rules? What about football? A relay race?

Exercise 2.20: Why are there so many team sports, but so few team boardgames?

Exercise 2.21: Choose three or four other broad categories of games (e.g., card games, arcade games) and discuss how often teamwork is found in games of those categories, and why. When there is teamwork, how much cooperative interaction is there? Why?

Exercise 2.22: Can you name any cooperative sports? How about cooperative card games?

Exercise 2.23: Choose four broad categories of games and discuss which are more suitable for cooperative play, which are less so, and why.

Exercise 2.24: Name some team sports where players frequently tell each other what to do. Name some others where advice giving is rarer. What about these sports causes them to fall into one group or the other?

3 Infrastructure

In this chapter, we discuss some of the basic systemic elements of games: ingredients of the game system that help make the game what it is. Games can be complicated, and some of our ingredients will be partially agential, but it's probably helpful to think of them as systemic first with agential overtones.

We begin, naturally enough, with a discussion of rules—what kinds there are, how they are enforced, to what extent they "are" the game (our feeling: less so than commonly supposed), and how they can sometimes become a barrier to play. Rules often fall in clusters, such as the rules surrounding shuffling, dealing, trick-taking, and the like common to so many card games. We refer to such clusters as "standards" and discuss them in the next section.

Games typically end at some point, and the different states in which they can end (with a unique winner, with several winners, with everyone assigned a numerical score) and the conditions that cause them to end (such as time running out, or a player checkmating an opponent's king) are the subjects of the next two sections. Going backward from the end of the game to its beginning, we then discuss different possible starting positions for games. Finally, we briefly discuss how games interact with the human senses.

3.1 Characteristic: Rules

Games, of course, have rules: instructions telling players what actions they can take and what the outcome (immediately, in terms of changed game state; ultimately, in terms of winning or losing) of various actions will be. Rules may be enforced by the players themselves (common in casual paper games), enforced by judges (common in formal sporting events), or enforced by the structure of the gameplay environment itself. This last can be seen in a football game, where the laws of physics enforce some outcomes (kick the ball just so and it will go through the goalposts), or in a computer game (where the code, if working as intended, ensures that only legal actions can be taken, and that they will have the appropriate results; in some sense both rules and

Figure 3.1

enforcement are the same here). In particular, note that we are not using *rules* in the narrow sense of "rules written in a rulebook" but in a broader sense that includes other instructions one might need in order to play, or that determine how one does play.[1]

There are many delicacies of definition involved, and many borderline cases (e.g., universally accepted play practices that are not in fact written in the rules—are they "rules" or not?). It's not our intention to focus overmuch on marginal cases, however. In keeping with a more practical approach, we wish to focus on how rules affect the play of the game, and how they interact with the other characteristics.

Before beginning, though, perhaps one slightly less practical observation is still worth making. People often tend to think of the rules of a game as equal to the game in some abstract sense. We don't like this point of view. Think of all the minor rule changes that have happened in, say, basketball over the last twenty years. Is it a different game every time? Only a pedant would say yes. To most people, it is still basketball (of course, if you change *enough* rules it would not be basketball, and rugby and football, say, are pretty clearly different games despite having evolved from the same roots). A better viewpoint is to think of the rules to a game as like the words to a story: a story can still be *Little Red Riding Hood* despite having different words from some other version. In fact it can even have a completely different ending. For example, Little Red Riding Hood herself sometimes lives and sometimes dies, but both versions are still *Little Red Riding Hood*! If enough elements are the same, the two versions are the same story. As always, there will be borderline cases (is *Clueless* the same story as *Emma*, or not?). And although the rules are not the game, the rules let one experience the game by playing it, just as the words let one experience the story by reading it.

Another way to see that the rules are not the game is in the common occurrence of changing rules in order to keep the game the same. If players find some strategy that changes the play of the game drastically, and there is a general consensus that this change is for the worse, the rules may be changed to disallow the strategy. Patches to eliminate exploits in computer games, or the banning of cards in *Magic*, are further examples: technically they change the rules, but they do so in order to make post-change play similar to the play experience before the exploit was discovered.

Just as *Little Red Riding Hood* is an entity having life outside its specific text, games are usually entities that live beyond their rules. The various rule changes to basketball adding a shot clock, making goaltending illegal, or adding a three-point line are rule changes universally designed to make the *rules* of basketball match the concept of the *game* of basketball—how it was initially played and how it is *supposed* to be played.

1. We do not use the term *rules* to include "rules of thumb" or other guidelines on how to play *well*, however. In other words, rules for us do not include heuristics.

The situation is not different in most other games. Many rule changes from patched computer games to professional sports serve as instructive examples that games are not defined by their rules. Most commonly the rules are defined by the games.

First-Order and Second-Order Rules

A useful practical distinction can be made between what we call first-order rules and second-order rules. First-order rules are rules that anyone needs to know in order to play (or profitably watch) the game. Second-order rules are rules that someone needs to know for the game to take place, but the player may not need to know them (of course, expert players often will know them).

Examples of first-order rules are how the pieces move in chess, that you score a point in soccer by kicking the ball into the opposing net, or that you die in *Diablo II* if your health goes to zero. Examples of second-order rules are the precise punishments for various rule violations in a chess tournament, the finer details of the offside rules in soccer, or how precisely different items that increase your attack speed in *Diablo II* stack. Classic boardgames and card games tend to have relatively few second-order rules, especially if formal tournament play is not considered (for example, *Othello* arguably has no second-order rules). This is almost a requirement for such games, given that they are so often not formally adjudicated. Sports tend to have more, with referees responsible for knowing them. Computer games have enormous numbers of second-order rules, adjudicated by the computer. Very often no one human being knows all the second-order rules for a computer game; only the code itself is completely authoritative.[2]

One way to see the difference between first-order rules and second-order rules is to imagine you are teaching someone how to play. In very few games would you want to teach someone all the rules initially. Typically you only want to teach them the first-order rules. And players often learn some basic heuristics before they learn second-order rules—for example, a beginning chess player might know the point values of the pieces but not be quite clear on en passant capture.

Some first-order rules for very complex games are slightly less important than most. In some games there are rules players have to know that come up rarely enough that in practice players are content merely to have access to them. Examples include parts of the rules in *Starfleet Battles* or the text on all the trading cards in *Magic*. Even the options in *RoboRally* form part of this rules space. While the player does not have to know them to begin play, they will come up and once they do, knowledge of them is required to proceed. Thus the burden on the player is somewhere in between most first- and second-order rules.

2. In the case of a bug, one could argue whether the "real" rule was the one actually implemented by the code, or the one intended by the designer.

Rules as a Barrier to Play

In general, rules are a bad thing in the sense that one would like to achieve the same gameplay results with fewer rules rather than more. Of course, this is not always possible. Too many first-order rules is especially bad: since every player needs to know them to start playing, they provide a real barrier to entry. Second-order rules are not as bad, although they are still pretty bad in games where you expect the players to adjudicate.

Expert players, including game designers, tend to misjudge how ordinary players interact with rules, and in particular with the learning of rules for a new game. Seeing new paper games being blind-tested[3] (rulebook and components handed to players who know nothing of the game and attempt to learn it from them) is a very sobering experience. Players typically do not want to read rulebooks, and very few people are good at learning how to play from written rules longer than a page. Most players learn from other people. This puts classic games, where there is a pool of people who already know the game, at a big advantage over newer ones. Computer games also have a huge edge here: because the computer adjudicates the rules, players can begin play knowing very little, and learn as they go. In particular, for most computer games little or no time must be spent reading or otherwise preparing to play before actual play begins.

Even for computer games, though, complex rules can be a barrier to learning or enjoying play. Computer adjudication (especially of second-order rules) takes a lot of the burden off the player, but a beginner can still feel lost if he does not understand what he needs to do to progress. And an expert player can become frustrated if it is impossible to figure out the details of the system in her efforts to play better (i.e., a lack of clarity in the second-order rules can make it hard for the expert player to keep climbing the heuristic tree). In single-player games, clarity of rules is especially important in those rules that apply to the players; sometimes a little more obscurity can be accepted in rules applying only to nonplayer parts of the system (for example, in an RPG a player will demand a more detailed understanding of how to build her own character, but may be willing to accept a more rudimentary understanding of how a typical AI monster is built, and may hardly care at all about rules restricting the kinds of level layouts that are possible).

3. The phrase "focus group" is also used, but this covers a wide variety of methods, and is most typically used to refer to a discussion group led by a moderator. In a blind test, nobody is in the room but the players themselves. The term *blind test* is perhaps unfortunate, because it's easily confused with the single-blind and double-blind methods of scientific testing, but it seems to be the most commonly used term for this type of rule testing in the paper game world. Beta testing for computer games is in some ways analogous, but it doesn't test the clarity of the written rules (which are of limited relevance for computer games in any case).

One danger to watch out for when designing or modifying a game is the impulse to fix things (problems in the other characteristics) by adding rules. Sometimes adding rules is unavoidable, but in general it's better to look for other fixes. Repeated little extra bits of rules, each added to fix a different problem, can add up to a quite messy game. Again, adding first-order rules is worse than adding second-order ones, and the more players (rather than referees or computers) must adjudicate, the worse adding rules becomes.

Counterintuitively, making a rule against some behavior and giving it an in-game penalty can in some sense legalize it. A delay of game call in football or kicking in basketball are activities against the rules, and yet commonly used in play. The rules in actuality are not "don't do x" but rather "when you do x, y happens." This distinction is important and has implications when designing rule systems. For example, the introduction of a rule that forces a move after a certain amount of time has passed could be intended to speed up a game. Instead, however, the rule might lead to players using all of that allowed clock time, thus actually increasing the average time it takes to play a game. The normal agential pressure that would be exerted in speeding up casual play can be short-circuited by a poorly thought out rule intended to have the same effect.

Exercise 3.1: Name some second-order rules in backgammon.

Exercise 3.2: Name some second-order rules in baseball.

Exercise 3.3: Does the average computer game have more or fewer first-order rules than the average noncomputer game? Why?

Exercise 3.4: How often do the rules change in computer games? How often do they change in sports? Compare this to how often they change in boardgames or card games. Why the differences?

3.2 Characteristic: Standards

Learning new rules is difficult. Learning new heuristics is difficult as well. Games can get around this by following *standards*: commonly accepted patterns that many players are already familiar with.

Some examples include putting a ball into some sort of net to score points, using the standard fifty-two-card deck in countless card games, having each player take turns moving a single piece in a boardgame, or using the keys W, A, S, and D to move around in a first-person shooter. Standards can be low-level details, like the WASD keys, or high-level ideas—the very idea of a first-person shooter is a standard, just as the turn-based boardgame is.

Figure 3.2

Innovation Considered Harmful

People often decry the use of standards and claim they represent a lack of innovation, especially when discussing computer games. The large software companies receive a great deal of criticism on this score. Oddly enough, in paper gaming standards are better respected—consider, for example, the European boardgames that are by and large well received[4] yet have very strong standards.

But in the end games are for people to enjoy, and most people enjoy games with which they have a certain comfort level. Innovation is sometimes appreciated, but convenience always is. So innovation is best saved for areas where it really pulls its weight—where the innovation improves the game experience in some way. If an innovation is no better than what it replaces, it can fail to be accepted for two reasons: first because it is new and thus harder to learn, and second because being new it is easy for the designer to get the details wrong so that the new feature may well be unpolished. And when successful games do have innovative elements, they usually have just one or two; more than that and the game may be too overwhelming for most people. (On the flipside, there is an audience that deliberately seeks out innovation for its own sake, but this audience is relatively small.)

4. Well received, that is, by the type of elite player who tends to be making the "where's the originality?" criticism. We're not speaking in this case of mass popularity but rather of critical reception.

Consider Blizzard Entertainment. They are almost universally viewed as one of the highest-quality producers of computer games in the industry. But their games are not unusually innovative: *Diablo* was preceded by other top-down action RPGs, *Warcraft* was preceded by *Dune II*, and *World of Warcraft* was preceded by *Everquest*, *Ultima Online*, and various MUDs. Blizzard's greatness comes from understanding what makes a game enjoyable for its players and from a willingness to put in the level of polish to achieve that end. Their games stand out because they are better, not because they are more innovative.

All this is not to say that standards must be respected at all costs. Rather, deciding how and when to use standards is an important part of the game designer's art. But the point is to consider standards as a good thing, to be deviated from when there is a real gain from doing so, rather than as a bad thing forced on unfortunate designers by an ignorant public or a cowardly publisher.

When innovation really does add a lot to a game, to the point where it overcomes any audience resistance to nonstandard games, the payoff can be big. Often the largest payoff comes not to the first game to exhibit the innovation, but to later ones: *Warcraft* rather than *Dune II*, the *Pokémon* trading card game rather than *Magic: The Gathering*, *World of Warcraft* rather than *Everquest*. Given the difficulty of perfecting the innovative elements on the very first try, this is unsurprising.

Bundles of Standards

Standards often come in groups or bundles, usually in accordance with the game's genre. Genre is itself a large and complex topic, and not one we want to tackle here. Instead, we take a naive working view of genre: everyone who plays games is comfortable with the idea that they fall into groups of similar games, such as "trick-taking card games" or "first-person shooters." These groupings can be at a very high level—for example, "boardgames," "sports," or "arcade games"—or at a more detailed level, such as "card games in the whist family" or "real-time strategy games." Games in such a grouping, at whatever level, will tend to have certain features in common, and these common features are standards for those familiar with the group. A few examples:[5]

Track boardgames with dice: Senet, The Game of Goose, *Monopoly*, Parcheesi, *The Game of Life*.

Standards: Track with squares, piece(s) to represent the player, progression on a track according to the throw of dice (or other randomizers).

Note this genre dates back at least 5,000 years (Senet), albeit with throwsticks or knucklebones instead of dice.

5. This is of course just a sampling—nothing like an exhaustive list, either in terms of genres covered or in terms of standards listed for the genres, is intended.

Alternating-move two-player boardgames: chess, checkers, go, reversi/*Othello*.

Standards: Two more or less identical sides of different colors, square grid board, players take turns moving or placing a single piece, no randomizers, some method for capturing opponents' pieces.[6]

Some of the standards here, such as taking turns, are so ingrained that they might seem required to someone who is not a student of games. Indeed, it seems that the standard of taking turns was "broken" fairly late, and for a purpose involving the simulation of reality rather than reasons of pure gameplay: the wargame, invented in the eighteenth century to train officers in the Prussian army. The wargame is now a genre of its own, with its own conventions (move all of your army when it's your turn, hex-based map, roll dice and look up the results on a chart, etc.).

Sports races: 100-yard dash, marathon, horse racing, regatta.

Standards: Multiple simultaneous participants, starting line, finish line, starting signal, measured time to finish.

An interesting example of standards being broken for a specific purpose comes from the bicycle time trial. In bike racing, drafting (following closely behind another racer to reduce drag) is such a large factor that simultaneous races are often team-based, with teammates helping each other out, and individual races are often "time trials": each rider starting at a separate time and riding against the clock rather than directly against the other players. The cost of breaking the standard is necessary if you want the race to measure individual performance.

Team sports with a ball: Football, basketball, soccer, rugby.

Standards: Two sides, team victory rather than individual, point-based scoring, goal or scoring line, concept of possession of the ball, allowable methods for moving the ball.

Baseball and similar games are probably best thought of as part of a different (but related) genre.

Real-time strategy games: *Dune II*, *Warcraft: Orcs & Humans*, *Command & Conquer*, *Age of Empires*.

Standards: Real-time play, rough simulation of cities/bases and armies (building both units and buildings in-game), tech trees, multiple unit types (both economic and military), multiple building types, rock-paper-scissors relationships among the unit types, group-selecting units by drawing a mouse box around them, a pulled-back overhead view.

6. Note that some of the listed games violate some of the standards—for example, in go or reversi the pieces are placed rather than moved, and in reversi the pieces (but not how each player uses them) are identical for each side. This violation of some standards by some members of a category is the norm (see Lakoff's *Women, Fire, and Dangerous Things*).

All these standards existed in *Dune II*, and they have continued throughout the life of the genre. Although the standards arguably arose as part of *Dune II*'s attempt to simulate a specific intellectual property, they stayed because they fulfilled other needs, such as pacing and complexity control. A "standard" from *Dune II* that did not survive for long (although it can be found in the first *Warcraft*) was the building of squares as a foundation for the player's base: logical from a simulationist point of view in a world where you are building on sand, but a gameplay annoyance. The standard of mining resources with peons to build military units works well in matching a Frank Herbert setting rather than any independent simulative principle. Its general utility in controlling the pace of the game and providing a multifaceted set of heuristics (namely the interplay between the economy and military) has made it a standard difficult to replace despite the jarring nature of its simulative qualities for most settings. This exemplifies the power and utility of standards—other pacing mechanisms that fit a particular property better may well be easy to find, but they must be weighed against the fact that following the standard allows players to enjoy the total experience more by shortening their learning curves. Notably the learning curve for designers attempting to balance complex games such as this is also shortened.

Shooter games: *Doom, Quake, Half-Life, Tomb Raider.*

Standards: First-person (or over-the-shoulder third-person) view, WASD maneuver keys (if on a PC platform), spacebar to jump, health and ammo bars, different weapons, possibility of being hit from behind,[7] importance of dodging and aiming, respawning after death.

Occasionally a shooter will try to make a game more immersive by eliminating UI standards such as health and ammo bars (e.g., *Peter Jackson's King Kong*). This can prove frustrating for players who were expecting such elements.

Card games (fifty-two-card deck): bridge, cribbage, poker, solitaire, hearts.

Standards: The standard fifty-two-card deck itself, shuffling, dealing, hands of cards, the discard pile. There are many subgenres within this genre, from trick-taking games (with standards such as bidding, tricks, trumps, and following suit) to poker to solitaire, these latter two really being families of games rather than individual games.

Early decks of cards varied widely, but over time they settled on a number of standard varieties in use today (besides the fifty-two-card deck used internationally, many countries have their own versions, with roughly the same structure but varying numbers of cards).[8] However, there has been one interesting drift away from previous standards: the low card in older games often becomes the high card in

7. That is, a full 360-degree environment as opposed to the shooting on rails common in earlier games (where your enemies were always in front of you).

8. David Parlett, *A History of Card Games*, chap. 3.

newer ones. So the ace, once the lowest card, is now the highest card in most games, and there are a number of games of more recent vintage (e.g., Dai Hin Min or poker with deuces wild) where the two is high.

In the last hundred years or so, card games with dedicated decks (*Pit, Rook, Uno*) have arisen. Sometimes these games had gameplay that really required a new deck, but often they were minor variants of games that can be played with a standard fifty-two-card deck. The trend toward these nonstandard decks is probably due to some combination of technology (it's much easier to print a unique deck of cards today) and financial/legal reasons (if a company makes a unique deck, it has ownership rights and can charge a premium for its game; it is essentially impossible to profit selling just the rules for a game to be played with a fifty-two-card deck).

Computer role-playing games: *Final Fantasy, Fallout, Knights of the Old Republic, Baldur's Gate.*

Standards: Player-controlled party of one to eight adventurers, character stats, levels and experience points, hit points, weapons/armor/equipment, paper doll interface.

Many of these standards are inherited from paper role-playing games (particularly *Dungeons & Dragons*). For massively multiplayer online RPGs, additional standards come into play, such as spawning monsters, respawning after death, and grinding to level.

Occasionally standards will cross from one genre to another, such as the standard of hit points. Also, sometimes interesting game features can come from pulling standards of one genre into a different genre, such as the adoption of turn-based strategy gaming standards into the real-time strategy game *Rise of Nations*. And of course occasionally a game is so successful that its features become standards, either in that game's existing genre or (occasionally) in an entirely new genre that game spawns.

Bundles of standards such as these provide a very powerful tool for learning. If you fire up an unknown computer game and you see a 3-D world with two hands close up holding a gun, your hand will naturally move to the WASD keys, and you'll know what to do. Or consider poker: a whole family of games called poker exist, all sharing some basic properties such as betting, a pot, and a certain ranking of hands. If you know how to play one of them, you can quickly learn another. Standards apply not only at the level of rules, but also at the level of heuristics: knowing something about how to play one game in the family will usually mean you have some heuristics you can apply to other games in that family as well (don't stand still for too long in an FPS; bluff occasionally when playing poker).

Individual games can sometimes be (deliberately) designed to have the variety that an entire (evolved) genre has. Consider scenarios in hex-based wargames, or different formats like draft or sealed in the card game *Magic*, or various PvP battlegrounds and arenas in *World of Warcraft*. Although normally viewed as variants of a given game, they can just as profitably be viewed as different games sharing a set of standards. Given that these games require a large amount of mastery of detail on the part of the user, it's very reasonable to try to leverage that mastery into a number of different play experiences.

Exercise 3.5: Think of three genres of games, and for each of them give example games and standards. Make sure at least one of your genres is high-level (e.g., "winter sports") and one is low-level (e.g., "electronic tactical RPGs").

Exercise 3.6: Pick one genre and try to give *all* the standards for it. (You are unlikely to succeed, but try to be as complete as you can!)

Exercise 3.7: What are some standards that cross multiple genres of computer games?

Exercise 3.8: What are some standards common to *all* of the following professional sports: football, baseball, basketball, soccer, and hockey? What are some standards common to all of these except baseball?

3.3 Characteristic: Outcomes

For most games—in particular, those we term *orthogames*—the game ends at some point and winners or losers are declared. The first examples one tends to think of are games like chess or football: two sides, and at the end of the game one of them is declared the winner and the other the loser, or perhaps a draw is declared. But there are a number of other possible game outcomes, especially when there are more than two players. After a short discussion of games without explicit defined outcomes, we'll discuss the basic kinds of game outcomes and their influence on the flow of the game. Finally, we close with a brief discussion of draws.

Nonorthogames

Some games—ones that are not orthogames—have no formally defined winners and losers. Typically players of such games define their own victory criteria, some of which

Figure 3.3

might look much like an orthogame's victory criteria and others of which do not. For example, in an MMO a player might decide to focus on gaining levels, defeating certain monsters, gaining skill in a trade, defeating opponents in PvP, griefing, accumulating gold, or accumulating equipment. Alternatively, she might decide to focus on role-playing, accumulating many friends, gaining political power in a guild, getting a certain visual look to her character, or helping new players. Most often, a player will focus on some combination of these goals.

With a physical or paper multiplayer game, the choice of goals will typically come not just from the one player, but from his community: a group of friends will decide to play in a certain fashion, perhaps playing *Hacky Sack* to keep the bag in play for as long as possible, or perhaps trying for spectacular stunts. In online games, a player may decide individually on a set of goals, and then pick a community based on that, joining a PvP guild if she is interested in those goals, or a raiding guild if that matches her personal victory condition better. Of course, the reverse can happen as well, but the relative abundance of different community choices online means players are probably relatively more likely to fit a community to a gamestyle preference instead of vice versa.

In single-player games, such as sandbox games (*The Sims*, *Roller Coaster Tycoon*), victory conditions tend to be purely individual, and sometimes highly idiosyncratic.

In all of these cases, there is no formal sorting of players into winners and losers, but rather varying levels of satisfaction for players depending on to what extent they achieved whatever goals they chose or had set before them.

Types of Outcomes

There are a variety of possible outcomes to an orthogame:

- Unique winner or team of winners (chess, football)
- Unique loser, with everyone else considered a winner (Old Maid, Skitgubbe, drawing straws)
- Subset of winners—that is, alliances are allowed to form, and anyone in the winning alliance is declared a winner (*Cosmic Encounter*, the *Dune* boardgame, qualifying races)
- Rankings: place, with first being best, but for example third still better than fifth
- Scaled performance: the game assigns players a score in some way
  - points, usually with more points being better (poker, many European boardgames)
  - time, with accomplishing some task in a shorter amount of time being better (very rarely more time is better, e.g., a dance marathon)
- In any of the above cases, draws may or may not be allowed.

The above categories are not mutually exclusive. In particular, rankings very often arise from scaled performance, as in a footrace or a boardgame played for points.

Sometimes, though, one has rankings not based on score, with the ranking arising perhaps from players being eliminated (the last person left in the game receiving first place). Occasionally, too, points may not result in ranking: in a poker game, one typically doesn't think of players coming in first, second, third, and so on, but each player simply considers how much she is ahead or behind at the end of the session.

One normally thinks of the rules surrounding winning, losing, and game outcome as systemic. But in fact they are often agential. For example, a multiplayer boardgame may have a point track, with the winner being the person who scores the most points. Some playgroups may treat the game as a "unique winner" game, caring only about who the winner is and caring nothing for points or second place versus third place. Other groups may choose to play for place, or play for points. So even though we normally think of how you win a game as systemic (after all, it's written right there in the rules), it can be agential as well (the rules don't tell you whether you should play to maximize your points if you are too far behind to win). For an extreme example, consider *Starcraft*: strictly speaking, the game is systemically based on scaled performance (it gives you a point score), but nobody plays that way, and instead there is all but universal agreement that only elimination matters.

Note that if the game has only two sides, there is almost always a unique winner. Thus the different game outcome types are the most relevant in the context of multiplayer games. Scaled performance, however, is still relevant. In two-player games it can provide a context for monetary stakes. In single-player games it gives a good way to compare across different games.

Game Outcomes and Politics

Games will have different gameplay characteristics depending on what type of outcomes they can have—and since those outcomes are often agential, so too are the resulting gameplay characteristics. Political characteristics are especially affected.

For a multiplayer game with a unique winner, the play can become different in character toward the end because the players will take crazy chances and make desperate plays to win. The game can also become political, with picking on the leader and kingmaking being an issue. If there is some natural way to determine position, players will often play for that, even if the rules don't support it. For example, in a game where first and second place get the same points (e.g., a qualifying heat), people may still vie for first. Some games have a condition where everyone loses (e.g., the card game *Nuclear War*), which can be problematic—is it better for you to come in second, or better for everyone to lose? If enough people in a playgroup feel the latter is better, games may end with everyone losing almost all the time.

Games where the goal is to avoid losing can tend toward picking on the player that is behind. As with all political problems, limiting the scope for targeted interaction can limit the negatives. Also, some games based on another outcome type (rankings, say) can agentially become games with unique losers: the playgroup can agree to quit as soon as someone is knocked out.

Games with a subset of winners may be very political as players jockey to be on the winning side. As with unique loser games, games of other types can be turned into games with subsets of winners by agreement of the players. For multiplayer boardgames that take a long time to play and have player elimination, this transformation happens quite frequently, and in fact some playgroups may more often agree to call a game over, with the players remaining as winners (perhaps ranked informally according to some score), than play the game out to the bitter end.

Scaled performance occurs in a great many games, even ones that are according to the rules in one of the other categories. Players, or player groups, may react in different ways, either focusing very much on first place (or highest point total), or focusing on trying to place as high as possible (or score as many points as possible) even when first is out of reach. Differing interpretations of the "right" way to play can sometimes lead to strife (see sections 2.3 and 2.4); money or other rewards can help here, because they make it clearer what value positions other than first place have. A poker player in fifth place[9] rarely worries about whether to sacrifice all his chips to help the second-place player come in first. Scaled performance when accepted by the players can go a long way toward mitigating unwanted effects of politics and kingmaking because very often players in a "lost" position with only their ability to affect the leaders to consider will have something more concrete to play for.

Draws

Sometimes the rules of a game specify no winner in certain circumstances, with chess being perhaps the classic example. Draws are sometimes seen as undesirable—after all, if players are playing an orthogame, they are expecting a winner, and if none is declared the game may seem unsatisfying. Sometimes explicit mechanisms are added to a game to prevent draws, such as penalty shootouts in soccer or noninteger komi in go.[10]

Games that allow draws are often fairly low-luck games, perhaps because there draws seem "fair": if the different sides are evenly matched, perhaps the draw is the best representation of the (minimal or nonexistent) difference in skill levels. In a game with lots of luck, it seems more natural to allow luck to determine the winner if necessary.

If a game allows players to play for a draw, players in danger of losing will of course attempt to draw if they feel they cannot win. This sort of play occurs, for example, in

9. Even the phrase "fifth place" sounds odd when applied to a poker player.

10. In go, *komi* is a point bonus given to one of the players, typically 7 1/2 points given to white to offset the advantage black has in moving first. The half point serves to prevent ties.

chess, tic-tac-toe, or *Nuclear War*. If a draw is too easy to get, the game may rarely reach a satisfactory conclusion.

In some casual games, especially children's games, draws can be desirable. The game has been played and no one need lose. The draw outcome can be a powerful incentive to play again, as long as there is some reasonable possibility of a nondraw in the future.

Exercise 3.9: Do NFL games have scaled performance as part of their outcome? Do NFL seasons?

Exercise 3.10: Do campaign structures tend to enhance or detract from scaled performance in individual games? Why?

Exercise 3.11: What is the primary reason that games allow draws? Why do games with less luck tend to find draws more acceptable?

Exercise 3.12: Often, the total prize purse in a tournament is fixed for cost reasons and the payout to the winner is fixed for marketing reasons. If the primary goal for distributing the rest of the money is to reduce kingmaking, what might the payouts look like?

3.4 Characteristic: Ending Conditions

At some point, an orthogame will end and a winner (or group of winners, or unique loser, etc.) will be declared. There are two basic ways this can happen:

• Winning ends the game—for example, checkmating your opponent's king means you win, and the game ends at that point.
• An end condition occurs, then the winner is determined—for example, when the *Scrabble* tiles run out, the game is over, and whoever has the highest score is the winner.

In both cases, the phrase "victory condition" is commonly used to mean "what a player needs to do to win." In the first case, achieving the victory condition immediately ends the game; in the second case, an independent ending condition occurs (e.g., nine innings have passed in baseball), and the victory condition is to be in the proper state (e.g., having the most points) at that moment. Games with an explicit end condition tend to have some sort of scaled performance as their victory condition; games where winning ends the game may be based on scaled performance (e.g., first person to 100 points wins) but may have some nonscaled victory condition (e.g., take all of the opponent's pieces).

Exercise 3.13: Give five examples each of games where winning ends the game and where an end condition occurs. Do you believe the generalization that end conditions tend to have scaled performance? Can you think of any exceptions?

Figure 3.4

Sometimes the end condition occurs more or less independently of what the players do, as when time runs out or a certain number of turns pass. Sometimes, though, the players have some control over when the end condition happens. The dynamics involved—with winning players attempting to hasten the game's end and losing players trying to delay it—can be intriguing or annoying depending on the details. Some problem areas to watch out for include an ability of losers to delay the game's end ad nauseam, or annoying calculations that potential winners feel compelled to make as they decide exactly when to end the game.

Points

Points—numerical scores assigned to each player, typically with highest being best (although sometimes lowest is best, as in golf or hearts)—are extremely common in games.[11] Even games that do not have points as an explicit part of the rules may develop point systems of some type—really state heuristics—such as the point value for pieces in chess (each piece is assigned a point value, and your total "score" is the total value of pieces you have taken from your opponent).

It's perhaps not surprising that even games without explicit scores may develop them, since reducing one's position to a single number is an extremely powerful first-order heuristic. It tells you both whether you are winning or losing, and by how much.

Exercise 3.14: Consider the games listed in appendix C. Of the ones you're familiar with, how many have formal point systems? How many have informal ones? How many have no point systems at all? Discuss two or three of the borderline cases that you find most interesting.

In single-player games, sometimes there is no way to "win," but instead one plays until one loses but tries to get as many points as possible before that happens (with time spent until one loses being a common alternate player-chosen metric). *Tetris*, or almost any arcade game, is an example of this style of play. Sometimes this lack of a clear victory condition feels a little unsatisfying, and so an explicit win condition (e.g., defeat the big boss, or clear all the levels once) is put in at a certain point during the game, and if one achieves it the game goes back to the beginning but with everything much harder—for example, *Donkey Kong* or *Diablo*.

Complex games such as RPGs and especially MMOs often have a number of different point tracks (gold, experience points, faction reputation, craft skill, PvP points), and the player can pick and choose which ones to go after. Even loot becomes a point track system in *World of Warcraft*, given the raid loot tier system—having Tier 8 gear instead of Tier 7 gear is a kind of advancement along a victory track.

Money and "Playing for Points"

Often points are spendable, either as in-game currency as in an MMO (not only gold, but perhaps also honor, reputation, or experience points) or as real-world currency as in gambling games. In this case, "playing for points" (playing to maximize one's point score, regardless of whether one is in a position to win the game or not) is very natural and in fact may seem more natural than playing for place. After all, most people would probably choose to be up $200 at the end of a night of poker with someone else at the table who has more, rather than being up $100 even though everyone else at the table has less. In fact, a game like poker is so connected with playing for points that it is hard to think of it differently.

11. Many of the remarks here in fact apply to scaled performance generally—both points and time—but are phrased in terms of points to avoid awkwardness.

Although monetary systems are the most obvious examples of systems where players will tend to "play for points," they are not the only ones. For example, many runners in a marathon (particularly those not among the top finishers) will care more about their time than about how they place—coming in under four hours for the first time will mean more to most people than placing 163rd rather than 167th.

"Playing for points" is extremely common. In games where the points have some explicit value, such as poker where the points have the real-life value that money has, playing for points is obviously natural. But even in games where the points have no such value built in (*Scrabble* or hearts, say), players will often track them over time (perhaps informally) in order to give them value. And even absent such a tracking system, players may continue to play for points or for position in individual games. Playing in such a way has a number of advantages: it reduces politics, and it gives meaning to the game for players who are out of contention. You may not be able to win the game—you may not even be able to move from fourth place to third—but you can almost always try to eke out a few more points. Playing to do so is not entirely satisfying (especially if the points have no intrinsic value), but it is still more appealing to most people than playing randomly. One can think of this phenomenon as a way—often player-adopted—of controlling the problems around player elimination and politics. In other words, the more valuable points are, either explicitly or implicitly, the less trouble the game is likely to have with player elimination, politics, kingmaking, and the whole complex of issues surrounding multiplayer play.

We'll have more to say about money in section 6.2.

Dual-Track Point Systems

Sometimes the point track simply records who is winning. Sometimes, however, the points also can be spent within the game to improve one's position, as in *Monopoly*. If the advantage to spending points to win is very great, it can lead to excessive snowballing; whoever is ahead spends points to get further ahead—that is, to get more points. One approach to control this problem is to use two (or more) point tracks, one for victory and one for power. This approach is especially common in European boardgames, which often have money (representing in-game power) and victory points (which are used solely for determining the winner). A similar dynamic appears less explicitly in go, where there is a balance between power/influence (roughly, outward-facing thickness, which is useful for scoring points in the future) and territory (the actual victory condition of the game), although the parallel is inexact since power is not easily converted into a point-based system. One can also think of an RTS in this way, with a measure of one's military strength representing victory points, and one's economic strength being the "money points" that influence victory only indirectly.

Separating money and victory points adds complication, of course, which is a disadvantage. But it can have some good effects as well.

• It can give a kind of catch-up, since the player behind on victory points may have more power points that she can use to close the gap. This is the flipside of the fact that single-track point systems tend to cause snowballing.
• There are often interesting strategic choices ("guns or butter") in terms of balancing the two. Typically investing in victory points means going for a quick victory, and investing in power points means giving up an early lead in the hope of winning in the end.
• Games may seem closer; the person who loses will often be ahead in power points and can say "I would have won in another turn or two."
• Having the most power points (or the most of any one kind of power point in complex games with multiple point tracks) is a kind of consolation prize or alternate victory condition—"Yes, I lost, but look how much more wood I had than anyone else!"

Victory Conditions

Games have countless victory conditions besides "amass the most points": checkmate the opponent's king, get rid of all the cards in your hand, control the hill for three consecutive turns. As mentioned above, such games tend to end on the achievement of the victory condition as opposed to having a separate ending condition.[12]

For deliberately designed games, tweaking the victory conditions can be an important way to solve various problems that might come up in a game. For example, in a game about battling armies, having the game continue until one army is destroyed might lead to players hanging back and avoiding a fight. Having the victory condition be control of a center area for a certain period of time can prevent that, while keeping the basic feel of the game the same (i.e., the new victory condition encourages players to have a large fight leading to the destruction of one army, the behavior that was hoped for with the initial victory condition). Another example might be a *Monopoly*-like game, originally designed to be played until all but one player is bankrupt. Such a victory condition could cause player-elimination problems (players who go bankrupt early have to sit out for a long time) or problems maintaining interest at the end of the game (the winner is clear, but it takes a long time to actually end the game by bankrupting everyone else). In such a case, changing the victory condition to amassing a certain amount of money might fix the problem, while leaving the basic gameplay intact: players are still trying to amass the most wealth, just as before. Fixes of this kind tend to come at a cost in increased complication, so there are always tradeoffs.

Some games have multiple victory conditions: in *Magic* you can run your opponent's life down to zero or you can run his deck out of cards; in *Age of Empires* you

12. This is just a restatement of "games with ending conditions tend to have scaled performance."

can destroy your opponent's civilization or you can build a wonder. The appeal of multiple victory conditions lies in the added depth and replayability they give the game; it's almost as if there are different games in the same game framework, one for each victory condition.[13] There is a real complexity cost, however: a moderate one for the players, who must learn each victory condition, and a large one for the game designers, who must balance the different victory conditions. Ensuring that two different routes to victory are both viable tends to be even harder than ensuring that two different game pieces, say, are both viable.

Asymmetric Victory Conditions

Sometimes the victory conditions of the opposing players are not the same. This is common in simulation wargames, but appears in other games as well. It is commonly associated with asymmetric sides, but does not have to be. Some games even have victory conditions known only to individual sides, as in some modern *Risk* variants. The asymmetry in victory conditions can be critical for simulations. For example, in recreating military battles it might be important to have initial conditions that presuppose one side as the winner, but by declaring victory in the game to be based on the losing (in the historical sense) side holding out for a certain number of turns, a relatively fair contest can be created out of an unfair one.

This is seen commonly in many sports with handicaps to score in order to make games fair. A game of HORSE may have the better player start with an H-O and thus his victory condition is to make five unrepeatable shots, while his opponent's win condition is only to make three unrepeatable shots.

A wide variety of changes in audience skill range, in styles of play, and in strategy can be created by varying victory conditions asymmetrically, often with minimal cost to the overall rule structure.

Exercise 3.15: Give an example of a game where sometimes winning ends the game, and sometimes an end condition does.

Exercise 3.16: Give some examples of games played professionally and casually where the type of end condition changes. Why is this the case?

13. A less appealing corner case occurs with victory conditions put in to cover holes in the rules, with the expectation that they will rarely come up. In reversi/*Othello*, one normally wins by having the most pieces of one's own color when the final sixty-fourth piece is played. But under rare circumstances one can flip all the pieces to one's own color at an earlier stage of the game and win that way. Such alternate victory conditions tend to come up too rarely to be relevant to normal play, and are often included in the rules mainly for logical completeness. Another example is the triple ko in go, which under traditional Japanese rules could lead to an automatic draw.

Exercise 3.17: Single-player computer games commonly have a variety of victory conditions throughout their campaign. Why are varied victory conditions more common in these types of games?

3.5 Characteristic: Positional Asymmetry

Almost all games have different starting states for the players. These range from something as simple as one player moving first in chess to something as grossly asymmetric as one player being a level 40 rogue and another a level 43 priest in a *World of Warcraft* duel. These asymmetries may come from the game itself (white starts first in chess), from the environment (wind in football), or from the players. Asymmetries coming from the players may involve different gameplay options each player has (what char-

Figure 3.5
©iStockphoto.com/Juan Escalante

acter class that player chose to play) or relations between the players (the ordering of various players around the poker table).[14]

The effects may become washed out over the course of the game, or they may stay in play throughout. In general, effects that might be washed out (like moving first in chess) are more likely to do so at lower player skill levels. Sometimes the asymmetries hardly seem to matter: moving first in *Monopoly* does not appear to make much of a difference.

To find a game without any asymmetries, one needs to have all players moving simultaneously and choosing from the same option set. Such games are rare; rock-paper-scissors is one example, and bicycle time trials are another as long as riders don't know how well other riders have done. Many games, though, are fairly close to symmetric—for example, in a marathon the initial positioning doesn't matter much given the length of the race.

Extreme Asymmetry

Positional asymmetry may be seen as "unfair," but some games use it deliberately to increase game variety and replayability. Games such as single-player RPGs are built around complete asymmetry: the player role and the (AI) monster role are wildly different. Simulation wargames are asymmetric for reasons of historical accuracy. Some games, like *Cosmic Encounter*, *Counterstrike*, *Magic*, *Starcraft*, or any MMRPG, allow players to pick from among different positions, or assign them to one, with the intention that these different starting positions are reasonably balanced.[15] There is arguably a trend toward more positional asymmetry in computer games nowadays, as can be seen in the increasing use of different character classes in first-person shooters like *Team Fortress* compared with the symmetry of *Doom* or *Quake*.

Although classic games are rarely grossly asymmetric, there are a few exceptions like Fox and Geese or monster chess (if one accepts the latter as "classic").

Moderate Asymmetry

Games with more modest amounts of player asymmetry—roughly equal player roles, but with a slight advantage such as moving first given to one player—usually try to

14. Strictly speaking, the fact that one chess player is better than her opponent is a kind of asymmetry, but we do not mean to include this case when we speak of positional asymmetries. For a slightly more formal definition, one can say there is a positional asymmetry when swapping the positions of two equally skilled players can change the likely outcome. Thus the presence of a weaker third player (on my left, but your right, say) might introduce a positional asymmetry between us, but we don't consider the weakness of that player relative to you as a positional asymmetry between you and that player (it is an asymmetry, of course, but it is not one based on position).

15. Or, in the case of *Magic*, a subset of the starting positions (decks) are reasonably balanced.

limit that asymmetry as much as possible, most often by rotating which player has the advantage. Teams take turns kicking off at the start of each half in football, the deal rotates in most card games, chess matches involve multiple games with players alternating black and white, and the go player who has white receives 7 1/2 points komi in return for going second.[16] In computer games, simultaneous play is usually possible, so asymmetry in board position is often the main concern in games that are close to symmetrical. In RTS games, for example, a common approach is to have slight asymmetry for aesthetic reasons, but to make the positions as symmetrical as possible otherwise (although in games with different races, the remarks above on extreme asymmetry apply to the choice of race).

If the game is short (or has short atoms), playing multiple times is an easy way to relieve the asymmetry. Note that atoms can have a very marked asymmetry even when the game is relatively symmetric (e.g., bridge and football, where there's an offense and a defense at any given moment). For any game, even a longer game without short atoms, say chess, asymmetries can be handled from a metagame point of view by the campaign, within which enough games take place to wash out positional advantages.

Sports and Equipment

One special kind of asymmetry, akin to that of the extreme asymmetry seen in games like *Magic* or *Everquest* but to a lesser degree, is the asymmetry found in sports equipment. In sports it is generally accepted that players or teams may bring their own equipment within some limitations. (In other game genres this is *not* entirely accepted, and some people object to games like *Magic* as a result. Another common point of view is that equipment obtained entirely in-game, such as through normal play in an MMRPG, is acceptable but that purchased equipment is not.) In many sports, the positional advantage obtained through equipment is minor (e.g., basketball, athletic shoe commercials to the contrary), but in some (e.g., bicycle racing, Formula 1) it's quite large. Stock-car racing (and, more recently, showroom stock racing) was initially in effect a rule modification to auto racing that limited the positional advantage due to equipment. *Magic* sealed-deck play is a similar development.

Further Examples

Almost every game has at least some amount of asymmetry, usually with advantages accruing to players in certain positions.

Chess Going first provides a massive advantage at high *and* roughly equal skill levels, and is generally washed out otherwise.

16. See note 10, explaining komi.

Bridge A full rubber of bridge is fairly symmetric. But players do bring a bidding system to the table, which can be thought of as like a *Magic* deck or an RPG character. During bidding, order matters a great deal (the same bid can mean something quite different in first seat versus fourth seat). When the play of the hand begins, the positions are highly asymmetric: one player (dummy) is out entirely, and another (declarer) is extremely powerful compared to the remaining two (the defenders).

Hearts In a game with players of varying skill levels, two players of equal skill may find themselves in asymmetric positions based on their positioning relative to the weaker players and to each other.

Poker Both the order of player action and the particular qualities and personalities of the other players might suit two otherwise equally skilled players in different ways. So in terms of positional asymmetry poker is much like hearts.

Scrabble Going first is a relatively modest advantage. Position compared to other players (in multiplayer) is, however, very important. In particular, going right after a weak player is extremely useful, because that player is more likely to give you good opportunities to score.

Most sports The home-field advantage is small but significant. Advantages in order of play range from nonexistent (basketball and hockey have symmetric starts) or modest (each team has one kick-off at the start of a half in football) to extreme (going second in baseball is very good, because you can react to what the other team has done; since this is tied in with home-field advantage, it's hard to untangle the two). The pure in-game advantages of these asymmetries, however, can be washed out by asymmetries from outside the game (e.g., the effects of crowd noise).

Races In most races, initial positioning is fairly important. Indeed, in auto racing there is even a term—*pole position*—given to the preferred starting position. Many races, especially shorter ones, have staggered starts to attempt to make up for the differences in starting positions. If the race is long enough, a marathon for example, any initial advantage may be largely washed out. Further positional advantages may arise from equipment (see above).

Single-player games When discussing single-player computer games, we mentioned that some of them felt like "pure" one-player games (e.g., *Tetris*), and others seemed like "one and a half" player games (e.g., *Starcraft* vs. the AI). With the language of positional asymmetry, we can phrase this more precisely: thinking of the computer as another player, a high degree of asymmetry means we have a "pure" one-player game, and a high degree of symmetry means we have a one and a half player game.

Exercise 3.18: What are some asymmetries commonly associated with RPGs?

Exercise 3.19: Why does baseball have the largest game mechanical home-field advantage and the smallest statistical home-field advantage of the major sports?

Exercise 3.20: What are some asymmetries that develop late in the average RPG (as opposed to the initial asymmetry in character class)?

Exercise 3.21: In collegiate freestyle wrestling, players in periods after the first start in asymmetric (referee's) positions. What are some reasons for this?

Exercise 3.22: What common features of RPGs make them ideal for extreme player asymmetry?

Exercise 3.23: What are some advantages that an extremely asymmetric game can have over a more symmetric one?

3.6 Characteristic: Sensory Feedback

Playing a game is not just the meeting of an abstract human brain with an abstract set of gameplay algorithms. The game's conceit is one reflection of that; the interface and aesthetics of a game are another. The game provides visual, tactile, and audio information to the player (but rarely taste or smell), and the player inputs her choices to the game somehow, whether it be by leaping to catch a ball, telling her opponent

Figure 3.6
©iStockphoto.com/Pei Ling Hoo

her letter choice in ghost, picking up a chess piece and moving it, or group selecting RTS units with a mouse. This flow to and from the user is extremely important for any game, regardless of genre, and it can be good or bad for the game depending on how it is done.

Note that there are really two axes on which to measure the sensory feedback a game has: how aesthetically pleasing it is, in and of itself, and to what extent it supports or inhibits gameplay. Aesthetic appeal and support of gameplay can sometimes work against each other—to grossly oversimplify, aesthetic considerations often push for a greater ornateness, and gameplay wants simplicity of interface. Examples of this tension include fancy versus simple chess pieces, spare versus decorative cardface designs in a TCG, 3-D zoomed-in versus isometric pulled-back views in an RTS, and spartan versus ornate buttons and controls in a computer game. Thus in some sense artists and game designers are natural enemies; they need to transcend this innate opposition of concerns to get truly great results.

People tend to think of the word *interface* as applying to computers only, but in the general sense in which we take it—all the ways the game sends and receives information to and from the player—every game has an interface.

Interface and aesthetics are both subjects worthy of books in their own right; we'll content ourselves with just a few comments and examples, organized by sense.

Visual

There is much appeal in well-done artwork in a paper game or good graphics in a computer game (with a computer game, the artistic quality is often more important than the technical sophistication measured by such things as polygon count[17]).

Examples of good visuals can be found in the following:

- *Playing cards* The standard designs are not too busy, but they aren't absolutely minimalist either.
- Pokémon *monster designs (say, on the GameBoy)* Rather like playing cards, a nice balance between simplicity and representation gives them an iconic character.
- *Sports* Players can instantly react to the physical acts of others due to the wonder of the interface that is real-life physics.
- *Casino games* These typically have a very clean and sophisticated-looking presentation that is very good for spectation.

When the visuals in a game go bad, it is often because they have become too complex, making it harder to read the game state (and thus making state heuristics

17. *World of Warcraft* is a fine example of this at work; most players think of it as having "great graphics" even though, on a technical level, they are by no means cutting edge. The artistic direction, however, is excellent. Web games are another example where one can see artistic excellence without cutting-edge technology.

more taxing to apply). The classic example of this is the fancy-themed chess set, which may make a nice gift or conversation piece, but is usually less good to play with than a more classic chess set. Note that this is partly a matter of standards—players are used to the traditional pieces—but partly a matter of simplicity and cleanness of the look of the pieces. Sometimes a game's visuals are "upgraded" by making them more complex, and thus actually worse; the transition in style from *Pokémon* to *Digimon*, and the shift from art to photos in the first U.S. edition of *Settlers of Catan*, are examples of this.

Some cases where visuals are especially likely to obscure gameplay include

• Newer games (older games have evolved a harmony between visuals and gameplay)
• Games made with art as a focus (e.g., the decks of cards one buys in a museum, with a different work of art pictured on each card)
• Gift items (e.g., a *Simpsons* chess set)

Computer games especially have an enormous number of issues to wrestle with. They are newer, art is often a very large part of them, and computer interface is hard enough already, even in applications like business software where aesthetics is not a major consideration.

Audio

Computer games use sound very deliberately, including music, voiceover, and all kinds of more or less naturalistic sound effects. But many physical games also gain aesthetic value from sound, from the clinking of poker chips, the shuffling sounds of cards, the roar of racing cars, the regular thudding of a tennis volley, to the brutal impact of bodies colliding in boxing or football. The roar of the crowd at sporting events has not only aesthetic value but also gameplay implications: it can affect gameplay (especially when very loud) and it can inform spectation.

It is easy to overlook the power of sound in a game. One can see evidence of it if one plays a web game with the sound off (perhaps at work), and then again with the sound on. Even if the game seems like "it doesn't really need sound," one often finds that one unconsciously enjoys the game more with the sound.[18]

18. Game designers often like to think that they can judge a game's quality even when it is in an unpolished state—and indeed it is part of their job to be able to do so. But an honest game designer who is paying attention can often find himself misjudging based on polish. (This same phenomenon occurs with visual polish as well, but it's harder to detect because one doesn't commonly turn visuals off and on.) It is very easy to find gameplay flaws in the no-sound game—or to overlook them in the version with sound. This effect is particularly powerful in games involving monkeys.

Tactile

The weight of chess pieces, the feel of shuffling and dealing cards, the tactile qualities of poker chips—noncomputer games have always had a good deal of pleasure and satisfaction coming from the physical feel of their components. Sports, of course, are even more physical, although the sensations involved are both pleasant and unpleasant. Until recently, computer games have had very little tactile feedback, although more recently force feedback joysticks, rumble packs, and special input devices like the *Dance Dance Revolution* dancepad, the *Guitar Hero* controller, and above all the Wii remote have begun to change this.

For another example, look at dice. Rolling dice is enjoyable to many people, and some games, like craps, are little more than an excuse to roll dice. But rolling dice isn't visually alone that much fun, for example with a computer. Paper role-playing games almost always use dice, and critical die rolls become a focus for player attention and excitement. Perhaps because they can't match the tactile input, computer RPGs don't simulate die rolling directly (although they borrow a great many other things from paper RPGs) and instead put the random number generation behind the scenes, probably because a direct translation of die rolling to the computer screen would be an annoyance rather than an enjoyable feature. More recently, though, floating combat text (where damage numbers spout up from the heads of the targets like water bubbling from a fountain) has become more common in MMOs, notably *World of Warcraft*. These numbers can be thought of as the analog to die rolling, an analog more suited to the computer medium.

Olfactory

Although not a large part of computer games or boardgames and card games, smell is a factor in sports. Aside from the obvious factor of the smell of humans exerting themselves, there are outdoor smells (grass, earth, the woods after a fresh snowfall) and the smells of animals and equipment (horses, cars, baseball gloves).

Even nonsports games may have some equipment-related smells, such as the scent of newly opened packaging. Although the scent alone may not be that important, it is part of an overall aesthetic appeal that can be strong for some people, especially with games where one frequently opens new packaging: an expansion to a computer game, or a booster pack of a trading card game.

Still, because smell in a game is rarely deliberately designed but is instead a side effect of other decisions, there's not as much scope for discussion as there is with the other senses.

Taste

Taste is not commonly a factor in games, except perhaps in sports if things go drastically wrong. Some specific exceptions might include *Fear Factor*–style games, chocolate Russian roulette, and drinking games.

Control Feel and Kinesthetics

When you give input to a game, the game can absorb that input and incorporate it into the game state in different ways. People can gain pleasure from the way their interactions match or surprise their internal physics calculation engines. Sometimes things are pretty straightforward: you pick up a chess piece and move it—although even there the heft of the chess piece can feel better or worse. Placing stones on a go board has a kind of tactile feedback. Playing pool, bowling, or using the Pop-o-matic dice in *Trouble* all provide distinctive sensations based on how your body is interacting with your environment.

With computer games, the most common "feel" is a sort of weightless responsiveness: click on a certain area or press a direction key, and you either go there instantly or you head in that direction at whatever speed the game allows. But some games do have a more distinct feel, such as the bouncing rhythms of *Q*bert*. So-called physics games, from the classics *Lunar Lander* and *Crystal Quest*, to the many modern physics games (especially common in the indie game movement) such as *Armadillo Run*, *Bridge Builder*, *Tower of Goo*, *Triptych*, *Crayon Physics*, or driving a Warthog in *Halo* have very strong feels.

Exercise 3.24: Before 1997 there were almost no examples of tactile feedback in console games. After 1997 the number skyrocketed. What changed? What does this say about the importance of this feedback?

Exercise 3.25: List the features of *Monopoly* that give good tactile sensations. Compare this list to other boardgames.

Exercise 3.26: Give some examples of how sound can be critical in gameplay. Give some examples where it hinders gameplay.

4 Games as Systems

If chapter 3 dealt with systemic ingredients of games, this chapter deals with emergent systemic phenomena: properties of games that are more large-scale, and that typically emerge from the rules rather than being included within them. The sections in this chapter look at games as an abstract whole rather than looking at concrete individual elements.

We begin with a discussion of abstract games (like rock-paper-scissors) and how they may map onto more concrete games or parts of those games. We then discuss the overall flow of the game: first from the point of view of the ebb and flow of victory, whether accelerating ("snowballing") or decelerating ("catch-up"), then from the point of view of complexity (does the game become more complex over its course, less complex, or does the complexity shift in some more complicated way?). Finally, we talk about game balance, and how the strategic choice in the game—that is, the experienced complexity of it—can collapse if the balance is wrong.

4.1 Characteristic: Abstract Subgames and Essential Games

Games are often disguised versions of other simpler games, or have other simpler games within them. An example of the former is when one says of a political game "it's really just the chip-taking game." An example of the latter is a rock-paper-scissors relationship between units in an RTS: perhaps melee beats ranged beats flying, but flying beats melee because the melee units can't hit back.[1] These abstract games may be good or bad for the game in question (depending on how they are integrated into the game, and whether they support or simply overwrite the other elements of the game), but recognizing them is always a help for understanding the game.

1. For the computer programmers among our readers, the first case can be thought of as an "is-a" relationship, and the second a "has-a" relationship. We might say of some game that it "is a" chip-taking game, or that it "has a" rock-paper-scissors subgame within it.

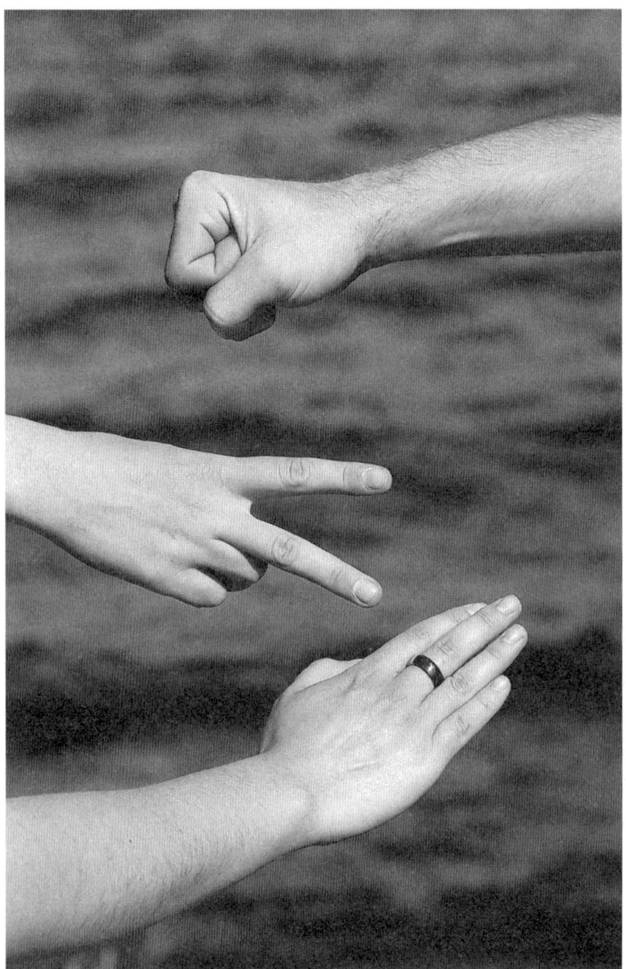

Figure 4.1
©iStockphoto.com/Troy Knox

Explicit Subgames

Sometimes a game is quite explicitly made up of distinct subgames. *Mario Party* and *Wario Ware* are collections of minigames. In the boardgame *Titan*, the main game involves traveling around the board building up an army, but when two armies fight, a tactical subgame with its own distinct rules is fought on a separate map. In some live-action roleplaying games[2] rock-paper-scissors is used explicitly as a conflict resolution mechanic.

Games with subgames fall into three rough categories:

1. *Games that contain subgames* *Titan*, most MMOs (buying from vendors, e.g., is a subgame), most *Final Fantasy* games, and many other examples.
2. *Games that are subgame collections* *Mario Party*, *Cranium*, *Wario Ware*, Barbu, dealer's choice poker.
3. *Staged games* Games that fall into stages so distinct, they are essentially different games. Examples include bridge (bidding and play[3]), *Magic* drafting (the initial draft of cards for your deck, followed by playing with the deck you drafted), or Skitgubbe (accumulate cards in the trick-taking phase, then attempt to void your hand in the rummylike phase).

There is a continuity between subgames on the one hand and metagame activities on the other, especially with staged games. Bidding and play in bridge definitely feel like subgames of one game. *Magic* drafting, *Magic* constructed (deckbuilding and play), *Warhammer* (army selection, painting, and play), and *D&D* (character creation and play) feel successively more like a game activity with an associated metagame activity. But for any of these games, one can think of them as a (smaller) game with a pregame activity, or a (larger) game that's made up of subgames. Note that each of the subgames of a given larger game will tend to have its own characteristics: length of playtime, interactivity, costs, rewards, and so on, and thus may appeal to different parts of the larger game audience.

Implicit Subgames

Although some games have explicit subgames, it's more common, as in the melee-ranged-flying RTS example, for the subgames to be implicit. Another example, found in many TCGs and RTS games,[4] is early-game units losing to midgame units losing to

2. Live-action role-playing games, or LARPs, are a form of role-playing game that is played while moving about and acting out the game, rather than using a computer or playing at a table with pencil and paper. The mobile nature of the game encourages mechanics that do not require any special equipment.
3. Or, for a few playgroups, three phases: bidding, play, and postmortem analysis.
4. Found in both because these games share a power buildup over time and player choice between immediate military buildup and investing in economic growth.

late-game units. Showing up a little later with a bigger army can win you the game; planning to show up much later with a huge army is bad for your chances, because you will lose to a fast army before your huge army is built. A related RTS rock-paper-scissors is the rush-eco-turtle (aka rush-boom-turtle) relationship, where a fast attack beats an economic buildup, which in turn defeats a defensive strategy.

These rock-paper-scissors subgames[5] do not determine the outcome of the game all by themselves; they are merely one element. Enough other things are going on that it is easy to miss the relationship of the elements in the subgame, because winning or losing a particular subgame can easily be washed out by losing or winning other subgames. But to some extent winning or losing the game as a whole can be thought of as winning or losing enough of the various subgames. Many elements of design can be broken down by looking at the subgames as well—for example, a balance problem in one of the subgames (like rush being too good against turtling, or ranged beating both air and melee) can spill out to break the game as a whole.

Another abstract game that appears as part of many games is the "resource commitment game," which can be modeled as follows: two players each have 10 points, which they simultaneously distribute into three buckets A, B, and C. Then they compare, and whoever wins two out of three is the winner. So for example if one player chooses 7–2–1 and the other chooses 4–3–3, the latter player wins the game since she won both B and C. Any military game where multiple areas are important and it makes sense to split forces potentially has this subgame. At a tactical level, *Diplomacy* is very much like this (at a strategic level, it is of course fundamentally political). Of course, in many military games having the largest army after the clash is most important, in which case each player brings his entire force, and there's no such army splitting and thus no abstract subgame, at least on this axis. Similarly any game where a player distributes points when designing a character, starship, or other game unit potentially has this abstract subgame. Again, this subgame can disappear if it's in the player's interest to invest all or almost all of his points in a single area. If a designer wants to preserve this subgame, it's important to watch out for this problem.

One can think of sports and other physical games as having physical skill subgames as well. For example, running a sprint, or throwing and catching, can be thought of as subgames of football. Note that many computer games (but few boardgames and card games) have some physical subgames, typically involving reaction time and eye-hand coordination, and some physical games (pool, rifle shooting, darts) have

5. When we call these "rock-paper-scissors subgames," we mean this in a general sense. There may be more than three strategies, for example. Really these are Von Neumann games (see appendix A).

relatively few of the physical skills we associate with sports (again, mainly eye-hand coordination is involved).

Essential Game

If the game can be viewed as a disguised version of some abstract game, we'll refer to that abstract game as the "essential game," as in "this game is essentially a chip-taking game." Essential games are most often found in multiplayer games with a lot of targeted interaction: the voting games and chip-taking games discussed earlier.

Note that when people say some game is "really just X" they usually mean to be dismissive. But having an essential game is not necessarily bad. What is important is that the essential game does not make all the other game mechanics superfluous, but instead integrates them into some kind of cohesive whole. Overly political games can fail on this account: how good you are at the various submechanics of the game may not matter, and instead victory is determined solely by the politics. Very often, the essential game of politics can be hard to uncover due to the slow but interesting process of the development of positional and directional heuristics. A game that is essentially a chip-taking game at a perfect level of play can in practice be far from that. Here casual play explains why there are so few "classic" games with a chip-taking essence relative to newer ones. Over time a player community will often be able to uncover the essential game, perhaps leading to its decline if that underlying game is unsatisfying, but a casually played game only a few years old is unlikely to encounter this sort of problem.

Exercise 4.1: Why do designers consistently add RPS (rock-paper-scissors) subgames to trading card games or miniatures games?

Exercise 4.2: Give some examples of implicit RPS in football.

Exercise 4.3: Give some examples of explicit subgames in football.

Exercise 4.4: Give some examples of computer games that contain explicit subgames (other than those mentioned in the text).

Exercise 4.5: What are some of the drawbacks of explicit subgames? Some of the benefits?

Exercise 4.6: Would you expect to see more RPS in a strategy game or a physical skill game? Why? Give some examples of RPS in physical skill games.

Exercise 4.7: What are some ways a turn-based game (without simultaneous turns) can include RPS?

Exercise 4.8: Would you expect to see more RPS in a simultaneous-turn game or a (nonsimultaneous) turn-based game? Give some examples of RPS in turn-based games. What about real-time computer games?

4.2 Characteristic: Snowball and Catch-Up

Many games, especially multiplayer games, have "catch-up features": features whose purpose is to help losing players catch up, such as the shells (missiles) in *Mario Kart* that let you shoot at the drivers ahead of you. And many games naturally have a tendency to "snowball": once you start winning, you win more and more due to your initial advantage, such as the ability of a winning *Monopoly* player to use her money to buy even more advantage. In *Chutes & Ladders,* one can think of the chutes and the ladders as a catch-up feature—the viewpoint is slightly problematic given that it is not obvious the chutes hurt the leader more than the other players, or that the ladders help the loser more than the other players (more on this later), but surely if one player were twenty squares ahead she would vote to get rid of all the chutes and ladders if she could, and the players who were far back would vote against her. And any political game tends naturally to exhibit catch-up in the form of "pick on the leader" and sometimes snowballing as well in the form of "eliminate the weak."

Figure 4.2
©iStockphoto.com

But if one thinks about catch-up and snowball features a bit more, it becomes quite tricky. Suppose you're way ahead of me. But the game has a lot of catch-up features. Then I still have a chance to win. Well, then perhaps you are not so far ahead of me after all. (For example, a twenty-square lead in *Chutes & Ladders* might be basically the same as a five-square lead in the equivalent game without the chutes and the ladders.) Or, if the game has a lot of snowball features, then you are even further ahead of me than it seems. In either case, how meaningful are the ideas of "catch-up" and "snowball" at all? If we both understand the game well, we understand that you are however far ahead of me you truly are, and "catch-up" and "snowball" are illusory.

There is partial truth to this idea that catch-up and snowball are illusory. But it will take us a fair amount of untangling to sort out what is really going on. We will start by looking at some more examples of snowball and catch-up. Then we will give a more precise way of defining the terms, look at how those more precise concepts reveal the illusion, and examine how that illusion relates to the perceived realities of games. Armed with our new (and hopefully more enlightened) viewpoint, we will look at a number of issues surrounding snowball and catch-up.

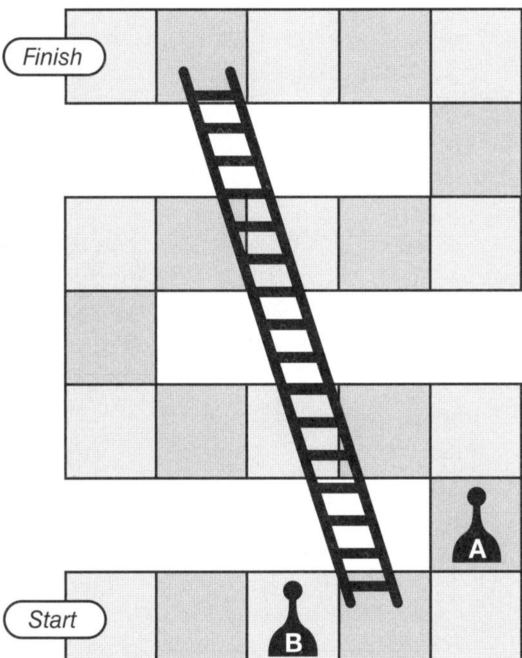

Figure 4.3
Is A really ahead? And if so, by how much?

More on Snowballing

Any game in which your score (either in the sense of official score that determines the winner, i.e., victory points, or "unofficial" score in the sense of a simple and easy to use metric, such as money) equals your power[6] tends to have snowballing. *Monopoly* is a classic example; more money helps you to make even more, until you are unstoppable. In no-limit poker, having a high score definitely increases your power. Chess can also be viewed this way, if you think of "score" as your lead in pieces. On the flipside, in go a territorial lead does not typically help you make even more territory. Players often trade away territory for power, in the hope that that power will allow them to get even more territory later in the game.

In most sports, having a lot of points doesn't really help you score more. You can't "spend" a touchdown you made in football to get a new player.[7] Boxing is one of the few exceptions (and indeed boxing is also exceptional in having an explicit snowball-handling mechanism: early ending of fights by the referee). In a PvP computer game with experience points and leveling up, snowball is the rule: win a few fights early, and you will be higher-level and win even more fights later on (*Defense of the Ancients* being an extreme example). In an RTS like *Starcraft*, if one thinks of army size, or army size plus economy size, as a kind of score, then one certainly sees snowballing.

Another natural effect that increases snowballing in some multiplayer games arises from players' reaction to randomness (although randomness itself is generally a catch-up feature; see below). If a game has a lot of uncertainty, knocking out a losing player can be beneficial to the winning players. His elimination means he doesn't have a chance to randomly get lucky later and defeat one of the leaders. Poker is a common example: players who are ahead in no-limit poker are typically happy to knock out a player in a worse position.

Snowballing is often considered bad by designers and players. Partly this is just a natural feeling of unfairness: why reward the player who is already winning? A more sophisticated point of view is to think of it as a problem in logical elimination. Nobody thinks it "unfair" simply because a game ends and someone wins it. What's bad is when someone who has little or no chance to win is forced to continue playing for a long time before the game is over. So a snowball feature that directly leads to the end of the game might be a fine thing (and in fact might not be perceived as a snowball feature at all, but simply as a mechanism for determining when the game is over).

6. Power meaning your ability to make the game go your way—your ability to affect the overall game state.

7. "Having points doesn't help you score more" is true here only to first approximation. Certainly one could argue that there are psychological gains from being ahead that might lead to scoring even more points: momentum, demoralization of the other team, and so on. But that's nothing compared to the advantages of being able to put hotels on all your property in *Monopoly*.

Less appealing is a snowball feature that pushes the game to a state where the winner has an even higher chance of winning, with the game still nowhere near its conclusion.

One way to limit snowballing is to unlink power and score, say by adding victory points that are used to determine the winner but that cannot be spent or otherwise used during the game. Sports and European boardgames commonly use this technique. The price of limiting snowballing in this way is often a more complicated game (gold and victory points as in many European boardgames rather than simply dollars as in *Monopoly*). Race games have this feature naturally: you typically can't "spend" your lead in the race to buy anything, so your lead in the race is simply a specialized and intuitive kind of victory point. In fact, many physical races have something like the opposite of spendable victory points in that not only can't the leader "spend" her lead, she is often harmed by her lead position due to air resistance and the ability of nonleaders to draft.

Although designers largely tend to look for ways to limit snowballing, there are often good reasons to increase it. If games are dragging on too long, or the game suffers too much from player-elimination issues, adding snowballing effects can be helpful. Rewards for knocking out a player (as in *Risk*) are one example.[8] These are strictly speaking snowball effects—they make losers lose by even more—but it's often better to have a 0 percent chance to win (and thus be able to go get a cup of coffee) than to have a 1 percent chance to win (and thus be forced to remain in the game with almost no chance for victory). Games that use the "eliminate the winners" mechanic (e.g., a footrace, or the card game known variously as Asshole, President, or Dai Hin Min) are similarly snowball games—once you drop out, you are no longer in any danger of being the loser.

More on Catch-Up

The dynamic of the rich getting richer means snowballing tends to appear naturally in games. By contrast, catch-up features are more often deliberately included, and less often appear as natural outcomes of game features put in for other reasons.

There are countless examples of deliberately added catch-up features in games. The shells in *Mario Kart* fire forward, so the person in the lead can't make use of them, but people who are behind can fire on those ahead of them. And the Spiny Shell specifically homes in on the person in first place. Some racing games go so far as to speed up the car of anyone who is behind. In *Warcraft III*, the upkeep tax on large armies is a catch-up feature limiting the snowballing effect of large-army dominance.

8. As mentioned above, some games (like poker) have these rewards naturally so they don't need to be added. In *Risk*, though, the odds of an all-but-eliminated player coming back and winning are fairly small, so encouraging the knockout blow makes sense.

As mentioned above, any game with voting or other political features will typically thereby have catch-up, sometimes to the point of making "in the lead" a meaningless concept for much of the game. If someone has a clear lead, it is in the interests of all the other players to stop him. Note that this kind of catch-up is especially agential—one playgroup may think it is fine to pick on the leader, but another may impose limits on it (similarly for political snowballing—various groups will be for or against knocking out weak players, say). But politics is surely a net catch-up feature, since picking on the leader in some form is all but universal in political games.

In general, randomness may be thought of as a kind of catch-up feature. Although a random event may not differentially help losing players over winning players, change in the game state is still appreciated more by the players who are losing than by those who are winning.[9] Reset buttons are one example: if a player is losing in a race game, she is happy to play a card that says "everyone goes back to Start," or that scrambles everyone's position around randomly. Note that although scrambling everyone's positions at random is in some sense "treating all players equally," it can only help the person in last place and only hurt the person in first. Even a seemingly equitable random jolt like "each player rolls two dice and moves forward that many spaces" is probably better for someone who is behind.

Expansion and Contraction of Win Probabilities

Saying that "each player moves forward a random number of spaces" is a catch-up feature is perhaps counterintuitive (although the fact that the player who's behind is in favor of it is evidence in favor of this viewpoint). And we still haven't addressed the question of how meaningful catch-up is once you take it into account: if I'm way behind you in *Chutes & Ladders*, but I might roll a 4 and land on a ladder and wind up ahead of you, then I'm not really so far behind you after all, am I? To address these issues, let's try to be a bit more precise about what catch-up and snowball really mean by creating a simple mathematical model of the progress of a game over time.

At any moment in a game, we can write down each player's chance to win. Typically those chances will start out more or less equal (for a fair game), change somewhat over the course of time, and then gradually shift toward 1 (for the winner) and 0 (for everyone else).[10] If we write the various chances for each player in a row, say for a

9. Indeed, a basic strategy common to all games with a certain minimum amount of skill is to look for highly variable lines of play when losing, and to try and make the outcome as simple and straightforward as possible when winning. Bridge is perhaps the supreme example—when losing, assume various low-probability distributions of the cards in an attempt to find some chance to win; when winning, try to find a line that succeeds no matter how badly the cards are distributed.

10. Readers with some knowledge of mathematical modeling will realize that, like most models, this one comes in a discrete-time and a continuous-time variety. We ignore such issues here, although with its emphasis on events, our model is essentially a discrete one.

four-person game that lasts ten turns, we might see something like (0.25, 0.25, 0.25, 0.25) at the start of turn 1, (0.3, 0.2, 0.15, 0.35) on turn 4, and (0.9, 0.03, 0.03, 0.04) on turn 9. We'll call this list of numbers a *state vector*. Note that the sum of the numbers is always 1.

If there's no chance[11] involved at all (i.e., the game is completely determined), then the vector will look like (0, 0, 0, 1, 0)—all 0s for the players who have no chance and 1 for the player who is certain to win.

In a two-player game, if I am 70 percent likely to win at a certain point (perhaps it's a simple race game and I am eight squares ahead), and then later I am only 60 percent likely to win (perhaps you've rolled well and I'm only five squares ahead now[12]), then you have caught up. If instead later I am 95 percent likely to win, then that's a snowball situation relative to the earlier game state.

What we're really looking at is the spread of the state vector: as it spreads out, the game is snowballing toward its conclusion. If the player who is behind catches up, the vector will be less spread out. The standard way of defining spread is by the *variance*:[13] the expected sum-of-squares deviation from the average. The average is just the sum of the values divided by n, so for a state vector that's $1/n$. Thus for a state vector $(p_1, \ldots, p_n)$ the variance is

$$[(p_1 - 1/n)^2 + \cdots + (p_n - 1/n)^2]/n.$$

This number represents how far the state $(p_1, \ldots, p_n)$ is from the "most caught up state" $(1/n, \ldots, 1/n)$. Naturally, the state $(1/n, \ldots, 1/n)$ has the smallest possible variance, namely 0. The largest possible variance[14] belongs to vectors like (0, 1, . . . , 0)—the most extreme snowball states.

So we'll define a catch-up event as one that decreases the variance of the state vector, and a snowball event as one that increases the variance.

It should be mentioned that ending state vectors like (0, 1, . . . , 0) represent a game with a unique winner. Some games, however, end in draws, thus ending with minimum

11. By "chance" we mean uncertainty in the outcome of the game, not overt chance elements like cards or dice. In this sense, even a game of chess has chance—in fact, quite a large amount of chance between two evenly matched players, for whom the state vector in the early game might be something like (0.47, 0.53). See section 5.1, on randomness.

12. Note that the number of squares until the end of the race factors into the probability estimate of each player's chances, in addition to the number of squares one player is ahead of the other. For concreteness, you might like to imagine the race as two players taking turns rolling a single die, with the winner being the first player to reach 100 total points.

13. The square root of the variance is called the *standard deviation*, and is another common measure of spread. The variance is more convenient for our purposes—it's easier to compute with—but it conveys essentially the same information.

14. $(n-1)/n^2$, not that it matters for this discussion.

Exercise 4.26: Compute this.

rather than maximum variance. This also happens in games with scaled victory conditions, for example poker, where the ending state of the players can be any redistribution of the total buy-in one likes.

Note that hurting the player in the lead and helping the player who is behind are exactly the same thing in this model: if we go from (0.7, 0.3) to (0.6, 0.4) we have both hurt the leader and helped the follower. Any increase in one player's chances must represent a decrease in the chances of some other player(s). Similarly, in a snowball event, the leader does better as the person behind does worse.

Thinking about games in this manner abstracts away a great many features, but a surprising amount of the flow of the game can be read from the time history of a player's chances to win. Some examples:

Here's a three-person game that progressed in a typical fashion (figure 4.4). One player (the thick black line) started out with a $1/n = 1/3$ chance to win, fell a bit behind, started winning, and then continued to widen his lead until the end of the game.

In the two-player game represented in figure 4.5 our player took a modest early lead, but eventually lost the game.

Figure 4.6 shows what a player's history might look like in a highly political game (perhaps the chip-taking game), where none of the early choices matter because an apparent lead results in getting "picked on." The player represented by the thick black line may have gained a lot of points early on, or he may not have, but none of that affected his chances to win. Each player had about as good a chance to win as any of

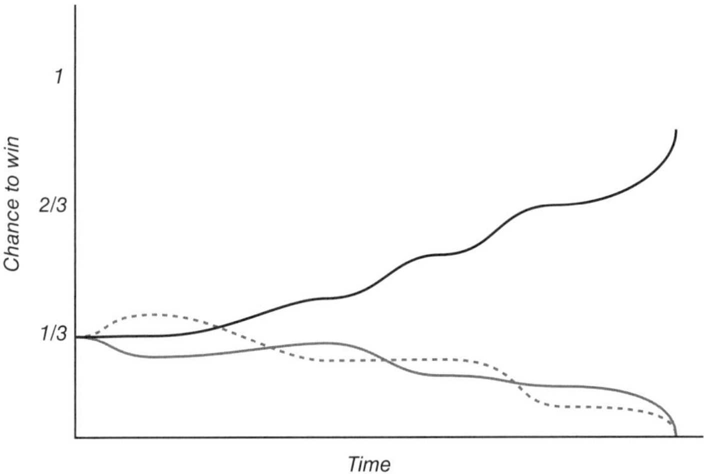

Figure 4.4
Typical win

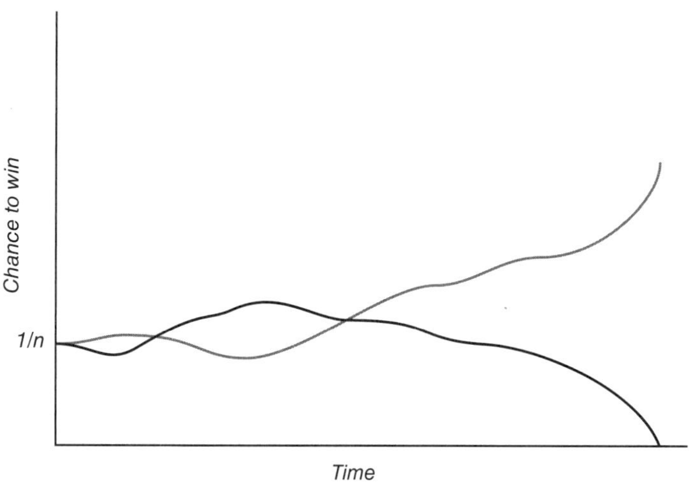

Figure 4.5
Typical loss

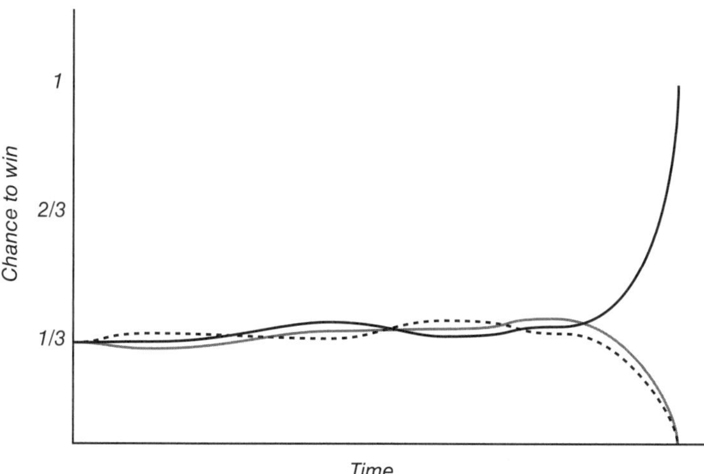

Figure 4.6
Only the end matters

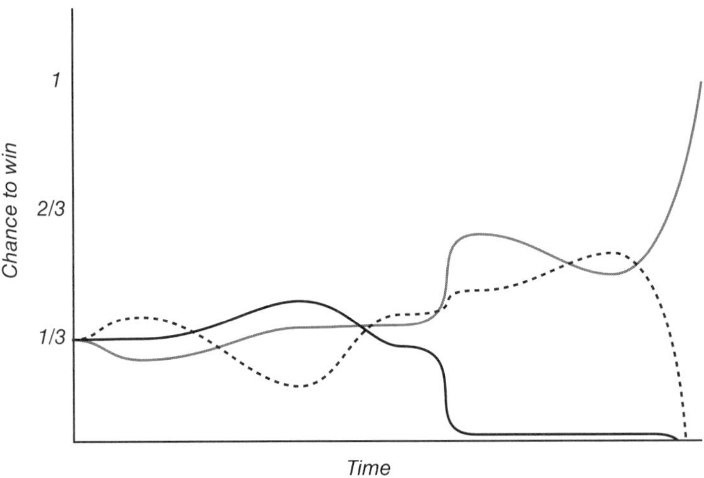

Figure 4.7
Effective elimination

the others throughout most of the game. The winner of this game was determined entirely at the end.

This same graph might also describe a game with extremely strong catch-up features—for example, a race game where cars behind the leader are given a significant speed boost.

In this unhappy game (figure 4.7), our player (the solid black line) was beaten down about halfway through the game. At that point, she had almost no chance to win, but she wasn't actually eliminated until the very end of the game. (Perhaps it was a race game in which she was so far behind that she had no real chance to win.)

Catch-Up: What Is Apparent and What Is Real?

One might ask the question of what part of catching up is real and what part is illusory. Imagine a game with an easy first-order state heuristic like a race. The game has a "catch-up mechanic" that helps people who are behind. Players enjoy playing because they feel like they can catch up if they fall back and remember pleasurably the number of great comebacks they have seen. But if players understand how this mechanic works, they should adjust their heuristics and when they evaluate their chances to win (i.e., use their new state heuristics) they will find there is no catching up from behind in the race—in fact there is no falling behind and never was, at least to the extent they once believed. It just means that a large lead on score really represents a small lead in chance to win.

Real catch-up features can come in two types. The first type is features that put some limitations on how big the variance can get (until the very end) and how fast it can get there. The second type is features that tend to reduce the variance in ongoing games by having events that either end the game in favor of the leader or reduce the variance going forward. For a simple example, consider a duel, with two duelists shooting in turn, each with a 60 percent chance to hit (which ends the duel). At the start, the first shooter has a greater than 0.6 chance to win, but if he misses, the other shooter is now ahead. Many games have features that work in this manner: the player who is ahead must press his advantage and attempt to win quickly lest the other player catch up.

It's true that for games with a unique winner, it is common that catch-up is the apparent catch-up that comes from imperfect state heuristics, not necessarily "true catch-up" (if one thinks of "true catch-up" as variance control).[15] But that's okay. It is important to remember that since it is rare for players to have perfect state heuristics, it may be true that there is no reason to draw a distinction between a "true" versus "apparent" catch-up feature. When a catch-up feature is put in, by and large what is happening, as we have stated, is partially actual variance control and partially catch-up relative to a particular heuristic—for example, the lead in *Mario Kart*. The feature's effect is one of muddying the heuristics, but as long as those heuristics don't change, for all practical purposes the effect is real—the player who thinks he is far behind thinks he is catching up. The danger lies in players developing new heuristics, perhaps seeing that there is no catch-up but instead only a nonintuitive ranking of the leaders, and placing themselves back into the state the designer was attempting to avoid—namely player dissatisfaction with their ability to come back from behind.

Catch-up features can still do good things:

• Sometimes skill can be used to apply the catch-up feature if you are behind (or avoid it if you are ahead).
• Catch-up features allow a nice first-order heuristic (score/position without the catch-up feature considered) and a more advanced second-order[16] heuristic. Since climbing the heuristic tree is a big part of the enjoyment of games, that's no small thing.
• Catch-up features keep more players in the game in the sense that they have a reasonable chance to win. In other words, catch-up features slow down the spread of the

15. And we'll generally just say "catch-up" from now on, since there's no point in making the distinction any longer.
16. Strictly speaking, it may not be first-order and second-order. It may be third-order and seventh-order, say—"first-order" and "second-order" are a stand-in for "lower-order" and "higher-order." Heuristics don't have absolute numbers associated with them in any case; at best one can say that a certain heuristic is more advanced than another (typically by taking the other one into account, along with additional information).

state vector. The catch-up feature may also put a cap on the variance of the vector until just before the end. (To see this is true, just consider a game with some catch-up feature, and delete that feature partway through the game; now the players' chances to win are as far apart as they would seem with the simpler heuristic, which is further apart than they would be with the more complex heuristic, i.e., with the catch-up feature implemented.) In fact this may be the most important true catch-up function—that at no time until the very end will any player have too great a chance to win. Features like this often work better if player heuristics do not fully take this lack of variance into account, so that players feel exciting "comebacks" are common.

• Catch-up features with the "maybe it fires, maybe it doesn't" coin-flip type event (the missile that hits or misses) make the point lead more random-seeming, make it change more, and make the typical game more exciting for most players. Pushed to extremes, this can backfire with some sophisticated players, who realize that the point lead is such a bad indication of the true game state that they lose interest in it—a race where nobody cares who is in the lead is probably not an enjoyable game. Worst of all is if there is no useful state heuristic left whatsoever.

• Catch-up features can have the real quality that at any time the state vector has too high a variance, the game will either end or shrink the variance. This effect is very important since generally the harshest problem of having a small chance to win isn't losing itself, but rather playing a game where one has too low a chance of winning. There are catch-up features that consistently deal with this problem by ending games or making them fairer. Either way is often a gain for the player behind, especially in a noncompetitive game.

Despite all these positive features of catch-up, it is worth remembering that it is often easy to see the bad in snowballing, but not the good (control of game length, better player-elimination characteristics), and the good in catch-up features, but not the bad (poor positional heuristics, relative irrelevance of early-game choices, opportunity for kingmaking because the last-place person has more power, overly long games).

Miscellaneous Catch-Up Topics

Now with more perspective under our belts, we can tackle several issues involving catch-up and snowballing.

Randomness and Catch-Up

Stirring the pot (e.g., resetting everyone's scores to the starting score, or adding a random amount to everyone's score) is somewhat like what people tend to think of as catch-up, and somewhat not: it doesn't differentially help losers and hurt winners, but it tends in practice to hurt winners and help losers simply because the winners are ahead and the losers are behind. Events of this kind tend to be "catch-up events" in the sense of decreasing the variance in the state vector when they happen (compared to the variance of the vector when they fail to happen). So one can think of random elements in a game as being in themselves a kind of catch-up feature—if a game has a lot of randomness, you are probably not as far ahead as the score (or other first-order state heuristic) might indicate.

Random features in a game often give rise to "press-your-luck" situations: cases where a player can choose to make the game more random or less. Typically a player chooses to make things more random when behind, less random when ahead. Hail Mary passes in football, going for three-point shots in basketball, guessing in *Clue*, or pushing for a risky *Yahtzee* combination are all examples, but perhaps the ultimate example of a press-your-luck game is Sid Sackson's boardgame *Can't Stop*.

Over-Catch-Up

Sometimes catch-up features are so strong that it is better to be second, or at the very least it does not hurt to be second. Race games with lots of ways to hurt the leader, shoot the person in front of you, speed up if you are behind, and so on, can have this problem. Highly political games tend to be this way, due to the "pile on the leader" tendency almost all playgroups have. Over-catch-up tends to be frustrating—people *want* to pump up their score, or get ahead in the race, and they do not want to be punished for it. In theory, jockeying for second (or should it be third?) and then jumping to win at the end can be a reasonable game, but in practice it is not much fun if it happens all the time. And games of this type tend to have all the play choices other than those near the very end of the game be irrelevant to the outcome.

A game with this attribute will generally become less fun when players realize it.

Catch-Up in Very Long-Running Games

Catch-up can take certain unusual forms in games that go on for a very long amount of time—typically one and a half player games (like single-player RPGs) or MMOs. Long one and a half player games tend to have a great deal of catch-up: if one thinks of the basic metric of player level compared to stage in the game (for an RPG), then grinding is a mechanic that lets the player freely "catch up" anytime she wants. The same applies to an MMO.

The reason very long games require catch-up is that if a game lasts ten hours (say), then without some form of catch-up, a losing player would be clearly losing for the last several hours, which is just too long to be in a state of all-but-certain loss. Of course, if the catch-up features are extremely strong, one gets the problems one often sees in these genres: choices in the early stages of the game may not matter very much, or the player may be discouraged on realizing that a painstaking and tedious method of play is most likely to guarantee victory. One common attempt to solve the problem of catch-up in very long games is to use dynamic difficulty adjustment. This basically amounts to catching up the player invisibly whenever she falls behind, and catching up the AI if the player moves ahead. The problem is that it is rather like your spouse cheating on you: arguably fine if you know nothing about it, but liable to make you feel bad if you do find out about it, which eventually you will (at least in the case of games, given the Internet). Players who are trying to play well want to feel that if they do play well, they will be rewarded. This feeling is hard to come by if the game tries to ensure equal outcomes regardless of player skill.

Even for games with a short game length, one can think of the ongoing metagame as a corresponding game with very long game length. This very long game has some of the same issues—for example, if a dozen people all learn to play chess together, as time goes on their skill levels will spread apart. After a number of months, some of the players may be in a permanently winning or losing state. Those players have (all but) won or lost the have-the-most-skill metagame, leading to a bad play experience. Better players in the group teaching weaker ones provides a sort of catch-up feature, arguably analogous to level grinding (the weaker players are spending more time improving their skills, the stronger players are spending less).

Targeting and Catch-Up

A catch-up feature may hit various targets: it may hurt the leader specifically, the player of your choice, the guy in front of you, a random player, everyone but you, everyone in front of you, and so on (likewise for catch-up features that help a player, although "help yourself" is by far the most common sort). Depending on whom the catch-up feature targets, different gameplay effects can occur. We'll give just a few examples of problems that can arise, especially if the catch-up feature is too strong.

Hurting the leader often tends to lead to over-catch-up and a "play for second" style of game. Each player hurts the leader, nobody else gets hurt, and thus the lead cycles regularly, but having the lead isn't necessarily meaningful. There are no choices, so the only skill increase comes from the disguise of the first-order "who's ahead" heuristic, a heuristic that may be so heavily damaged as to be almost useless.

Hurting your choice of player tends to lead to highly political games. As with any targeting mechanic, carried to an extreme it may result in a chip-taking game.

Hurting someone near you (in whatever sense the game defines "near": a player sitting adjacent to you in a boardgame, a car driving near you in a racing game) can be good in that it is less political, although of course it does represent some diminishing of player choice. However, such a mechanic—say the Green Shell in *Mario Kart* (which, being unaimed, typically is used against players who are close)—may not give large-scale catch-up. Instead, it may cause clumping: groups of players who are close together keep shooting each other, forming clumps, but one clump can't affect another far-off clump (although occasionally a player will break away from one clump and push ahead or fall behind until pulled into the orbit of another clump). In this sense *Mario Kart* is almost exactly like a large bicycle race, with the Green Shell playing the same role as drafting: something that pulls together nearby vehicles but does not affect faraway ones. They are a catch-up feature within a given clump, but less so when viewed from the point of view of the race as a whole.[17]

Conclusion: Limitations and Effects of Catch-Up

The limitations presented on catch-up are interesting for both player and designer. The most critical of these is the idea that catch-up relative to a fixed state heuristic is real even when the situation relative to winning percentage is not. Any time a player is in a game that he perceives to have a catch-up feature, there is some indication that his state heuristics may be insufficient and there is a possible gain in strategic understanding to be had by altering them. Similarly the designer needs to take care that adding a catch-up feature relative to a state heuristic continues to serve the basic intention of keeping players excited and hopeful without eliminating some core element of the game. It is probably true that you don't want to naively add a catch-up feature to maintain player hope at the expense, for example, of actually wanting to be in the lead in a race, or gather the most power in a political game. While the simple state heuristic of the lead being good in a race is arguably more important than keeping all players involved, there is often a lot of leeway for players maintaining naive state heuristics depending on the player audience. It is much more likely that adding a catch-up feature to a race for children or casual players will be seen as a true catch-up feature relative to the lead heuristic, rather than causing a shift in player heuristics to devalue the lead in favor of a more complicated formula. Even for a more hardcore game, features like dynamic difficulty adjustment may cause players to believe they "caught up" due to good or lucky play when in fact the existence of the feature meant they were never really behind. This situation can break down in a game meant to be highly replayable as players refine their state heuristics. Few players are interested in a game where they see they always have a 50 percent, or even 95 percent, chance of winning no matter what they do.

True catch-up in the sense of limiting state vector variance has an important place as well. Very often this will achieve the goal of continuing player involvement while maintaining clean first-order heuristics. The difficulty here lies in the potential to disenfranchise competitive players who may feel slighted they can only be a limited amount better than a truly bad opponent. Again the audience is the key. A feature that limits a player's downside to 1 percent of the leader's chance to win may not go

17. This whole clumping phenomenon only arises if the outcome of the catch-up affects future targeting, as in a race game with missiles. If the two are unlinked, as in a card game where you can only affect players sitting next to you, the clumping won't happen.

far enough to keep many people interested in the game. Conversely, a feature that sets that limit at 40 percent may scare away more competitive players.

Catch-up features that either end games or make them fairer can work especially well in achieving the basic goals for player hope in a long game. They may have the tendency, however, to create a lack of control over the length of the game, since by their nature they achieve their leveling by ending some games early. Still, it is encouraging for many to know that there are no bounds on how good they can get at the game while at the same time worse players will never have to be in a game they feel they can't win for long.

Exercise 4.9: Give some examples of pressing your luck in baseball and hockey.

Exercise 4.10: Give some examples of pressing your luck in a chess tournament.

Exercise 4.11: What types of audiences would be more interested in games with catch-up features?

Exercise 4.12: Do games with catch-up features tend to have poor or good state heuristics? Why?

Exercise 4.13: What are the risks of dynamic difficulty adjustment? Do all the risks go away if no players know that the difficulty is being adjusted?

Exercise 4.14: For a game to have a "true" catch-up feature what needs to happen? How might this be beneficial for the player audience? (*Hint*: Think about the elimination qualities inherent in such a game.)

4.3 Characteristic: Complexity Tree Growth and Game Arc

Game Complexity Trees

One can think of a game as a series of choices.[18] In fact, the game designer Sid Meier famously defined a game as "a series of interesting choices."[19] There are certainly games with no interesting choices, and in fact examples of games without any choices, but these tend to be limited to the sphere of gambling. For logical completeness, one would typically consider all possible choices at any given node (decision point). But from the point of view of human players, what matters is the number of meaningful choices. "Meaningful" is of course an inherently agential concept: for the exact same game state, a beginning player might be choosing at random (no meaningful choices), an intermediate player might feel pressure to examine a great many choices, and an

18. This point of view is quite explicit in the Nash/Von Neumann game theory's extensive form, the definition of game in combinatorial game theory, or the game state trees one searches through in a computer chess program.

19. Rollings and Morris, *Game Architecture and Design*, 38.

Figure 4.8
©iStockphoto.com/Baris Simsek

expert might need to examine only a few. Imagine, for example, the number of meaningful choices for players of various skill levels at tic-tac-toe or chess.

Exercise 4.15: How many meaningful choices are there for a beginner at tic-tac-toe? For an expert? What about a beginner at chess? An expert?

Exercise 4.16: Pick two different games and give a reasonable estimate of how many choices there are at any point. Do this for both beginner and expert players.

If the number of choices is too low, you hardly have a game at all (Conway's Life, or tic-tac-toe or Nim between expert players) or you have a boring one from a strategic point of view. If the count is too high, you may have a game that is not fun for most people (go, or an RTS).[20]

We speak of the game tree as being *sparse* if there are relatively few choices, and *bushy* if there are relatively many. Of course these terms are not absolute, but relative (say to the number of choices likely to be enjoyed by a particular audience, or compared to other games in the same genre, or compared to some particular other game). Often we compare the sparseness or bushiness of the game tree at one point in the play of the game, say the opening, with another point, say the endgame.

Bushiness and sparseness are largely systemic—how many legal actions are there at a certain point in the game tree? But they are also somewhat agential, because players

20. Of course, these games are fun *for those who choose to play them*. But that's a self-selected audience. The people who find the complexity tree daunting have chosen not to play.

will not necessarily consider all possible choices, but will *prune* the game tree by eliminating certain choices from consideration. Pruning can come from eliminating duplicate moves (i.e., recognizing symmetries) or from quickly recognizing some moves as bad ones. Pruning can also come from the recognition that some choices are effectively though not exactly the same—for instance, the exact spot to stand on a large playfield.

Games that are very sparse or very bushy can be unsatisfying to players. Too sparse, and players may not feel they have any interesting choices to make—in the extreme case, where a player always sees a single correct move (as in Nim or tic-tac-toe, say), one might hardly feel there is a game there at all. Too bushy, and the player may feel overwhelmed by all the choices and may feel they are left making moves essentially at random (as happens to beginners in go, or in building certain complex RPG characters[21]).

The Game Arc

The game arc is how the bushiness of the tree fluctuates throughout the course of the game. Commonly the tree will start out sparse, get bushier, and then become sparse again. This is basically a good thing—it provides the game with good pacing, and a kind of narrative arc. A typical example would be *Monopoly*: initially one simply rolls the dice and makes relatively few decisions (it's often right just to buy whatever one can at the start, and houses, hotels, and mortgaging properties are not relevant in the early game). In the midgame one is deciding on trades, deciding how to invest in one's properties, and in general making most of the decisions one makes in the game. Toward the end things typically settle down again, and one rolls to see who lands on whose developed properties, along perhaps with continuing to develop the properties one has decided to focus on. An extreme example would be the card game Oh Hell, where the expanding and contracting of the game tree is built in directly, as the hand size (and thus the bushiness of the game tree) changes from round to round.

One can use diagrams showing the relative number of choices available over the course of the game as a visual aid to help one understand the game arc. So, for example, a classic game arc like that of *Monopoly*, where one starts out with a modest number of choices, those choices increase, and then finally the choices decrease until the game ends, would look something like the arc shown in figure 4.9.

Note the rough resemblance to pictures of a narrative arc, with an opening, a climax, and a denouement. Many, perhaps most, boardgames fall into this pattern. An RTS can as well, with basic opening build patterns, a complex middle game, and

21. In the case of building RPG characters, one often gets around the feeling of being overwhelmed by following flavor rather than trying to build a powerful character.

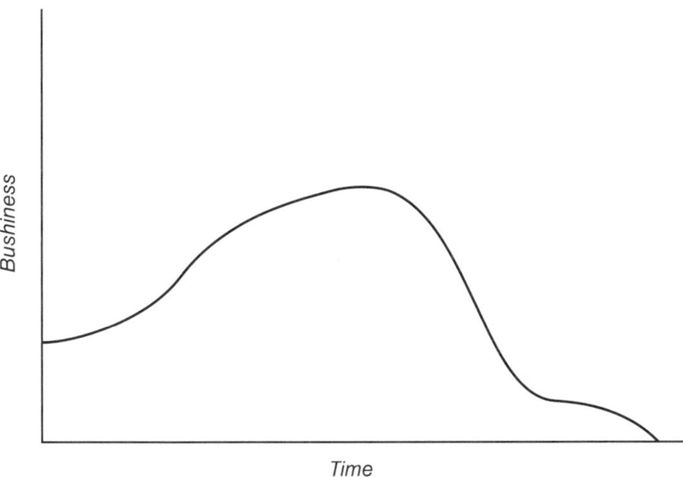

Figure 4.9
Classic game arc

relatively fewer choices at the end (perhaps because a max tech level has been reached, or perhaps the definitive battles have been fought and a mopping-up phase has been reached).

Even a crossword puzzle might fall into this pattern, with some easy clues answered early on, then a number of tough clues that don't cross many other completed answers needing to be tackled, with the last few clues coming fairly quickly as the final portions of the board are filled out. Similar remarks can be made for card solitaire.

Sometimes a particular game, say of chess, may end suddenly, before the bushiness decreases. In this case the overall game arc rises as the bushiness increases, and then suddenly terminates, with no "calm" phase at the end (figure 4.10).

Beginners may experience the game arc somewhat differently. To them, the opening phases may seem quite confusing—they haven't learned the standard opening patterns, and so may need to think as hard about the opening as about the middle game, leading to an arc somewhat like the one in figure 4.11.

One might think of the arc in figure 4.11 as representing a beginner's chess game, say. There are slightly fewer possibilities in principle for the opening moves (certain pieces simply cannot be moved because they are blocked). Still, there are many moves to consider—for instance, opening rook pawn moves forward two—that an expert can simply ignore. If one thinks of go, the situation for the beginner is even worse. Even the theoretical number of opening moves is larger, and the end does not collapse much either—in fact, when the game is over is not terribly clear, giving rise perhaps to a diagram as in figure 4.12.

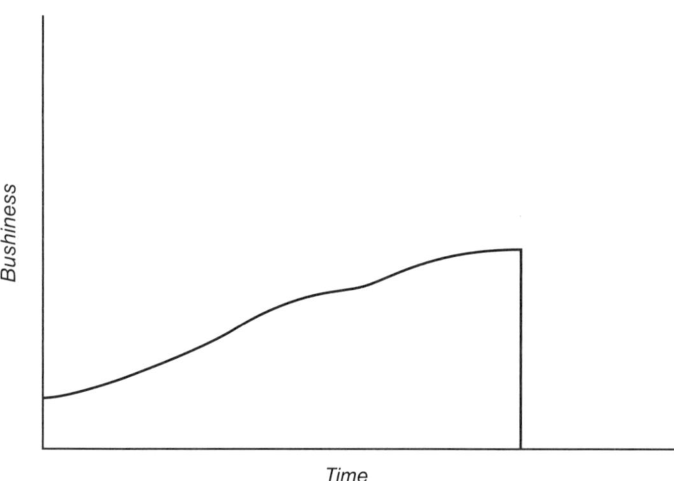

Figure 4.10
A game ending suddenly

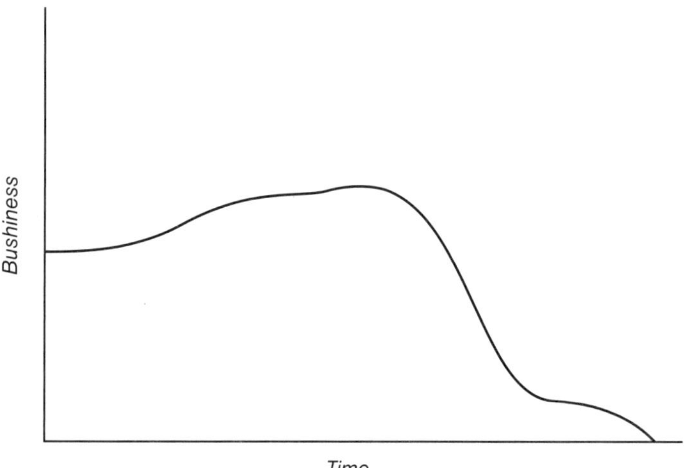

Figure 4.11
Game arc—a beginner's view

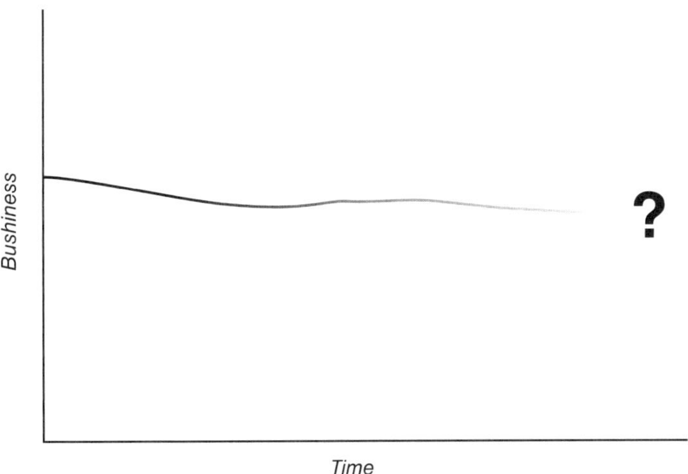

Figure 4.12
The confusion of the beginning go player

Games in which one places a large army on the field that is then gradually destroyed (*Risk, Warhammer, Myth*) often start at maximal complexity and gradually decrease (figure 4.13).

Some minis games or wargames have rules for reinforcements, which is a way of getting closer to the classic game arc: more choices for later on, with a somewhat simpler starting position.

Sports often have a more or less steady game arc. Basketball is not noticeably more or less complex in the first quarter than in the third (perhaps slightly more right at the end due to management of the clock) (figure 4.14).

Any game with very short atoms will also tend to have a flat arc like the sports one. That's because there's not much room for an arc inside such a short atom, and each atom being the same means the overall game arc is flat. Another example of this flatness of arc can be seen in a tournament (thought of as a game in and of itself): what a player is doing in the first hour of the tournament is not that different from what she's doing in the fifth hour.[22] Flatness of arc might be one of the few disadvantages to the otherwise strong game feature of small atoms.

For a paper RPG or an MMO, one has to decide what time period one is looking at, since the game length is not well defined. Looking at, say, an MMO over the lifetime of a single character, one might say the game arc gradually increases in bushiness

22. Of course, zoomed in the arc may be more complex: it will be the arc of whatever game the tournament is for (chess, say). But we are speaking here of the large-scale view.

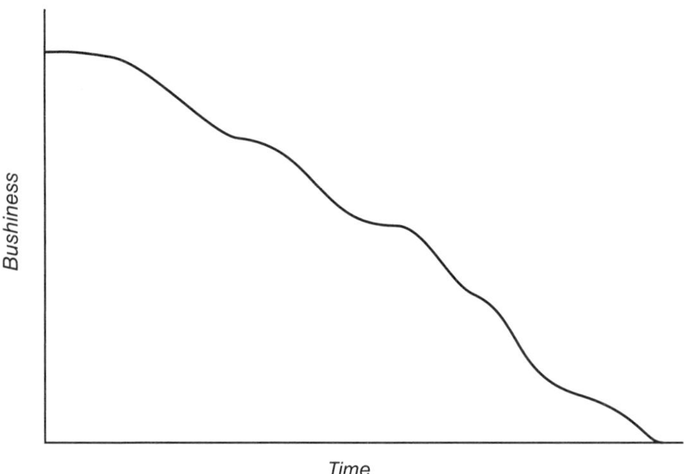

Figure 4.13
Complexity progression in a miniatures battle

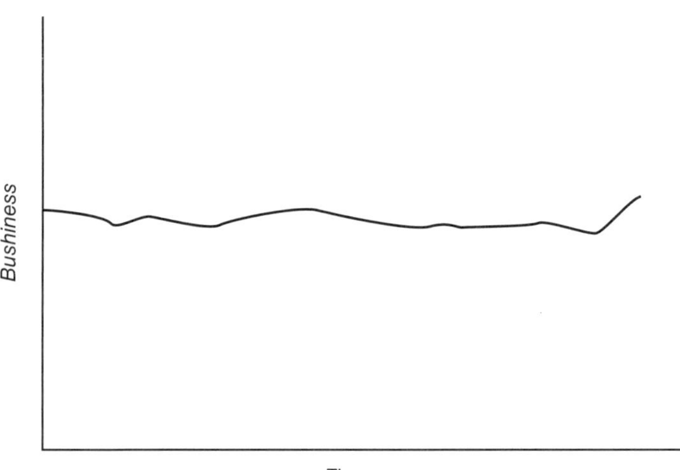

Figure 4.14
Sports—roughly constant complexity

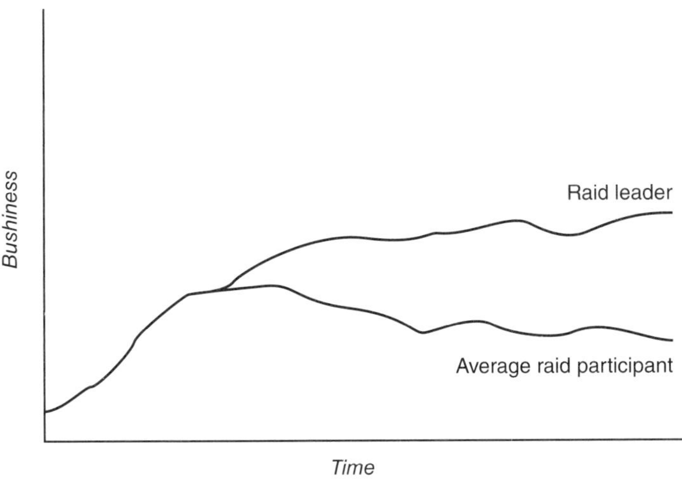

Figure 4.15
MMO—lifetime of one character

(higher-level characters have more options and more difficult challenges) until raiding starts. In most cases, raiding involves fewer real choices for an individual character, and indeed the game arc can sometimes get very sparse. The raid leader, however (who is managing the raid as a whole) is typically engaging in a very complex task. His game arc might show an increase in bushiness.

Thinking of a single MMO raid as one event, it often follows something like the classic arc: not too many decisions early on (gather, buff everyone), some choices further on culminating in a boss fight, after which things are quickly over.

The one-session measure coming from a raid is probably the more important one: that's where the narrative-like satisfaction of increasing tension followed by a denouement is at its best.

As mentioned above, some games, like miniatures games and chess, violate the usual game arc pattern in that they start with a great many pieces on the board and then gradually shrink as those pieces are destroyed—in other words, their game tree appears to start maximally bushy and then decrease. Sometimes, however, the early phases of the game have fewer choices than it might appear: in a minis game, the pieces start far apart, and the early moves may consist largely of closing the distance, which is relatively simpler than the midgame. (Although this is true for average minis players, for very expert players the early maneuvers are extremely complex and telling, so the game arc pattern of maximal and decreasing bushiness is probably closer to the truth.) In chess, the mobility of pieces is restricted early on, and opening

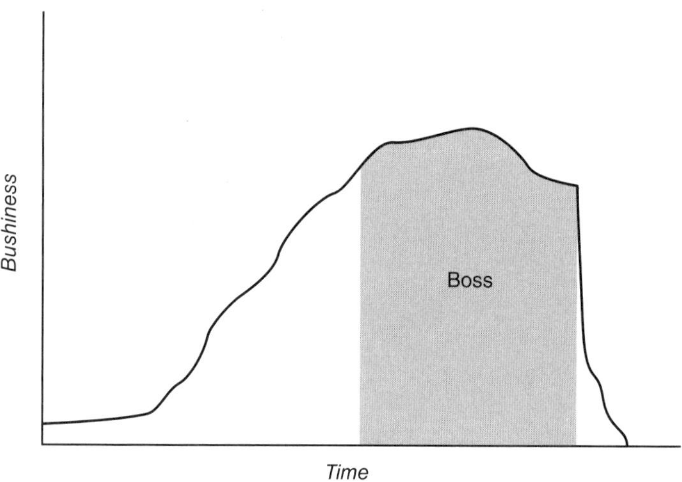

Figure 4.16
MMO—a single raid

patterns are available to tell you what to do, thereby narrowing the meaningful choices.[23]

Many, perhaps most, games are like chess in that the opening moves become at least partially standardized over time. For example, think of the standardized opening build patterns in an RTS. These openings have the effect of pruning the game tree during the early game for nonbeginners, but beginners are often more at sea in the early game. Once again this points out the value of good zero-level heuristics, for without them beginners will have a worse game arc than more experienced players.

Some games, like RTS games and trading card games, have a very explicit early arc built in: many game options are simply unavailable early on and must be slowly enabled. Games of this sort may have the later arc extremely bushy, and sudden endings are possible: a *Magic* or a *Warcraft III* game may end suddenly, with the game tree still uncollapsed.

One large and important category of games that do not follow the standard game arc well is sports (and computer games based on the sports model, like *Mario Kart* or *Street Fighter*). Although there is sometimes a collapse at the very end, due to time

23. Go appears different at first, since there are more and more pieces rather than fewer and fewer. But since those pieces don't move, the options are really the empty spaces on the board, and the end result is somewhat like chess: opening theory to guide players in the beginning, and collapse toward the end as fewer options are available. However, at the very top levels of play openings in go are perhaps harder than they are in chess, so go can be quite bushy for expert players—and for beginners with no opening ideas to guide them.

running out or to the outcome being inevitable, by and large the sorts of decisions players make at the beginning of a soccer game, auto race, or tennis match are similar to the ones they make during the middle or toward the end.

Exercise 4.17: Think about the complexity tree for Nim. What does it look like for a beginner? For an expert? For an intermediate player?

Exercise 4.18: Draw some parallels between the "classic" game complexity arc and the standard three-act narrative structure common in plays and films.

Exercise 4.19: What drawbacks for the player might a game with many options have?

Exercise 4.20: Give an example of a game where the number of meaningful options increases with player skill.

Exercise 4.21: Construct an example where adding an option to the game decreases the number of meaningful options.

4.4 Characteristic: Game Balance and Strategic Collapse

Often players and designers worry about game balance or criticize a game for being unbalanced. Lack of balance can be thought of as a problem with the complexity tree: the bushiness of the tree is much less than intended because a small number of strategies are much better than the others. Phrased another way, the game seems to be offering a large number of interesting choices, but on closer examination it turns out only a few of them are viable, so the fun of the game is not realized. Players just use those few choices again and again. The heuristics of the game have been reduced from the potentially rich and satisfying collection that might have existed to a very simple heuristic: play only with the much better strategies.

Phrasing the problem in terms of complexity trees lets us make some additional observations we might otherwise have missed. First of all, saying the tree's bushiness is less than "intended" raises the question of intended by whom. The answer is some mixture of designer intent and genre convention (player expectation). For example, in an RTS players expect that almost every unit has some use. If one can always achieve victory by building nothing but one particular unit, that game is considered unbalanced. In fact, players and designers often feel so strongly about this problem that they will refer to the game (or the unit) as "broken," meaning that once you discover the strategy of just building that unit, the game is no longer working as intended, to the point where it is analogous to a broken machine. If a unit in an RTS is so bad that one never builds it, that also fails to meet players' expectations (although the game as a whole is rarely declared "broken" merely because of that—a single bad unit does not cause the decision tree to collapse the way a single very good unit can, so the rest of the game remains reasonable). Most RTS games have a modest number of units,

Figure 4.17

and the conventions of the genre are such that players expect, or at least hope, that all will be useful, at least in some situations. Designers generally try to adhere to this expectation, so the "intention" is indeed some mix of player expectation and designer intent.

In an MMO, on the other hand, there are an enormous number of items, and the genre convention is that most of them are not that good compared to the best items. Because this is expected, players and designers do not usually consider it a problem that many items are so bad that one would never want to use them. However, items that are so good that they are the only thing one would consider using (in that particular item slot) are sometimes considered "broken." The ideal, perhaps, is that of all the items for a given slot, there will be a handful that are reasonable to decide among, and a large number that are not worth considering. The end result is that the question "What item do I put in this slot?" has a reasonable bushiness, at least for those in the know. (Those not in the know are probably not choosing from the entire set of possible items, but just from some smaller subset available at their level of play, so the bushiness of the decision node is reasonable for them as well.[24]) Again, what is "intended" is a mix of player expectation and designer intent.

In other words, the amount of balance expected in RTS units and in MMO items are examples of standards. Of course other genres have widely differing standards of balance—for example, those in *Magic* or other trading card games.

Saying imbalance is a problem with the decision tree's bushiness also reminds us that imbalance must be relative to some set of heuristics, because the tree's bushiness for a given player is dependent on the heuristics that player is using. Thus balance is not only an expert phenomenon. It is perfectly possible for an imbalance to occur at the level of beginner heuristics: some strategy may be executable by a beginner, and all but unbeatable by the things a beginner can do in response. One example might be the strategy of rushing in an RTS where rush defense requires at least an intermediate level of skill. An imbalance at the beginner level is bad—it may cause the beginner to quit before gaining a higher level of skill—but at least there is some way out, namely to become a more expert player. Moreover, small advantages of one strategy (or unit, or item, etc.) over another tend to be more telling at an advanced level, so serious imbalances are more likely to occur there. All this means designers tend to worry more about imbalance at the expert level, which is quite natural. But a bit of worrying at the beginner level is also appropriate.

Options Offered, Options Received

Good game designers have some idea of the choices players might make, and they try to offer enough choices to make the game fun and interesting.

But because of the risk of imbalance, there is a paradox that offering more options does not necessarily lead to the player having more options. At least for players in the know, the real options are the "good" ones, and adding an additional bad one doesn't really increase the available options. Adding one that's much better than the others is even worse—it destroys all the previous options as viable choices. Think for example of an MMO where one is faced with a choice of six character classes: add a new class

24. Note that a similar phenomenon occurs when playing *Magic* in a constructed environment versus a limited one. In a constructed environment, the entire card pool is available in principle, so you consider only the top cards, and a great many other cards are not good enough to be worth considering. In a limited environment, you are choosing from a smaller pool of cards—the ones that are in front of you at that moment—but more of them will make the cut. The difference is that in an MMO, typically high-skill players play "constructed" and more casual players play "limited," whereas in *Magic* a high-skill player might deliberately choose to play limited, because it is set up as a specific environment with its own rules. One could imagine doing the same thing for an MMO, but to our knowledge it has not been done formally yet (it happens casually all the time, of course, any time an expert decides to level up a new character "just for fun" without twinking).

that is not as good, and the expert player still has six choices. Add a new class that is better, and she now has one choice (i.e., no choice at all). Beginners might still have choices to make, but they will not be so happy when they eventually learn they made the "wrong" choice. And they surely will learn if the game has multiplayer play, although a beginner who has made a "bad" choice might never know in a single-player game (assuming he never goes online for hints or tips and tricks, and he does not learn too much over the course of the game). But even then the designer is left with a quandary: Are the other parts of the game (e.g., the monster difficulty) balanced for the player making the "right" choice (destroying the poor soul who's chosen unwisely) or for the player making the "wrong" choice (boring the player who has chosen well)?

Balance problems can occur at the strategic (large-scale) level, like picking a character class or a style of *Magic* deck. They can also occur at the tactical (small-scale) level, like picking an item for your character or a card for your deck. And imbalances don't have to be item-based: they can also be choices in game actions you take, such as disc jumping in *Tribes*[25] or rushing in a badly balanced RTS. For another example, expert players in tournament no-limit poker can find themselves playing against less skilled players who go all in when they have a good hand and drop out otherwise. If this strategy works too well, then the rich strategic area of postflop play suffers—and for that reason there are experts who prefer pot-limit poker, which they would view as "more balanced."

Just as adding an extra choice (such as an unbalanced RTS unit or RPG character class) can actually reduce the real choices in the game, eliminating a choice can sometimes increase the number of real choices. In *Magic*, a low-level example would be banning a specific overpowered card; a high-level example would be the color wheel itself (which restricts the cards you can play with in any given deck, but increases the number of viable decks overall).

Kinds of Imbalance

A gameplay choice can fail to be balanced in roughly three different ways, in increasing order of severity:

1. It can be too weak. As discussed above, sometimes this is okay, or even desirable (to keep the decision node at a reasonable size). What's important are not violating standards for no reason and having the right number of choices remaining when the weak ones are discarded.
2. It can be too strong, to the point where it drives out other choices of an equivalent type, but not all choices in the game. An example might be a flying unit in an RTS

25. In *Tribes*, you could shoot one of the weapons (the Spinfusor) into the ground, which in conjunction with the jetpack allowed you to spend a large amount of time in the air, making you much harder to hit.

that's better than all the other flying units. If you build a flying unit, you'll build this one, but you still have the choice of whether to build a flying unit, and when you build nonflyers you have choices of which ones to build (assuming they are still balanced with each other). In an MMO, a helmet that's better than any other helmet (at the level cap, say) might drive out all your other helmet choices, but you still have choices for all your other item slots (and choices of character skills, which abilities to use in combat, and so on). In *Magic*, there might be some two-mana green creature card that every green deck will want four copies of, but there are still all the nongreen decks, and even the green ones have lots of other cards to choose from for the other slots.

3. It can be so strong that it drives out a huge number of other choices, perhaps to the point of determining the winner of the game. In a badly balanced RTS, you might have a single unit that's so good, your best strategy is to build nothing but that one unit. In an MMO, the "Helmet of Always Winning" would be so powerful you wouldn't care about your other equipment choices—or a spell that did far too much damage might be the only spell you ever bothered to cast. In *Magic*, a blue card so powerful that everyone played blue, and games hung on who drew that particular card first, and the other cards in the deck all went toward supporting that card, would turn a game of making choices in deckbuilding into a game with one choice (i.e., no choices): play the broken blue card.

Games with Explicit Costing Systems

Some games have explicit systems built into them that require a player to pay an in-game cost in order to use some object in the game (by "objects" we mean a collection from which a player chooses—cards in a deck, spells an MMO character can cast, units in an RTS, equipable items in an RPG).[26]

Such games tend to have two properties: there are many objects in the game, *and* players choose from among those objects as part of creating their strategy—they create a deck, or a character, or an army. Typical examples are trading card games, plastic or metal miniatures games, RTS games, and MMOs. Such games are a fairly modern phenomenon, perhaps because to reach a large enough player base they more or less require mass production and large amounts of leisure time. The earliest examples are probably military simulation wargames, which date back only to the eighteenth century.[27]

26. For further details, see Gutschera, "Costing and Balancing Game Objects."

27. One could consider a professional sports team as an example also, although the issues are somewhat different in that the costs are not set by the game designer, and relatively few people get to play the game at the team-building (object choice) level. In any case, the time period is not that different.

Games such as these, with their large number of objects and player freedom to choose among them, present special balance problems. In chess, the queen is better than the other pieces, but each player only has one and is not allowed to bring more. If a player is allowed to bring as many queens as he wants, something must offset the queen's power. That something is the explicit costing system.

So the first advantage of the explicit system is that it allows units to be of different power levels without the game being unbalanced—the game simply needs to charge more for the more powerful objects. This cost differential is what allows a game like *Starcraft* to have both battlecruisers and marines, even though the former are much more powerful than the latter on a unit-by-unit basis.

A second advantage of an explicit costing system is as a balance aid to the designer. By separating cost from effect, the designer can choose the effect she wants based on criteria other than balance, and then tweak the cost separately until the balance is right. This is much easier than trying to tweak a whole number of different effects on an object until that object is perfectly in balance with other comparable objects.

On the downside, the explicit costing system typically adds to the complication of the game.[28] And it never works perfectly in a game with a very large number of objects. Such games always need adjustments if the competitive pressure is large, lest the game suffer some amount of strategic collapse. There are always cards in *Magic* that need banning, and there are always balance fixes needed in a large MMO. A game with fewer units, like an RTS, can eventually reach a more or less stable state, but even that takes an enormous amount of time and energy if one desires a level of balance suitable for competitive play.

Implicit Subgames as Balance Mechanisms

No one needs to worry about strategic collapse in rock-paper-scissors. All three choices will be constantly viable. Even if one were to construct a version of RPS where Rock had a 10 percent chance of beating paper, the game would still contain all three choices as viable options, albeit ideally chosen at different rates than the standard game. There are many balanced implicit subgames whose existence can help to guarantee a minimum degree of choice for the player. These can be built in somewhat explicitly (e.g., color A beats color B beats color C beats color A in a trading card game) or can be included more subtly as a general strategic truism (e.g., ranged units beat slow armored units, which beat fast melee units, which beat ranged units). By building in many copies of these uncollapsible games, the designer is able to set maximum

28. The burden of the added complication for the player can be modest if the costing system makes sense intuitively—charging gold to buy things in a game that is simulating an economy is natural enough that players will understand it quite quickly. But in a game like *Magic*, where the costing system is more abstract, the mental burden is much greater.

levels of strategic collapse. As in political games, which tend also to be inherently balanced, the art of the designer is in making these subgames not overly obvious or dominant so there is still much play left in climbing the heuristic tree.

Exercise 4.22: For a general manager in professional sports, what prevents strategic collapse in terms of team construction (i.e., think of constructing the best possible team roster as a game in itself—what prevents strategic collapse in this game)?

Exercise 4.23: What are some rules and restrictions added to basketball after 1945 intended to prevent strategic collapse?

Exercise 4.24: What are some drawbacks of eliminating certain cards, miniatures, or digital objects from a game's play environment, when done to prevent strategic collapse?

Exercise 4.25: Does every character class in an RPG need to be played equally to avoid strategic collapse? In a game with four character classes, what usage data for the classes played should cause a designer to worry? A game with ten character classes? With fifty?

5 Indeterminacy

We promised a certain agnosticism as to game definition—what was and wasn't "really" a game. But if we had to pick one ingredient that was necessary (although not sufficient) for something to be a game, uncertainty in outcome would probably be it.[1] Without getting into the mires of definition, it is safe to say that most if not all games have some uncertainty as to their outcome. But what does that really mean? Where does that uncertainty come from?

We begin by talking about uncertainty, or randomness, by itself. It is a truism that some games have more randomness—more luck—than others. Nailing down what that means is a bit tricky. Classic random elements like cards or dice are relevant, but they are not the sole determiners of the amount of luck in a game. We try to categorize some of the others. Classic games often have large amounts of luck, computer games and sports quite a bit less; we try to examine the effects of luck in a game and to make the case that luck is not necessarily a bad thing that must be eliminated.

People often speak of luck and skill as being opposing forces. We don't agree with this point of view, and we try to untangle what is really going on, and how luck and skill relate.

Lastly, we look at one particular source of uncertainty in a game's outcome, namely hidden information, and tease out the relationship between it and other sources of randomness.

5.1 Characteristic: Randomness

Some games have a great deal of randomness, and others have much less. If an average chess player plays a game against Kasparov, the outcome is all but certain; similarly

1. The other candidate would probably be being done "for fun"—that is, not for a serious purpose but rather for entertainment or enjoyment. There's lots of unpacking to be done here to pursue these thoughts properly. See for example Salen and Zimmerman's *Rules of Play*, chaps. 7, 22; Caillois's *Man, Play, and Games*, chap. 1; or Huizinga's *Homo Ludens* (especially the first two chapters).

Figure 5.1
©iStockphoto.com/Akadiusz Iwanicki

for a game of tennis or a game of *Starcraft* in which an average player goes up against a pro. But in a game of backgammon or a hand of poker, the outcome is by no means certain, although the better player certainly has some kind of advantage.

Although everyone has the intuition that some games are more random than others, putting one's finger on what that means is difficult. We won't build a perfect formal definition, but we will try to clarify the concept of randomness in games. Then we'll talk about the different ways randomness can arise in games. Finally, we'll talk about some of the effects of having more or less randomness in a game. The relationship between randomness and skill is a large enough topic that we will save it for section 5.2.[2]

What Is Randomness?

We define randomness (or "luck"—we use the terms synonymously) in a game as uncertainty in outcome. In particular, randomness is not the same thing as random elements such as dice or cards. Random elements tend to increase the amount of randomness (uncertainty). But games can have other sources of uncertainty—rock-paper-scissors has no overt random elements, but it is highly uncertain. And even chess has some uncertainty to it, although it has no random elements of any kind built into its game mechanics.

Luck is also not by any means the opposite of skill. Chess and poker both have a lot of skill, even though the first has very little luck and the second has a great deal. Tic-tac-toe and *Candyland* have very little skill, even though the first has very little luck (essentially none among decent players) and the second has a great deal. Note that in some sense, if there is no uncertainty in outcome, there is arguably no game at all. If you understand how to play a perfect game of tic-tac-toe or Nim, playing seems more like performing an algorithm than like playing a game. Most games tend to exist in the space where there is some opportunity to make meaningful decisions, which means it is possible to play better or worse, but not possible always to play 100 percent correctly.

A few games exist where one makes no decisions at all (one just declares certain random outcomes as "wins" and others as "losses" and then rolls the dice or pulls the slot-machine lever to see which outcome one gets), but people almost never play predetermined games.

Randomness—a Slippery Concept

Uncertainty in game outcome is a slippery concept for several reasons. One is that uncertainty itself is philosophically difficult. Generally, we think of a die roll as

2. Much of the material in this section and the next first appeared in Garfield's "Getting Lucky."

random. But perhaps that is simply a reflection of our ignorance. Perhaps if we knew more about the exact shape and weight of the die, how it was thrown, the air currents in the room, and so on, the die's outcome would be deterministic. This is the viewpoint of classical (prequantum) physics—the deterministic world machine, the clockwork universe of Newton.[3] It's generally held that there exists "true randomness" in quantum mechanics, but it is not clear that it is relevant for things like die rolls or other game randomizers.

A fairly practical approach is to think of uncertainty as arising in situations where, due to ignorance or to some deeper reason, we simply do not know the outcome, but various rules of probability apply. This approach is the one we will take. In this sense, chess is very much random: for a given game, the standard Elo rating system (see section 5.2 on luck and skill for details) in chess gives a probabilistic prediction for the outcome of the game based on the difference in ratings between the two players. And for players whose ratings are reasonably close, one cannot predict with any certainty who will win.

Note that taking a probabilistic approach to game randomness means that many of the usual perspectives of probability are available to us. For example, it is well known that people tend to see nonexistent patterns in random sequences, and the same phenomenon occurs in games, where people often see hot or cold streaks that don't really exist.[4]

Chess is one example of a game without overt random elements where luck (as uncertainty in outcome) arises. For an even more extreme example, recall our toy game "Guess the Digit," where each player tries to guess a specific digit of pi (e.g., the millionth digit). This game is completely deterministic in principle, but in actual practice it's a coin flip. So as actually played, the game is completely random, in the sense that its uncertainty in outcome is maximal (and the outcome follows the simple 50/50 probability distribution). One might imagine that in theory knowing something about the distribution of pi's digits could make the game have some skill, and certainly having a perfect memory or access to a powerful computer would help, but absent such advantages there's not much to the game. Although "Guess the Digit" seems highly artificial (and admittedly its main value is as a thought experiment), note that

3. For a game analog, consider clock solitaire, where the entire tableau of cards is laid out (face down) in the form of a clock, and then the game is played in a completely deterministic fashion to see if the tableau is a winning one or a losing one. We consider the outcome of the game uncertain, and thus random in our sense, because it is uncertain to the player, even though the outcome is predetermined once the cards have been laid out.

4. See, for example, Kahneman, Slovic, and Tversky, *Judgment under Uncertainty*, chap. 3; Gilovich, Vallone, and Tversky, "The Hot Hand in Basketball"; and Levine, "Do Baseball Players Have Hot Streaks?"

in some sense every computer game that uses pseudo-random number generation as a source of randomness has a game like "Guess the Digit" as a subgame.

In general, "What is randomness?" is a complex question. A great many people have analyzed it at great length.[5] We aren't planning to go any further into the philosophical points, but the reader should be aware that there are deep waters here.

Aside from philosophical and mathematical issues, another way luck in games is hard to discern relates to exactly what one says is uncertain. It can't be just an individual match: the outcome of a game between two evenly matched chess players or two evenly matched *Candyland* players (i.e., any two *Candyland* players) is equally uncertain (50/50), but we don't want to say chess and *Candyland* have the same amount of luck. A better point of view is that a game has more luck if a beginner can often beat an expert. Of course, the way we can tell someone is an expert is that she wins more often, so at this point the interplay between skill and luck starts to matter. We'll say more about this subject in the next chapter.

Amount of Luck

The amount of luck in games varies by genre. Gambling games typically have a lot of luck. Sports typically have very little luck.[6] Computer games sometimes have some luck, but often they have very little—think how unlikely it is for someone who learned to play *Starcraft* last week to beat one of the top players, for example. Classic games have widely varying amounts of luck, and it's often quite easy to see how much: simply look for random elements. In games with dice or cards, it's quite possible for a beginner to beat an expert. In games with no overt random elements, such as chess or go, it's almost impossible.

Not quite impossible, though. If one assumes that even against Kasparov there is some line of play that will defeat him (after all, he does sometimes lose), then the odds of stumbling into that line are around 30^{50} (assuming about thirty choices per move, with a game lasting around fifty moves). But to win the New York State lottery, you need to pick six numbers, each 1–59, so that's about 60^6. So your odds of winning

5. The interested reader might look at Bewersdorff's *Luck, Logic, and White Lies*, chap. 8, for a gentle introduction, and at Knuth's *Art of Computer Programming*, vol. 2, section 3.5, "What Is a Random Sequence?", for a much more intense treatment.

6. This remark may seem counterintuitive to some readers. After all, many sports outcomes in practice may seem to be determined by luck. But any given matchup (be it a tennis match or a chess match) between equally skilled players will, by definition, be close to 50/50—that is, its outcome will seem determined by luck. And sports matchups very often involve relatively closely matched players (indeed, the matchups need to be close due to the lack of luck in sports). To see that sports are more like chess than backgammon in terms of luck, just ask yourself how likely a player who learned to play tennis last week is to beat a pro. In chess and tennis, it's essentially impossible. In backgammon, it wouldn't even be surprising.

n times in a row are 60^{6n}, which is roughly equal to 30^{50} when $n = 7$. In other words, your odds of beating Kasparov (assuming only that you know enough to make legal moves; if you know a bit about chess it goes way up) are about the same as your odds of winning the New York State lottery seven times in a row. It's interesting to note that most people would describe the first as "impossible" and the second merely as "very unlikely."[7]

We tend intuitively to think of a game (say in chess) between two beginners as being "more random" than a game between two experts. If both matchups are even, then the chances are 50/50, so how can we make sense of this intuition? One way to think of it is to imagine swooping down early in the game and altering the board somewhat, say by removing a pawn. The two beginners will probably still be around 50/50, say 55/45 in favor of the player whose opponent lost a pawn. But the game between the two experts will become significantly more predictable; perhaps it will now be 70/30 in favor of the expert who is now up a pawn.

In general, games thought of as "hardcore" or "serious" (ones where the typical player devotes a great deal of time and energy to playing the game and to improving his skills) tend to have less luck than games thought of as "casual." Typically this is because the lack of luck in the game means that the only way to win is by devoting a great deal of effort to the game, which tends to drive out anyone who doesn't want to put in that amount of effort. The causation can run the other way, though: if the game is being designed (or redesigned) to suit hardcore players, luck will often be removed from it. More on this below.

Sources of Luck

Randomness arises from a number of sources. The most obvious are overt random elements—game features that cause the game to move from one state to another in an unpredictable (to the players) way.[8] Dice and cards are random elements that very clearly add uncertainty to the outcome. In sports, weather, lucky bounces, and similar effects provide randomness. In computer games, random number generation in prin-

7. In fact, your odds of beating Kasparov are probably quite a bit higher than what's computed here, because with even a little chess knowledge you are playing much better than randomly. For example, if you had an Elo rating of 1200 (a bright beginner), then given Kasparov's roughly 2800 rating, Elo predicts your chances as 1 in $10^{((2800-1200)/400)}$, or 1 in 10^4. A computation like this is surely pushing beyond the boundaries of the Elo system's reliability, and we don't mean to present it as authoritative, but it does suggest that 1 in 30^{50} is a gross underestimate.

8. One might argue that any game, even chess, has random elements in the sense that what other players will do (and perhaps even what you yourself will do!) is unpredictable to you. But when we say a game has random elements we mean something beyond this—some more overt randomizer such as cards or dice. For the more general concept of uncertainty of outcome, we use the term *randomness*.

ciple provides uncertainty of outcome, but in practice there are a very large number of numbers generated and the differences often tend to wash out—think, for example, of random damage in an RTS.[9]

Many games, even those with no other overt random elements, have random elements in the setup. For example, in chess or football one might decide randomly who goes first. In some multiplayer games, the exact choice of seating is important, and it may be randomly determined. Also, the identity of one's opponent may be thought of as a random setup choice: in a tournament, there are often random pairings, and poker is a different game if, for example, a table of experts happens randomly to have one very poor player as well.

Another source of randomness comes from the randomness of von Neumann games: players making simultaneous choices and then resolving the outcome.[10] Rock-paper-scissors unit matchups and fog-of-war[11] in an RTS are examples. Note that although there are no overt random elements involved, these kinds of simultaneous choices do add uncertainty to the outcome (turn-based rock-paper-scissors, in comparison, has very little uncertainty), so they constitute randomness in our sense of the word. It is worth mentioning that, in practice, these choices can be made sequentially as long as the choices aren't revealed right away—for example, choices of which unit to build in an RTS (where certain units counter others) tend to work this way.

One last source of randomness arises from human nature itself. Even games like chess and go that have no overt random elements and no simultaneous choices still involve human nature, and humans are notoriously unpredictable. Sometimes chance will arise from one player being more "on" than another that day—perhaps she had her morning cup of coffee and her opponent did not. Or perhaps a chess player will choose an opening that, unbeknownst to him, is a particular weak point of an otherwise strong opponent.

Often a human player's "game-playing algorithm" can be thought of as looking at different choices, discarding the ones that are noticeably inferior in any way, and then choosing more or less randomly among the remaining (apparently equally good) choices. This approach is especially common in games that seem "hard," in the sense that there are multiple equally plausible choices, such as chess or "guess the digit of pi." Often, as in chess, there is some underlying combinatorial complexity to the game that makes it difficult to analyze completely. But in fact these various choices may not all be equally good, and thus luck enters in.

9. See the discussion in section 5.3 on hidden information.

10. See appendix A for more on Von Neumann games and the mathematical theory behind them.

11. One can think of fog-of-war as a Von Neumann game based on the choice of the first player to explore a given section of the map, and the second player to explore another section.

Summary: Some Sources of Randomness

Overt random elements
Dice
Cards
Random number generators
Weather
Physics (e.g., ball bounces)
Setup (e.g., choice of opponent, or who goes first)

Von Neumann (simultaneous choices)
Rock-paper-scissors
Fog of war
Movement in an FPS
Units built in an RTS

Human nature (often make random choices out of ignorance)
Guessing from apparently equal options (e.g., in chess)
Pure guesses (e.g., guessing digits of pi)
Beginners playing instead of experts
Politics

Political choices in multiplayer games are highly complex, but in general can be thought of as falling into this third category.

Costs and Benefits of Randomness

Players, especially more serious or expert players, will often object to random elements in a game. Some sources of objection, and some negatives to luck that players may not consciously notice, include:

- Skilled players may want to be more often rewarded for their skill—that is, want to win more often compared to unskilled players.
- Players may wish to feel they are masters of their own fate, perhaps best expressed by the chess player who, after playing his first game of backgammon, said he was never playing the game again, because it was a game "where you can not only make the right move and lose, but lose *because* of it!" Of course, any game with random elements has this property. At an extreme, randomness can make players feel their choices don't matter.
- People like predictability.
- Random elements can add complexity:

  - Random elements are additional game features and complex simply for that reason.
  - Probability is naturally hard for people to understand; we're not wired to think probabilistically.[12]
- Luck can make it harder to climb the heuristics tree:
  - Heuristics involving probability tend to be more complicated.
  - It's harder to learn any of the heuristics (even those not directly involving probability)—if you make a move and lose, was it a bad move, or did you just get unlucky?

One additional comment on the first item on the list: although players often want to be rewarded for their skill with a higher victory percentage, in fact skilled players *don't* necessarily win more in games with less luck. Although in a given matchup, the more skilled player has a better chance of winning the less luck there is in the game, in practice players tend to play with others at about their own skill level, resulting in a roughly 50/50 win chance even for skilled players. Moreover, in games with very little luck, the less skilled players are often driven out (one sees this in online FPS and RTS games, for example), and the skilled players are left playing each other. Of course, if you have a fixed pool of opponents, it is to your advantage to gain skill more quickly than others in your pool, and the less luck the game has, the more rewarding it will be for you. For online games, though, that fixed pool typically does not exist.[13]

But adding more luck to a game has many benefits as well. These benefits tend to be much appreciated subconsciously (many games that have stood the test of time have a great deal of luck in them), but not always consciously, so that deliberately designed games do not always take full advantage of the good things luck has to offer. Given the less obvious nature of the benefits, we will examine them in some detail.

Some of the benefits of luck are

- Increased range of competition
- Ego crutch: something to blame losses on
- Increased variety of gameplay
- Catch-up mechanism
- Control of calculation
- Additional psychological interest to outcomes

12. See, for example, Kahneman, Slovic, and Tversky, *Judgment under Uncertainty*, chap. 1 and throughout.
13. Note that a solid automatic matchmaking system makes the problem of not being rewarded for skill worse: everyone is being matched with players of equivalent skill, and thus each player's chance of winning is pushed toward 50/50. On balance, it is still an extremely good thing to have, though; it creates better matches (both players have a chance to win) and without it the bottom tends to drop out entirely in high-skill, low-luck games.

Range of Competition

If a game has very little luck, it's much harder to find a good matchup. You won't have much fun playing chess against Kasparov unless you yourself are an extremely good chess player—indeed, the range of chess players with whom you can have a reasonable game (in the sense that both people have a decent chance to win) is quite narrow. But you could play backgammon or cribbage against a wide range of people. Even if they were a lot better than you, you would win at least some of the time.

Note that increased range of competition is an advantage in several ways. If you bump into a random person and play with them (whether informally, or at a tournament), you're more likely to have a good game. Perhaps more important, if you want to play with a specific person you already know (a friend or spouse, perhaps) you are both more likely to have a good experience.

Increased range of competition is extremely important for games requiring physical presence, because of the more limited choice of opponents—you can play cards with your spouse, but you will probably have to go to the club to find a chess opponent. Again, this is not because there is less skill in cards, but because there is less luck in chess. With a very large pool of potential opponents and a good matching system (a large tournament or online[14]), the need for a large range of competition in a game is less pressing. But it is still a valuable asset for a game—people may want to play in other environments, such as with a group of friends, and no matching system is perfect.

Ego Crutch

It is a natural human tendency to take credit for our wins and blame the fates for our losses. In a game with overt random elements, it is easier to do that. In chess, you can hardly say you lost to Kasparov due to bad luck. In backgammon, you can say you *would* have beaten the world champion, if you just hadn't made that terrible roll at the end (conveniently forgetting all the terrible rolls he made, or the terrific rolls you made, earlier in the game).

Also, players with a more casual attitude can feel easier about experimenting with different playstyles or tactics. After all, it's not as if they're expected to win every time.

Variety of Gameplay

Luck causes odd situations to come up during the course of the game, situations that might not occur in a game where the gameplay state is due to the conscious choices

14. Online matching isn't always great, but the best systems are pretty good, and the potential is clearly there. The old-school system of "list of games, pick one to join" is a disaster in terms of getting a reasonable game (where it works, it is typically because the less skilled part of the community has simply been cut out, leaving players of similar skills), but it is thankfully becoming less and less common.

of the players with little intervention from random elements. Dealing with these odd gameplay states (typically by applying more general heuristics) is often more interesting than becoming ever more expert at a very narrow set of gameplay states (typically by memorizing patterns that have been worked out in advance). Fischer Random Chess (Chess 960)[15] is just one example of using randomness to solve this problem of stagnation in play.

Luck also increases the number of situations where a good player may have to struggle to come from behind, or a bad player may need to play steadily to have the best chance of maintaining a likely win. Play in these situations tends to be different from normal play in interesting ways. One sees this, for example, in bridge, where one takes risks to make an unlikely contract or plays conservatively to bring home an easy contract.[16]

And of course anything that increases the variety of gameplay tends to increase the replayability of the game. So additional randomness increases replayability. A classic example is the replayability of NetHack and *Diablo* due to their randomized dungeons and items.

Catch-Up

As discussed in section 4.2, random elements can provide a kind of catch-up feature, without some of the disadvantages other catch-up features can have.

Control of Calculation

Games with more randomness often (although not always) have less pressure for players to perform difficult calculations, such as the detailed reading out of moves in chess or go. We discuss this further in section 5.3 on hidden information and section 6.5 on reward/effort ratio.

Add Interest to Outcomes

Random elements often galvanize player interest. Players become excited to see how the event will turn out. A typical example is the focus all players at a *D&D* table have on an important roll to hit in a difficult battle. Late in a *Monopoly* game, there is a

15. A chess variant invented by Bobby Fischer, where the starting positions of the pieces are chosen randomly.

16. Playing aggressively when behind or conservatively when ahead is a general phenomenon—it happens all the time in chess and go, for example. Randomness simply means it can happen more often, and (in an uneven matchup) it can happen to the player one would not expect it to happen to. One can think of this advantage of randomness as a special case of the range-of-competition advantage—randomness allows an uneven matchup to have the same variety an even matchup would have.

great deal of interest in a player's roll, as the other players look to see if he will land on their property and pay them a great deal of money.

Player Acceptance of Randomness

Since the benefits of randomness are less clear than the costs, players may not be that accepting of it. This is especially true of highly enfranchised players, say in a game that is a sequel or more generally a game that is in an established genre. There is certainly a place for the low-luck game (although historically it has tended to be a small niche, at least in the case of boardgames and card games[17]—the intensity of chess does not appeal to everyone). But for designers who want to take advantage of what randomness has to offer, it's worth looking at what tends to make it more or less palatable.

The most important factor in acceptance of randomness is the nature of the player base. More expert players tend to dislike random elements because they make them lose; less expert players tend to like them because they help them win. Of course, over time a game will tend to attract a player base that fits it, so a game like chess or *Quake* will have a high proportion of very serious players (the more casual ones having been driven out by their high rate of losing), and games with more randomness (like poker or *Parcheesi*) will have more casual players. If you make a new game in an existing genre, it is very hard to overcome players' expectations. If you add randomness to such a game, players who already like the genre will usually not be pleased (they are experts who want to demonstrate their skill as much as possible, and they are an audience already selected for not liking luck). The new players you might want to acquire are unlikely even to try the game (they have already made up their minds that this genre is not for them). All this goes double for a sequel to an existing game.

There is some evidence that individual games and game genres evolve so as to reduce luck, perhaps due to the pressure of their more serious players. The existence of the dummy in bridge (a feature not found in whist, from which bridge evolved), for example, serves to reduce luck. Even chess once had dice.[18] If casual players, however, prefer games with more luck, it may be that expert players are pushing games to evolve in a direction that makes fewer people want to play them, somewhat like the proverbial peacock's tail.[19]

17. At present, computer games have tended on balance to be more low-luck, like sports, rather than high-luck, like most boardgames and card games. It's interesting to speculate if that's because computer games really do have more in common with sports (so that being low-luck is perhaps "natural" for them), or if it's because computer games are deliberately designed, and designers, being generally expert players, tend to prefer games with low luck.

18. Parlett, *A History of Card Games*, 13.

19. More generally, see the discussion of "grognard capture" in the section "Excessively Increasing Costs" in chapter 6.

Game designers in particular tend to be fairly serious players, so they are often inclined to remove luck from games rather than to add it. It is important for designers to be conscious of this tendency so that they can add luck when the situation calls for it. Computer games in particular tend to suffer from this tendency to short-change randomness. Boardgames and card games usually fare better here, whether because of a greater appreciation of the advantages of randomness or simply because the traditional mechanics of the genre include random elements (rolling dice, shuffling cards).

When a new genre is created, or when an existing genre is ported to a new platform, the audience is more fluid, and adding randomness can be more acceptable. On balance there are probably more players who enjoy games with random elements than who enjoy games without them, so it is certainly worth considering whether extra randomness is appropriate.

Player expectations and the conventions of the genre are the main factors that influence player acceptance of randomness. But there are some other factors as well. Players who dislike overt random elements like dice and cards will often accept von Neumann–style randomness. Indeed, many will not even perceive it as random, since it stems entirely from choices that they or their opponent have made.[20]

When a game does have overt random elements, it is often best if they are front-loaded. Players may enjoy being dealt a hand and then figuring out how to play it more than they enjoy arranging a complex attack and then rolling the dice to see if their plan succeeded or failed.[21] If it gets to the point where the entire game feels predetermined fairly early on, though (e.g., if the outcome of an RTS match is determined by the initial choice of races), it will be too much for most players unless the game is very short.

All this said, many players are quite happy to have luck in their games. Although it may be appreciated more by casual players, it brings expert players many benefits as well, particularly in terms of a larger pool of opponents and increased variety of play. The main cost they must accept is that they will sometimes lose to players worse than themselves. They may still win just as often overall, simply because they will

20. And indeed although there is much randomness in, say, rock-paper-scissors, there is also some potential to predict one's opponent. Furthermore, many games with Von Neumann randomness offer ways to get around it, such as scouting in an RTS.

21. Random damage in an RTS might seem to be an acceptable mechanic that violates this rule, but keep in mind that the randomness in this case is very slight. The outcome of most RTS battles is at least 99 percent determined by the preparation and in-battle management of the players, as opposed to random number generation during the battle. A better example might be a paper RPG battle, where a great deal can hinge on the roll of the dice, but again there are many die rolls, and if one plan fails it is expected that the players will come up with a new one—the failure rarely represents a permanent defeat.

more often encounter players worse than themselves—players who would not even play them if the game had very little luck.

Team Fortress 2 is an interesting case of applying luck to a game. After reading an article[22] covering much of the material above, the development team decided to add some wild critical hits to the game and see how it went. Their goal was to broaden the appeal beyond niche players. After a couple weeks they had glowing reviews from the playtesters, who couldn't put their fingers on why the game seemed so much more fun. At that point the developers became committed to having luck injected into play through critical hits. Once the extent of the critical hit system was understood, however, the hardcore players had many complaints. Two years after the product's release, the development team still considers the addition of critical hits a success.[23]

Exercise 5.1: Pick a low-luck game. What sources of luck does it still have? How can you tell it is nevertheless a low-luck game?

Exercise 5.2: Choose a high-luck game. What sources of luck does it have? How can you tell it is a high-luck game?

Exercise 5.3: Estimate the chances of achieving perfect play in checkers by moving randomly.

Exercise 5.4: Estimate the chances of achieving perfect play in tic-tac-toe by moving randomly.

Exercise 5.5: Think of a game you like to play. What is its biggest source of luck? Would you remove or reduce that source of luck if you could? How?

Exercise 5.6: In general, card games tend to have a lot of luck. Boardgames may have very large or very small amounts of luck. Sports and computer games tend to have relatively little. Why?

5.2 Characteristic: Luck and Skill

People often speak of luck and skill as if they were opposites of each other. And indeed in the case of individual events they can be: one can speak of some success, such as catching a ball, as being due either to luck or else to skill (although it is more often due to some combination). But when looking at a game as a whole, the two concepts are independent (or, as a mathematician might say, orthogonal): a game can have a large or small amount of skill, and it can have a large or small amount of luck. Knowing the amount of luck there is in a game tells you nothing about the amount of skill, and knowing the amount of skill in a game tells you nothing about the amount of luck.

22. Garfield, "Getting Lucky."
23. Chris Green, Valve Software, personal communication.

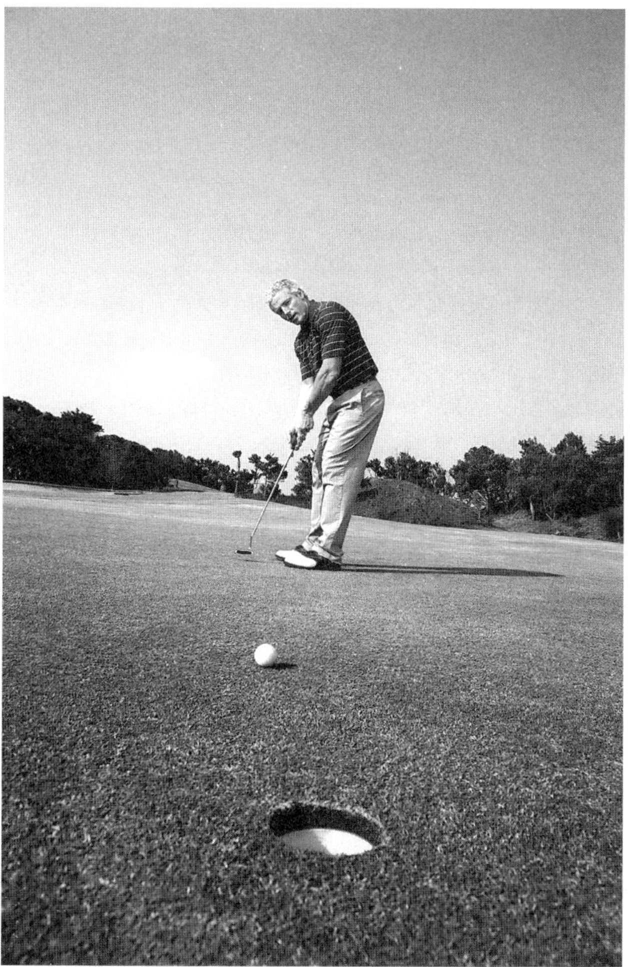

Figure 5.2

Table 5.1

Game	Amount of luck	Amount of skill
Poker	High	High
Chess	Low	High
Tic-tac-toe	Low	Low
Slots	High	Low

For example, poker and chess both have a lot of skill, even though poker has much more luck than chess. Tic-tac-toe and slot machines both have very little skill, even though the former has essentially no luck and the latter is essentially all luck.

For another example, consider "die-rolling chess": Two people play a game of chess (replaying draws). Then a die is rolled; 1–2 means the first player wins, 3–4 means the second player wins, and 5–6 means the winner of the chess game wins. This game has all the skill of regular chess—every book written about regular chess still applies to die-rolling chess—but it certainly has more luck. In fact, this game would likely have the same world champion as regular chess—after all, he would still have a higher win percentage against everyone than the second best player would. However, because of the noise in the system, more matches would need to be played before the rank order of chess players coalesced to (roughly) the same ordering as in regular chess. What, then, is the relationship between luck and skill? The short answer is that luck decreases, not skill, but the returns to skill. In this section we explore that relationship.

Returns to Skill

If there's a lot of luck in a game, then the best player may not always win. The more a skilled player can win at a game, the higher returns to skill we say that game has. So returns to skill is naturally enough a function of both skill itself and luck.

Unlike skill alone or luck alone, there is a relatively simple way to measure returns to skill: the "skill chain." Consider the set of all people who play the game (in particular, these are all people who can play correctly according to the rules). Choose one of them, and then choose another one who beats that one 60 percent (say) of the time. Then choose another player who beats that person 60 percent of the time, and so on, until you've reached the best players in the world. Go in the opposite direction as well, finding a person that your original player defeats 60 percent of the time, and so on. Now you have a long chain of players, each beating the next. What does the length of that chain measure?

At first glance it measures skill. Certainly the players higher up on the chain are better than those lower down. But think again of die-rolling chess: if you beat me 60 percent of the time at regular chess, then at die-rolling chess you only beat me 53

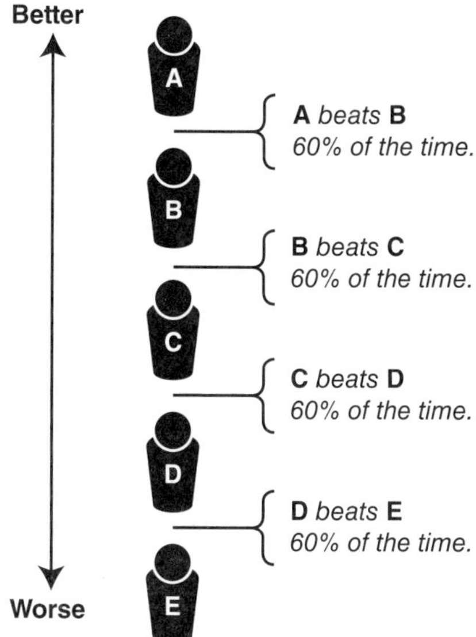

Figure 5.3
The skill chain

percent of the time, even though there is the same amount of skill in each game. In fact, what the length of the skill chain is measuring is return to skill: how much a player can hope to leverage whatever skills she may have in order to achieve victory.

Exercise 5.7: Check that winning 60 percent of the time at regular chess means winning 53 percent of the time at die-rolling chess.

The skill chain may be short because there is not much to the game: tic-tac-toe has no luck, but it would be hard to find a dozen adults, each of whom had a 60 percent chance of beating the next. Or the chain might be short because of luck: a two-player card game might have a lot of skill, but the luck of the deal could mean that even a very skillful player didn't win 60 percent of the time against an average opponent.

A game like chess, with a lot of skill and very little luck, will have a long skill chain. And indeed given a good set of match results (one that covers a large number of games from players at all skill levels), one can actually compute the skill chain. The Elo player rating system is precisely a measurement of any player's chance of beating any other. (This system is used in many games, but most famously in chess—see Elo's *The Rating of Chess Players Past and Present* for more details. Chess currently utilizes a modified version of the system.) Given a set of Elo ratings, the chance for one player to beat another is directly based on the difference in ratings. More precisely, if D is the difference in ratings between two players, Elo tells us that the chance for the stronger player to win is

$1/(1 + 10^{(-D/400)})$.

Setting that equal to 0.6 and solving for D, we find the players are roughly 70 Elo points apart.[24] In chess, nobody keeps Elo ratings for the worst players (a bright beginner is considered to have an Elo of roughly 1000), but if we guess that the scale goes down to about 700, and up to about 2800, we find the skill chain has length around 30.

In die-rolling chess, for comparison, one needs to win 80 percent of the time at regular chess (a difference of about 240 Elo points) to win 60 percent of the time at die-rolling chess. So the skill chain for die-rolling chess has length about 10. The amount of skill hasn't changed, but the rewards you get (in terms of winning) in return for your skill have gone down, because of the addition of luck to the game. And the skill chain's length decrease from 30 to 10 reflects this.

It is possible to partially correct the Elo ratings for the randomness of die-rolling chess. One can see this intuitively by realizing that the current world champion would still be the world champion even under die-rolling chess or that player A will still be better than player B despite adding the die roll if he was better before. If the Elo system were modified so that the number of points awarded to the winner (and subtracted from the loser) was based not on their true Elo ratings (which gives their actual chances to win), but on a modified one where the point difference was equivalent to their chances to win without the die roll (a simple calculation for every ratings differential), then you would recover the full rating scale from before. This works for the simple die-rolling chess because the effect of the overt randomness on win percentage is so transparent. In a way it is differentiating "skill chain" from "winning percentage chain" or more precisely "skill chain with die roll" from "skill chain without die roll." This gives a clear example of the fact that there is no cure-all rating system, and systems can be tailored to specific games. This tailoring is quite common in the world of professional sports. Analogously to the comments on standards, crafting new types of ratings can be a burden for players to understand, and the costs and benefits must be weighed individually.

Exercise 5.8:

a. Compute that 240 Elo points difference gives an 80 percent win chance at regular chess.

b. Compute that winning 80 percent of the time at regular chess means winning 60 percent of the time at die-rolling chess.

24. See section 8.43 of Arpad E. Elo, *The Rating of Chess Players Past and Present*, 1978, which has recently (2008) been reprinted by Ishi Press International.

Skill Is Agential

Implicit in this point of view is the idea that skill is agential. Skill is something that a community of players has more or less of. It is not something inherent in abstract properties of the game itself (although it is certainly influenced by those properties), like the number of options at each stage or overall size of the abstract game tree. For example, there may be a great deal that could be brought to bear in "guess the digit of pi" (facts about pi and the various infinite series one uses to compute it, perhaps), but the skill chain for (unaided) human players is length 1: nobody can beat anyone else 60 percent of the time.

Two related thought experiments may further illuminate the agential nature of skill and the skill tree. Imagine that, on the planet of geniuses, the very brilliant beings there see the entire game tree of chess. Perhaps they show chess to very young children (as we do tic-tac-toe), but at least for adults, there's not much to the game: they play perfectly, knowing the game is a win for white, perhaps, and their skill chain has length 1. Meanwhile, on the planet of morons, the very stupid beings there play tic-tac-toe as their favorite game. They have great tic-tac-toe tournaments and write books of tic-tac-toe strategy. Their skill chain for tic-tac-toe is quite long—certainly their tic-tac-toe amateurs, even the very good ones, have little hope of beating a true tic-tac-toe professional!

These two hypothetical planets should not be taken too seriously, especially the second—it is not clear there is enough going on in tic-tac-toe to support that many distinct levels of skill, even among very stupid beings. But for games like Nim where the strategy is not immediately obvious, but the game can in fact be "solved," a given community of players can essentially make a transition from the planet of morons to the planet of geniuses as they learn the game's strategy. With the recent solving of the game of checkers, our own planet has undergone a similar transition, at least if one allows artificially assisted play.

In general, increasing knowledge within a community can either increase or decrease the skill chain. If more is learned, but only by a subset of the community, that gives more different available skill levels. Something like this has arguably happened to chess and go over time.[25] One also sees expansion of the skill chain when a new RTS, for example, is released, and the players start to separate as they learn the game. Early on, a middling player can be matched up against a random player and have a decent chance of winning; later on, as skills start to diverge, random pairings are more likely to lead to very one-sided games. Although the overall skill chain has

25. There is some evidence of this in famous go games such as that of Yara no Satanoshi versus Honinbo Dochi (or more to the point, Satanoshi versus one of Honinbo's students), where a top player from a distant province came to the capital only to discover that go had evolved far past what he knew (Ohira, *Appreciating Famous Games*, Game 2).

increased, it's questionable whether the skill chain of the active players has increased, or whether so much of the bottom of the skill chain has dropped out that the length has stayed the same or even shrunk.

Occasionally, however, increasing knowledge can collapse the skill chain. This certainly happens when a game like tic-tac-toe or Nim is "solved." In principle, it can also happen in nonsolved games if some powerful and relatively easy-to-learn set of heuristics spreads throughout the community. It could well be that greater knowledge of chess openings or the relative value of pieces had a contracting effect on the skill chain (but it's also certainly arguable, especially in the former case, that the net effect was expansive).

Measuring Luck

Luck, unfortunately, is less easy to measure than applicable skill (measuring pure skill directly seems hardest of all). One approach is to look at how often the worst player beats the best player: the more often that happens, the greater the luck in the game. Given that the very ends of the skill chain are problematic, and especially the lower end (how low can you go before you don't want to count someone at all?), it might be best to compare, say, the 25th percentile and 75th percentile players. However, this is an agential measurement. If hardly anyone plays the game, the 25th and 75th percentile players might be quite close in skill, and thus be fairly evenly matched, giving a low measure of luck; as player skills increase, the skills spread, and the luck measured in this way goes down. Another problem is that for actual data sets, there may not be a lot of good data for players spread that far apart. And if the amount of luck in the game is low, one may be trying to distinguish between various extremely low win rates where statistical noise may drown out the signal (how many games of chess would one need to look at to get a good read on how often a weak player could defeat Kasparov?). Perhaps a better approach is to look at chains of three players, say A, B, and C, each beating the other 60 percent of the time, and ask how often A beats C; the more luck there is in the game, the better chance C should have.

Roughly speaking,[26] though, we know that

Applicable skill = skill – luck.

Given that one can numerically measure applicable skill (with the skill chain) and luck (perhaps with some measure of bad players beating good ones, although it's not clear which measure would be best), one could hope to compute the actual amount

26. Very roughly. In particular, we're not saying you can really find numbers and add or subtract to get the other numbers; it might just as well be division, square roots, or some other more complex function. More precisely, applicable skill is a function of both skill and luck, and tends to increase as skill increases, and decrease as luck increases.

of skill in the game (i.e., the amount of brainpower—or physical prowess—the players are bringing to the game) from the other two measures. Then one could hope to answer reasonably questions such as "Is there as much skill in poker as there is in chess?" that have been the topic of much debate. However, it's not obvious how best to proceed.

Skill and Longer Game Sessions

When one wishes to know which of two players is more skillful, one typically has them play a series of games rather than a single game. That's because if the better player has, say, a 60 percent chance to win a single game, there is still a 40 percent chance that the inferior player will win and be judged the victor. But the chance that the inferior player wins two out of three games is less, and for three out of five still less.

Exercise 5.9: If the better player has a 60 percent chance to win one game, how likely is she to win best two out of three? Best three out of five?

Exercise 5.10: How many games must be played to ensure the better player has at least a 90 percent chance to win?

But if we are thinking of games in terms of how much skill is required to play them, there is nothing magic about a single game. Why compare one game rather than best two out of three? Going in the other direction, for games like basketball or tennis, one could compare atoms—possessions or games in a tennis match—just as well as full games. And for games like poker, it's very unclear what the right measure is. A single atom (hand)? A session (evening of play)? How long a session? Ultimately, then, the real measure is skill per unit of time. If one wishes to compare the skill of two different games, one should first pick a unit of time long enough to allow some measurable amount of play in each of the games (i.e., for which one can measure some number of wins and losses in that time period, and declare the winner of the time period to be the player with the majority of the wins). For example, if one game takes three minutes and the other takes five, one could choose fifteen minutes as the time period and look at best out of five for the first game and best out of three for the second. Then one can compute the skill tree length, chance of a bad player beating a good one, and any other related information, all based on that time period.

Another way to say all this is to note that one can make a skill chain to be as long as one likes simply by allowing players to play for long periods of time (thereby making two players who would otherwise have a 51 percent difference in skill instead have a 60 percent difference). So to keep things meaningful one has to disallow that, or correct for it by using a standard amount of time for a particular match.

Gaining Skill over Time

Players often wish to improve their skill at a game over time. One might think of this roughly as how many hours of study or practice it takes for a player to gain 100 Elo points. Of course, the more luck in the game, the less the return to skill, so the harder it will be to gain those Elo points. Other factors enter the picture as well: if the game is utterly incomprehensible, like "guess the digit of pi," it will be hard to gain skill.[27] In addition to systemic factors like luck and comprehensibility, there are agential factors. If the player community is weak (maybe the game has just been released), the Elo points per hour of studying will tend to be very good. Good tools, such as strong players to play with, teachers to study under, strategy books, or libraries of famous games, can all increase one's rate of skill growth. We'll have more to say about the returns players get for their efforts in section 6.1 on costs and section 6.5 on reward/effort ratio.

Returns to Skill: Luck vs. Politics

The astute reader may have noticed that, although we have described luck as causing a decrease in return to skill, we have made much the same claim about politics (see section 2.3). How are politics and luck similar and how are they different?

Partly it is the other effects of luck and of politics. For example, luck tends to increase play variety, whereas politics decreases it. As another example, the psychological negatives behind the "gang-up" behavior often found in political games might strike many players as less appealing than the vicissitudes of fortune found in games with luck. Just looking at the change in returns to skill itself, however, there is often a significant difference between luck and politics: luck tends to gradually decrease returns to skill, whereas politics more often reaches a point where it completely cuts it off any return to skill. This is perhaps because the effects of politics sometimes require advanced heuristics before the essential game is revealed. It would be far less common to have a situation where luck would at some point give zero return to skill without having this be immediately recognized. Recall our examples of die-rolling chess (where your chess skill still helped, albeit less than in regular chess) and chip-taking chess (where your chess skill didn't help you in the slightest).

In pictures, we have the curve in figure 5.4.

Your return to skill goes gradually down as more and more randomness is added to the game (figure 5.4).

27. It has been argued that *Othello* suffers from this to some extent: the flipping nature of the pieces makes it hard for humans to visualize (see Norvig's excellent *Paradigms of Artificial Intelligence Programming* for a discussion and a short program that nevertheless plays *Othello* well). And indeed computers are better than humans at *Othello* (although difficulty in human visualization is not the only reason; the relatively small size of the game tree means minimax, a strategy computers excel at, works better as well).

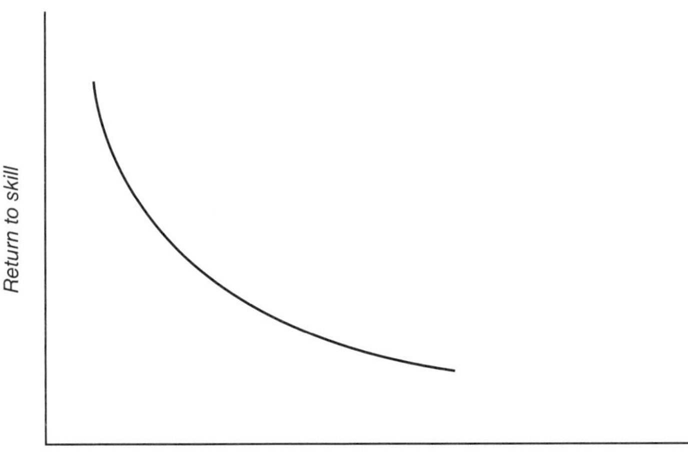

Figure 5.4
Adding randomness to a game

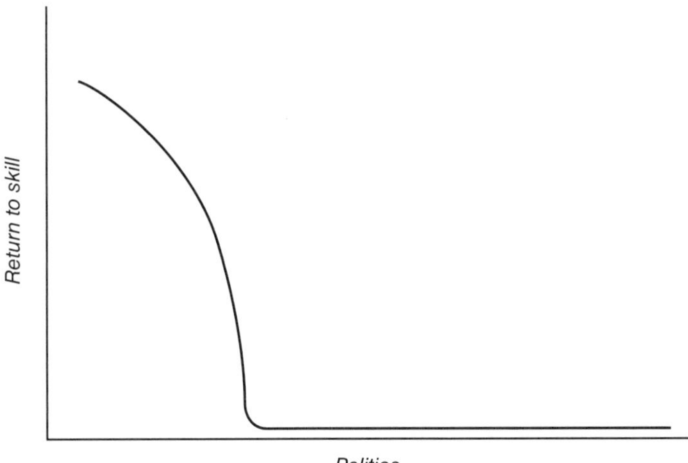

Figure 5.5
Adding politics to a game

With enough politics in the game, your skill (again, excepting political skill) doesn't help you at all. If you were to add enough luck to a game that return to skill got zeroed out, it is likely there would be no interesting beginning part to the curve.

This difference is an important one: in the first case, the player always has at least some incentive to improve and to learn more about the game. In the second, if the level of politics is great enough, there are no rewards at all for the player's further study of the game.

It's perhaps also worth mentioning that the simple fact of returns to skill declining is not by itself terrible—it is actually all but inevitable, even in a game of "pure skill." Players will tend to learn the most productive heuristics first, and gradually add more and more esoteric heuristics that yield ever smaller benefits, with the end result that almost all games give smaller rewards, in terms of increased win chances, for the thousandth hour of study than for the first hour. More on this in section 6.5.

Is Poker a Game of Skill?

People often argue whether a given game is a game of skill or a game of luck. If the game in question is a gambling game (gambling in the sense that it is commonly played for money, not in the sense that it has any particular amount of luck in it), the argument is even more frequent, sometimes taking place in the courts. By way of wrapping things up, let's take a look at this common question in the case of poker.

The simple answer is that poker has both luck and skill in it. But it's better to note that the question has in it a subtle but incorrect assumption: that luck and skill are somehow opposed. The fact that poker has a lot of luck in no way decreases its skill. The fact that it has a lot of skill in no way decreases its luck. Poker has a great deal of both luck and skill.

The luck in poker means that a highly skilled player may not defeat a less skilled player in any given hand. But over the course of many hands, eventually the skilled player will tend to win out. One could hope to measure the amount of luck by seeing how often the less skilled player did manage to win. All these measurements are best made on a per-hour basis, at least if one hopes to compare the skill and luck involved in poker with that of another game. One might even dream of comparing the skill in poker with the skill in chess, but that would require some way of "subtracting out" the luck buried in the skill chain for poker—since the length of poker's skill chain, like that of any game's, combines both luck and skill together in a single measurement of applicable skill.

In any case, the *rewards* a skilled player can get for her skill are lessened by the luck in poker, even though the skill itself is not.

Exercise 5.11: Assume that a round of head-to-head elimination poker between two players lasts an average of twenty minutes. If Player A wins two-thirds of the time versus Player B, how long would two players need to play (i.e., how long would a match have to last) in order for Player A to have an Elo rating 300 points higher than player B?

Exercise 5.12: Consider the following alternate version of die-rolling chess: each player rolls a die, highest roller wins, and only the ties are settled with games of chess (for simplicity, assume the chess games never result in a tie). What would the highest Elo rating be in this form of die-rolling chess? What would the skill chain look like compared to regular chess?

Exercise 5.13: If the luck in poker decreases the return to skill, why do skilled people who wish to make money through gaming nevertheless play poker? Why don't they play some game that has less luck?

5.3 Characteristic: Hidden Information

Types of Hidden Information

Many games contain *hidden information*: things about the game state that are not known to all players. (The contrasting term is *public information*: things that are known to all players.) For our purposes, hidden information falls into at least three rough (nonexclusive) categories:

1. *Private information* (e.g., a card I hold that you can't see, or a portion of an RTS map that is fogged out to you but not to me)
2. *"Puzzlelike" hidden information* (e.g., what damage type the boss is weak to)
3. *Randomness* (any of the sources of randomness as discussed above)

Because some of the above are not generally thought of as hidden information, let's briefly discuss each in turn.

Private Information

This is what most people commonly think of as hidden information. One player sees it, another does not. Note that for the information to be private, it can't be generated in a completely obvious and deterministic fashion (or both players would know it), so it is usually generated by some sort of random process. A card that I draw from a deck and put into my hand without showing it to you is hidden information; so is a *Mario Kart* power-up I drive over.[28]

"Puzzlelike" Hidden Information

Sometimes the game has information that the player does not know, and part (or all) of the game is figuring out this hidden information, based on some mixture of

28. Unless we are both playing *Mario Kart* from the same screen, and you are particularly attentive.

Figure 5.6
©iStockphoto.com/Alexander Garaev

experimentation and clues provided by the game. The crossword puzzle is a model example, but many one and a half player games like *Super Mario Brothers* have hidden elements in them, and some single-player games, such as *Myst*, are almost entirely made up of this kind of gameplay.[29]

Indeed, discovering how to play the game is such an essential part of any game that the line between hidden information and simple knowledge of the game can become quite blurry. When one thinks of all the knowledge it takes to play *World of Warcraft*, some things like the technique for beating a given boss or where to buy a certain crafting recipe seem much like hidden information to be uncovered, and other things such as the best order in which to cast one's spells seem like gameplay skills to be learned, but really there's no absolute distinction.

In general, puzzlelike hidden information does not tend to make for very repeatable gameplay. You typically don't want to do the same crossword puzzle twice or play *Myst* again and again; once you know the secret, it's time to move on. There are a few exceptions where the hidden information is regenerated each time you play and thus you can rediscover it: Roguelike games (items and maps) and *Mastermind* are examples.

Randomness

One doesn't normally think of randomness as hidden information, but it can often be useful to take this viewpoint. If private information is something one player knows and another doesn't, the outcome of a die roll is something no player knows: information hidden from everyone.

Recall that we divided sources of randomness into three groups: explicit random elements (e.g., dice or cards), von Neumann games (e.g., rock-paper-scissors), and human ignorance (e.g., guessing between two apparently equal lines of play in chess). Each of these can yield hidden information. Even visible randomizers like dice generate hidden information in the sense that no players know what the die roll will be before it is made. And other randomizers, like cards, typically are not revealed to all. Thus cards or *Mario Kart* power-ups can be thought of as adding hidden information in two ways: once because of their unpredictability before they are drawn or run over, and again afterward because one person knows what they are and the others do not.

Any time two players make a choice at the same time, as in rock-paper-scissors, and the game has some mechanism for comparing them, the outcome is rather like the roll of a die. Thus Von Neumann games yield hidden information of the "unknown

29. It's a moot point whether these examples are "really" games: common usage would say the crossword puzzle is not, but the other two are. Yet it's not clear there's anything in the gameplay itself that distinguishes a crossword puzzle from *Myst* in terms of either one being a game.

future" sort, much as a die roll does. That "die roll" is itself coming from private information: the intention of each player, known only to himself or herself, as to what Von Neumann choice he or she will make.

The situation involving choices made out of ignorance is similar, if one imagines them as being made in effect by some sort of randomizer in the brain.

In general, when people speak of "hidden information" they are thinking of private information. But any way of producing information that is not known to the players is in some sense hidden, and there is some value to discussing all such game features as a group.

Randomness and Hidden Information

Random elements, randomness, and hidden information are related to each other in a number of ways.

As mentioned above, implementing hidden information in a game typically requires putting some sort of random element into the game. This may be an explicit random element, as in the case of the draw of a card. It can also be the kind of random element that secret simultaneous choices give, as in the secret choices that players in an RTS make (such as which units to build). A common example of the first type is the hidden draw of a victory point chit found in many European boardgames (as discussed in section 6.5). Examples of the second type are rarer in the boardgame genre, but they do exist—for example, *Stratego*. In sports, explicit randomizers are rare (other than the occasional coin flip to start the game), but simultaneous decisions happen all the time—prominent examples are penalty kicks in soccer[30] or play-calling in football. Another interesting example of secret simultaneous choices occurs in tournaments where a player can bring a strategic "package" of some sort to each match: an army in a miniatures game, a deck in a trading card game, or a race in an RTS.

RTS games have several further interesting examples of von Neumann–style hidden information built into them. There's very little in the way of significant explicit random elements in most RTS games (they commonly have random damage, but that doesn't affect the outcomes of most battles; instead it serves to wash out breakpoints that might otherwise exist along upgrade paths[31]). But a large amount of hidden information arises from player choice. That hidden information may arise directly

30. Goalies may need to guess which direction the kicker will aim, with the kicker guessing simultaneously which direction the goalie will leave open.

31. For example, if units always did the exact same damage, then a small upgrade in unit A's damage or unit B's hit points might mean a large jump: unit A can now kill unit B in two hits instead of three, or four hits instead of three. Keeping track of all these breakpoints (for all upgrades on all unit pairs) would be a large memory burden.

during building, as players choose to create units, upgrade them, or follow entire tech trees, with their opponents not necessarily knowing. Fog-of-war means the position of a player's army may not be known to his opponent, which also yields hidden information and a Von Neumann game of "where is the army." The choice to set up a base is a decision only the player who makes it knows (until his opponent discovers it), and it also leads to further hidden information: that part of the map is revealed to the player who set up the base there, but not to his opponent. Of course, good players do everything they can to learn as much of this hidden information as possible through scouting, much as good card players try to deduce as much as possible about their opponents' hands.

Effects of Hidden Information

Hidden information can do a number of good things for a game:

- Provide (a perhaps more acceptable form of) randomness
- Control calculation (by diminishing returns to calculation)
- Give a sense of discovery or pacing (as the hidden information is revealed)
- Provide surprise
- Provide an excuse for losing ("How was I to know he had the jack?"), valid or not
- Provide gameplay in
  - The deduction of the hidden information from clues
  - Planning out lines that take into account various values hidden information might have
  - A psychological game of bluffing and insight

Note that this list of advantages is much like the list for randomness. Given the close relationship between hidden information and randomness, this similarity is hardly surprising.

The negatives of hidden information are also very similar to those of randomness, but perhaps a few points are worth mentioning separately. Although hidden information can, as mentioned above, help control calculation, it may sometimes increase busywork or calculation, either due to memorization of occasionally revealed data or due to the necessity of reading out various alternate lines of play based on possible values of the hidden facts ("if the king of spades is on the left, I'll play this way, but if it's on the right I need to play that way"). Hidden information can be harmful to spectation—the question of what hidden information to let the spectators see is often hard to solve. And certainly games like chess or go, with completely public information and no overt random elements or simultaneous choices, have a kind of purity to them that is appealing to many players despite the difficulties inherent in such a style of play.

Exercise 5.14: In bridge, one player (the dummy) "plays" with an open hand. How does this elimination of hidden information affect the skill in the game? In other words, would bridge have more or less skill without the dummy rule, and why?

Exercise 5.15: If all players in bridge played with open hands, how would it affect the skill in the game?

Exercise 5.16: If all players in poker played with open hands, how would it affect the skill in the game?

Exercise 5.17: Give examples in baseball of hidden information.

Exercise 5.18: Give examples in football of hidden information.

6 Player Effort

Games can be rewarding for players, but they also require effort. Those efforts impose a cost on players that they may or may not be willing to pay. We open with a general look at costs, and then go into more depth on two: the cost of downtime (time not spent playing) and of busywork (rote activities in the game that aren't perceived as fun). Lastly, we look at the rewards players get—first what kinds of rewards a given game might offer, and then how rewards (particularly the reward of winning) scale with effort.

6.1 Characteristic: Costs

If there's a game you want to play, you might be dissuaded if the cost of playing it is too high. By cost, we mean not just monetary costs, but every possible obstruction to your playing the game, including how long it takes to play, how difficult the game is to learn, injuries you might incur playing, how much physical space is needed to play, and so on. So for example *Starcraft* might cost $30 for the box, but you also have to buy and maintain a computer (and a net connection if you want to play online), you'll need to spend some time to learn the build tree, you'll have to put up with annoying people if you play online, and so forth.

Costs will vary not only in how high they are but also in how necessary it is that you pay them:

Required: a ball and at least one bat for baseball
Effectively required: a certain amount of stamina to play basketball (the amount will depend on the group you are playing with)
Helpful: a fast Internet connection to play *Quake*
Optional: a really nice graphics card for the latest MMO

The largest costs are usually either time and effort, or money and materials. Time and effort include not only the time it takes to play the game, but the time it takes to learn it, and any time that needs to be spent practicing or preparing. Practice and

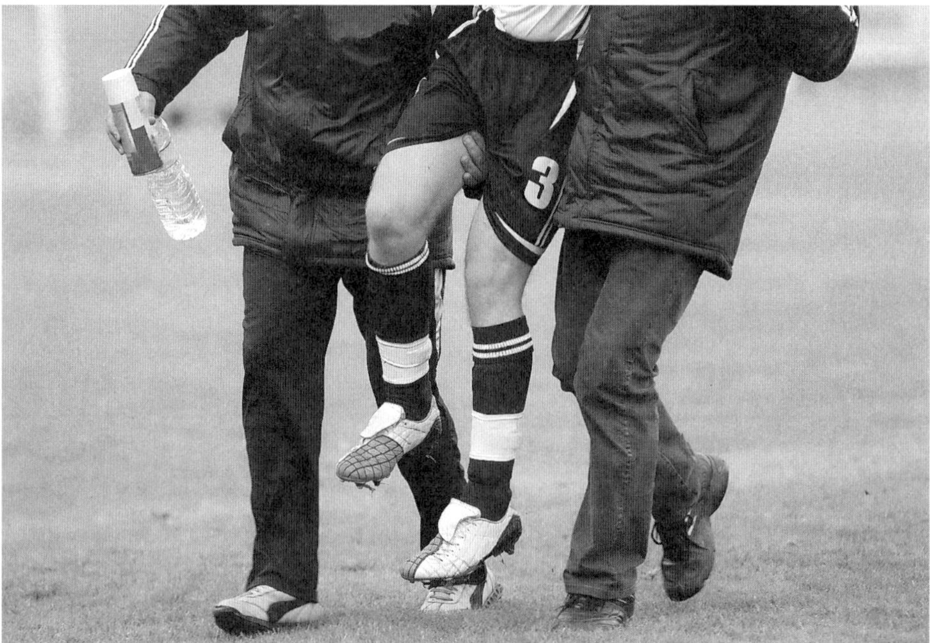

Figure 6.1
©iStockphoto.com/daniel sainthorant

preparation costs tend to be more agential than in-game costs: one playgroup may spend slightly more or less time than another in playing the game, but preparation time will differ vastly. NBA games do not take that much longer than the average pickup basketball game, but the preparation time needed is hugely different. A certain amount of preparation is often forced on the player by the game system: you need to come with a well-equipped level 80 character to go on certain *World of Warcraft* raids, and you need to come with your own deck to play *Magic*.

In terms of money and materials, there may be relatively little required, as in tag, where one only needs a place to play, or twenty questions, where one needs nothing at all. More often one needs some basic equipment, as in most sports games. For paper games, all the equipment and rules typically come in a box, and if you've bought that box you're all set.[1] Electronic games typically need the "game itself" (software in a box, or downloaded over the Internet) and some sort of platform: a PC, a console such as the Xbox or Wii, or a handheld device like a GameBoy or Nintendo DS.

1. Except for a place to play and an opponent, which one might think of as material requirements, and some time.

The platform costs can be amortized over many games, but definitely present a barrier to entry. For consoles, there are a number of tricky issues for the platform maker. Is it best to make as little money as possible on the console, and make it back on the games ("give away the razor, sell the blades")? How much should other people be allowed to enter the game market (more means more market power for your console, but perhaps fewer sales for your own games)? If you do let others enter, how much freedom should you give them (for example, limit the games they can make to protect your IP and marketing message, or let them create whatever they think is profitable and take a cut)? How should you market the console compared to the games?

The cost of a PC is particularly hard to analyze, because the PC typically has other uses, and might be thought of as "free" (you have one anyway), except for the fact that a PC used for PC gaming[2] needs additional hardware, such as a high-end video card and perhaps some specialized controllers. The success of web games is due not just to their broader appeal as games, but also to the fact that (like the much-played Minesweeper and FreeCell) no additional hardware is needed to play them.

One way to think of the money cost of games is in terms of the business models behind them. In other words, if there are people making money selling the game, how are they doing it, and how does it look to the consumers? Some possibilities:

- It's all but impossible to make money off of the game (e.g., tag).
- Equipment sales (Go Fish, baseball).
- The equipment is the game, "game in a box" (chess, *Settlers of Catan*).
- Rental (equipment, as in skiing, or a place to play, as in golf).
- "Pay to play": arguably a variation on rental, but may be perceived differently (gambling, *World of Warcraft*).
- Object model: a version of equipment sales. The game requires many (possibly consumable) objects to play (auto racing, *Magic*, many Asian online games).

If the game is owned (in the legal sense) by the seller, he can hope to charge a premium for it; if it is in the public domain, the seller will face competition from other people selling the same game. The market for *Settlers of Catan* is very different from the market for chess sets (of course, if the seller owns the game, he has game-design costs to recover that the chess-set manufacturer does not).

Many games follow multiple business models, sometimes with the same company involved in each case, sometimes with different companies. If there are two different costs to play, a player might need to pay them both (rent time on the golf course *and*

2. "A PC used for PC gaming" sounds redundant, but in fact "PC gaming" has come to mean, not any game played on a PC, but one specifically written for its hardware, as opposed to browser-based web games.

buy clubs), in which case overall costs tend to be high, or she might have an option (buy a game *or* rent it), in which case the costs will probably be lower for her.

The possible combinations are endless: Nintendo sells both game consoles and games for the console. Other people may rent either of those things to players. Nvidia sells you a high-end video card you can use in many different games, and other people sell you the individual games. Golf-course owners rent course time, and different people manufacture golf clubs. Blizzard sells you a box containing the game *World of Warcraft*, and then charges you each month to play.

Trading Costs

Often players can exchange one cost for another. The risk of getting injured in football is a cost, but you can pay money for pads. If you don't want to buy skis, you can rent them. Carrying your clubs around, and walking, are costs to playing golf, but there are caddies and golf carts. Particularly interesting are situations where you can trade time for money, since many people have more of one than of the other. Letting both money-rich, time-poor and time-rich, money-poor people play your game can expand your audience a great deal. For example, in *Magic*, you can buy some cards, and then do a lot of trading to improve your collection, or you can spend less time trading by just buying a lot of cards. In *World of Warcraft*, you can play a great deal to get all the gold you need, or you can save time by purchasing gold from Chinese gold farmers.[3]

Skills Players Need

One cost players must bear is that of developing (or possessing already) certain skills or abilities. Of course, developing one's skills can be part of the enjoyment of a game, but for the moment we'll be thinking of it as a cost.

Most games fall into three broad categories in terms of the skills players need:

- No physical skills needed: chess, bridge
- Only eye-hand coordination: many computer games, like RTS, FPS, darts, pool
- Broad physical skills needed: basketball, soccer

Games in each category may require more or less mental skill: go versus slots on the nonphysical end, *Starcraft* versus target shooting in the eye-hand category, or football versus sprinting on the physical end.

In general, physical skills are needed for sports, but not for card games or boardgames (with a few exceptions like Spit). Computer games are sometimes purely mental (e.g., *Civilization*) or sometimes involve eye-hand coordination (e.g., *Starcraft*), usually because they take place in real time. When discussing a game in a category that may

3. Although purchasing gold is frowned on (but commonplace) in *World of Warcraft* and most Western online games, Asian games such as *Maple Story* often have it built right into the system.

or may not require eye-hand coordination and quick reflexes to play, we say the game has "twitch" or is a "twitch game" if it is at least in part reflex-based: so *Starcraft* or *Quake* is a twitch game, whereas *Civilization* or *Minesweeper* is not.[4]

Non-twitch skills include skills like reading out moves, memorizing openings, political skills (fast-paced games often lack time for politics), and so on. Non-twitch games are often rich in conscious game heuristics (control the center, don't draw to an inside straight). As games get faster, more of the heuristics need to be unconscious and automatic, although they are often trained consciously and then executed automatically.

Twitch skills in computer games include aiming, splitting your attention, timing attacks, or simply performing many actions in a short amount of time. This last is often referred to as "apm" (actions, i.e. clicks, per minute) in the RTS community and is especially powerful in certain kinds of games: in an FPS, shooting fast is limited by ammo, but in an RTS being able to perform 200 actions in a time period where an average player can only perform 10 is an overwhelming advantage.[5] Player tolerance of games that demand these kinds of skills varies widely: some players want no time pressure at all, some are willing to accept a certain amount of aiming or quick thinking but no more, and only a few are willing or able to play a game at a level that demands a hundred or more productive clicks every minute.

Of course, there are a huge number of different skills in sports and other highly physical games: catching, throwing, running, and so on.

In addition to skills per se, there are also attributes that players may need that are not amenable to training and thus are not generally thought of as skills: height in basketball is the classic example. But the line between what is trainable and what is not is by no means hard and fast: although anyone can hope to increase his *Starcraft* apm, it is certainly imaginable that 200 apm is simply out of reach for many people. And while anyone can increase her muscle mass with exercise (or steroids), there are limits that only some people can reach. And who is to say whether a given person has, even in theory, the ability to memorize as many chess openings as Karpov? The more a particular attribute seems unreachable, of course, the more players who feel they do not have it will be discouraged from playing the games that demand it—short

4. An intermediate case is a normally nontwitch game like *Civilization* or chess played with a timer: some speed is required, but typically more speed of thought rather than reflexes and coordination. In general we think of these games as nontwitch, but obviously the faster the timer runs the closer the game becomes to a twitch game, and in some sense *Starcraft* is *Civilization* with millisecond turns (thus *Starcraft* has made a tradeoff by reducing downtime but increasing the skills needed to play). The dividing line is somewhere around the point where the turn length equals the physical time needed to make whatever moves are allowed in a turn.

5. An apm of 10 might be fairly quick for a beginner, and top players do indeed reach 200.

people may choose not to play basketball, or slow people not to play *Starcraft*, even if the game otherwise seems appealing. The unattainability of certain skills may seem to players very similar to out-of-reach monetary costs, such as those required to participate in yacht racing or polo.

If a game has different roles available to players, the skills required may vary quite a bit by role: a football linesman has different skills from a running back, and a *World of Warcraft* rogue has different skills from a priest. If there are leadership roles available, the differences can become even more pronounced: a quarterback or a *World of Warcraft* raid leader needs a number of specialized skills. One can think of coaches or managers as "playing" a game as well (and indeed some sports-themed computer games and card games have the participant take on that role rather than that of a player in the game itself), again with a very different set of skills needed.

Besides the skills needed to play the game, there are often quite different skills needed in the metagame: discipline in training, building of social networks among other players, "gaming" the tournament system for greater rewards, finding the right instructors, and so on.

It is worth looking twice when the skills needed to play a game vary widely. If the variance is too great, it can cut down the potential player pool dramatically. Sometimes this is deliberate—for example, chessboxing.[6] Mostly, though, it is probably inadvertent—think, for instance, of the players who like strategy games generally but gravitate toward turn-based ones because they feel RTS games are out of reach. Other potentially "incompatible" skills might be character building and grinding in MMOs, or logical thinking and rote memorization in chess. Of course, what is incompatible with one group may be perfectly acceptable, even enjoyable, to another.

Excessively Increasing Costs

It will usually take a while to acquire skill, so one important cost to a game is how much time and effort it takes to become good enough at it that you can find a reasonable game. This cost is highly agential: if you are surrounded by very casual chess players, you can quickly get up to speed and have some fun. But if everyone you know is rated 1800+, you have a lot of work to do before you will be able to enjoy yourself.[7]

Over time, in the absence of other forces, players who are not good at a (low-luck) game will tend to leave if they are constantly playing with good players—losing all the time is no fun. But as more low-level players drop out, the game can get harder and harder for new players to enter: the amount of effort to become an okay player

6. Exactly what it sounds like. See, for example, http://site.wcbo.org.

7. Once again, games with lots of luck shine here. Their barriers to entry are lower because a modest amount of effort on your part will allow you to play and win at least a few games.

of the game goes up. Or, to put it another way, small amounts of effort on the part of new players aren't rewarded—only the very large amount of effort required to bring them up to the level of the pack gives noticeable rewards. So more of the new players who do enter may drop out. And as bad players drop out, players who once were near the middle of the pack may find themselves near the bottom, losing much more often than they had been, and they may drop out too. At its worst, the game-playing audience may become a smaller and smaller group of ever more skilled players.

If a game is one that is deliberately designed, and part of a larger genre, further iterations of the game will typically be made to appeal to this more elite audience. The game design shifts in this way partly because that is the audience that is available, and not appealing to them makes the new version highly likely to fail, and partly because the game designers themselves are likely to be members of the elite and will tend to design for themselves. But this new game filled with features for the elite is likely to be even harder for a newcomer.

This two-pronged narrowing of the audience—more casual or less skilled players dropping out as they lose, and new game designs appealing to a narrower and narrower group of elite players—has been termed "grognard capture" by the game designer Greg Costikyan[8] (the term *grognard* is a term for old-school wargamers, from a French word meaning "veteran soldier" or, literally, "grumbler"). One sees it in many game genres, such as RTS games; the push for ever-larger feature lists as seen on box copy ("Now with 437 different units!") and the nature of online play (players of all different skill levels in the same pool[9]) make computer games especially vulnerable. Another notable example is the fighting game, where entry into the genre for a new player is extremely difficult.

Costs can spiral out of control in other ways as well: raiding in an MMO requires enormous time costs, more so in the time costs of building a character suitable to go on the raid than the costs of the raid itself. The cost in time or money to build a suitable *Magic* deck has gone up greatly compared to the original vision, where it was imagined that most people would have only a modest number of cards and nobody would have them all. *Magic* in particular made a concerted and expensive effort to cap these costs in order to keep the game accessible to newcomers. While costing more than originally intended, the cap placed on player expenditures was a drastic reduction from what it had become shortly after its launch.

When costs spiral, once people understand these costs they may choose not to play at all, even though they would have been perfectly happy to play at a more modest cost level.

8. http://www.costik.com/weblog/2003/08/grognard-capture.html.

9. Good matchmaking solves this. Unfortunately, few online computer games have good matchmaking, although the situation is improving.

Controlling Spiraling Costs

The basic way to prevent players from leaving a game as the costs spin out of control is to have good player matching. If players are matched against players who want to pay about the same amount that they do (in time, money, or some combination of the two), they are more likely to have good games and more likely to perceive the game as fair.

People sometimes think of player matching as a new thing, but it's really very old. Players choosing to play with their friends (who are more likely to want to invest about the same amount), regional microclimates (where an informal consensus about how much to invest can build up), different levels of leagues in sports, and beginner tournaments in chess are all examples of matching systems of one kind or another.

With electronic games, many of the traditional matching methods break down to some degree, due to anonymity. In a vast undifferentiated sea of players, it's hard for microclimates to form. Friend lists help; so do matching systems based on explicit ratings systems such as Elo. Guilds and guild migration can be thought of as a kind of online matching solution. However, the fluid nature of identity on the net leads to phenomena like smurfing (where an experienced player creates a new, low-rated, account in order to be matched against other low-rated players and thus win more often), and the problem of player matching is by no means completely solved.

Online or offline, although matching (broadly construed) is the main solution, other things help as well. Having more luck in the game is extremely useful, because the beginner can reach a point where enjoyable games are possible much more quickly and with much less effort. Explicit training, be it coaching on a sports team or a tutorial for a computer game, can also help beginners get up to speed.

Exercise 6.1: Purely from a monetary cost perspective, would you expect single people or people in families to spend more time playing PC games (consider how the costs are spread out)? Why? How does this difference compare to the difference you might see in other kinds of games, such as sports or boardgames?

Exercise 6.2: Purely from a cost perspective (both monetary and otherwise), would you expect younger people to play more basketball or more golf? What about older people? What costs change absolutely and relatively for people as they age?

Exercise 6.3: Describe from a cost perspective (monetary and otherwise) what type of demographic differences you would expect to see in the player populations of an MMO and of online poker.

6.2 Characteristic: Rewards

Offsetting the costs of playing a game are the rewards. Often the rewards stem simply from the enjoyment of playing the game itself, but many rewards go beyond pure in-game enjoyment and connect with various factors outside of the game.

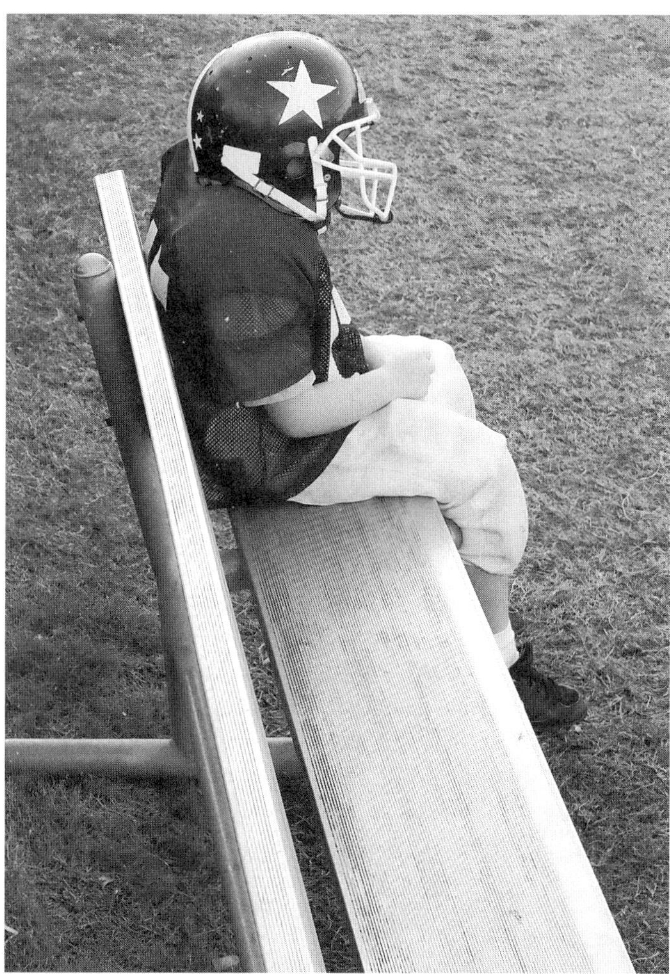

Figure 6.2
©iStockphoto.com/Catherine Key

In-game rewards can include

- Pleasure from winning
- Satisfaction from playing well
- Enjoyment of mental or physical challenge
- Aesthetic enjoyment of the game experience (computer graphics, well-crafted game pieces, etc.)
- Excitement or adrenaline rush (more common in sports and first-person shooters, less common in boardgames)
- Escapism
- Enjoyment of social interactions during the game

Note that we do not include *fun* as an item in the above list, because the term is too broad to be useful as a specific reward category. For us, the term *fun* is simply a casual synonym for enjoyment or in-game reward. If a game is said to be "fun," the question to ask is "in what way?"—that is, what rewards is the game offering?[10]

Much of the pleasure of games comes from out-of-game analogs to these various in-game pleasures. For example, many playgroups keep track of who won (and how often, and how spectacularly) over time. Most often, the tracking is done informally, simply by remembering notable events and occasionally telling stories about them. Sometimes it's done more formally, with written records being kept. Computer games, and arcade games especially, typically record high scores. Getting on the high score board, or better yet getting the highest score, is a special sort of achievement.

Although players have always talked about special accomplishments in their games (spectacular catches, winning from behind, winning several games in a row), and often tracked them explicitly (think of baseball stats), computer games recently have extended and automated achievement tracking with systems like Xbox Live Arcade's Achievements or the *City of Heroes* badge system.

Parallel to the satisfaction of playing well is the pleasure of seeing improvement in your skills over the long term—that is, in climbing the heuristic tree. This pleasure ties in with that of winning, since as your skills improve, you either win more often, or at the very least you win against opponents you could not defeat before. It also connects with the enjoyment of challenge, since you can tackle tougher challenges as your skills improve.

If you play soccer, you may be enjoying the challenge of doing so. One part of that challenge is exercise. But even if you do not enjoy exercise, you might still enjoy

10. For other breakdowns, see Marc LeBlanc's list of eight kinds of fun at http://algorithmancy.8kindsoffun.com/, or the discussion of typologies of pleasure in Salen and Zimmerman's *Rules of Play*, 334–346.

the fitness it causes. So parallel to the physical or mental challenge within a game is the larger physical or mental fitness that may result. Physical games are widely acknowledged to provide physical fitness; mental games are more often viewed as "wastes of time," but they surely provide mental fitness.[11] Some games are specifically designed to be "educational" and provide a specific knowledge base, but many non-educational games have such knowledge benefits as well (e.g., *Civilization* or *SimCity*), and all games that involve effort to achieve victory are exercising the mind or body to some extent.

The social benefits to gaming may be fairly modest during the game—everyone's too busy playing—but can be quite large before and after the game. The bonds that form around a high school football team, or a *Dungeons & Dragons* group, can be very strong, and they may even last a lifetime. A further reward is the status one can get from the group, be it from winning in general or from knowledge or skill in some specific subtask (see also section 7.1). These status rewards for players may extend beyond the playgroup, especially if the game is frequently played before spectators.

Tangible Rewards

Sometimes there are tangible rewards for winning—the most obvious of these is money. In a society where money matters, a victory that is rewarded by money may seem more real, more valuable, than one that is not, even on a purely psychological or status level. And the money itself is certainly a reward. Many games have tournaments with cash prizes. Some games, such as poker, are built on top of money in such a way that it's hard to play them satisfactorily without money. Others, like backgammon, improve with money (mainly because the doubling cube is then of more use, and the doubling cube adds a great deal to the game). With some games that can be played for money, playing for points works quite well also—bridge is one example. This phenomenon is in large part agential, in that bridge players accept that points are important, and play to some extent as if the points were backed by money even when they are not. Poker players and backgammon players do this less often.

Money is so powerful as a reward that some games that use it can be popular even though they would be completely uninteresting without it. It's hard to imagine playing slots, for example, if no money were involved.

Strictly speaking, while money is certainly a reward for professional baseball players, say, it is probably better to say that the dream of money, or the opportunity to fantasize about money, is the actual reward for gambling games. Most people who gamble do not do so in the expectation that they really will have more money afterward (and

11. See, for example, Johnson's *Everything Bad Is Good for You.*

of those who do, most of them are wrong). And perhaps even more important than the fantasies of money are a certain status gain for playing—a kind of conspicuous consumption—and above all the thrill of risk.[12]

Besides money, certain games offer other tangible rewards. In the case of *Magic*, the cards are a reward, and while they can be purchased they can also be won as tournament prizes. In-game "material rewards" such as virtual loot, virtual currency, or even experience points are an interesting borderline case. They can be thought of simply as part of the game's mechanics, or as a kind of achievement, but it is also natural to think of them as a reward. Certainly the players think of them that way. The fact that they give in-game power distinguishes them from other achievements such as having slain a particular monster without assistance, or passing a level by popping only red and blue balloons.

Exercise 6.4: What are some rewards in bridge? *Monopoly*? Party games? What correlation might you expect with high downtime and rewards?

Exercise 6.5: What are some rewards in *Myst*? Other puzzlelike games? What correlation might you expect with these games' rewards and replayability?

Exercise 6.6: What are some rewards in playing high school football? What are the costs?

Exercise 6.7: What are some rewards in playing high school chess? What are the costs?

6.3 Characteristic: Downtime

Downtime is time during a game when a player is not actively playing (she may or may not be considering strategies, but she is not making any moves, or even about to do so[13]). It is often seen by players as a detriment—usually they would rather be playing than waiting around—but it can sometimes be a benefit, as when it provides scope for socializing. Also, no downtime at all can sometimes be a detriment, as we'll discuss below.

The most typical example of downtime is waiting for your turn to come, perhaps in a boardgame or card game, or perhaps in a sports game where some players sit out

12. Compare putting $10 on the roulette wheel with, say, seeing a scary movie for $10. In each case you get a thrill (and in the case of roulette you even have a chance of getting your $10 back). If seeing the movie makes sense, then betting the $10 on roulette can make sense, even for someone who understands that in the long run they are not going to come out ahead monetarily.

13. In particular, we don't consider it downtime when you're thinking about what move to make while it is your turn.

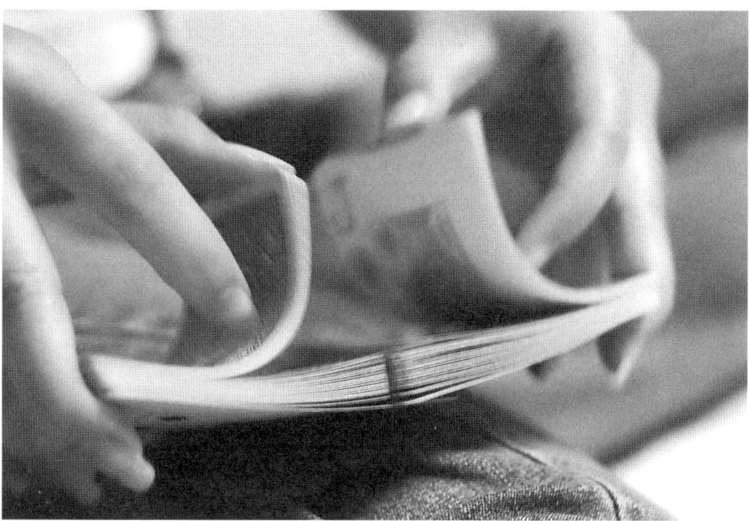

Figure 6.3
©iStockphoto.com/Tom Nguyen

for some part of the game. Playing dummy in bridge is another example. Downtime is not necessarily imposed by strict lines in the rules saying you can do nothing: less sharply defined examples include a soccer goalie waiting while the ball is at the far end of the field, an RTS player waiting for an early building to be finished, or an MMO player waiting for mana to recharge.

Downtime is often at its most problematic with multiplayer turn-based games (e.g., multiplayer boardgames), especially as the number of players increases. If there is not a lot of interaction among the players, then the total downtime is enormous, as each player waits for a succession of other players to take their turns before he can play again. Even if there is player interaction, it is very often one-on-one, and all but those two players experience downtime while the two of them interact. An extreme case of this may be found in the boardgame *Titan*, where every so often two players essentially stop the game and play a one-on-one miniwargame before normal play continues.

When considering player tolerance of downtime, note that both the total percentage of downtime (i.e., how much time the player is playing versus not playing) and the length of a stretch of downtime (i.e., what the longest stretch of time is that a player must wait) matter. The two of course are related, but not absolutely—there are games where one sits out a lot, but never for that long (poker), or where one spends most of one's time playing, but every so often sits out for a good chunk of time (hockey).

Exercise 6.8: Suppose a turn-based game has n players, and turns last t minutes. Also suppose there is essentially nothing to do on an opponent's turn. What percentage of a player's time in the game is downtime? How long is a given stretch of downtime?

Downtime turns players into spectators. This is not all bad—watching other players play can be a fun part of the game, and the fact that you are participating in the game yourself makes the fates of the other players particularly interesting to you. Of course, if a game is very interesting to watch (see section 7.3, on spectation) the downtime may be more bearable. However, in general downtime looks very different to players and to (true) spectators. On the one hand, players are more likely to need a rest, or to be willing to think about the game when they aren't actively involved, and in that sense are more likely to benefit from downtime. On the other hand, spectators are less committed to the game, and may be happy simply to step away for a few moments (e.g., getting a drink during a break in the action). And of course for sports on commercial television, there are economic incentives to have downtime in which the networks can sell commercials. Also, downtime for just one player hardly matters to spectators—they can simply watch another player. It is only downtime that affects everyone, such as a time-out, that matters.

Downtime—Good and Bad

Since generally players want to be playing, designers should, and do, attempt to minimize downtime. However, it should be recognized that too little downtime can be bad also.

In some games, downtime varies with player skill, with weak players sitting out more. *Counterstrike* and *Defense of the Ancients* both can have very high amounts of downtime for weaker players.[14] Such a situation is very punishing for beginners and other weak players (not only is sitting out discouraging, but it also makes it harder to improve one's skill), and such games tend not to make good casual games.

Waiting a long time between turns is not so bad if you can plan your strategy during that time. Some games with a lot of calculation, such as chess, almost require this downtime in the sense that the game would take almost twice as long without it in order to get the same quality of moves.[15] Games without overt random elements are more amenable to this kind of analysis: it is much easier to read out one's moves if those moves don't rely on, say, the unknown roll of the dice at the start of one's turn. Some games with random elements, such as *Scrabble*, can still benefit in this way if

14. In a very different way, team sports have the same issue, with weaker players being forced to sit on the bench.

15. Go players can use this downtime even more effectively than chess players can, because different regions of the board are more independent. Thus a player can read out one portion of the board while his opponent is (most likely) playing in another.

the random elements are placed at the end of one's turn rather than the beginning (drawing a new card or tile at the end of one's turn rather than the start[16]), or if the influence the random element will have on one's turn is not too large. The utility of this downtime can vary agentially with skill. Waiting for the other player in chess can be painful to a weak player, but a highly skilled player may relish every extra second he has to think about the board.

Turn-based multiplayer games with many players suffer in terms of a player's ability to use downtime, because the board state on one's next turn may be very different from what it is at the end of one's current turn. In such games, one often starts thinking about one's turn only during the turn of the player immediately preceding, rather than as soon as one's own turn is over. (One way to think of this is that the state heuristics of the game, as applied by me at the end of my turn, are damaged by all the intervening players, forcing me to apply them later.) However, the more interested I am in what happens during other players' turns, the less onerous the downtime. One particularly good example of this is *Monopoly*: the best thing that can happen to me—namely someone landing on my property and paying me lots of money—happens on my opponents' turns. So I am excited to watch the turns of other players.[17]

Downtime can also be useful for pacing. It allows the game to be less high-pressure and lets players take a break. No downtime at all makes for an exhausting game. Anyone who has played indoor soccer, where the ball never goes out of bounds, can appreciate how much more exhausting it is than regular soccer, which is itself more tiring than games like football where one sits out frequently, or baseball, where one essentially sits out almost the entire game.

Computer games are both better and worse in terms of downtime. If the computer game has fast AI opponents, the downtime problem is essentially solved even for multiplayer (more precisely, one-player, multiple simulated opponent) turn-based games: you take as much time as you want on your turn, playing as quickly or as slowly as you like, and then the AIs all quickly complete their turns. But if such a game is ported directly to true multiplayer form, it becomes all but unplayable: every-

16. This can have an unintended consequence, however: a player may get a bad draw, and then spend considerable time feeling sad that her fate is sealed. Drawing at the end of the turn is more likely to be a positive in games like *Scrabble* where any draw will have some use, and less likely where, as in *Magic*, a draw tends toward "success" or "failure."

17. *Monopoly* tends to come in for a lot of criticism among game designers. (A highly popular game that the "experts" all hate should be a warning flag for the thoughtful designer—if the game is so bad, why do so many people like it? Some answer beyond "people are stupid" is required.) While the game certainly has plenty of flaws, this one innovation, of exciting downtime in a turn-based multiplayer game, is enormously powerful and still not as widely appreciated as it should be.

one is spending an enormous amount of time waiting for others to take their turns, turns that tend to be very long in a game originally designed with a one-player focus.[18]

Computer game players tend to be less tolerant of downtime in general. Partly this is the faster pace of the computer world, and partly it is due to being accustomed to the lack of downtime in the single-player computer game experience. But perhaps the greatest part is due to the computer as a gaming interface: there are far fewer social cues, less of a sense of another human being doing something rather than doing nothing, less to watch as the other person is taking her turn, less of a sense as to how the other player's turn is progressing (is she thinking hard, or did she just leave and get a cup of coffee?). Indeed, often most of what the other person is doing is not even visible.

The computer enables various solutions to the downtime problem, though: automatic clocks are easy to build in, simultaneous turns are possible, real-time play is possible. Strategy games are an interesting case: early on, turn-based single-player strategy games against AI opponents were the norm (e.g., *Civilization*). The downtime situation was good. But when made multiplayer, the downtime was awful. The RTS was a solution to the downtime issue:[19] no downtime at all, just keep doing what you want! But now you are playing indoor soccer, with no resting of any kind allowed. And the twitch skills required, in terms of clicks per minute, were out of reach of the vast majority of players. One's skill at the game was influenced more by one's ability to click quickly and efficiently and less by thinking strategically, at least at all but the very highest levels of play (and those high levels of play absolutely required outstanding clicking skills). The whole situation was rather disheartening if you were originally interested in playing a strategy game—the promise of "*Civilization* without waiting around" was never entirely met. An interesting new genre of games arose, but one with an awkward tension between fast clicking and strategic thinking.

Lastly, one interesting and unusual approach to downtime can be seen in poker. Poker has a lot of downtime, which is bad for the enjoyment of the game. One indication that poker's downtime is probably more than is optimal can be seen from the tendency of many people to play multiple games simultaneously in online poker (not many people want to play simultaneous games of online chess). But poker's downtime provides part of the economic engine on which the game is based: most players at the low and intermediate levels probably play too many hands. Poker's approach to down-

18. One of the authors still has nightmares about a particularly stressful game of multiplayer *Masters of Orion II* in which he played against a much more experienced (and thus much faster) and very irate opponent.

19. Except in the early phases of the game, where one had to wait, for example, for resources to be gathered and buildings to finish. These problems weren't too hard to fix, though; see section 6.4 on busywork.

Figure 6.4
©iStockphoto.com/Gustaf Brundin

time is very capitalistic—you can always simply pay to eliminate your downtime, by staying in a hand you shouldn't be in. Many weaker players will occasionally call simply because they have sat out several times in a row, and they want to have the experience of being in a hand to the end.

Exercise 6.9: How much downtime is there in chess? For advanced players? For beginners?

Exercise 6.10: Why are turn-based multiplayer games dominant in the world of boardgames and card games and virtually nonexistent online?

Exercise 6.11: How does player elimination affect downtime differently in online games versus party games?

6.4 Characteristic: Busywork

Busywork in games consists of the rote activities that the player must perform, which are not part of what they would consider the fun of the game. As such, it is in principle an agential characteristic, since what one person considers rote or boring another might enjoy. In practice, though, much busywork is fairly clear from a systemic point of view. For example, setting up the board before the game begins (or between rounds for more complex boardgames), shuffling and dealing out the cards, adding up scores, or making change in *Monopoly* all count as busywork.

Busywork is like downtime in that the player is not "really playing," with the difference that the player is doing something mindless rather than doing nothing at all. If downtime is a player doing nothing, busywork is a player doing nothing much.

One way of attempting to decide what's busywork is to look at the decisions involved: if there aren't any, or if they are arbitrary from the players' point of view, that's busywork. In other words, players are not using any heuristics to do busywork. In games where physical skill is relevant to victory, players can't be using any of that either for a task to count as busywork—basically, busywork can't be done well or badly, at least not in the sense of it affecting one's chances of victory.

Activities that may eventually seem like busywork are rarely considered so when players are first learning a game. This is because exploration provides interest before a game's limitations are well understood. Standards can accelerate a player's identification of activities as busywork for themselves. For example, in the first RPG you ever played it was probably more exciting to walk around the town finding armorers and apothecaries than in later ones where the constant walking between them can become numbing.

Busywork does not always have to be bad: some players might enjoy the feel of shuffling and dealing, or setting up the pieces on the board. Rounding the bases after hitting a home run is busywork, but most people would say they enjoyed doing it, and it provides nice pacing and underlining for a big game event. But busywork by definition does not feel like the core activity of playing the game, it doesn't involve any decisions or skills, and it cannot be done better or worse (as far as the player can see).[20] Too much busywork will usually be seen as an annoyance.

Usually when we use the term *busywork*, we mean that there is enough of it for a player to notice (perhaps negatively). Strictly speaking the act of rolling the dice and moving one's piece around a (nonbranching) track is busywork, but it is rarely seen as onerous.

Types of Busywork

Busywork can be divided into three basic types, the third of which is only barely busywork (or arguably not busywork at all, although it may be perceived by the players as such):

20. An interesting borderline case is painting miniatures in a game like *Warhammer*. For many players, this is a core part of the game (or, more properly, the metagame)—both enjoyable and significant. For some, though, it's an annoying thing one is sometimes forced to do in order to play (either because other players demand it or tournament entry requires it). One might think that painting doesn't affect the game directly, and can't be done well or badly from the point of game victory, thus pushing it toward busywork. But some tournament rules do allow painting to have an impact, at which point perhaps painting is better viewed as a subgame.

1. *"Pure" busywork* Completely mechanical operations that must be performed according to some deterministic algorithm. No choices of any kind are involved. Shuffling and dealing, setting up the board, making change, or looking up results in a table.
2. *Incomprehensible busywork* Actions that involve gameplay choices that are completely opaque to the players and are made essentially randomly. Logically these are quite different from pure busywork, but the effect on the player is much the same. These are actions that must be performed for the game to continue, but that don't involve any meaningful choices and cannot be done better or worse,[21] and hence seem like work unrelated to the play of the game.
3. *Very low reward/effort ratio activities* Not strictly speaking busywork, these sorts of activities might seem close to busywork to some players.

Note that incomprehensible busywork is particularly agential, and depends very much on the heuristics of that particular player (players will, however, often agree as to what constitutes "pure" busywork). For a beginner, some choice may seem quite arbitrary, and thus amount to busywork, even though the choice might be meaningful to an expert player. To a very expert player, the choice might seem logically determined, and thus busywork again. Some examples:

• *Dots & Boxes* Initial choices seem completely arbitrary to all but an extremely expert player (see the discussion in section 1.3), so the opening phase of the game has a busywork feel. To an expert player, the late phase of the game is deterministic, hence is busywork (although it can simply be skipped and the score counted).
• *Chess* The opening seems somewhat arbitrary to the beginner, but probably not enough to qualify as busywork. To a more advanced player, though, if a standard opening line is chosen, making the moves in that line is simply playing through the opening and could be considered busywork.
• *Go* A beginner is often so at sea in the opening moves that they may seem like busywork. A strong player might find it to be busywork to play through a known opening, but choosing which opening to use in which corner[22] based on the situation elsewhere on the board is definitely not busywork. A really expert player might be

21. Note that simply saying "involves no (meaningful) choices" is not enough, since running quickly in a footrace may not involve any choices, but it is certainly not busywork—it's what the race is all about.
22. Opening patterns in go are typically patterns played out in a given corner rather than whole-board openings as in chess. In fact, there are two words for "opening" in go, one meaning the corner openings (for which there exist dictionaries like the opening dictionaries in chess) and the other meaning whole-board opening strategy (for which books also exist, but focused more on general strategic principles than on specific fixed sequences of moves).

essentially rederiving and modifying an opening sequence as he goes, thus making the play of even a standard opening no longer busywork.

• *Nim* If you don't know how to play, the majority of the game is all incomprehensible busywork. Once you do, it's deterministic, and thus busywork again (or simply not a game at all).

Exercise 6.12: Briefly discuss three to five other games in terms of busywork. Some possibilities:

Tic-tac-toe
A European boardgame
A highly complex computer game
A sport
A game of your choice

In the extreme, the general pattern that occurs is something along the lines of (incomprehensible) busywork becomes interesting play becomes (pure/deterministic) busywork. The first and last phases are obviously unfortunate. Avoiding the first is a matter of having good beginner heuristics; avoiding the last is a matter of having good expert heuristics.[23]

Busywork and Game Evolution over Time

In general, games (and game genres) tend to evolve over time to reduce busywork. Some noteworthy examples:

• *Backgammon* Originally one began with the pieces off the board and had to bear them on (move them on as part of game play). Later, the pieces started on the board, and later still they started on the board with the opposing pieces interspersed in an immediately interesting position (as they are today). The addition of the doubling cube early in the twentieth century, although it did many things for the game, can partially be thought of as reducing the busywork of finishing an almost certainly won game (see also section 2.1 on player elimination). In each case, the game underwent an increase in popularity.[24]

• *Chess* Increased movement of the pawns, castling, and more powerful pieces like the queen all reduced the "busywork" of early forms of chess where the opening moves consisted of a great deal of pawn pushing. (Other forms of chess solved this problem

23. Again, "good" in the sense of "good for the game," not "strong/powerful" or "good for the player who uses them." In this case, the designer wants the beginner heuristics to be strong enough to provide at least some guidance, and the expert heuristics not to be so strong as to be deterministic.

24. See the historical survey in the introduction to Jacoby and Crawford's *The Backgammon Book*.

in other ways, with Chinese chess opening its pawn structure and Japanese chess allowing players to use captured pieces as paratroopers.)

- *MMOs* An increase of questing over grinding and a general increase in the ease of leveling are part of what made *World of Warcraft* so popular, producing features likely to dominate the genre. Moving around the virtual world is also a form of busywork or downtime, and newer MMOs (or even later versions of the same MMO) tend to have more ways of moving around quickly (teleporting, various mounts).
- *RTS games* The initial build patterns (once they are discovered by the players) are often seen as "busywork." Later RTS games seem more likely to have various ways around them: starting with some basic buildings and units in play, automated worker management, or no workers at all. Build queues, rally points, and hotkeys can all be thought of as ways to reduce busywork.

The trend toward decreasing busywork is by no means absolute and one-directional, however. To take one interesting example, consider inventory management in computer RPGs. Before the advent of graphical RPGs, one's inventory was a simple list, and managing it involved relatively little busywork. Once graphical interfaces became common, the typical interface was a large box showing what one could carry, and individual items took up more or less space, introducing the busywork of arranging one's items in order to use the space efficiently. Arguably the new interface made designers reimagine things from scratch, and since the evolution from more to less busywork is often unconscious, they did not realize the costs of the new way of managing inventory—or perhaps they were seduced by the lure of greater "realism." In any case, over time the graphical interfaces had less busywork, first with the addition of buttons that autoarranged one's inventory, and later with the simple expedient of making every item take up one inventory slot, regardless of how big it "really" was. Additional inventory space (especially in banks), easier mailing to one's "mule" characters, and increasing stacking of items all pushed toward reducing the strains of inventory management. Ironically, though, these very things that make inventory management easier also encourage people to keep larger and larger inventories, worsening the problem again—whether the end result is a net decrease in inventory busywork is anyone's guess.

On average, busywork seems relatively low in sports and classic boardgames and card games, somewhat higher in newer boardgames and card games, and highest of all in computer games.[25] This is, perhaps, further evidence of a tendency for busywork to be evolved out over time—the older the genre is, the less busywork it has.

25. Interestingly, although computer game players are relatively tolerant of busywork, they are highly intolerant of downtime.

Ways of Controlling Busywork

In general, there are many methods of reducing or eliminating busywork depending on the details of the busywork in question. Some have been mentioned above, such as converting a large amount of marginal busywork into a small amount of pure busywork in the case of backgammon setup, or automating certain busywork processes in computer games in the case of the inventory autoarrangement button.

Sometimes busywork can be reduced by assigning it to a third party. This is especially common in sports, where referees do a certain amount of busywork (like moving chains in football) in addition to their primary duties. A more straightforward example is that of the ball boy or ball girl in tennis. Examples in the worlds of paper and computer gaming are rarer, but they do exist: Chinese gold farmers in an MMO are one. In general, if large-scale farming out of busywork makes a big difference in how players enjoy the game, it may be a sign the game design needs further attention to ways of eliminating that busywork.

If busywork is farmed out to a third party, it often means that the player who would have had the busywork now has *downtime* instead. Less commonly, busywork can become downtime when marginal busywork is converted into pure busywork, which is then done by another player: the bridge dummy being the classic example.[26]

Exercise 6.13: Choose a game that has all three types of busywork, and explain how it has each type. Are there activities in the game that some players see as busywork and that others do not?

Exercise 6.14: How does the player elimination common in many games (e.g., *Monopoly*) affect busywork?

Exercise 6.15: Is traveling in an MMO busywork—is it busywork to walk from place to place? The first time? The tenth time? The thousandth time? How might an MMO deal with these changes over time in busywork?

Exercise 6.16: Is "grinding" for experience in an RPG busywork? How might an RPG deal with these changes over time in the busywork associated with a repetitive task?

Exercise 6.17: Would you expect beginners or experts in chess to resign earlier? Why?

Exercise 6.18: Why might computer games have relatively more busywork but relatively less downtime compared to other kinds of games?

26. It is arguable whether dummy's play (if required to be performed in the normal fashion) would really be boring enough to qualify as busywork, but it would almost certainly be less interesting than the play of any of the other three hands. So, since someone needs to go get more drinks, declarer's partner seems like the best choice.

6.5 Characteristic: Reward/Effort Ratio

Things that players do in an attempt to win a game will typically require some amount of effort, either during the game (e.g., counting cards played in bridge) or in preparation (practicing your basketball foul shots again and again). That effort may be mental or physical. Any given effort will yield some amount of reward. Players will tend to prefer doing things that give a high amount of reward for a small amount of effort.

Choosing to engage in a certain effort is executing a heuristic ("in thus-and-such a situation, do this activity") but the effort itself may not be: it may be a calculation (counting cards), a purely physical activity (running as fast as possible, or throwing a ball through a hoop), or some other kind of activity (grinding in an MMO).

We wish to examine the relationship between the amount and kinds of effort players exert, and the reward they get for that effort. In general, the reward we're focused on here is that of doing well at the game (and whatever other rewards, such as prestige or money, might stem from that), but of course players can make greater or lesser efforts directed at any of the rewards a game might have to offer.

Sometimes the ratio of reward to effort is low enough that the players don't wish to do the effort, and they will say things like "it's just too much work." Of course, the most competitive players will seek every advantage they can, but depending on where they fall on the casual-to-competitive scale, some efforts that players may reject include

- Counting cards played in trick-taking games
- Memorizing openings in chess
- Diving for the ball on a muddy field
- Extensive physical drill in team sports
- General physical conditioning
- More generally, any outside of game training ("I just want to play")

Many games will or won't work for a certain audience based on their perceptions of the reward/effort ratio for the common activities in the game. At a very general level, people who find physical things easy and are good at them will enjoy being rewarded with victory in physical games, and will be more likely to play them, while their more cerebral and less athletic counterparts may prefer boardgames over sports. But even among boardgame players, many will avoid games like chess because activities like memorizing openings or reading out complex lines of play seem more like work than like fun.

The reward/effort ratio is of course agential in that how much work is too much is a player perception. But it is agential in another perhaps more interesting way: different playgroups will have their own ideas about which heuristics are worth the effort,

Figure 6.5
©iStockphoto.com/diego cervo

which will affect a new player joining the group. If the group is very casual and feels counting cards (or diving for the ball) is not really worth it, a new player who wants a relaxed game will be content. If the group counts cards on a regular basis, the new player may feel obligated to do the same. Even if he does not, he may suffer increased downtime from the players who do, decreased chances of winning, and a generally less relaxed atmosphere. The group is pushing him toward an escalated level of play that is less enjoyable than the more casual experience would be. If the new player is instead more serious than the group, she may be encouraged to "relax" or "take it easy" as the group tries to preserve the style of play they enjoy and to avoid having to engage in what they see as unpleasant activities just to stay at the same level of winning.

Calculations

One type of effort common in many nonphysical games is calculating. We use the term here broadly, to mean mental efforts that are particularly formulaic, efforts where having a computer or even just paper and pencil would be a help. Examples include

- Counting cards or memorizing other game data
- Playing a memorized opening in chess[27]
- Reading out a series of moves ("if she goes there, and then I go there, and then she goes there, then I go there, and then she takes my rook")
- Actual calculations in the mathematical sense (e.g., calculating the odds in poker or blackjack)

Calculations tend to be particularly unappealing to players. Fortunately they usually have decreasing returns to scale. In hearts, for example, there are a number of things a player might keep track of, such as

1. Has the queen of spades been played?
2. Have the ace and king of spades been played?
3. How many spades have been played?
4. Is someone out of a suit?
5. Which key cards are outstanding in some particular suit I care about?
6. Who has taken a heart?
7. Have any cards I've passed been played?
8. How many cards of each suit have been played?
9. Exactly which honors have been played?

27. Note that calling this a "calculation" is overloading the English definition of the term, but it makes sense to include these sorts of activities in our discussion at this point. Strictly speaking, perhaps it is better to think of executing the opening as busywork and the "calculation" as the memorization work involved in learning it.

10. Exactly which of the lowest cards (say 2–4) have been played?
11. Exactly which cards have been played?
12. Exactly which cards have been played, when, and by whom?

Only the last step means the player has all the information he could possibly need, and few players would go that far. Keeping track of just the queen of spades gives a big payoff. Keeping track of the high spades, or the numbers of cards played in various suits, or who is out of each suit, all give a good payoff. Keeping track of every single card played and who played which one when—immensely more effort—gives only a modest payoff beyond that. Games where each additional effort in calculation gives a smaller marginal return will give experts something to do, but those more advanced calculations won't be absolutely required for beginners to keep up.

Returns to Effort

If we graph the reward a player receives for a given amount of effort (whether from calculation, from study and preparation, or from some other source), decreasing returns to effort would mean we would expect a graph something like the one in figure 6.6.

Learning the first or the second technique gives a lot of reward for relatively little effort. Learning the third or the fourth technique gives somewhat less reward, and so on.

Graphs of this sort are very rough, and are meant only to provide a guide to one's intuition. Effort should be taken to include both effort spent in game and effort spent

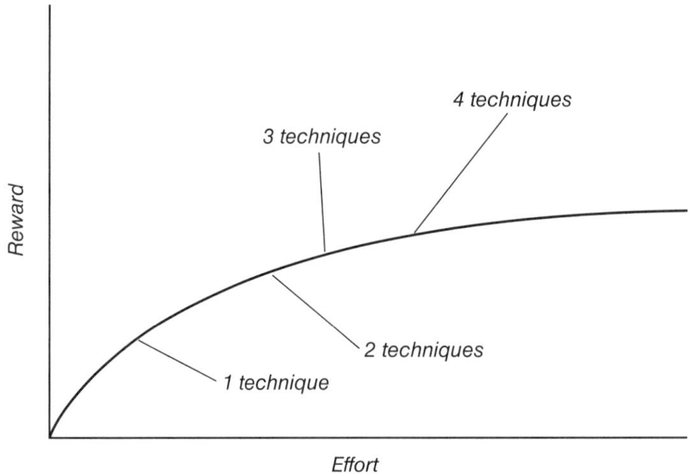

Figure 6.6
Rewards for effort in hearts

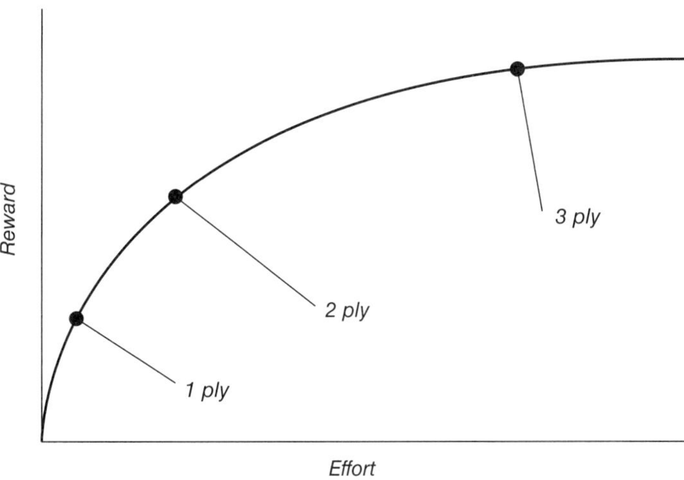

Figure 6.7
Rewards for reading deeply in chess

out of game (say by memorizing strategies, studying books, doing practice drills, or working out in the gym). Reward here represents an increased chance for the player to win, as compared with a player of his own level.[28] At the level of abstraction we are using, the graphs may equally well be thought of as graphs of returns to skill (see section 5.2).

For another example, think of chess. There are great returns to being able to read out sequences of moves. These advantages are enormous if you compare being able to look ahead a move or two versus not looking ahead at all. But the difference between looking ahead four moves and looking ahead five or six is perhaps not so great. And given that looking ahead five or six moves is vastly more difficult, the gain *per unit of effort* in looking ahead five or six moves instead of four is very small indeed when compared to what you gained looking ahead one or two moves (although still large enough, perhaps, to matter in a game like chess without overt random elements that decrease payoffs to skill).

In fact, it is quite natural that effort should have decreasing returns to scale in general. Players, as they attempt to improve their skills, will tend to look for the way to gain the greatest improvement with the least amount of time and effort. So if two different calculations are possible, each involving the same amount of effort, the player will naturally choose first to make the one that has the biggest payoff. Thus, because of the order in which players choose to learn their skills, there will naturally

28. In other words, one can think of rewards as being measured in Elo points.

Reward/Effort Ratio and Randomness

As discussed in section 5.2, the payoff to skill goes down in the presence of randomness: a given amount of skill (or effort spent to acquire skill) will not yield as high a winning percentage in a game with a lot of randomness. Figure 6.8 shows chess and hearts, but the diagram comparing chess and die-rolling chess would have essentially the same form.

One can look at the ability of beginners to play with experts in games with randomness using these diagrams. Let's pull apart the two curves above for chess and hearts. Imagine a game like hearts, poker, or *Monopoly* with large amounts of randomness. There, the returns to effort are modest, so an expert gains only a limited improvement in chance to win over a beginner (figure 6.9).

However, for a game like chess or go, the additional effort put in to become an expert yields a very large payoff in increased winning chances. This larger spread means beginners and experts are too far apart to play together (if one wishes for both to have a reasonable chance to win) (figure 6.10).

Although it's a natural impulse to want effort to be rewarded as richly as possible, the game designer needs to be cautious: Who is her intended audience? How will her players be finding opponents? Will all the players who want to play be able to have a good experience?

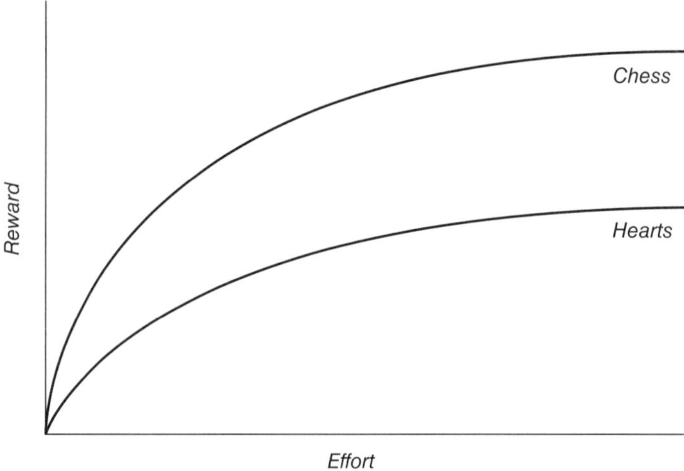

Figure 6.8
Rewards for effort in chess vs. hearts

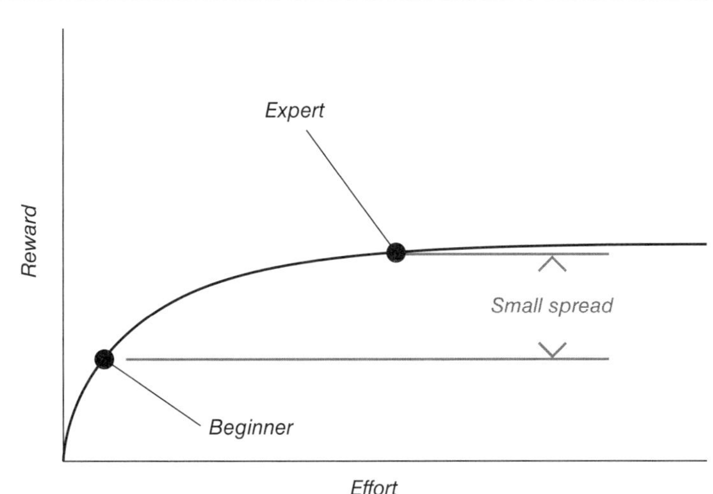

Figure 6.9
Low rewards for effort in high-luck games

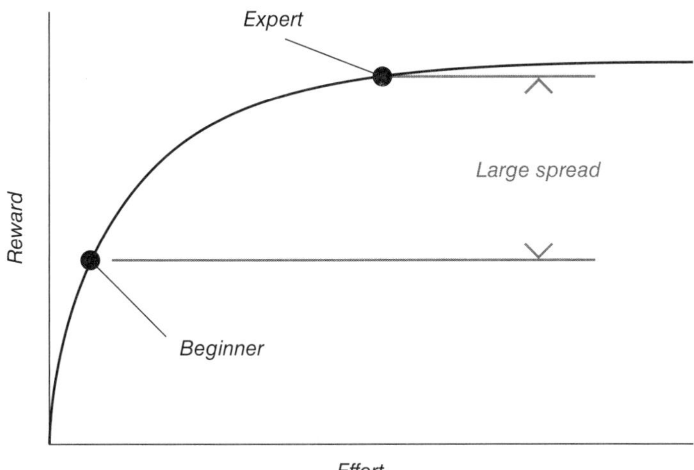

Figure 6.10
Greater rewards for effort in low-luck games

be decreasing returns to effort in most cases.[29] This may not hold, though, if logic dictates that certain skills need to be learned before certain others—see the discussion below on the need to learn basic techniques in sports.

In general, additional rewards to calculation decrease with effort. Sometimes, though, games may have calculations where the rewards increase as you go up the difficulty scale. Such games severely punish beginners. Increasing returns to calculation may happen when reading out a series of moves, where the returns to being able to read out to the end of a sequence, or to be able to read just a little bit further than one's opponent, can be quite large.[30] This sets up a sort of arms race where players feel they have to be very good at calculating to be able to play, and that will drive out many players (again, think of chess or go). That said, certain people are definitely attracted to games with no overt luck and no hidden information, and in such games reading out the game tree will always be an important element. In general, though, games with lots of calculation for a big reward are at a disadvantage, since most players don't like calculating.

Aside from the reading out of moves, another place where calculations can be powerful occurs toward the end of many boardgames with a point-based victory condition. Early on, rough estimates are a reasonable guide to play, and these estimates can be heuristic-based. Toward the end, one can see exactly how far other players are based on the score, calculate exactly how each possible play will modify that score, and choose one's plays accordingly. One sees this problem in go and in many European boardgames.[31]

Heuristics can to some extent limit the need for calculation. Any chess heuristic is an example—with perfect calculation, chess heuristics would be irrelevant because one could simply follow the game tree. Or, in hearts, the heuristic "play the highest non-winning card" offsets a good deal of calculation and memorization. Good heuristics can move a game from "lots of calculation gives a big payoff" to a state where lots of calculation gives a diminishing payoff.

29. For the mathematically inclined, if R gives reward as a function of effort, then because further effort generally gives further reward, we expect $R' > 0$. Since in general the size of that reward will decrease, we expect $R'' < 0$. In other words, R is typically rising but concave down.

30. For example—admittedly an extreme case—in tic-tac-toe or Nim, a player who can execute exactly the perfect strategy has an enormous advantage over a player whose ability falls just short of that. More realistically, being able to read to the end of a life-and-death problem in go is very useful, but being able to read four-fifths of the way through it is of relatively little use.

31. Really this is just a special case of reading out the game tree. In go, it's probably fine, since the game is heavily reading-based anyway. In European boardgames, it leads to an endgame that may not be appealing to the sort of audience that most of the gameplay appeals to. For one possible solution, see the last section in this chapter.

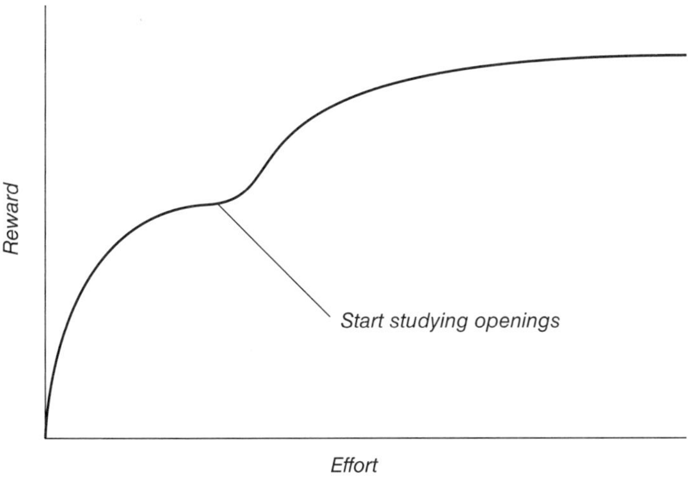

Figure 6.11
Chess reconsidered—rewards for opening study

All other things being equal, players will enjoy a steep reward-for-effort curve. That is, they will like it if it is readily apparent that extra effort is yielding strong results. In the abstract, this is true for both casual and competitive players—a highly competitive player focused on a game's rewards will appreciate the extra effort being a clear differentiator. The problem is that while steep curves in isolation are enjoyable, so is winning. Thus games are saddled with the problem that steep curves are not casual-friendly. Single-player games break this unfortunate situation with a player pool that is matched to the effort of a casual player and that doesn't care about its win percentage—namely computer AIs. Thus casual single-player games can have very steep reward-for-effort curves that multiplayer casual games in general cannot.

Further Examples of Reward for Effort

Although returns to effort typically get smaller and smaller for the reasons discussed above, there can be exceptions. For example, one arguably gets a relatively large bump up in chess skill when one begins studying openings. Occasionally this phenomenon causes problems in playgroups, when some people in the group embark on this study and others do not, with the end result that people cannot continue to play together satisfactorily.[32]

32. Of course, this separation of player skill more often happens simply because some people just start putting in a lot more effort than others.

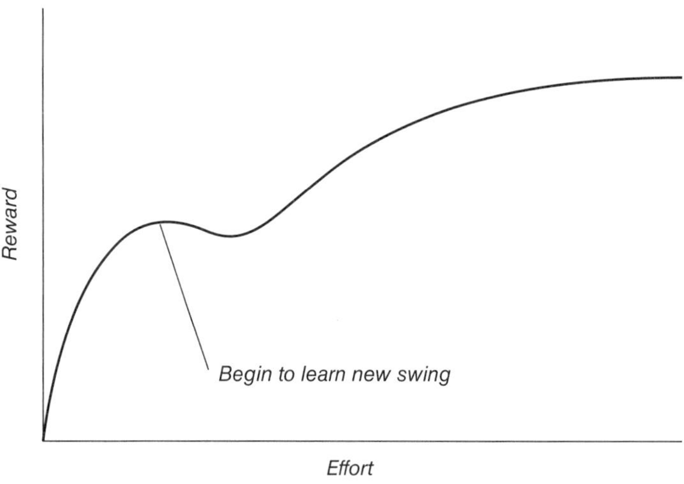

Figure 6.12
Tiger's new swing

In general, effort in a game improves performance, or why would players make the effort? But occasionally a player may make an effort that sacrifices short-term performance in the hope of a long-term gain. Fundamental technique adjustment in games requiring physical skill can fall into this category. For example, if a skilled golf pro like Tiger Woods changes his swing, he very well may be worse for a while until the new swing is perfected. At a less advanced level, any beginning console fighting game player may find that, when first transitioning from simple button mashing to deliberately trying to perform combos, there is a temporary decrease in performance. Other techniques that might at first make a player worse include starting to learn openings in go (unlike chess, it's possible to choose the "wrong opening" in a given situation), memorizing *almost* all the cards in hearts, or learning a new race in an RTS game.

Of course, when a player tries a new technique, she cannot know for certain if it will improve her situation. Perhaps the new technique is worse than the old one! (See figure 6.13.) Some games, simple slot machines for example, do not reward effort, or, if you like, there is simply no effort to be made (figure 6.14). Progressive slots, it turns out, can offer very slight rewards after a great deal of study. Of course, if those rewards take you from 49 percent against the house to 51 percent, they can be quite exciting to some (figure 6.15).

Another exception to the general rule of decreasing rewards per unit effort can occur in games where there is a big startup cost. This is especially common in sports. If you are learning tennis, snowboarding, or bicycle riding, you spend a lot of effort in the beginning for essentially no reward at all—you can hardly do the activity at all

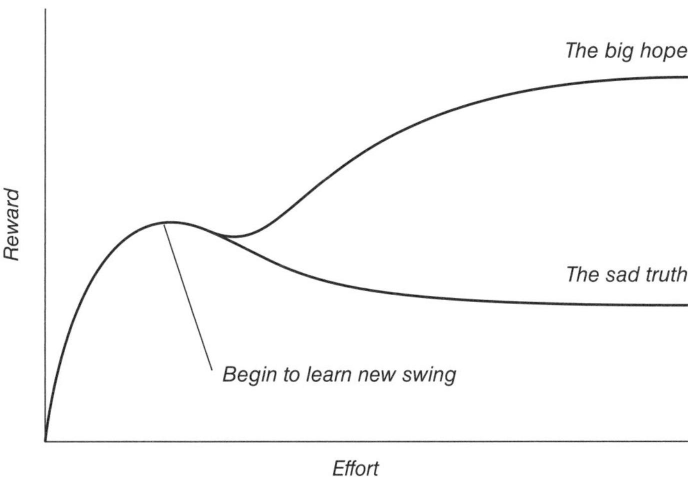

Figure 6.13
New golf swing—disaster!

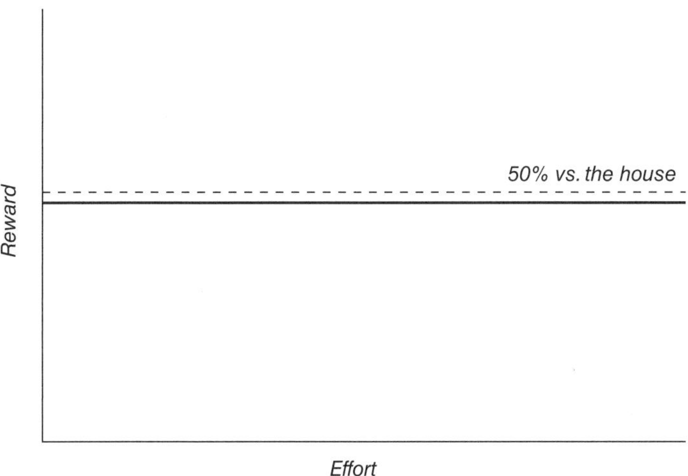

Figure 6.14
No useful effort to be made

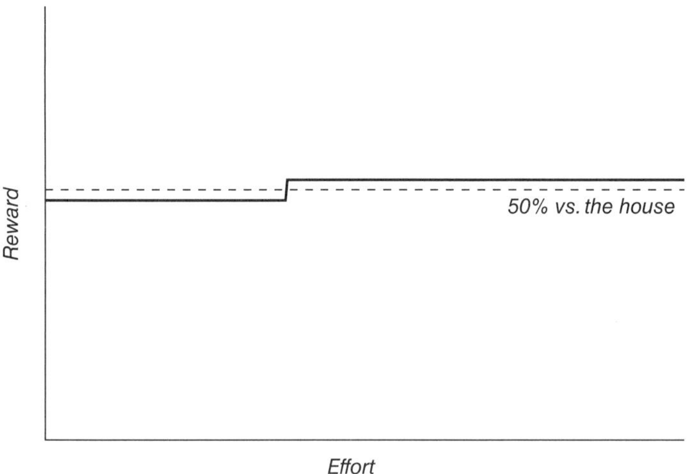

Figure 6.15
Much effort for a small reward—but worth it!

yet! But none of the more rewarding intermediate techniques can be learned before you learn the basics, so you must spend the time and effort on these low-reward activities first (figure 6.16).

Note that it is not hard to learn twenty new boardgames a year, but hardly anyone learns twenty new sports a year. This upfront cost is why.

Controlling Low Reward/Effort Ratios

Particularly frustrating for players are game activities that they see as having low reward/effort ratios, but that they feel they must perform anyway to be good players. Calculations, like counting cards or memorizing chess openings, often fall into this category. If one is designing or modifying a game, there are various ways to deal with this problem.

The simplest in principle is to eliminate the activity entirely. One might wish for this solution, say, with grinding in an MMO. But replacing all the grinding content with some more interesting way to level would require either an MMO game design breakthrough or a much larger budget for content generation (more quests, more boss fights, more zones, and so on), and so many MMOs have at least some amount of grinding in them.

Occasionally one might want simply to increase the reward. If the effort is not unpleasant, but does not seem to provide enough return, making the reward worth the effort might be all that is needed. Beware of this method when the effort is intrinsically unenjoyable, though: if grinding in an MMO is not fun, giving it greater XP

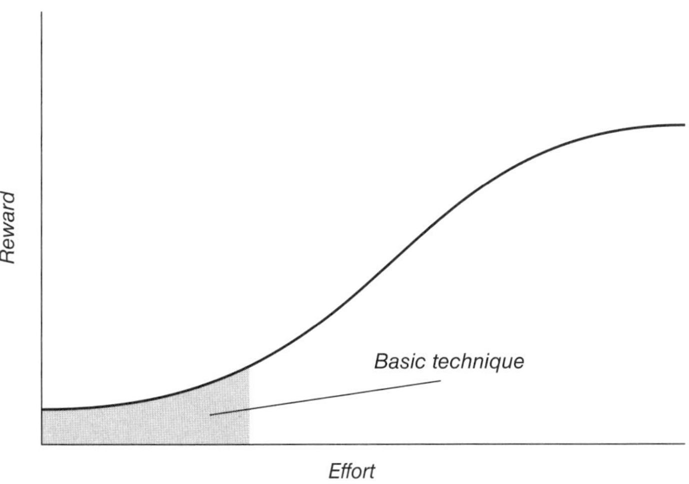

Figure 6.16
Sports—some rewards come slowly at first

rewards does not fix the problem. It just makes it worse. The underlying principle is that the most fun way to play a game, and the way that is "best" in the sense of helping you win the most, should be the same. If playing in a boring or unpleasant fashion is the best way to advance in a game, that game will become unenjoyable for many players. Some players may be able to ignore the efficient but boring playstyle and just play to have fun, but others will feel the pressure to "play correctly" and then eventually quit the entire game in disgust.

One can look at the effort involved and find some way to decrease it. One example is in card games where the discard pile may be freely examined: such a rule means that memorization of cards played is less necessary. Now any decision based on knowing what cards have been played requires less effort. However, this lessening of effort may have the unfortunate side effect of slowing the game down as players look at the discard pile frequently. The game designer has to balance the positives and negatives of that decision.

Oddly enough, the dangers of decreasing the effort or increasing the reward suggest another way to improve the situation: increase the effort, or decrease the reward, to the point where very few people will engage in the activity. For example, in some European boardgames where players need a certain amount of gold (or some other game resource) to win, the amount that each player has is kept secret from other players. This prevents the unenjoyable activity of players counting everyone's gold before taking any important action near the end of the game. Of course, players could try to memorize how much gold each player has earned during the course of the game.

This problem is sometimes addressed by having some money be earned secretly (e.g., by being written on a card that a player earns during the game without ever showing it to other players),[33] thus decreasing the reward for the activity of memorization. If done properly, tweaks like this can take unpleasant activities—that is, ones with a low reward/effort ratio—and largely eliminate them from the game. If done improperly, they can take unpleasant activities and make them even more unpleasant. Which result you get depends as much on the audience for your game (at what point do they decide to just not engage in the activity?) as on the tweaks themselves.

Further examples of decreasing returns from calculation include the randomness of die rolls in miniatures games (without the die rolls, such games might have the same rewards from calculation that chess does) or random damage in an RTS (without it, memorizing exact break points on damage and hit point upgrades would become a much greater memory burden). A reverse example is the dummy in bridge: here, the revealing of dummy's hand increases the rewards from calculation in the exact play of the hand. In general, randomness and hidden information tend to decrease calculation rewards.

Sometimes the heuristic or activity can be disguised with randomness. This has the effect of decreasing the rewards, and probably increasing the effort of discovering the heuristic as well, both of which will mean that players will feel it less necessary to engage in it.

Exercise 6.19: Why would someone find their overall reward/effort ratio decreased when learning a new golf swing?

Exercise 6.20: What would you expect of the player audience for games with a (low) horizontal asymptote[34] in a reward/effort graph? Why? Can you give examples of such games?

Exercise 6.21: What would you expect to happen to the chess player audience at the point where the study of openings begins (i.e., how many chess players are there who inhabit the points just before and just after that point on the reward/effort graph)?

Exercise 6.22: How might the reward/effort graph of *Magic* have changed over time? For example, how might the graph have looked on release compared to how it looks now?

33. Note that this also relies on randomness: if the amount of money on the hidden card is completely predictable, it can hardly be secret.
34. An asymptote is a line in a graph to which the graph gets closer and closer without ever quite reaching it.

7 Superstructure

A great deal of what matters in a game takes place outside of or alongside the gameplay proper. There may be preparation before the game, crowds of people watching it, stories told about it, modifications made to it, or behavior that goes against the official or accepted practices of the game. In this chapter, we discuss various phenomena that might be thought of as somehow "outside" the game. This is in no way meant to be a value judgment, but merely a way of grouping content—many of these phenomena are just as important, if not more so, than the ones "internal" to the game.

We begin with a general discussion of the metagame: all those activities relating to the game that aren't part of the play of the game itself, such as preparation for the game. We then talk about game conceits: themes that give the game cohesion and identity, even if they aren't included in the rules directly. Sometimes these themes are story-based, especially in computer games, but very often they are not. We follow with a discussion of ways players can customize games, and then we look at ways players may violate expectations: whether by actually breaking the rules, or by breaking norms of "acceptable" behavior. Finally, we examine some factors that influence how long a player wants to keep playing the same game—does the game seem infinitely replayable, or does it at some point "run out" of content?

7.1 Characteristic: Metagame

The metagame is the "game outside the game." It includes all the activities connected with the game that aren't part of playing the game itself, such as tournament programs, online forums, magazines about the game, training and preparation players might do before the game, or even daydreaming about the game or staring lovingly at game equipment. If the game is the skeleton, the metagame is the "soft" structure outside the game, linking the game with other life goals such as status, self-expression, gaining mastery, money, socialization, or collecting. Many of the rewards for gaming come in whole or in part from the metagame, not the game itself.

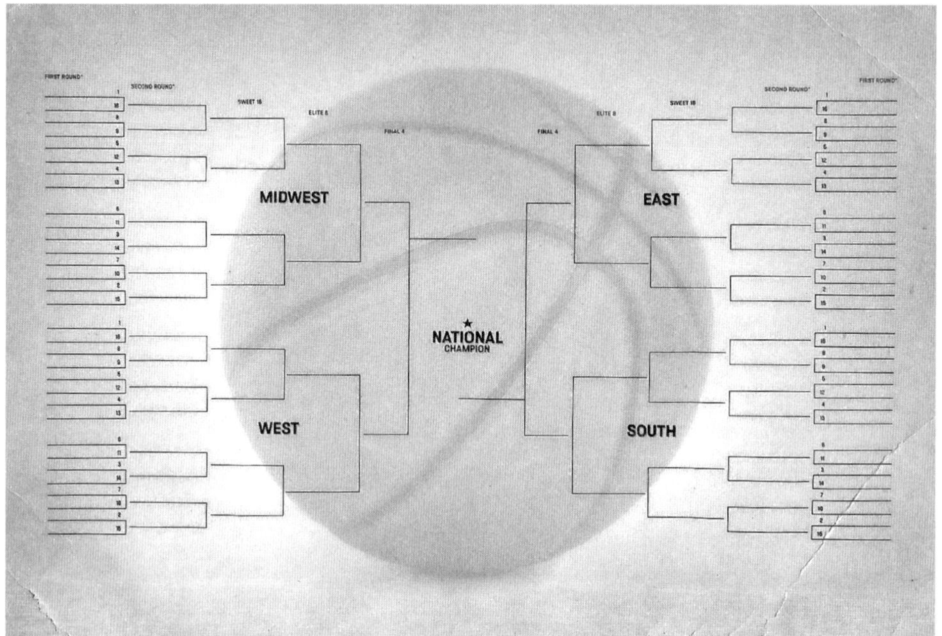

Figure 7.1

The term *metagame* isn't that common outside of hardcore gaming circles and is almost never used, for example, when discussing sports. So typically people will use the term *game* to discuss both the game proper and the metagame. But we will generally try to distinguish the two: if you are on the field trying to score a goal during a game, you're taking part in the game of soccer; if you are practicing penalty kicks, or you are buying cleats, you are taking part in the metagame of soccer.

Hardcore gamers often use the word *metagame* in a narrower sense. If a game allows very specific preparation before the match, like building a deck in a trading card game, the "metagame" is the current environment resulting from all these preparations (e.g., perhaps people are playing a lot of fast red decks at the moment, and not many people are playing slow blue ones). With this usage, "metagaming" is game preparation done to prepare for the current environment (perhaps you'll choose to put anti-red cards in your deck, or cards that will slow down a fast deck).[1] We won't use the word *metagame* in this more narrow sense.

1. Note that special preparations because of a specific game environment, although especially common in games such as trading card games, exist in many other games as well. One might study specific chess openings to prepare for a certain opponent, or field a slightly different starting football team when the weather is very bad.

Some Metagame Activities

- Preparation
  - Drills
  - Reading strategy books
  - Preparing equipment (building a *Magic* deck, waxing your skis)
  - Discussing strategy with others
  - Formal instruction (classes, coaching)
- Hanging out with other players
  - Chatting while playing the game (happens during the game, but we group it with metagame activities because it's not a necessary part of playing the game)
  - Reading or posting in online forums
  - Reading, watching, or hearing stories of famous players
  - Watching live games or replays
  - Arguing about how you would have done something differently
  - Entering a tournament (everything involved other than the actual play during the tournament)

Some Metagame Rewards

- Status
- Socialization
- Self-expression
- Gaining mastery
- Explicit player rewards
  - Money
  - Prizes (including items usable in-game)
  - Trophies

The (broader) metagame is an extremely complicated subject, but an important one for a game designer or game critic. A great deal of the enjoyment of a game, and thus of its success or failure, comes from factors outside the game. For example, one can take a crowd of adults who would not normally enjoy rock-paper-scissors, put a tournament structure around it, and turn it into an entertaining experience.[2] Given all the possible structures that can be added to a metagame, knowing where to put one's effort—which structures are worth adding and which give little or no benefit—is extremely important.

2. One of the authors actually did this experiment at the annual Game Developers Conference several years ago.

Player Communities

Different players will have different preferred styles of play. The most obvious distinction is casual versus serious, but communities may have preferences around rule variants, formats, times and places to play, and so on. Unless a player is playing a single-player game in complete isolation,[3] she'll be influenced by some sort of community. One can think of these different communities as forming different game environments or player microclimates—environments that may vary enough as to be almost different games. A player may very well be happy in one microclimate but not enjoy another microclimate at all, for reasons that may be social or convenience-related, or that may stem from the style of play the group prefers. Sometimes a player is unaware that her enjoyment or lack thereof is coming from the microclimate, and may say "chess is great" or "chess is boring" when really it is the microclimate that is great or boring, and a different environment might lead to the opposite reaction.

So for a player to enjoy a game, finding the right player community is very important. At the most basic level, it's finding the right opponents: ones who aren't too much stronger or weaker, and whose approach to the game is similar enough to be congenial. If you play Ultimate Frisbee, say, you will probably want to be with people who are not too much more or less dexterous than you are. If you don't care to dive into the mud to catch the Frisbee, you will not want to be with people who will berate you for that choice—if you do go all-out, though, you may not want to play with people who "aren't trying."

For games that take place in the physical world, communities are dependent on physical location. You may not have a wide choice of different Ultimate Frisbee leagues where you live (indeed, you may not have any). But for popular sports, there are often multiple leagues, often in a fairly organized way: A leagues and B leagues, leagues separated by age or gender, leagues where the teams are formed around the workplace, and so on. For boardgames and card games, the choices aren't as wide, and often not as formalized. But enter any game store and look at the postings for role-playing groups and you will see players trying to sort themselves into the right microclimates.

Online, there are bulletin boards, guild websites, wikis, and other player communities. But when it comes time to play the game itself, since geography is not a limitation, players are often thrown into one big hopper, and then some kind of player matching occurs. Perhaps players deliberately select people they already know to play with; perhaps they look at a list of games and choose to join one. More and more, though, some sort of algorithm is used to match people, although these algorithms currently use far fewer kinds of information than players use in offline matching.

3. Note that many single-player games have communities, such as online bulletin boards that trade strategy tips, or a group of people at the office who are obsessed with *Tetris*.

When looking at a metagame, one thing to watch out for is how much it fragments player communities. Many games have deliberately built in choices about how you play them: different player settings (e.g., game speed, or starting money) when spawning a game in an RTS, different PvP battles available in an MMO, different formats to play *Magic*. Each new format choice is appealing, because it lets players customize their experience that much more, and there is always someone who wishes you could tweak this or that setting, or play on some new map. But too much of that, and there is the risk that none of the different formats will succeed: players will not be able to find the choice they want, or the minimum number of people required to join the game won't be available. Smaller game communities—often physical ones—are especially vulnerable. If twelve players show up at your store to play *Magic*, you can run a tournament. But if half of them want to play sealed *Magic*, and half want to play constructed, and you need at least eight people to start a tournament, you may have nothing. And then next week they won't come back. So it is important that there be a balance between having enough options for players to find something they like[4] and having few enough options that players can make a choice and expect to find someone else to play with. Newer games, games that take place in the physical world, and less popular games have to be most careful about having too many formats; established games, online games, and very popular games have more leeway.

Metagame Support for Player Goals

Features of a game and its metagame can support different player goals in a variety of ways. For example, in an MMO socialization is supported in-game with chat and guild systems. Apparently simple features like the ability to create a custom chat channel (and how the channel is moderated, and whether it is persistent through logoff, and so on) can make a real difference in how well players can socialize. The basic gameplay structure of an MMO supports socialization as well: there is a lot of downtime, such as while waiting for a raid to form, and not much to do during it. That downtime has a real negative side, as lengthy downtime generally does, but the socialization benefits are large (whether it is a net win is hard to say for certain—it's almost certainly agen-

4. Keep in mind that most players will prefer to have their second choice actually happen than have their first choice on offer but fail to take place. And for some minor format tweaks, players won't miss them if they aren't there—the choice to build all possible variants into a game under the theory that "it can't hurt to have it available" and "someone might like it" is generally misguided. If your RTS has a dozen binary settings, letting your formats be all of the 2^{12} possible ways of playing is not a good choice. Better to carefully pick three or four choices from the 2^{12} possibilities and have those be your formats. Now your players can figure out which of those three or four choices they prefer, and they can hope to find a game that matches their preference.

tial). Out-of-game, there are forums, informational websites (both official and fan-created), guild websites, and so on.

Exercise 7.1: For various sports, give some examples of game features and metagame features that support socialization.

Exercise 7.2: Pick a game you know with a lot of downtime that players use to socialize. Is the downtime a net benefit or a net loss? Why? Would more downtime be better? Would less?

Human beings certainly like accumulating stuff, and again there are both in-game and out-of-game ways to support that. Some games have collecting as part of the gameplay itself (e.g., the *Pokémon* handheld games), which is not a metagame feature per se. Some games (*Magic*, golf, bicycle racing) have a great variety of equipment available for players to collect—the equipment is useful in-game, but collecting it is a metagame activity and, for some people, can become an end in itself.[5]

Games can have monetary benefits as well: playing for money (poker, backgammon), tournament prizes (many games), professional play. Even the dream of such rewards can be enticing for many players—certainly far more players are inspired by the idea of making a living playing basketball than can actually do so. If professional play is out of reach, players can still make money in the metagame: repairing bikes for other people, or trading for *Magic* cards and then selling them on the secondary market.

Besides money, other prizes may include goods useful in ordinary life, items useful to play the game, and of course trophies. Although trophies are strictly speaking a physical good, they are really more about status than wealth. Any prize, though, can help fulfill a player's desire for status. Wealth is powerful in this way, since saying you have won a large sum of money is more convincing to most people as a sign of achievement than almost any other prize (especially people outside of the game's community—many a game player has finally gotten some sort of understanding and respect from his nonplaying relatives by winning a tournament with a large cash prize). Ratings, rankings, and titles are another way for players to gain respect, although of course such achievements are better understood inside the game community than outside of it. If the game has any kind of media coverage, that will increase status as well.

5. If that is *all* those people care about in regard to your game, and they stop playing the game itself, then you have the odd situation that they are players in your metagame but not players in your game. One might think of retailers as being in this category, but kids who collect *Pokémon* cards but do not play are probably a better example. These people are not necessarily bad for the game—thinking about ways to convert them into players is probably a good idea, but trying to chase them off entirely is usually a mistake.

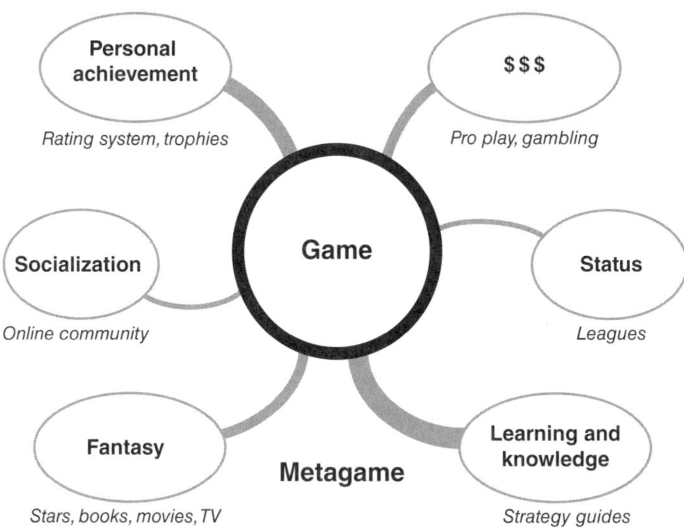

Figure 7.2
A general metagame diagram

If a player can develop signature moves, a unique play style, or even a notable personality, that can enhance his status. Poker players and sports figures do this a great deal, but it is part of almost any gaming community. These sorts of reputational benefits also provide self-expression, and sometimes gameplay benefits (e.g., intimidation) as well. Distinct player styles can arise out of the richness of the game itself if there are enough different ways to play (basketball does well here, but sprinting, say, does not). Sometimes features can be put into the game deliberately to support player expression and style, as with special titles or visible armor in an MMO.

We can graphically represent various player life goals, and how metagame features connect their achievement to the underlying game, by drawing circles for the goals and connecting lines for the supporting features (thicker lines represent stronger support for those features) (figure 7.2).

Note that depending on the limitations of the game, it can be hard to support some of these things. There is not much call in a game like roulette, say, for rating systems, professional leagues, or strategy guides.[6] On the other hand, a richer game like soccer has enormous scope for supporting almost any goal a player might have (figure 7.3). Or, directly comparing the metagame strengths and weaknesses of the *Pokémon* trading card game and the *Pokémon GameBoy* cartridge, see figure 7.4.

6. Which is not to say they don't nevertheless exist—but most roulette players don't give them much thought.

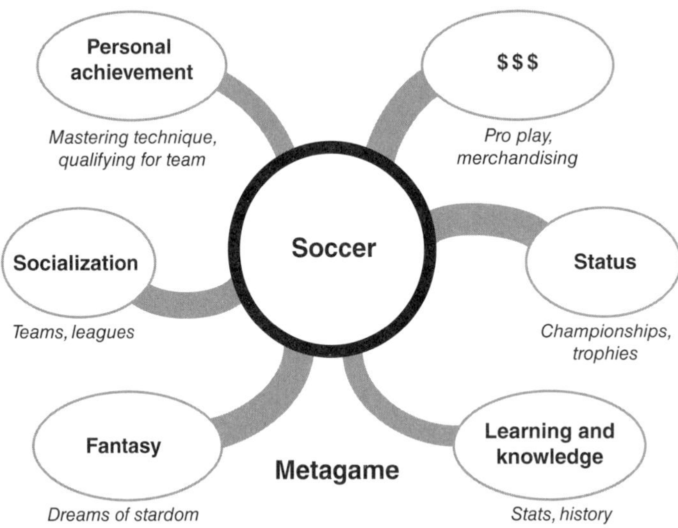

Figure 7.3
Metagame diagram for soccer

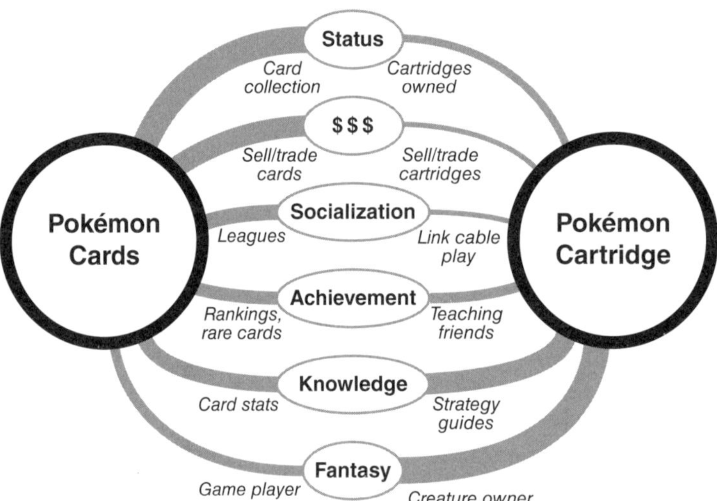

Figure 7.4
Comparing the *Pokémon Trading Card Game* to the *Pokémon* Cartridge Game

Status and money are better supported by a card collection than by a cartridge collection or even the collection of Pokémon creatures in-game. On the other hand, during gameplay, the fantasy of owning and caring for creatures exhibited in the cartridge game is stronger than the one presented in the card game. Socialization is best supported by the face-to-face play of the card game; achievement and knowledge are well supported in both games.

It can be useful to detail as completely as possible the metagame potential of a game. Along with the thickness of the arrows, one can consider how expensive the various metagame aspects are to produce for the game's publisher. For instance, a player's desire to achieve money or its equivalent might be efficiently satisfied in a trading card game by making sure price guides are published and well distributed. Perhaps the underlying skeleton of the trading card game can be changed, for example by increasing the relative rarity of certain cards, in order to facilitate this. Caution must be exercised because changing the basic skeleton of the game might alter the metagame in many ways. The above change to card rarity could potentially make the game less amenable to the goal of personal achievement if it nudges the game away from one of skill for the average player and toward one of initial monetary commitment.

Of course, none of these diagrams comes close to listing all the features that support the various goals (and many features support multiple goals, so a perfectly accurate diagram would be an impenetrable thicket of arrows). Any value the diagrams have comes more from the process of making them and thinking consciously about which features support which goals and how, rather than in the end result.

Exercise 7.3: Choose two different games and draw the metagame diagrams for them.

Exercise 7.4: How might you increase the reward of money in Little League soccer (assuming direct monetary awards are forbidden)?

Exercise 7.5: How might you increase the reward of money in a children's trading card game (assuming direct monetary awards are forbidden)?

Exercise 7.6: Discuss from a metagame perspective what you would expect to happen to sales/play of *Dungeons & Dragons* with the release of the *Lord of the Rings* movies.

Exercise 7.7: In 1968, the U.S. Open tennis championship had a total prize purse of \$100,000. What might the effect have been on the general (not just professional) tennis metagame if the purse were upped by \$1,000,000? What if that money were spent on local tournaments instead?

Exercise 7.8: Discuss how Tiger Woods changed the golf metagame for the average local player.

Exercise 7.9: What are the advantages for the golf metagame of the golf rating system (golf handicaps)? What are the advantages for the chess metagame of the chess rating system (Elo ratings)?

7.2 Characteristic: Conceit/Motif

When we speak of a game's conceit, we take *conceit* in the sense of an extended metaphor. Some games are purely abstract, such as go, *Tetris*, or poker, but most nonsports games are at least metaphorically "about" something. Games with a conceit might

Figure 7.5

have a very light one, in the sense that chess is vaguely about medieval warfare, or they might have a more elaborate conceit, in the way that *Starcraft* is about science fiction warfare or *Tomb Raider* is about swashbuckling archeology. If the game also tries to model its (possibly imaginary) conceit, it is to some degree a simulation: *PanzerBlitz* surely qualifies, *Tomb Raider* probably doesn't, but *Counter-Strike* probably does. In any case, a game's conceit can provide a great deal of motivation and explanation for the action: imagine, for example, how much less compelling *Clue* would be as a purely abstract boardgame.

Many games (e.g., almost all computer role-playing games) have stories, which are a special kind of conceit. We don't use the word *story* to refer to conceits in general, though, because chess and *Monopoly* don't have stories, but they do have conceits. *Conceit* for us carries a similar meaning to what is often called "motif" or "theme."

Sometimes people talk about the "intellectual property" of a game, meaning something similar to what we mean by conceit. We'll only use the term intellectual property when the conceit is something licensed or licensable—that is, something ownable. So a Star Wars RTS has Star Wars as its IP, but chess does not have an IP—its conceit, medieval warfare, is in the public domain.[7] Note that even a game not in the public domain can have a conceit that is public, and thus not "IP" in the sense that we use the term. For example, the game *Squad Leader* is not in the public domain, but we consider it a game whose conceit is not intellectual property, because World War II (which is *Squad Leader*'s conceit) is in the public domain—you can't own World War II or license it out (although you could license the *Squad Leade*r name itself).

Sports, and many older boardgames and card games, have no real conceits. But from around 1900 on, most deliberately designed games have had conceits. There have been a few exceptions, such as *Scrabble*, *Pente*, many party games, *Othello*, *Sorry*, and *Uno* (note, however, that many of these are repackagings of classic games). But there are far more games that do have conceits. Some examples, just to name a few at random, include *Clue*, *Doom*, *Risk*, *Battleship*, *Starcraft*, and the various *Final Fantasy* games. One of the early examples of a conceit that was added on top of an existing game mechanic (in this case, the race boardgame) was the Royal Game of Goose, which dates back to the sixteenth century.[8] Today most games have conceits added to them—

7. Note that from a legal point of view, intellectual property includes things like trademarks and copyrights, and (controversially) even the code itself in a computer game. We don't use the term in this way (or in any legally sound way—we aren't lawyers), and when we say IP we just mean "the ownable part of a game's conceit." Our apologies to those with legal knowledge; our use of the term IP, while doubtless quite odd to a lawyer, is very common in the game design community.

8. See Murray's *A History of Board-Games Other Than Chess*, 142.

sometimes in a manner that is tightly integrated with the game mechanics, but sometimes simply to give the game more flavor.

The same game can come in different versions, one with a conceit and one without. For example, *Uno* has no conceit, but *Doctor Who Uno* does.

In some cases, particularly with sports, an abstract game almost becomes its own conceit or even its own IP. Think of baseball, say: the rules are public domain, and the game has no conceit in that it is not a specific representation of something else in the way chess is a representation of medieval battle. But there is a whole world around professional baseball: history, legends, heroes, customs, and so on. And in fact Major League Baseball itself is owned, and people can and do license it. Similar comments apply to most popular sports, and to a few other games like poker as well (to some extent, they apply to almost any game that's played professionally, such as chess, *Magic*, or *Starcraft*). Perhaps the right way to think of this phenomenon is as an IP for the metagame more than for the game itself.

Note that very generic conceits, ones that are in the public domain or at least are well known to the players,[9] provide to the players a lot of information about how to play the game. For example, in *Magic*, you know to expect that a dragon is more powerful than an ogre, which in turn is more powerful than a goblin; you have a rough idea what to expect from a card named Fireball or Lightning Bolt; if a card is named "Sword of X" or "Shield of Y" you'll know it somehow helps attack or defense respectively. Similarly for chess: you know that the king is the most important piece, followed by the queen, and that the pawns are least important (the middle pieces are vague, though, and you may be surprised by the weakness of the king). If you create a unique, nonstandard IP for your game, you have the advantage of something that's easier to own from a legal standpoint, but it will be harder for people to understand how to play your game, even if the mechanics are no more difficult: this is what makes *Sid Meier's Alpha Centauri*, for example, harder to wrap your head around than *Civilization II*. In particular, abstract games (those with no conceit at all, such as tic-tac-toe) need to have very simple rules[10]—playing a purely abstract game with the complexity of *Civilization II* or *World of Warcraft* would be all but impossible. One way to view all this is as an example of standards—conceits provide standards that help players know what to expect, but the information is coming from the real world (or well-known fantasy worlds) rather than from the world of game rules.

9. Examples of conceits that are not in the public domain, but that have fairly general cores and thus are very familiar to the players, are the generic fantasy conceits of *Dungeons & Dragons* and of *Magic*. Although these worlds are rich in detail, the basics—goblins, dragons, ogres, knights, and so on—are known to everyone.

10. Note that although it must have simple rules, the game *itself* need not be simple—go is perhaps the ultimate example.

At an extreme, there are simulations: games that have a conceit and attempt to model it very closely. The more rules that are in the game not for pure gameplay reasons but because "that's how it works in real life," the more the game is a simulation. In *Uno*, there are no rules that model "real life"; in *Civilization* or *World of Warcraft* there are quite a few; in *Squad Leader* there are an enormous number. Full simulations tend to be very complex, and thus tend to have fairly small audiences. But games that are partially simulations are much more common. For games that are not in any way a simulation, worries about realism are not an issue—no one complains that *Uno* is "not realistic," because it is not trying to be. But once a game begins to simulate reality, the issue of how far to go in that direction rears its head. Partial simulations often have issues revolving around the compromises between "realism" (modeling the world they simulate) and optimizing the fun of the gameplay. Different players will have different ideas of where the game should fall. For example, different editions of *Dungeons & Dragons* have been more or less focused on simulation, and versions that have made *D&D* more like an abstract game have sometimes been met with dismay by those who want the game to be more of a simulation of a fantasy world.

When a game is highly realistic, those who don't like realism tend not to complain, but simply go elsewhere. As an extreme example of realism over gameplay, there are hex wargames that model one-sided historical battles in such a way that the forces that won historically are essentially guaranteed to destroy the opposing forces during the course of the game (the player controlling the losing side "wins" by staving off defeat for a longer time than would normally be expected). Such a game, with its

Scale of Intensity for Conceits

Conceits in a game can range from none at all, or a light conceit, all the way to full-blown simulation.

1. Purely abstract: tic-tac-toe, *Scrabble*, *Othello*, most sports, most classic card games
2. Theme only: *Bejeweled*, *Candyland*
3. Very light conceit: chess, fox & geese
4. Slight modeling of conceit: *Battleship*, *Asteroids*
5. Some modeling of conceit: *Clue*, *Donkey Kong*
6. Just barely a simulation: *Monopoly*, *Diablo*
7. Very light simulation: *Starcraft*, *Quake*
8. Simulation, but many sacrifices to gameplay: *World of Warcraft*
9. Simulation, minimal "unrealistic" elements: *Counterstrike*, *Civilization*
10. Full-on simulation (attempt to maximize modeling): *Squad Leader*

built-in loss for one side, would be unsatisfying to many, but those who desire accurate simulation will accept the odd gameplay logic.

Licensed Games

Many boardgames and computer games have for their conceit an intellectual property that they have licensed from someone else. This is a modern phenomenon and thus is not found in classic games (in their original forms) or sports. A game that uses a license has the advantage that it can get started more quickly—it comes with a built-in potential audience. However, when the licensed property dies, so does the game. Also, the game is unlikely to be successful with people who do not care for the IP; people rarely buy a Babylon 5 boardgame if they don't like Babylon 5 (although they might buy a generic merchant trading game or an Egyptian-themed boardgame just because they like boardgames, even though they don't care for mercantilism or Egyptology).

As an example, in 1965 Milton Bradley released a card game based on the TV show and movie *Voyage to the Bottom of the Sea*. It was based on Crazy Eights. It's long since forgotten. Six years later, another game based on Crazy Eights was released, but it did not have a license, or indeed any conceit at all. It was called simply *Uno*. The two games were not identical, and it would be wrong to assume that the difference in licensing was the only cause of the differences in the two games' fortunes. But although being nonlicensed is by no means a sufficient cause for achieving classic status, it is close to a necessary one.

So using an existing license usually means gaining some initial success at the cost of breadth of appeal and potential for longevity. If you're the first to market with a new and exciting kind of game (e.g., you've invented the first-person shooter or the trading card game), you might want to avoid licensing and have a fairly generic conceit (which might evolve into a real IP over time, as with Warcraft). If the market is already crowded with games like yours, you might want to license a popular IP to help you stand out. However, even in a crowded market one can sometimes be successful with a nonlicensed game and perhaps have a long-run hit; licensed games will almost never be long-run hits.[11]

Note that if a conceit gives a great deal of added value to the consumer, to the point of being one of the main reasons for buying the game, that conceit is almost always a licensed IP. Being able to interact with that IP is one of the rewards for playing the game. You buy a Battlestar Galactica game because it's about Battlestar Galactica. You don't buy *Fallout* because of the Fallout IP; even with a very powerful property

11. Computer games are rarely long-run hits anyway, due to technology (although there are exceptions like *Tetris* and *Starcraft*), which might be a factor pushing more computer games toward licensing.

like Warcraft, not many people are buying it for the Warcraft IP (they might be buying it because of the Warcraft name, which they feel represents quality, but that's a different matter).[12]

In general, games are not the best format in which to get people to like a new IP—something else had to get you to like Battlestar Galactica before you bought the boardgame. Books, movies, and television are all much better, probably because they are better at telling stories, and stories are what make people love IPs.

Licensed games are often not very high-quality,[13] perhaps because goodness is not why people buy those games, so why spend money making them that good? There are of course exceptions—for example, there are several good Star Wars computer games. Perhaps the reason is that the Star Wars license is worth so much money, and costs so much money, that you can afford to spend some cash making the game good as well; perhaps it's because there are enough other Star Wars games out there that you have to compete; or perhaps it's because the Star Wars license is long-lasting enough that you can hope to have your game last longer, so that making it a good game is a better investment.

Sometimes an IP is deliberately designed to fit together with a game. This is fairly common for (nonlicensed) computer games, but less so for paper games. One notable group of exceptions includes a number of Japanese trading card games: *Pokémon*, *Yu-gi-oh*, and *Duelmasters*, for example.[14] These games are also notable in that there is a game inside the IP itself, with the game the player plays being a mirror of the game the characters in the IP play. Done right, the presentation of the IP in various ways—books, comics, TV, various toys, and perhaps multiple games—can become powerfully reinforcing. Oddly enough, the dynamic here is not that different from the dynamic of sports, where a person who likes a sport might play, watch, and follow the "back-story" (personal lives of players, personalities of coaches, and so on), with all of these activities potentially supporting one another.

One tension between many licensed IPs and the games that use them is the so-called Batman problem:[15] if you have a game that uses the Batman IP, who gets to be Batman? Many strong IPs have just one or two main characters, and most have a rela-

12. Also, while not many people may have bought existing Warcraft games for the IP, it's imaginable that significant numbers of people might buy the *next* Warcraft game for the IP, because of the power of *World of Warcraft*. It's possible that MMORPGs (or RPGs generally) do a better job of getting people to fall in love with an IP than other kinds of games.

13. Granted, as Sturgeon's law says, 90 percent of everything is trash. But licensed games seem to do even worse than average.

14. People think of the Pokémon IP as being designed for the original *Pokémon* GameBoy game, but in fact it was designed with both the handheld game and the trading card game in mind.

15. See Damion Schubert's discussion at http://www.zenofdesign.com/2005/07/18/monday-morning-design-question-working-with-licenses/.

tively small number (which is what makes for good stories). Games, however, often call for more characters, and they may need more flexibility with those characters than the story allows. So making such a game involves some tough choices. If, in your Batman game, the user is not allowed to be Batman, it probably will not feel much like a Batman game. You might have Batman appear in cameos throughout the game, but then the player will not feel very important or heroic in comparison. On the other hand, if the player is Batman, you are pretty much locked into a single-player game (unless you want multiple Batmans running around), and if the game has its own storyline, it will be constrained to some degree (both by the licensor and by player expectations). These restrictions can all be fine for a platformer or a single-person FPS, but become very problematic for a paper RPG or an MMO. This is yet another example where a single-player game's requirement to satisfy only one person at a time is a powerful advantage.

Story/Narrative

Story or narrative is often part of a game's conceit, but it does not have to be. Chess, for example, has a conceit but no story. Story in games is a fairly new phenomenon, and almost exclusive to the computer world. Traditional boardgames and card games never have explicit stories, and newer ones very rarely do. Even computer games rarely if ever had stories in the early days (e.g., Space Wars, NetHack). Now almost all computer games have significant story elements, and the exceptions tend to be confined to certain genres, such as rhythm games, simulations (including sports), and puzzle games.

Although many computer games have stories, those games may take the story more or less seriously. At one extreme, *Doom* and *Quake* lead programmer John Carmack has said that "story in a game is like a story in a porn movie; it's expected to be there, but it's not that important."[16] And in *Doom*, this statement is arguably true—but the many fans of the *Final Fantasy* games, well known for their stories, would probably not agree with Carmack's viewpoint. Some players who enjoy games like *Doom* gnash their teeth in frustration at the many cut scenes that games like *Final Fantasy* use to tell their stories, and yet there are players who enjoy both types of games. Even games like *Doom* or *Diablo* that have fairly minimal stories can get good value out of them, in terms of setting player expectations, helping to make mechanics more understandable, and providing some extra motivation for gameplay goals. Such basic stories, however, are a far cry from the ones that the best of the story-rich games create, stories that create truly memorable characters that players care about.

There are a few examples of story in noncomputer games, such as paper role-playing games, choose your own adventure books, and murder mystery games like *How to Host*

16. Kushner, *Masters of Doom*, 128.

a Murder. However, these are exceptions rather than the rule, and they are all fairly modern.

Why are detailed stories so rare in precomputer games? Part of the reason is that a simple conceit can provide much of the help a game needs, in terms of adding interest and flavor to a game and helping the player understand more complex rules. So story is not absolutely necessary. And before the computer, options for presenting story in a game were very limited: mostly pure text, which many players might not want to stop and read during the play of a game. Reading chapters of *Le Morte d'Arthur* between turns of chess, for example, would not make a very satisfactory game experience. Another factor is that story is hard to present in multiplayer games—whatever method is used to present it will require time, and some players will be more inclined to spend that time and others less so, leading to problems with downtime. Since single-player games were less common before the computer era, that may have left less scope for story. Lastly, there is some difficulty in combining story and game generally.

There is a certain tension between some of the elements that make for a good game and those that make for a good story. Playing a game involves choices, and those choices can go in different directions; repeated plays of the game will be different.[17] These different outcomes are all equally valid (or at least many of them are). But with a good story, the outcome will feel in some way inevitable—other alternative outcomes will not represent as good a story. And a good story can be read again and again, even though it is the same every time. If a game plays the same way every time that is usually not a good thing—games rely on uncertainty in outcome in order to work. When a strong story is included in a game, it can sometimes make the game less replayable—a game like *Final Fantasy VII*, with strong story elements, may be less appealing to play again (you know how the story will come out) than a game like *Diablo* that has a weaker story.[18] All that said, the powerful visual and audio presentations possible in a computer game make presenting story very enticing. Many highly successful computer games rely heavily on story, and much academic work examining the role of story in computer games has been done.[19]

17. As Chris Crawford puts it in *The Art of Computer Game Design*, "The difference between [stories and games] is that a story presents the facts in an immutable sequence, while a game presents a branching tree of sequences and allows the player to create his own story by making choices at each branch point" (p. 10). This book is available online at http://pdf.textfiles.com/books/cgd-crawford.pdf.

18. Adventure games, such as *The Longest Journey*, are inherently less replayable due to their puzzle-solving nature. Thus they make a natural home for a strong story, since any lessening of replayability due to story does little harm.

19. The interested reader might wish to look, for example, at some of the essays in Salen and Zimmerman's *The Game Design Reader* as well as at their *Rules of Play*, chap. 26; Wolf and Perron's *The Video Game Theory Reader*; and Crawford's *On Interactive Storytelling*.

Exercise 7.10: How does a game's conceit affect the metagame?

Exercise 7.11: How does a licensed game affect the cost to the player in terms of time and money?

Exercise 7.12: Would you expect single-player or multiplayer games to have stronger conceits/motifs? (*Hint*: Think in terms of rewards.) What types of conceits might be best for multiplayer games?

Exercise 7.13: Name three games with the same basic conceit, but that use it in very different ways.

Exercise 7.14: Name five classic games without a conceit. Name five modern games without one. Which list was harder to come up with? Why?

7.3 Characteristic: Spectation

Two games might be equally fun to play, but one is much more enjoyable to watch than the other. This characteristic of a game—how amenable it is to watching—we call "spectation."[20]

Spectation includes everything from a TV audience for poker, to fans at a baseball game, to people at a bar casually watching a game of darts, to family members at home watching a game of *Monopoly* that they've decided to sit out of. Variables include the size of the audience, the formality of the viewing (e.g., purchased tickets to a sporting event versus watching a game between friends), and the game itself (watching chess is different than watching soccer). Normally people think of sports when they think of people watching a game, but in fact almost any game can be watched.

Sports do, however, generally have very good spectation. The initial demands placed on the viewer in terms of specialized knowledge tend to be fairly low: a five-minute explanation could be enough for someone to watch a soccer game. Imagine watching a chess game after a five-minute explanation. And yet the watcher of a sports game will still gain considerable extra enjoyment by being highly knowledgeable—sports do no worse than nonsports games in this regard. As we will discuss below, sports tend to have relatively few impediments to spectation in other areas as well.

In general, single-player games are not as good for spectation as multiplayer ones. Much of the enjoyment of the spectators comes from watching the human drama of competition. So even if a single-player game is easy to follow—think, say, of card solitaire—it may not be as exciting to watch as a head-to-head battle. Even for single-player games, though, spectation still matters, because it is a big part of how new players are brought into the game. If it is easy to watch someone else play, understand

20. We will also use the word *spectation* to refer to the act of watching a game. Context should make the intended meaning clear.

Figure 7.6

what they are doing, and imagine oneself having fun doing the same, the game is more likely to spread. So even a game that will never become a spectator sport can gain from spectation as a form of marketing. In the digital world, on average, arcade games do best here, followed by console games, with PC games in last place—this rank order is natural enough, given the physical environments (and in particular, the availability of spectators) where each of these game types is found.

If one thinks of games as evolving and competing organisms, in the sense that they change over time and become more or less prevalent, it's clear that good spectation is a big bonus for a game. Players will usually feel better about their choice of game knowing that people want to watch it. An audience may inspire them to want to play better, which in turn may make them spend more time playing and practicing so as to improve their skills. Members of the audience are in some sense participants in the game, and some of them may decide to become players later on.

Spectation After and Before the Game

Spectation does not even have to happen at the same time as the game itself. Watching a game can be interesting even if one knows the outcome. A newspaper article written about a game that happened the previous day is an example of delayed (and filtered) spectation—a friend describing the game to you is another.

Games that have distinct highlights rather than a more or less continuous stream of action tend to do better here, because they are easier to recount in a condensed yet still interesting form.[21] In this sense, football is probably better than soccer, which is still better than basketball, and a marathon is worse than any of them. Another reflection of how easy it is to condense the events of a game can be seen in the amount of information that can usefully be given in something like a box score. Poker as commonly played at home is decent in terms of how well it can be recounted—many roughly similar hands are played, but there are often some big wins and losses to talk about—but tournament poker is even better, because players can be eliminated on single big hands.

Games can be interesting to talk about or watch even before they happen: witness the pregame shows so common in sports. These can vary widely in content, from human-interest stories (the troubled home life of the big star who is about to play) to very detailed analyses of game strategy. Note that this variation is, like so much else that we discuss, both agential (How much does the intended audience know about the sport? What will they be interested in hearing?) and systemic (there is more to say about different plays to execute in football than there is about different ways to run fast in a sprint).

Impediments to Spectation

One way to think about spectation is to consider what factors impede it. Agential impediments tend to revolve around the amount of technical knowledge required to watch the game. Must I be a player to watch effectively? Must I be a good player? Can expert commentary make up for lack of knowledge on my part? Can I even understand the expert commentary if it's provided?[22] How much attention do I have to pay to enjoy the game—can I take breaks?

21. This is a sense in which narrative construction is extremely important for all kinds of games, including ones not thought of as having a narrative. Usually when people discuss narrative in games they mean something much narrower: a story that is contained within the game, such as the plotline of an RPG. As discussed above, there are pros and cons to story in games in this narrower sense, but in the broader sense of being able to talk about what happened in a game, story is an entirely positive feature.

22. Note that camerawork can be thought of as a kind of commentary: a selection for the viewer of some subset of information out of all the possible information available. Anyone who remembers the atrocious camerawork in the early days of televised soccer in the United States will know what a difference it makes. Both commentary and camerawork can help or impede spectation, either because of quality or because of the level of audience knowledge they assume.

The amount of attention one must pay is not entirely systemic—it depends on how the game is presented and on what the viewer knows—but some systemic impediments are important. Obviously the overall complexity of the game is a big factor. It's more work to watch and understand a game of chess than a footrace. Even at the same complexity level, though, the amount of game state information in a single moment is a big factor. Poker is a complex game, but between hands the state information is very simple: How many chips does each player have? Someone who stops watching and then starts again is at no great disadvantage. Chess is a lot worse, but at least all the state information is directly visible, if not easily comprehensible. An RTS is horrendous: a highly complex visible state, plus much state information that may not be visible at all (e.g., unseen areas on the map, or how far into each tech tree a player is).

Most sports tend to have a very simple and easy-to-understand state: there is just one really important thing to know, namely the score.[23] Other things might also be important, like who currently has possession, but they are quickly gleaned from looking at the game by someone whose attention has wandered (or who has just returned from the restroom). Football is somewhat of an exception: one wants to know the current down and the number of yards to go until a first down. It is not a disaster if one loses track, since a viewer can simply wait until the next first down, at which point she again has complete state information. But television spectation in football made a big leap forward with the introduction of the strip at the bottom of the screen listing the down and yards to go (not just the score), and another step forward with the electronic colored line showing the location of the line to gain the next first down. So presentation improvements can make up for systemic difficulties.

Spectation relies on the viewer's understanding not just of positional heuristics but strategic ones as well. What is a good move? What is an amazing one? Sports have an advantage here again due to people's innate understanding of real-life physics. A brilliant move in an RTS may return only blank stares from all but the most hardcore spectator. A Dr. J dunk from the foul line will be seen as amazing by everyone. Similar situations occur with a diving catch or with the thunderous roars and amazing speeds of racecars.

Systemic impediments are often visual. How easy is it to see the game from a distance? Is it easy to use cameras and microphones to good effect? Are the results of player actions clearly visible (computer games often score especially badly here—think of a player using hotkeys to build something in an RTS)? Is there important hidden information in the game?

23. Arguably, two things: score and time remaining. The latter can be at least roughly estimated, though, even by someone who has otherwise lost track of the game state.

> PC games often fare poorly at spectation, with small screen sizes and little use of the spectators' physical intuition. Contrast this state of affairs with sports, where the "screen size" is very large, and much activity is easily understandable due to the spectators' unconscious understanding of physics. The spectation problems of PC games are not necessarily critical given that opportunities to view other people's games in progress are often limited anyway. Coin-op arcade games, however, give better opportunity to view others' games, and enhanced spectation can lead directly to increased revenue due to the ease of impulse purchases. Taken together, all these facts imply a higher value to ease of spectator understanding for arcade games. Perhaps the emerging dominance of fighting games with humanoid characters and motion-capture technology appears more predictable from looking at spectation than from looking at any other gameplay characteristic of the progenitor of these games, namely *Karate Champ*.

Spectation and Hidden Information

Hidden information's impact on spectation is perhaps worth a few more comments. Here we are considering the common case of a game with multiple players, each of whom has access to her own private information. In general, the more information is hidden, the worse the game's spectation—draw poker is less interesting to watch than stud poker. Audience members don't necessarily want to follow the game from the point of view of a single player, but revealing information belonging to multiple players for the benefit of the audience can annoy the players. Both of these facts can be seen in the common occurrence of the bridge kibitzer who stands behind each of the players in turn. However, if the problem can be solved in some reasonable way, such as the hole cam in televised poker, the audience may find the revelation of secrets quite appealing, leading to good spectation.

Computer games often do badly on spectation due to hidden information. The standard setup of each player having his own screen, with information that only he knows, creates an enormous amount of hidden information. Indeed, there may be no public information at all, at least not in a systematic way—just hidden information that both people happen to have at a given moment (such as the progress of a specific battle in an RTS while both players are watching it). However, arcade games or split-screen console games avoid the hidden-information problem, and of course single-player games (whatever other spectation problems they may have, such as lack of drama) avoid it as well.

Improving Spectation

To make a game's spectation better, the most basic thing to do is make the game better in general. Most things (but by no means all, e.g., adding hidden information) that would make the game more enjoyable to play would make it more enjoyable to watch. Special emphasis should be placed on heuristics, especially beginner heuristics (since watchers typically have lower levels of skill than players). Good, and very simple, positional heuristics make it easier for viewers to understand the state the game is in, which is especially important since the viewers are typically paying less attention than the players and may even be absent for a time. Good directional heuristics let viewers say "I would have done that differently!" and thus become more involved in the game.

Removing specific impediments can help. It's important to limit the knowledge burden for the viewer: either systemically, by keeping the basics of the game simple (which goes back to beginner heuristics), or agentially, by presenting the game to viewers with helpful commentary or summary lines of key information. Another important point is visual: making sure that hidden information is revealed where appropriate, that player choices are clearly visible in results within the game, and that important game events visible to the players are made visible to the spectators as well.

In addition to designing games with spectation in mind, a game can be designed specifically for spectation—Roman gladiatorial combat and TV game shows spring to mind—or modified after the fact for better spectation. Sports appear once again as examples in this latter case: modifications like the shot clock in basketball, tiebreakers in soccer and tennis, and the instant replay rules in football are all designed in greater or lesser part to improve spectation. An older and more extreme example of adaptation to spectation comes from Tokugawa Japan: the annual go games played before the shogun were eventually played out entirely in advance, the players sequestered to prevent knowledge of the results from leaking out, and then the games replayed before the shogun, all to prevent the games from lasting too long for the spectators.[24] The shining modern example is the use of instant replay in football. The rule change occurred not mainly because of the increased accuracy of calls, but far more importantly so the game watched more closely equaled the game officiated.

Exercise 7.15: Choose a game and describe its spectation. What could be done to improve it? Would it be worth it, or would it be a net loss for the game as a whole?

Exercise 7.16: Consider computer games. Break them up by genre (or according to some other grouping that seems helpful). Which categories have good spectation? Which don't?

Exercise 7.17: How did lax rules on steroid testing and punishment help the spectation of baseball? How did they hurt it—or did they?

Exercise 7.18: How did the lipstick camera (aka hole cam) help the spectation of poker?

24. See Power, *Invincible: The Games of Shusaku.*

Exercise 7.19: What are the advantages of stoppages of play in football versus soccer for spectators? What are the disadvantages?

Exercise 7.20: Why do so many game shows feature three or fewer contestants?

Exercise 7.21: Discuss some reasons for the number of contestants on *Survivor.*

Exercise 7.22: Why do game shows often have bonus rounds?

7.4 Characteristic: Game Customization

We have mostly been thinking of players as choosing a game that meets their needs, or even adapting themselves to the needs of the game. Often, however, players adapt a game to their own needs, by customizing that game in some way. On the narrow end, this can be the very mild customization of choosing to emphasize one part of the game over another, as when a chess player memorizes only very aggressive openings and always opts for an attacking style of play. On the broad end, sometimes the entire game is built around player customization, as with trading card games or role-

Figure 7.7

playing games. When the scope for customization is very great, the original game may feel more like a family of games than like a single game, with each customization representing a different member of that family.

Sometimes the players are customizing the game as a whole—for example, when a group decides to play *Monopoly* with money going to whoever lands on Free Parking. Sometimes each player customizes his own play—the aforementioned aggressive chess player, or a person making his own character in *World of Warcraft*. In the former case, the customizers are taking on (perhaps unconsciously) the role of game balancers, by choosing a modification that they feel makes for a fun game. In the latter case, though, each customizer is trying to make a choice that will benefit herself in some way (often, though not exclusively, by making her win more often), so game balance gets quite tricky. It is very hard to make a system that allows players to make all kinds of individual choices but still ensures that all possible choices are balanced in the end.[25]

The customization may take place outside the game, in a preparatory period (building a *Magic* deck, deciding on a house rule). Or it may take place during the game (building all air units in *Starcraft*, getting as much +Strength gear as possible in *WoW*).

We'll break game customization into three rough categories:

- *Personal style* Favorite chess openings, or always rushing in *Starcraft*
- *House rules* Playing by some variant set of rules
- *Built-in customization* Where the game allows individual players to choose specific rules or game pieces for themselves, as in *Magic* or *World of Warcraft*

Afterward, we'll also discuss one particular type of rule variant: handicap systems.

Personal Style

Almost any reasonably complex game allows players to develop some kind of personal style. In chess a player might be more or less aggressive; in go a player might choose to emphasize territory or power. In either game a player might choose to memorize some openings rather than others. More explicit choices might be built into the game: an FPS might allow a player to be a medic, sniper, or heavy weapons specialist; an RTS might allow choices of different races, and surely will allow choices of different units.

If a player makes only light use of these kinds of options—perhaps attacking aggressively when he sees an opening, but playing a very positional game otherwise—it may not be clear where personal style ends and simply trying to play well begins. With heavy use—say the player always plays a medic no matter what—it starts to look like the kind of built-in customization an RPG might have.

25. In practice, for highly complex systems, it is essentially impossible. But often, *enough* of the options can be balanced for the game to still work.

House Rules

Another common customization option is for players to play some variant of the game given to them, whether for variety's sake or as a way of fixing perceived flaws. Sometimes the variants are given within the game (as optional rules or alternate scenarios). But sometimes the players simply make them up. The *Monopoly* variant where players get money for landing on Free Parking is perhaps the most famous example—this variant is so common many players don't realize it is not an official rule.

Some games are meant to be modified: informal games such as "playing house" or (fictionally) Calvinball, or more structured games such as *Eleusis*, *Icehouse*, *Fluxx*, or dealer's choice poker.

If the variants are different enough, the new "homebrew" is essentially a new game built from the parts of the old game. Paper RPGs tend to attract this kind of attention. More recently, computer games are often built with an open architecture allowing fans to build all kinds of mods, from minor tweaks to so-called total conversions. These mods may look somewhat like the original game, or they may look wildly

Figure 7.8

Calvinball. CALVIN AND HOBBES (c) 1990 Watterson. Dist. by UNIVERSAL UCLICK. Reprinted with permission. All rights reserved.

different: a new *Quake* level might be quite similar to other levels, *Counterstrike* is fairly different from *Half-Life,* and *Defense of the Ancients* is wildly different from *Warcraft III.*

Some game structures are so much of a whole that it is difficult to modify them. For example, it is hard to see how to change a game like go without just having a completely different game. Chess, on the other hand, has a basic structure (move your pieces to checkmate the opposing king) plus many pieces with different characteristics, lending itself to countless modifications: just create new pieces!

Built-in Customization

Some games have built in the opportunity for players to customize their own individual experiences. This can be thought of as a form of personal style, but much more than that. Allowing players to customize at this level can lead to a very strong attachment to "my character" or "my deck," but at the price of greater complexity and more difficulty in game balance.

Basic customization would include a choice of character type in an FPS, a race in an RTS, or the different player abilities in *Cosmic Encounter.* More serious customization tends to be found in RPGs (paper or online), trading card games, and miniatures games. However, the concept has been experimented with in many other genres—for example, in the RTS *Impossible Creatures* players bring to each game their own army design, created in advance of the game much like a *Magic* deck.

Games with heavy player customization are much harder to design and balance. As mentioned before, letting every player have some of the power of the game designer, but with personal goals rather than game-level goals, puts enormous pressures on balance. Also, players are likely to expect a stream of new content, to keep the game fresh, in a way they would not with a less customizable game such as a standard boardgame.

The player skills involved in customizing a game are often quite different from the ones involved in playing the game, and players may choose to specialize: some players may become quite good at building decks or characters, and others might choose to simply use those builds rather than make their own. Occasionally this state of affairs can become discouraging for players who would like to make their own custom game experience, but are intimidated by all the expert templates running around. To help protect such players a bit, it is often a good idea to balance choices based on templates people will want to play (for flavor reasons, say) so that they are within striking distance of choices built purely for power.

Games that allow a lot of player customization also tend to have a lot of scope for personal style and house rules—*D&D* and *Magic* both have lots of game variants and different play styles. Even when the technology does not seem to allow house rules, as with an MMO that does not allow modding (player modifications to a game), house rules nevertheless may crop up: that, after all, is what guild rules (such as DKP[26]) are.

These types of games have structures that allow a rich metagame experience to develop around the player desire for creativity and personal expression. It is easy to be aggressive in a game that gives you explicit choices to do so as a standard variant in your play. The rewards of self-expression present in-game tend to be magnified in the metagame. Players can buy and paint miniatures representing their characters, post blogs about their RPG adventures, or publish their favorite TCG decks to fan websites.

Handicaps

Handicaps are a kind of rule variant, but one deserving of separate discussion. They may be made up by players on the spot, or there may be an official handicap system as part of the formal rules of the game or metagame. The goal is almost always to take an uneven player matchup and make it more even, so that the outcome is not a foregone conclusion. Examples include golf and go.

Since the purpose of the handicap is to give both players a chance to win, games with a lot of luck don't need a handicap system as much. Handicaps are usually found in low-luck games.

Even if a game could use a handicap system, it is not always easy to give it one. If the game has some uniform resource, you can give a player more or less of it without altering the game too much: hence go (stones), golf (points), and horse racing (weight) all handicap fairly well. Chess, on the other hand, does not: taking a piece away from someone really changes the character of the game. But speed chess is fine: just give the two players different amounts of time.

With computer games for two or more players, it is often not that hard to put in some sort of handicap system, perhaps a tax of some kind on the stronger player, or making all the weaker player's units 10 percent stronger. Such systems are not all that widely used, though. Perhaps that is because most handicap systems need more than a mechanism for altering player strength in-game: they also need a rating system and a correlation between rating and handicap (indeed players often rate themselves by the handicap they need—again look at golf or go). When two players meet, if they can instantly understand what handicap would give an even game, they are much more likely to use the handicap. Such systems do not generally exist with computer games, and worse yet, many games are one-shot affairs with no follow-up, so there is

26. DKPs, or "dragon kill points," are MMO guild point systems to determine which guild members gain valuable in-game items based on the previous participation records of those members (how many "dragons they've killed"). DKP systems vary widely and are created and managed by each guild rather than built into the MMOs themselves.

no chance to institute a handicap in a second game (let alone adjust it in a third). Besides, the larger pool of people online means it is easier to look for someone else to play rather than tweaking a handicap with a given opponent.

Computer games for one player, though, do typically come with a handicap system, namely difficulty adjustment. Here the player usually chooses for herself what the right handicap is, making a more systematic structure involving exact ratings less necessary. Dynamic difficulty adjustment is also an option in computer games. This may turn out to be fine if the player never realizes what's going on, but has the potential to lessen the sense of achievement one might feel if it is revealed.

Exercise 7.23: What are some advantages and disadvantages of easily customizable games in terms of strategic collapse?

Exercise 7.24: What are some advantages and disadvantages of easily customizable games in terms of reward/effort ratio?

Exercise 7.25: What are some of the advantages of personally (as opposed to group) customizable games as far as the game's rewards are concerned? What are some of the disadvantages?

Exercise 7.26: What are the customizable aspects of NFL football?

7.5 Characteristic: Misbehavior

Game players engage in a wide variety of behaviors that may be viewed negatively by other players. We divide those behaviors into three broad categories: cheating, sharp play, and griefing.

Cheating

Games have rules, and rules restrict players. It is easier to win without those restrictions, so sometimes players cheat: they disobey the rules. One might think there is not that much more to say about cheating, but it turns out cheating is a surprisingly rich metagame area. How hard it is to cheat, how effective cheating is, and what costs (both in-game and out-of-game, both formal penalties and informal ones) are associated with cheating all vary widely. Perhaps surprisingly, even the acceptability of cheating varies widely, to the point where certain violations of the rules are not even considered cheating.

Cheating is hardest in turn-based games with no hidden information. As long as your opponent is paying attention, it is hard even to imagine how you could violate the rules of chess unnoticed. If the game contains random elements or hidden information, cheating becomes more practical because it is less detectable, although it is not always easy—manipulating dice or cards often requires some skill. If the game

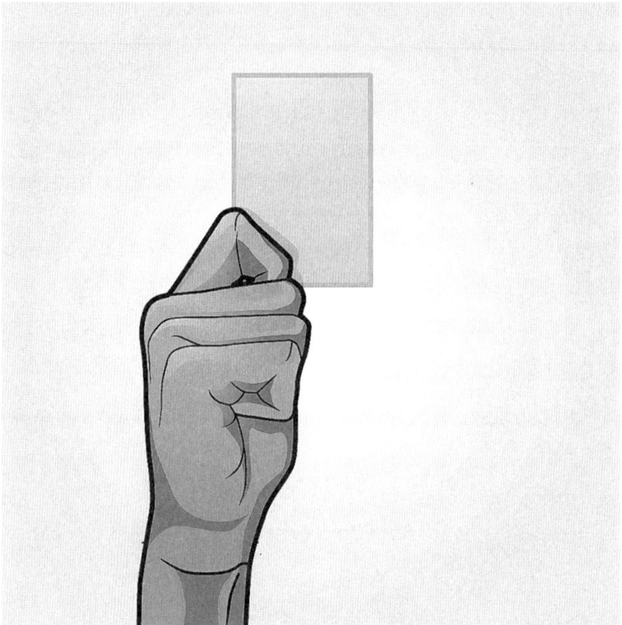

Figure 7.9

takes place in real time, that often helps enable cheating as well, since the pace of the game gives less chance for opponents to detect it.

In informal games, penalties for cheating are usually not precisely defined. They range widely, though, from eye rolling and a demand that the game revert to its pre-cheat state, to outrage and loss of friendship (or even risk of physical harm, if money is on the line). In more formal situations such as tournaments and refereed games, there are usually very explicit penalties for various violations of the rules. When the game has more at stake, the penalties for cheating tend to go up, and all the more so if money is involved.[27]

Usually violations of the rules are met with social disapproval on the part of most of the player community. Sometimes, however, they are not, and occasionally the violations are so widely accepted that they are not considered "cheating" at all. For example, being offsides in football is against the rules, but not many people would call it cheating. Factors that push a violation into the "not cheating" category include: the violation is relatively easy to catch, there are referees available to penalize it, an

27. See Friedman's *Law's Order* (especially chap. 15) for an interesting discussion about some of the relationships between the severity of penalties, the chance of getting caught, and any costs or benefits to committing the offense.

appropriately severe penalty is applied, the violation is not a deliberate attempt to injure someone, and the violation is possible to commit by accident. All of these factors mean that people's sense of fairness is less likely to be upset, and the rule violation may be seen more as a reasonable strategic choice or an unfortunate accident rather than cheating. Another example of a violation that might not be considered cheating is using your hands on the ball in soccer (when you are not the goalie) in a desperate attempt to stop the other team from scoring. Taking steroids, on the other hand, is more widely viewed as cheating. Although it does have severe and established penalties, it is hard to detect, it involves injury (although mainly to the perpetrator), and it is hard to do by accident.

Note that small and moderate rule violations tend to be punished in-game (foul shots, sitting out for two minutes). More severe violations involve penalties that go beyond one game (being banned for several games, or even for several years). Violations with more severe penalties are more likely to be viewed as "cheating," although it is arguable which way the causation runs.

One normally thinks that the less cheating possible in a game, the better, and in general this is surely true. Certainly large amounts of cheating are unsustainable: noncheating players don't want to be at a constant disadvantage, so they will leave the game, and the cheaters are looking for an advantage over the majority, so they will ultimately be dissatisfied as well. However, some of the most exciting metagames have a moderate amount of cheating, at least of the "perceived as okay" rule violations discussed above. Much excitement in sports comes from the tension and drama (often involving heroes and villains) of rule violations and the resultant penalties. Pro wrestling (which might be thought of as spectation for a game with no actual game underlying it) has elevated this to an art form. Note that having this tension correct in a metagame all but requires refereeing of some kind, so that the cheaters (or rule violators, if one prefers not to think of it as "cheating") can be caught and punished, at least a fair amount of the time.

With computer games, cheating takes on different forms. Since generally speaking the computer is the referee, cheating is often impossible for an average player, but for a player sophisticated enough to modify the game code,[28] cheating can take place that may be difficult to detect. Sometimes so-called cheats are built into the game code for single-player games, but given that these are part of the shipped game, using them is probably closer to using an alternate game mode or alternate difficulty setting rather than actual cheating. For online games, the owner of the game code can serve as a kind of referee, but often cheating becomes ill-defined—in addition to modifying the

28. Or any player, if they download a modification someone else has written. But in either case, serious preparation is required.

game code, any behavior the game owner dislikes (see the discussion of exploits in the section on "Sharp Play" below) might be labeled cheating.

A few more examples:

• *Card games (bridge, say)* Simple forms of cheating, such as not following suit, are easily detectable by good players. More sophisticated cheating, such as altering shuffles and deals, or illegal signals during bidding, can be hard to detect but is also hard to do.
• *Battleship* Cheating is very easy in *Battleship*, and all but impossible to detect if done carefully. With such temptation, people who might not otherwise cheat will do so, and the game can break down as a workable enterprise.
• *Baseball* Baseball has a rich history of cheating: steroids, corked bats, pine tar, spitballs, and of course the Black Sox.
• *Starcraft* The cheat of choice is the "map hack" (an add-on program that reveals the parts of the map normally hidden by fog of war), which shows the dangers of trusting the game client. Because the client knows the full game state, there is no way to be certain the player is not using that knowledge to reveal hidden information.

This last example, of the map hack in *Starcraft*, brings up an interesting point: the perception of cheating may be more damaging than the cheating itself. It is possible for cheating to be relatively rare, but perceived as much more widespread. A good *Starcraft* player, with a strong intuition for what his opponent is likely to do and where (or simply with a strong tendency to build observers[29]), will often be accused of map hacking even if he is completely honest. Both accuser and accused are likely to feel their game experience has been tainted, and too much of this sort of thing and many players will quit. This is why it is so important to stamp out cheating in multiplayer online games: not so much because of its direct effects, but because of the discouragement it causes among honest players, who feel either that they are falling behind or that they must work harder than the cheaters to achieve the same results.

Sharp Play

Sometimes certain in-game practices are acknowledged as being within the rules, but still somehow "disreputable"—as taking advantage somehow. In older books about games, these practices were often described as "sharp." A classic example from poker is sandbagging—that is, opening with a check when you have a strong hand. Nothing in the rules forbids it, and many players now would consider it simply a possible way to play with no moral connotations at all, but in the past many people considered it slightly shady.

29. One player of the authors' acquaintance referred to observers as the "broken unit" because he felt the ability to secretly see his opponent's activities was so powerful and game-changing. He was very frequently accused of map hacking.

Other examples of play that some playgroups will find disreputable:

- Rule lawyering: using the rules of complex games to one's advantage, perhaps by bringing up certain little-known rules only when it helps one's position.
- Rushing in an RTS: some casual RTS players feel rushing (attacking very early in the game) is unfair, or not fun, and expect it not to occur in "casual" games (typically meaning the game they are playing in). Sometimes this policy will be announced with a statement like "20 minute no rush," but sometimes it will merely be assumed, leading to bad feelings if other players don't share the assumption.
- Playing an especially powerful strategy in a casual environment: more generally, playing very aggressively or using very powerful gameplay techniques can be seen as unsportsmanlike. A typical example is bringing a tournament-quality *Magic* deck to a more casual play environment, but even just being a much better player (say at one-on-one basketball), or bringing a "ringer" to a team game, can evoke a similar reaction.
- Simply trying too hard to win
- Counting cards in blackjack[30]
- Some political behaviors, especially kingmaking

As mentioned above, in sports with explicit penalties for certain rule violations, violating those rules (and paying the penalty) is often not perceived as "cheating." However, doing so deliberately (because the benefit gained in some particular instance is perceived by the violator as being greater than the penalty) is often seen as sharp play, especially in casual games.

Computer games, where essentially the game code is the rules (i.e., the things the code lets you do are ipso facto what you are allowed to do), have the concept of "exploits": things you are capable of doing within the game, but that you are "not supposed to do." MMOs are especially prone to this problem. Sometimes it is quite clear that a certain game action is leading to results the programmers did not intend (clicking five particular buttons in a particular order to make a million gold pieces land in your lap), but sometimes it is not clear at all (finding a path that avoids several dangerous monsters but still reaches some valuable loot). Since players are always trying to find clever ways to do better at the game, it is a real burden on them if some of these ways—and how can they know which ones?—are deemed "too clever." Removing the possibility of the behavior in a patch is one thing, but branding the players as cheaters and punishing them is quite another. After all, one person's exploit is another person's clever play.

30. Sometimes card counting is officially against the rules, but it is certainly awkward to have a rule against a player strategy. The situation is quite similar to the concept of "exploits" discussed below. For one account of this interplay between casino and gambler, see Kushner's *Jonny Magic and the Cardshark Kids*.

So what counts as sharp play is highly agential. Some playgroups (typically more serious or "hardcore" ones) will accept a given practice; other groups (typically more casual ones) will feel the practice is unfair or inappropriate and will disapprove of it. An interesting example that highlights this difference is the practice of taking back moves. In very serious groups, it is usually considered cheating (although it may not be mentioned specifically in the written rules), in fairly serious groups it might be allowed occasionally but frowned on, and in very casual groups *not* allowing your opponent to take back a move might be considered "sharp": technically a player may forbid her opponent to take back his move, but doing so is the mark of an unpleasant player, one who is "too serious."

If sharp play is seen as "taking advantage," what is it taking advantage of? One view might be that it is taking advantage of holes in the rules, weaknesses that prevent the specific and exact written rules from fully reflecting the "spirit of the game." Since the spirit of the game will seem different to different players, what violates it and what does not will seem different as well. Looked at this way, it is further evidence that "the rules are not the game." And it brings out again the parallel to law brought up by the phrase "rule lawyering": a common objection to law is that laws are supposed to represent just outcomes, but too often an outcome is in accordance with the law but still unjust. Similarly, players may see certain behaviors as in accordance with a game's rules but against that game's spirit. Since it is impossible to get complete agreement on what a game's spirit (or societal justice) is—insofar as it is possible, those agreements tend to be encoded in the rules (or laws) already—some disagreement is inevitable.

Griefing

Sometimes players engage in gameplay behavior that does not benefit their own position in the game, but instead merely makes another player miserable. In online games, especially when done out of pure vindictiveness, such behavior is referred to as "griefing."[31] Although meanness has always existed, in games as in life generally, the anonymity of online gaming has made griefing much more common (and, in particular, common enough to receive a name).

In a way, griefing can be thought of as kingmaking's evil twin: it is political in the sense that it is gameplay behavior not intended to help the perpetrator win. It's done to make someone else lose rather than to make someone else win.

Common forms of griefing include repeated dominance of a weaker player (a lower-level player in an MMO, or a much weaker player in a high school football game) and refusal to concede (see the discussion of "hide the farm" in section 2.1 on player elimination).

31. One of the authors claims the definitive book on the psychology of Internet gamers was presciently written by Joseph Conrad over 100 years ago—*Heart of Darkness*.

Note that griefing, although an in-game problem, often requires metagame solutions. It is hard to prevent griefing purely from in-game mechanics, because there are just too many things a creative player can do to annoy others. In offline games, griefing is typically controlled by other players refusing to play with the griefer, or applying out-of-game repercussions, from social shunning to even (in extreme cases) physical violence. Current online systems make it hard to avoid griefers or to shun them in out-of-game contexts, but examples like eBay's reputation system or Facebook's friend networks show that it is possible in principle. Even in practice, griefing can be controlled where the same group of people play together regularly. For example, MMO guilds effectively limit griefing within the guild itself—someone who frequently griefed his guildmates would simply be ejected from the guild. It is imaginable that a more general reputation system, properly fed into online player matchmaking, could help control griefing further. As players start to have more consistent online identities, and thus reputations to protect, perhaps online griefing may become not that much more common than offline griefing.

Restrictions on Misbehavior

It is easy for game designers to get upset about misbehavior: they have a vision of how they think the game should be played, and player behavior can disrupt that vision.

The important question, though, is whether the behavior is actually making the game less enjoyable for most players. In that sense, adjusting a game to stop misbehavior is like fixing game balance: the important point is not whether some element in the game is working differently than how it was foreseen (some amount of that is inevitable in any complex game), but whether the element is creating a bad experience. Moral outrage is unlikely to be useful—in the case of sharp play, it may be misplaced, and in the case of griefing or cheating, the perpetrators are unlikely to pay attention.

If the game system allows too much bad behavior, the fault is with the game design and not with the players. Part of game design is understanding what incentives the game system presents to players, and understanding how the players are likely to react to those incentives. Players will try to push the game system as much as they can to win (whatever "winning" means to them), which is only to be expected, and demanding that players "play the game as intended" is unlikely to yield good results.

So the approach most likely to be effective is to adjust the game's incentives—ideally before the game is released, but sometimes afterward. Proper rule enforcement, perhaps done automatically (for an electronic game) or by judges (for a paper game or sports), is key so that players who want to follow the rules don't feel driven out by the success of those who do not. In MMOs, restricting PvP by zones, consent flags, and no-PvP servers are all examples of systems that restrict play automatically. Deck registration rules in *Magic* tournaments or rules about touching a piece in chess require human enforcement, but similarly serve to limit behavior that most players would rather not see become widespread.

In small groups of people that play together regularly, behavior rules can be made up on the spot and enforced by social pressure. With larger and more anonymous communities, such as online games, sports leagues, or boardgame tournaments, the temptations to misbehave and the lack of social enforcement mean formal structures are needed—hence the existence of special rules for tournaments and leagues that are not part of the rules of the game itself. Some of these rules are needed strictly for the running of the tournament (e.g., rules about how players are paired), but some are extensions of the game rules (e.g., explicit penalties for various violations of the game rules) needed because of the misbehavior-prone anonymous environment.

Exercise 7.27: What are some examples of griefing in nononline games? Why is it more prevalent in online games?

Exercise 7.28: What are some advantages to the metagame (especially spectation) of the existence of cheating in sports? What are some of the disadvantages?

Exercise 7.29: Name some games you (or your friends) have cheated at, and how.

Exercise 7.30: Give some examples of games that are hard to cheat at in face-to-face play, but easy to cheat at online.

Exercise 7.31: Give some examples from sports of "sharp play" (legal behaviors that are nevertheless often viewed negatively). Is it easier to think of examples from casual play or from professional play? Why?

7.6 Characteristic: Play Lifetime

Some games are bought, played for a few hours, and then set aside and never revisited. Others are played for months, years, or even a player's entire life. A great many factors go into the lifetime of play a game can have—every characteristic we've discussed can affect it. Perhaps a player set the game aside because he felt it had unsatisfying heuristics; perhaps the rewards were not worth the effort. Another player might have kept playing for years because she enjoyed the amount (large or small) of randomness in the game, or because she found the metagame compelling.

For digital games, being technologically up to date can make the difference. *Asteroids* is not as popular now as it was when it was cutting-edge arcade technology. Many older digital games have all but vanished today. Some of the best ones, though, survive, whether on emulators, on carefully preserved old hardware, as ports to new platforms (the web games and handhelds of today often make good platforms for the

Figure 7.10

console games of yesteryear), or in new versions (sometimes these sequels capture the magic of the original and sometimes they don't).

Beyond these issues of overall game quality and (for digital games) of technology, there is the question of the game's content—how easy is it to exhaust the possibilities the game has to offer? Can the player eventually explore everything interesting in the game, or is there always something new to discover? Tic-tac-toe and chess are in some ways similar games structurally—two-player turn-based games with no overt luck—but one has at most an hour or two's worth of play for an adult, and the other has more than a lifetime's. *Myst* may be very enjoyable the first time through, but once a player reaches the end, she may not want to play again, since she now knows how to solve all the puzzles. A *Final Fantasy* game offers more than *Myst* on a second playthrough, but enough of the pleasure is in the story that many people might decide not to play again. A game like *Starcraft*, though, can be played again and again, and indeed it has continued to be played long past its expected technological lifespan.

A long play lifetime is perhaps better thought of as a goal that a game may or may not have, rather than as a "defect" of the games that lack it. Play lifetime varies based on the type of game. Classic games and sports tend to have long lifetimes, arguably because ones that do not are unlikely to reach classic status. Classic games with short play lifetimes are often meant for children, for example tic-tac-toe and war, but there are exceptions such as sliding-block puzzles and the like.[32] Online subscription games and digital object sales games need long play lifetimes to support their business models. Digital games that rely on boxed sales do not—if a player buys the game, plays it through, feels it was a good value, and never plays again, the game can still be successful. However, a game that people can keep playing is often perceived as a good value, and a boxed-sale game can succeed by giving long-term play value. For example, *Diablo II* is a boxed-sale game but has an enormous amount of repeat play value: new character classes to play; nightmare, hell, and hardcore difficulty modes; an enormous item-chasing subgame; and online play. It has sold well for ten years after its launch, despite being technologically far behind more current games.

Game Content, Exhaustible and Otherwise

Why does someone quit playing a game? If you ask them, they will often say it's because something else intervened: perhaps another game that came out, or perhaps some real-life event. But there are always interruptions of one kind or another, so it is worth looking at the game in question to see if there is anything that made it easier to put down, or less likely to be picked up again afterward. In multiplayer games by far the most common answer is "because my friends stopped playing it" or "I can't find anyone to play with anymore." This is of course a second-order effect—somebody had to stop playing it first.

There are two basic reasons to stop playing a game: you're bored with it, or you've finished it. In the first case, there may be a weakness (or just a bad fit with your tastes) in one or more characteristics—unsatisfying heuristics, or reaching a very flat part of the reward-for-effort curve, for example. In the second case, the game must be of the sort that can be "finished." Such games are especially common in the digital arena, and are rare among sports or classic boardgames and card games: one doesn't say of soccer or chess that "I've finished the game"!

A game has two basic strategies to hold a player's interest. It can provide content for the player to consume, content that, after being experienced by the player, may not have further appeal—*exhaustible content*. Or it can attempt to provide *intrinsic variability*: play patterns that differ from play session to play session without a game designer having to create new material. Most often, intrinsic variability comes from other players (for digital games, possibly including AI opponents): soccer and chess

32. However, if one thinks of the sliding-block puzzle genre as a game type, like crossword puzzles, and the individual puzzles as new "layouts" within that game type, like a card solitaire layout or a specific crossword puzzle, then sliding-block puzzles as a whole are far from exhaustible.

remain interesting in large part due to the constant and yet ever-changing pressures that opponents bring to the game.

Although exhaustible content is more common now than it used to be, it is by no means a new phenomenon. A crossword puzzle[33] is exhaustible content: having done it once, a person is unlikely to want to do it again. As with any game built on exhaustible content, to keep a person interested in crosswords, puzzle creators must keep making new puzzles.

If a game relies on content, there are a number of ways to extend that content's reach. Sometimes content can be created randomly: the random layouts of card solitaire, the random minefields of *Minesweeper,* and the random dungeons of NetHack and *Diablo* are examples. Other times the content can be reused by means of various game modes. A single-player RPG with multiple character classes gives one way to reuse game content; multiple difficulty levels are another. If the game allows extensive customization, players may replay it several times, customizing it differently each time. While all these things take some effort to create, they can be very efficient ways of extending content, because they serve as content multipliers rather than merely adding to the existing content.

One game feature that pushes against replay is having an explicit ending. Some games, like *Tetris,* most arcade games, or chess, don't have an explicit end. Puzzle games do: they end when you've solved the puzzle. Computer role-playing games usually do: single-player ones have an ending point when you finish the story, and massively multiplayer ones have a level cap. Often RPGs have ways to keep playing past the end: replay using a new character class, replay to find hidden areas or complete some in-game collection, replay on a higher difficulty, or continue playing an MMO through PvP or raiding (and the equipment-collection game associated with them).[34] Even if there are options for continued play, though, many players will take the "end" as a natural time to stop.

In general, it is the games with an explicit end that are built on exhaustible content, and the games without an explicit end that are built on intrinsic variety. (For a counterexample, think of a paper role-playing game, where there may be no specific end, and the game carries forward based on the gamemaster creating a continued stream of content.)

33. Note that here the "What is a game?" question rears its head again. People don't normally call crossword puzzles "games" or say that you "play a crossword." But the issues surrounding crossword puzzles and exhaustion of content aren't really all that different from, say, those surrounding *Myst.* And as stated in the introduction, we see no benefit in saying that either crossword puzzles or *Myst* (or both, or neither) is "not really a game."

34. The very concept of "replayability" subtly assumes an ending. One does not "replay" soccer or chess; one simply plays them. To "replay" a game typically means it had an end the first time one played it.

How Goals Drive Play Forward

Games, and their associated metagames, have goals that give players reasons to keep playing. Nowadays these goals are often formalized in explicit achievement systems, such as those found in Xbox Live Arcade or in *World of Warcraft*—or in the certificates, ribbons, and trophies found in children's sports. However, games have always had goals, the most basic one being simply to win a given game. Achieving a certain level of skill—being able to run a marathon in under four hours, or mastering the Caro-Kann opening in chess—is another common goal that players set for themselves. Defeating a particular opponent, say beating grandpa at checkers, is another.

Goals in a game may be primarily linear: defeat a succession of harder and harder opponents, beat the game on an increasing series of difficulty levels, or complete a series of story quests in order. They may also be nonlinear (i.e., independent of one another): win a battle using only marines, complete a task without resorting to combat, or find the hidden flower.

Goals are very appealing (indeed, every game has them in some form) as game elements because they keep players interested until the goal is reached. But goals, especially powerful overarching ones like "finish the storyline" or "reach the level cap," also provide stopping points for players. Chess doesn't have a big overarching goal, so it doesn't get the benefits that such a goal can provide. On the other hand, it doesn't have a point where a player thinks "now I'm done" either.

Goals have evolved a great deal in computer games. Originally, there may have been no goal other than finishing the game, if it was the type that could be finished, or perhaps a high-score list was provided—especially common for arcade games, where "finishing" was undesirable for business reasons. Nowadays, there are explicit achievement systems, campaign frameworks (e.g., a global battle map framing a game centered on small tactical battles), and RPG frameworks (e.g., world exploration, leveling up, and collecting equipment for a game centered on snowboard racing). There are still high-score lists, or leaderboards, but often there are many of them for many different categories. As mentioned above, if there is a single overarching goal, such as completing a story or reaching a level cap, there are often postcompletion goals such as PvP. All these things provide additional goals for players. One danger, however, is that as online play (or offline play with online performance comparisons) becomes more common, many of these goals, if they involve comparison with other players, seem unachievable to the vast majority of players. It's one thing to get the high score on *Pac-Man* at the local arcade, where you're competing against dozens or hundreds of local players; it's much, much, harder even to make the top ten on a leaderboard that shows everyone on the Internet. Comparison against smaller pools (everyone in your guild, everyone on your server, everyone in your friends network) can make achieving these goals seem possible again.

Goal Chunking

Players' progress is often tracked by very fine scales: ratings (e.g., the Elo system) and scores (computer game scores, golf scores, race times, etc.). Such tracking is very good for comparing player performance, whether it be comparing one player with another, or comparing a single player's performance today with her performance last week. These comparisons are especially useful for races—it is often how you tell who has won—and for single-player games, where it supports a multiplayer metagame based on score comparison.

On the minus side, though, it is often hard for players to care about fine distinctions in points. So it can be useful to "chunk" fine scales into coarser ones. For example, *Dance Dance Revolution* gives players not only a point score, but also a letter grade. Many players do not care about their exact point score but do care if they have managed to get an A or a B on a particular song. When games do not do this explicitly, players will often do it for themselves by setting cutoff points: perhaps they will strive to get over one billion points in a certain pinball game, or to run a marathon in under four hours. In direct head-to-head games, chunking is less relevant (or if you like it comes built in): beating the other player is a clear and satisfying goal. Even in chess, though, when you consider the single-player metagame of improving your rating, there are chunks: one can be a master, an international master, or a grandmaster.

While chunking goals can make them more compelling, completion of such chunks does give a game "stopping points." Having chunked goals in a game may simply result in players playing until bored, and then continuing to play until the next chunk is finished, only quitting after that. Still, some kind of grouping of fine-scaled goals is probably a net benefit, especially for a single-player game.

Play Lifetime and Number of Players

Very often (although there are many exceptions) single-player games tend to be content-oriented games, and have the issues surrounding completable goals, explicit endings, exhaustion of content, and so on. In other words, single-player games are most prone to being "finished." Multiplayer games are more likely to be based on intrinsic variability, in large part through the medium of the other players.

Thus formal goal systems (achievements, collections to complete, different game modes, and the like) are especially useful in single-player games. Players need goals, and without other players to provide them, it's up to the game itself to do so.

In a game with two or more players, the other players provide the goal: win against them. This goal always renews itself, and if a player's skills increase and he wants a more difficult challenge, the goal comes naturally in more difficult versions: win against more difficult opponents.

With single-player games, simply winning may not be the best goal for long-term play. That's because (even without issues of content exhaustion) once a player has won once, future victories may be too easy. After a few wins, a player needs new goals, such as winning on Very Hard, getting the "Blasted Lands" achievement, or collecting every Pokémon in the game. Typically the game designer needs to add these goals directly, unlike games for two or more players, where to a great extent the opponent does the work.

One can see enormous evolution here. For example, look at arcade games. Thirty years ago, a typical Asteroids player's goal might be simply to get the highest score he could. Today, a *Dance Dance Revolution* player has not only score, but chunked goals (the letter grades) and subgoals (each song is a goal in and of itself), all of which come in various player-selected difficulty levels. Players will continue to set goals for themselves, or choose them based on the competitive and social influences of other players, but they now have a lot more material to work with.

Exercise 7.32: What's the game you have played for the longest period of time? What features gave it that longevity?

Exercise 7.33: What's a game you enjoyed very much but only played briefly? Why didn't you play it longer?

Exercise 7.34: Think of a game you play that has a great many different in-game goals. How many of them do you pursue? What value to the game, if any, do the other goals have?

Exercise 7.35: Name a game whose "standard" way of evaluating performance is very fine-grained. What are some ways players of that game chunk this fine-grained measurement into pieces that they care about?

8 Appendixes

A. Von Neumann Game Theory

I. Brief Overview

Two different subjects go under the name of "game theory." One is the theory due to John von Neumann and John Nash, which at its core focuses on simple abstract games like rock-paper-scissors, where two people make a single move simultaneously. The other, combinatorial game theory, is more recent and deals with games like chess where two players take turns until one player loses. This appendix covers the former and appendix B covers the latter. Our tone is fairly informal—each of these theories is a big subject in its own right, and we can't do much more than give a taste. References are provided at the end of these two appendixes for those who want to learn more.

The first, and better known, theory is almost always called simply "game theory," but one might call it "von Neumann game theory" if one needed to distinguish it. The theory is largely due to John von Neumann and John Nash and dates back to the 1940s. Economists like to use this kind of game theory for economic modeling, so much of the current work comes from them and other more application-oriented types, such as policy analysts and biologists.

The typical game that this theory is good for is a two-player game where each player moves simultaneously just once, and then the moves are compared and each player gets a payoff. This whole setup is usually encoded with a "payoff matrix" (examples follow shortly). Rock-paper-scissors is a classic example, but most of the games in Von Neumann game theory are made-up examples constructed to illustrate the core of some more complex situation. Such games are more objects to analyze than games one would play for fun.

The big idea is to look for "equilibrium points": strategies that are, in some sense, the ones that players "should" play if they are trying to avoid losing (which, oddly enough, turns out to be not quite the same as trying to win). The big result of the theory is a theorem saying that these equilibrium points, suitably understood, always exist.

II. The Basic Setup

The simplest way to present a von Neumann–style game is to write the game in grid form, with Player 1's strategies along the left and Player 2's along the top. Each box in the grid shows the payoff in the form *x*, *y*, where *x* is Player 1's payoff and *y* is Player 2's payoff.

Example 1: *Rock-Paper-Scissors*

Player 2 / Player 1	Rock	Paper	Scissors
Rock	0, 0	–1, 1	1, –1
Paper	1, –1	0, 0	–1, 1
Scissors	–1, 1	1, –1	0, 0

Here if Player 1 plays rock, and Player 2 pays paper, the payoff of –1, 1 means Player 1 loses $1 (or a victory point, or whatever you imagine the players are playing for) and Player 2 wins $1.

In general, one makes some assumptions about any game one analyzes:

1. Each player is trying to maximize his or her own payoff (they don't care either way about the other player's payoff[1]).
2. Each player is smart and knows that the other player is as well (each will play the best strategy she can, and will expect the same from the opposing player).

As an aside, rock-paper-scissors is *zero-sum* (what one player gains, the other loses) and *symmetric* (each player has the same options as the other). These two properties can be important for some results in the overall theory, but won't concern us in our brief overview.

1. Not caring about the opponent's payoff seems like a big restriction. But it fact it's more of a convenience than an actual restriction. For example, if we say the players are trying to maximize their payoff minus half of their opponent's (each player wants to get ahead, and cares a little about keeping the other player down as well), we can just tweak the payoff numbers to reflect that. So, for this example, a payoff of 6, 2 would become a payoff of 5, –1. The new game that results is exactly the same as the original game, but now each player cares only about his or her own payoffs—the amount that they cared about the other player's payoffs has been encoded in their own.

Rock-paper-scissors relationships come up frequently in games of all sorts. For example, in *Warcraft III* melee units beat ranged units, ranged units beat air units, and air units beat melee units.

Example 1′: *Rock-Paper-Scissors, Warcraft III style*

Player 2 / Player 1	Melee	Air	Ranged
Melee	0, 0	–1, 1	1, –1
Air	1, –1	0, 0	–1, 1
Ranged	–1, 1	1, –1	0, 0

Example 2: Matching Pennies

Player 2 / Player 1	Heads	Tails
Heads	1, –1	–1, 1
Tails	–1, 1	1, –1

This game is a simple alternative to flipping a coin or playing rock-paper-scissors if you want to see who is going to pick up the bar tab. One player (in this case Player 1) is hoping to match, and the other is hoping not to match. Each player secretly chooses heads or tails with a penny, and both players simultaneously reveal their choices. If the choices match, Player 1 wins; if they don't, Player 2 wins.

Note that matching pennies (along with rock-paper-scissors) is one of the few game-theory style games that people actually play in a more or less "pure" form in real life.

In real-life games—think for example of an RTS or a console fighting game—the abstract subgames[2] contained within them tend to be referred to as "rock-paper-scissors." In fact, they are often matching pennies, especially when they have a move-countermove feel to them. To take an example from game designer David Sirlin,[3] in *Virtua Fighter 3* one player might have the option to throw his opponent, which

2. See section 4.1.

3. At http://www.sirlin.net/articles/yomi-layer-3-knowing-the-mind-of-the-opponent.html. Sirlin refers to the move-countermove reading of your opponent's intentions as *yomi* (from the Japanese word for "reading").

she can defeat by using a throw escape. He can counter this by using double palm, which she can defeat with a block. The block is in turn countered by the original throw (as Sirlin points out, being able to counter the fourth move with the first is a general phenomenon; thinking in terms of matching pennies helps one see why).

Example 2′: Matching Pennies, Virtua Fighter style

Player 1 \ Player 2	Block	Throw Escape
Throw	1, –1	–1, 1
Double Palm	–1, 1	1, –1

III. Analyzing Games: Dominance and Nash Equilibria

Example 3

Player 1 \ Player 2	X	Y
A	1, 2	6, 1
B	5, 2	3, 1
C	2, 1	1, 8

There's no name for this example (based on an equally nameless example in Kreps's book, *Game Theory and Economic Modelling*); we've created it just to illustrate some points. Let's think about how our presumably clever players would play this game.

Looking at the game, we see some spots Player 1 would like to get to, like that juicy 6 payoff if Player 1 plays A and Player 2 plays Y. Similarly Player 2 would love to get the 8 payoff in the bottom right. (Remember neither player cares about what payoff the other player gets.)

One thing to notice is that for Player 1, strategy B is better in every way than strategy C: if Player 2 plays X, then Player 1 would rather get 5 than 2, and if Player 2 plays Y, then Player 1 would rather get 3 than 1. So (for Player 1, which is all that matters since they're her strategies) strategy B *dominates* strategy C.

Thus Player 1 will never play C (remember she's smart) and Player 2 knows it. So really the above game is as shown below.

Example 3: Continued

Player 2 / Player 1	X	Y
A	1, 2	6, 1
B	5, 2	3, 1

But in this game, we see that for Player 2, X dominates Y (in each case, it's a payoff of 2 for Player 2 rather than a payoff of 1). So Player 2 should definitely play X.

Knowing that Player 2 is paying X, Player 1 now knows to play B rather than A.

So the end result is that Player 1 should play B, and Player 2 should play X. They will receive payoffs of 5 and 2 respectively.

Many simple games can be analyzed using this method: deleting the dominated strategies one after another until the answer emerges.

Note that the B/X outcome of 5, 2 has an interesting property: neither player would want to move away from it unilaterally. In other words, knowing that Player 1 is playing B, Player 2 can't improve her position by switching from X to some other strategy (in this case, Y is the only other choice). Likewise, knowing that Player 2 is playing X, Player 1 can't improve his position by switching from B to some other strategy (A or C). An outcome with this property (that neither player can improve his or her position by changing strategies unilaterally) is called a *Nash equilibrium* (or occasionally just plain "equilibrium").

One naturally thinks of Nash equilibria as the "best" solutions, since neither player can improve by switching. There's some truth to that, but there is some trickiness going on as well, as we'll see by looking at some more examples.

IV. A Few More Examples

Example 4: Prisoner's Dilemma

Player 2 / Player 1	Keep Quiet	Betray
Keep Quiet	1, 1	–5, 2
Betray	2, –5	–3, –3

Two criminals are arrested on suspicion of a robbery, but there isn't enough evidence to convict them. They are both taken to separate rooms and interrogated. If they both keep quiet, they'll be released (and get to split the money they've stolen). If one of them betrays the other, the betrayer will get off free (and get all the money) while the other goes to jail for a long time. If they both betray each other, they both go to jail for a while.

Note that for Player 1, the strategy Betray strictly dominates the strategy Keep Quiet: if Player 2 keeps quiet, Player 1 gets 2 instead of 1, and if Player 2 betrays, Player 1 gets –3 instead of –5. Similarly Betray dominates Keep Quiet for Player 2.

So each player should (given our assumptions about how our players will operate) choose Betray. And –3, –3 is indeed a Nash equilibrium: neither player can move off it and do better. But it's hard to think of it as the "best" result: each player does worse than they'd do if they both kept quiet! Nevertheless, the "game-theory answer" is that –3, –3 is the "right" place for the game to end up.

This analysis bothers a lot of people. If one wants to support the idea that it's rational for both players to keep quiet, there are a number of approaches. Perhaps the players do care about supporting each other, or perhaps they expect they will pay some penalty for betrayal (maybe in future games). In either case, the payoff structure will change (options involving betrayal now give fewer points to the betraying player), presumably leading to a different equilibrium. Or perhaps one wants to look at different ideas of "best" or "rational" solution, ones other than the Nash equilibrium. But it's hard to escape the logic that *if* the above grid accurately represents the interests of the players, and *if* the players pursue their own interests exclusively, the result will be the (nonoptimal) –3, –3.

A multiplayer analog to this situation is the classic "tragedy of the commons" from economics: many different actors share a common resource—say common land for sheep grazing—that they can profit from individually, although the costs are borne by all. Each actor has an incentive to overuse the resource, with the result that it is "irrationally" destroyed (irrational in the sense that everyone is worse off than if all had decided to use the resource moderately), even though each individual acted rationally. Overfishing, pollution generally, and global warming in particular are all examples of this problem in the real world. The lesson of the tragedy of the commons is generally taken to be one of the failure of unregulated access to common resources, but the suggested cures vary widely: from privatization of the common resource to government regulation limiting the ability of the actors to exploit it.

Example 5: ***Battle of the Sexes***

Spouse 2 / Spouse 1	Opera	Football
Opera	5, 4	1, 1
Football	0, 0	4, 5

A married couple wishes to spend an evening together. Spouse 1 prefers opera; Spouse 2 prefers football. But each cares mainly about spending the evening together. If for some reason they had to decide what to do without communicating, what should happen?

Note there are two Nash equilibria, Opera/Opera and Football/Football: given that the couple has landed on either one, neither spouse at that point wishes to move off. But which equilibrium? Spouse 1 hopes for the first; Spouse 2 would prefer the second. In the absence of some sort of prior coordination (i.e., if they really are deciding independently and simultaneously as we've been assuming) it's hard to see how they can decide. If they each go for their own favorite, they could wind up separate and unhappy; if one decides to pick the other's favorite, there's no way to know if the other has done the same, leading also to an evening spent separately. This game is a very simple model for a problem in coordination.

Example 6: *Hawks and Doves*

Player 2 / Player 1	Hawk	Dove
Hawk	–5, –5	2, 0
Dove	0, 2	1, 1

Some birds (or perhaps nations) have a choice between two strategies: be very aggressive in confrontations over some resource like food, or give way. Two hawks will have a terrible destructive fight that leaves them both much worse off. Two doves will share food and each gain a little. A hawk that meets a dove will frighten it off and gain the whole meal for itself. (This game can also be thought of as the teenage driver's game of "chicken" with Hawk as Drive Straight and Dove as Swerve; it sometimes goes by that name in the literature.)

Hawks and Doves is quite similar to Battle of the Sexes with its two Nash equilibria. The focus here, though, is on the desire to be the Hawk: each bird would like to be the Hawk if only it could be sure the other bird would be the Dove. But both birds being the Hawk is a disaster, whereas both birds being the Dove is fine.

It's hard to make much sense of this until you start thinking of populations. In a population of Doves, a single Hawk will do very well (and presumably will start reproducing more and more, leading to more Hawks). In a population of Hawks (constantly fighting and hurting each other) a single Dove will do very well. With some work, one can compute what the end percentage of Hawks and Doves should be (i.e., the percentage at which a new Dove or a new Hawk entering the population has no special advantage over its opposite number). The Hawks and Doves game is a foundational example for the application of game theory to evolutionary biology.

This same population-based thinking can be applicable in real-world games, particularly those like *Magic: The Gathering* where people show up with a preset strategy—in the case of *Magic*, their deck. Specific decks have various degrees of advantage over specific other decks, which one can think of as a large game-theoretic payoff matrix (your payoff in this case being your chance of winning against a specific deck type, a chance that you naturally would like to be as high as possible). Then the numbers of various deck types at *Magic* tournaments evolve in essentially the same way as the numbers of Hawks and Doves in a population of birds, but with the difference that a clever player can hope to predict imbalances in the population beforehand, and show up with a deck to take advantage of those imbalances.[4]

V. Back to Rock-Paper-Scissors: Mixed Strategies and the Existence of Equilibria

We've been looking at Nash equilibria in various games, and we claimed at the start that the big idea in the theory was to look for the equilibria in whatever game we were trying to analyze. But it's possible to have a game with no equilibria in it. In fact, we already know such an example: rock-paper-scissors.

In rock-paper-scissors, no matter what strategy I pick, there is a strategy you can pick that will beat it, and vice versa. So by definition a Nash equilibrium is impossible.

But is there a rock-paper-scissors strategy, in the more general sense of "a method of play," that would prevent one's opponent from gaining an advantage? Certainly: one could roll a die and then choose one's strategy via 1–2: Rock, 3–4: Paper, 5–6: Scissors. If I choose this overall strategy, I can even announce it to you beforehand and (so long as I don't reveal my die roll to you beforehand) there's nothing you can do to take advantage of it.

So let's define a *mixed strategy* as a set of probabilities (totaling 1, i.e., totaling 100 percent), showing how likely you are to play each strategy given in the game's grid (which we'll call *pure strategies* if we need to distinguish them from mixed strategies).

So our "unbeatable" rock-paper-scissors strategy is 1/3 Rock, 1/3 Paper, and 1/3 Scissors.

Probably the most basic result of game theory is the following:

Theorem: Every game has a Nash equilibrium once you allow mixed strategies.

A few caveats about this Nash equilibrium:

(a) It may not be unique.
(b) It may not be the "best outcome" in terms of payoff.

4. However, if the field is at equilibrium, then it won't matter what deck you bring (see caveat (e) below on Nash equilibria—you can think of the field as a whole as playing an equilibrium strategy). But given the complexity of the game, the field will never be at perfect equilibrium.

(c) It may be hard to find for more complex games.
(d) Any dominated pure strategies won't show up in the mix—that is, they'll have probability zero.
(e) If you play the Nash equilibrium strategy, it turns out that although your opponent won't be able to "beat" you (get a better result against you), you won't be able to "beat" them either (i.e., no matter what, you'll both get the expected result). Untangling what this really means takes more time than we have here, but you can get a feel of it from the rock-paper-scissors example: play the die-rolling strategy, and on average you'll never do worse than 50/50, but you'll never do better either, even against a terrible opponent who always plays rock.

Note we already knew (a) from the Battle of the Sexes, and (b) from the Prisoner's Dilemma.

Despite its limitations, the existence of Nash equilibria is still a powerful and perhaps somewhat surprising result: it means there is a kind of stability in even the most complex games.

VI. Concluding Remarks

This survey of game theory has been a very brief one (see the references below for further information). Many of the limitations of the theory as we've presented it can be relaxed with some more work. Among the things people look at are

- More than two players
- Allowing players to take turns
- Looking at what happens under repeat play (this really changes the best strategies for games like the Prisoner's Dilemma)
- Allowing hidden information
- The differences between theory and experiment (i.e., how do real people actually play these games if you give them the opportunity?)

If one's main interest is actual games people play (e.g., chess or *Starcraft*), what relevance does game theory have? In terms of the detailed techniques of game theory, the answer is usually "not very much." But the point of view of game theory can be instructive when looking at subgames within a larger "real" game. Also, when doing balance work, one is often mentally deleting dominated strategies (such as equipping the trash items in *World of Warcraft*), and what's left can be thought of as a large and complex version of rock-paper-scissors: more than three strategy options, of course, but with each option beating some other options and being itself beaten in turn by yet other options.

If you understand this point of view—perhaps instinctively, or perhaps with the help of some mental tools like game theory to help you along—you can guide your game's development. If you think of the game's strategic choices as a large rock-paper-scissors structure, it's important that all the strategies you want to remain viable (i.e., used at least occasionally by good players) neither dominate nor are dominated by the other viable strategies. If, on the other hand, you can delete dominated strategies one by one, and are then left with only one choice for each player, your game has suffered complete strategic collapse—a grim fate indeed.

References

Arranged roughly in increasing order of difficulty.

Game Theory: A Very Short Introduction, by Ken Binmore. The "Very Short Introduction" series is quite good in general, and this intro to game theory is particularly nice. Lots of good examples, very readable.

Game Theory and Economic Modelling, by David M. Kreps. Another fairly accessible text. Don't let the *Economic Modelling* in the title scare you; it's not a heavily mathematical text, and it's fairly user-friendly. It's more a general text than an economics-specific one. A little more academically oriented than Binmore, but not by that much.

Luck, Logic, and White Lies: The Mathematics of Games, Part III, by Jörg Bewersdorff. An excellent survey that applies three different kinds of math to games: basic probability theory, combinatorial game theory, and Von Neumann game theory.

Evolution and the Theory of Games, by John Maynard Smith. Game theory is also used in biology to explain how the behavior of animals can evolve (the Hawk-Dove game is an example). This is the classic book by one of the founders of the field. Not too much math—very much focused on evolutionary biology.

The New Palgrave Game Theory, edited by John Eatwell, Murray Milgate, and Peter Newman. A collection of essays about game theory by and for economists (the *New Palgrave* is a series of books for economists on various econ-related subjects). The essays vary widely in accessibility—some friendly survey articles, some pretty hardcore stuff. The fact that the articles are all independent makes it useful for finding short bits on specific topics that interest you. A good place to get a survey of how game theory is used in economics.

Game Theory for Applied Economists, by Robert Gibbons. A good intermediate-level survey of game theory. A nice place to find careful and precise statements of definitions and theorems (if you're the type to find such things helpful) but definitely requires some ability to read math.

Game Theory, by Drew Fudenberg and Jean Tirole. The standard reference in the field. A serious graduate-level text.

Theory of Games and Economic Behavior, by John von Neumann and Oskar Morgenstern. The book that started it all back in 1944, and still in print (in fact, a commemorative edition was published in 2004). Not an easy read, in part due to its density and in part due to the fact that notation has changed since the 1940s, but still a classic.

B. Combinatorial Game Theory

I. Introduction

Dating back only to the 1970s, combinatorial game theory is more recent than Von Neumann game theory. Combinatorial game theory was invented primarily by John Conway (also known for the 0-player game of Life). It's still an active, albeit small, field of mathematical research. No real-world applications of the theory have been found (other than applications to games themselves), so not many people outside of mathematics know much about it. It's approachable enough, though, that recreational mathematicians (who are often the sort of people who like games anyway) have some interest in it.

It's best suited for two-player games where players alternate moves, until finally one of the players wins and the other loses. The games need to have no overt luck (no dice or cards or other randomizers) and no hidden information. Games like chess, checkers, and go fit into this category.

Chess and checkers, although the right sort of games, turn out not to be the best ones to analyze using combinatorial game theory. There is, however, some good work using the theory on go.[5] Other games that the theory works well on include Fox & Geese, Nim, and Dots & Boxes, plus a great number of more obscure games such as Hackenbush, Chomp, Kayles, and Sprouts, the kinds of abstract strategy games that recreational mathematicians like to invent and play. As in von Neumann game theory, many of the games studied are made up for purposes of the theory; however, the made-up games in combinatorial game theory feel much more like games one might actually play as opposed to the pure thought experiments one sees in the von Neumann theory (imagine actually playing Hackenbush as described below versus playing the Hawk-Dove game described above).

The big idea of the theory is that game positions or states can be analyzed in a way that lets you think of a game state as a kind of generalized number. The Conway game theory is a type of math for these generalized numbers (sometimes called "surreal numbers," a term invented by Donald Knuth, who also wrote a book by that title on the theory). If you can decompose the board position into pieces, evaluate the (surreal) numerical value of the pieces, and know how to do (surreal) addition, you can win games that would utterly baffle people who don't know the theory.[6]

5. It's possible to construct (admittedly somewhat unnatural) go positions that even a professional go player can't solve, but that can be solved with the aid of the theory. See Berlekamp and Wolfe, *Mathematical Go*.

6. This approach is why games like go or Dots & Boxes, where the board sometimes breaks down into different independent areas, are more suited to the theory than games like chess, where one piece often affects another piece all the way across the board.

The numbers involved include the usual numbers we all know and love (or hate, as the case may be). But they also include numerous oddities, including many types of infinite numbers, and even stranger beasts such as

* star
↑ up
$+_2$ tiny-two

Very roughly, the number you associate with a game position is the number of moves that you're ahead, but that can be a bit puzzling for a position with value 3/4 (what does it mean to be 3/4 of a move ahead?) and even more confusing for a position with value * or ↑.

We'll begin by describing a game many of our readers may not know, called Hackenbush,[7] that will help make some sense of the link between games and numbers. Once you understand Hackenbush, you will see why it makes sense to assign values of 3 or –2 or 0 (or even 1/2) to game positions. Then we'll redo what we did for Hackenbush from a more general point of view. In particular, we'll define *game* in the general sense of combinatorial game theory, and explain what it means to add two games together. Lastly, we'll talk a bit about another simple game, called Domineering, where some of the stranger numbers like * and ↑ will make their appearance.

II. Hackenbush

In this game, there are two players, Black and White (later we will call these players Left and Right). A game state is a series of black and white lines (called "edges") each connected to the ground or to other edges.

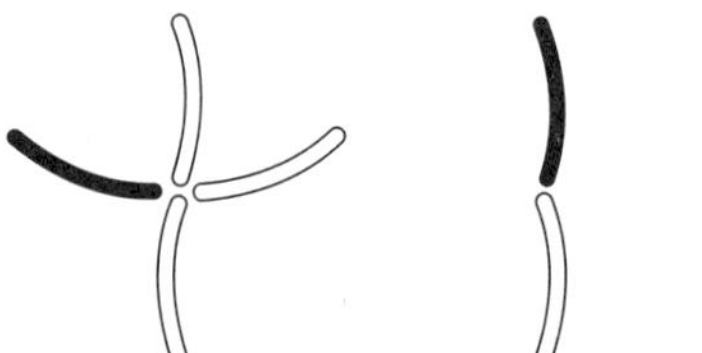

Figure 8.1
A typical Hackenbush position

On her turn, a player must remove an edge of her color, and any edges that lose their connection to the ground fall down and disappear. If a player has no edges left to remove (e.g., if it's Black's turn but only white edges are left), then that player loses.

7. Strictly speaking, we will be showing a variant called Blue-Red Hackenbush or Black-White Hackenbush; there are other variants as well.

For instance, in the above position, if it's White's turn, he might take the rightmost white edge (killing the black edge above it). Then Black would be forced to take the only remaining black edge. Then White would take any edge he liked. Now it's Black's turn and she has no edges to take, so she loses.

Now that we have this game, let's try to understand it better by analyzing some very simple positions.

Our first trick will be to think of positions as games in their own right: this makes sense because for any position, we can play a game starting from that position. So from now on we'll be referring to positions as games, and we'll try to figure out, for each such "game," who will win. Of course, that may depend on who gets to play first. (We'll assume each player plays perfectly, i.e., always makes the best possible move.)

Figure 8.2

In this game (no edges of either color available), if it's Black's turn to move, she'll have no move and thus she will lose. But the same thing will happen to White if he must move first. So in this game, whoever moves first loses.

We call this game, naturally enough, 0.

Figure 8.3

In this game, Black wins going first (she takes her edge, and then it's White's turn to move in the game 0). But if White goes first, he still loses. So this game is a win for Black no matter who goes first.

We name this game 1, and we think of it as a 1-move advantage for Black (more on that below).

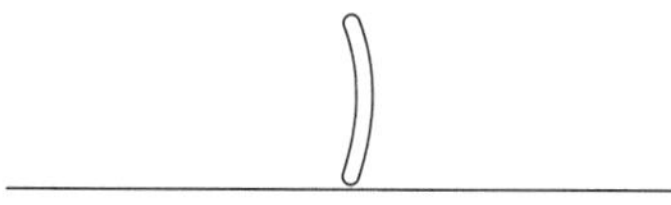

Figure 8.4

This game is a win for White, no matter who goes first. We call it –1.

Figure 8.5

This game is even better for Black than the game 1. It will, we trust, surprise no one that we are going to call it 2. However, it's not clear yet if all these names mean very much.

Figure 8.6

Here is a game that looks like 1 and –1 standing next to each other. Let's interpret "standing next to each other" as + (we'll expand on this idea of adding two games together as we go . . . it's the core of combinatorial game theory, appearing here in a very simple form). Well, what should 1 + (–1) be? Surely it should be 0!

Well, how does this game work? If Black goes first, she takes her edge, then White takes his edge, and then Black loses. If White goes first, he takes his edge, then Black takes hers, and White loses. So whoever goes first loses, just like the game 0!

The big trick: we will declare *any* game (not just the special game with no options at all) where the first player always loses to be equal to 0. So even though this game *looks* different from the game with no options at all, we will still call it 0.

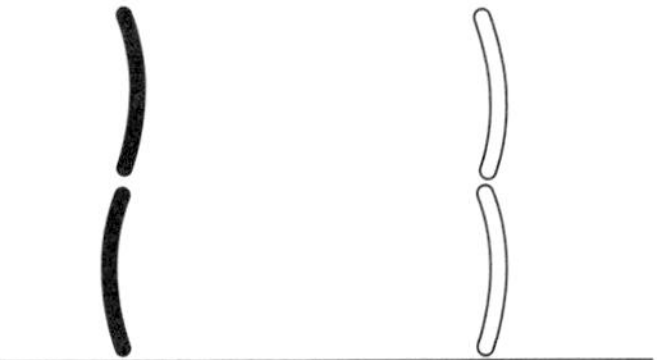

Figure 8.7

Here's $2 + (-2)$. Try playing it Black first, and then playing it White first (each player is playing smart, so she or he will of course chop off their upper edge rather than their lower edge), to see that the first player always loses. So $2 + (-2) = 0$, just as we'd hope.

Figure 8.8

This one's a bit strange. It's not hard to see that Black wins no matter who goes first (try it!). So far we've been assigning positive numbers to Black-favorable positions, and negative numbers to White-favorable ones, so this game should be a positive number. Let's call it x for now. Note this game is worse for Black than the game 1 (there's a white edge in it, which can only help White). So presumably $0 < x < 1$.

Well, maybe $x = 1/2$? What could *that* possibly mean?

It turns out we already have the tools to answer this question. If $x = 1/2$, then surely $x + x + (-1) = 0$. And that's something we can explicitly check.

Figure 8.9

Here we have $x + x + (-1)$. If this game is 0, we can feel we are on the right track assigning the value 1/2 to x.

So we should check to see that the first player always loses. If Black goes first, she takes one of her edges. Then White should take the edge he has on top of the remaining black stalk. Then Black takes her remaining edge, White takes his last edge, and Black loses.

If White goes first, he takes a white edge on one of the black stalks. Black takes her other stalk (killing a white edge). Then an edge for White, an edge for Black, and White loses! So whoever goes first does indeed lose, this game is indeed 0, and so we are happy to say $x = 1/2$.

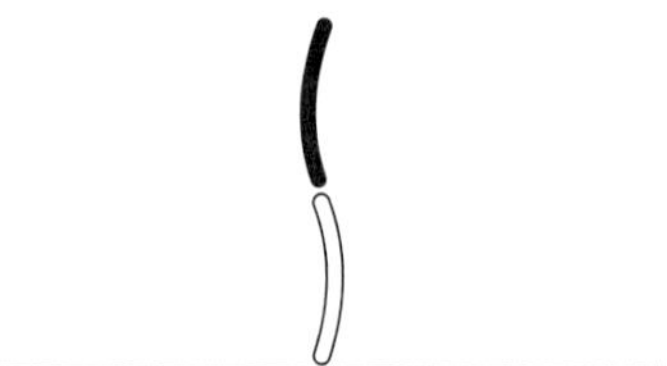

Figure 8.10

Similarly, this is –1/2 (try checking it by showing (–1/2) + (–1/2) + 1 = 0).

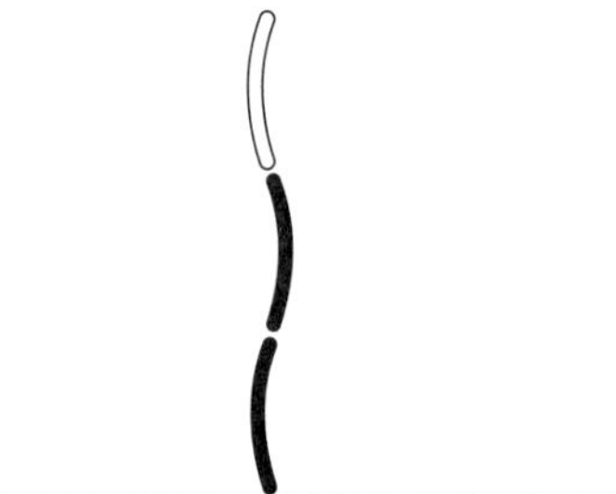

Figure 8.11

You might want to try showing this is 1 1/2.

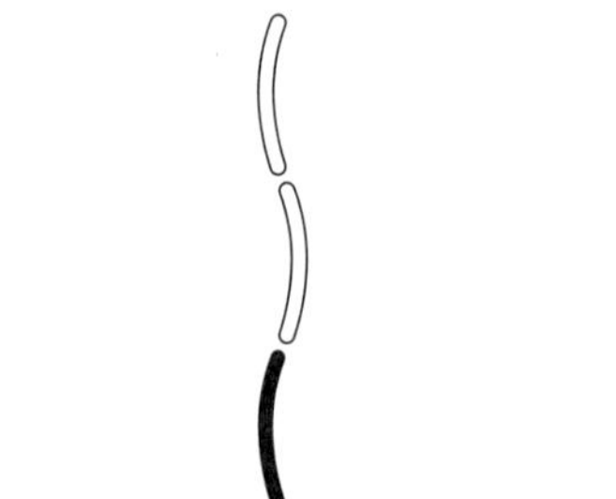

Figure 8.12

And this, it turns out, is 1/4 (try it!). (You might think this would be 1/3, but if you check, you'll find $y + y + y + (-1)$, where y is this game, is a win for White no matter who goes first! That means the game must be less than 1/3, which might lead you to try 1/4. And if you check, you will find $y + y + y + y + (-1)$ does indeed equal 0.)

Exercise 8.1: Check the various statements above regarding –1/2, 1 1/2, and 1/4.

There's a lot more to say about Hackenbush, but we'll stop here. Let's summarize the main ideas of our analysis, and then we'll use those ideas to develop a general theory that applies to any two-player game of the appropriate type (players take turns, someone eventually wins, no randomizers, no hidden information).

• *Games = positions.* We think about a position in a game as a game in itself (start playing from that position).
• *Look from both points of view.* Think about who wins the game when one player goes first, and then when the other player goes first.
• *The 0 game.* Call all games where the first player always loses 0.
• *Adding games.* If a game/position is made up of two unlinked games/positions, think of the big game as a sum of the two little games. Use this idea (sometimes with help from the 0 game idea) to assign the right numerical values to unknown games.

III. The Theory

A *game* G is denoted by {A, B, C, . . . | P, Q, R, . . .} where A, B, C, . . . and P, Q, R, . . . are games. All games are built up in this way. (Think of this as like set notation, but there are left elements of G and right elements of G, and we want to keep them distinct in our heads.)

The game is played by Left (formerly known as Black) picking one of the games A, B, C, . . . if it's her turn, or Right (formerly known as White) picking one of the games P, Q, R, . . . if it's his turn. We call the games A, B, C, . . . the *left options* of the game G, and P, Q, R, . . . the *right options*. Play continues with the players taking turns—for example, if Left picks B, then Right picks one of the right options *of B* (not of G), and so on. A player who has no options loses.

If all games are built from other games, how do we get started? How is it that there are any games at all?

The answer is that we "build up from nothing"—that is, we start with the game { | }, which we will call 0. This is the game where neither player has any options (so it's true, in a formal mathematical sense, that all of its nonexistent options are games, as required by the definition, i.e., 0 is a game by our definition). So whoever moves first in this game loses.

Then we define some more games from that:

1 = { 0 | }

This is the game where Left can move to 0, but Right has no options. Note that this game is a win for Left, no matter who moves first.

2 = { 1, 0 | }

–1 = { | 0 }

1/2 = { 0 | 1 }

Quick detour: Let's compare this with some of our Hackenbush games. We claim it's the same thing, just with different notation.

The game with no options for Left (Black) or Right (White). So it's the game $0 = \{ \mid \}$.

Left can move to 0, but White has no options at all. Thus this game is $1 = \{ 0 \mid \}$.

Similarly this is $-1 = \{ \mid 0 \}$.

Left can move to 1 or to 0, but White has nothing. So it's $2 = \{ 1, 0 \mid \}$.

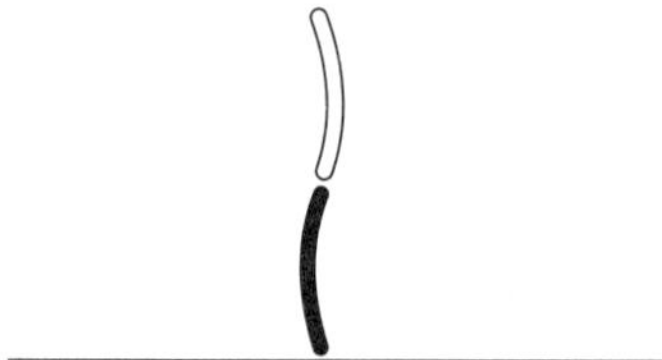

Left can move to 0, and White can move to 1. Thus it's $1/2 = \{ 0 \mid 1 \}$.

Back to the more general case. If we have some game G, and we assume both players play perfectly, then there are only four possibilities:

1. L always wins (whoever goes first).
2. R always wins (whoever goes first).
3. Whoever goes first always loses.
4. Whoever goes first always wins.

We will say $G > 0$ in the first case, $G < 0$ in the second case, and $G = 0$ in the third case. We haven't encountered the fourth case before, but let's label it $G \parallel 0$ and say "G is fuzzy" or "G is confused with 0." (Fuzzy games never come up in Hackenbush, which is why we haven't seen them before.)

Here's an example of a fuzzy game:

$G = \{ 0 \mid 0 \}$

(Convince yourself that whoever goes first wins this game!) This game is called * ("star") and it comes up a lot. (If you know the game Nim, you can think of * as a Nim game where there is a single pile with just one stone in it.)

Addition: If G, H are games, we define G + H to be the game where players can move in either G or H on their turn (and they lose if they have no moves anywhere).

Negatives: We define –G to be the game with the roles of Left and Right reversed (just like switching Black and White in Hackenbush).[8]

Equality: We say $G = H$ if $G + (-H) = 0$.

Note that two pretty different looking games can be "equal" in this world. You might want to try checking that $\{ 1 \mid \}$ is equal to $\{ 1, 0 \mid \}$, for example (the game we've been calling 2).

If you are trying to do all this with mathematical rectitude, there are a bunch of facts to prove, like

$G + 0 = G$

If $G > 0$ and $H > 0$, then $G + H > 0$

$G + H = H + G$

$G - G = 0$

8. Note that you have to switch the roles of Left and Right "all the way down," not just at the very top level. More formally, if $G = \{A, B, C, \ldots \mid P, Q, R, \ldots\}$ then $-G = \{-P, -Q, -R, \ldots \mid -A, -B, -C, \ldots\}$. If this seems weird, try it out on a few simple Hackenbush positions, or just ignore it for now.

One might try to define multiplication of games as well (multiplication turns out to be rather tricky, although proving the above addition facts isn't too bad). We won't delve into multiplication, or go through all the formal proofs, since that would take us too far afield (see the references below for more details). We'll give the outline of the last one, though, because it's short and appealing, and it actually shows a good strategy in some games (e.g., two-pile Nim).[9]

Theorem: G – G = 0.

Proof (sketch). By definition, G – G = 0 means G + (–G) = 0. So we have to show G + (–G) is a win for whoever goes second. Suppose R goes first. Then, because –G is just G with the roles of L and R reversed, L can make the exact same move R made in the other game (if R goes in G, L goes in –G and vice versa). Now it's Right's move again. L can continue to mirror Right's moves until R finally runs out of moves, and then L wins! But R can do the exact same thing to L if she moves first. So whoever goes first loses.

So in Hackenbush, our games are all nice things like 2 and –3 and 1/2, but we've seen there are games like * that are weirder. We can sort out the actual numbers from the nonnumbers as follows.

We say a game G is a *number* if G = $\{X_1, X_2, X_3, \ldots \mid Y_1, Y_2, Y_3, \ldots\}$ where all the X_i and Y_j are numbers, and $X_i < Y_j$ for every i and j. In other words, G is a number if it's built out of things that you already know are numbers, and each left option is less than each right option.

Remembering that vacuous statements are automatically true (the same trick that made 0 = { | } a game), we find

0 = { | } is a number

2 = { 1, 0 | } is a number (all the left options are less than all none of the right options)

– 1 = { | 0 } is a number

1/2 = { 0 | 1 } is a number

If the "vacuous statements are true" bit feels awkward, one can just think of it as a special rule that G is a number if it has no Left options and all the Right options are numbers (or vice versa), and that 0 is a number by fiat.

There are some weird numbers too. One interesting one is

$\omega = \{ 1, 2, 3, 4, \ldots \mid \}$

9. Also see note 32 in chapter 2.

and its friend

$-\omega = \{ \mid -1, -2, -3, -4, \ldots \}$

So ω is the game where Left picks any whole number she wants (and Right has no options). In Hackenbush terms, ω is the game.

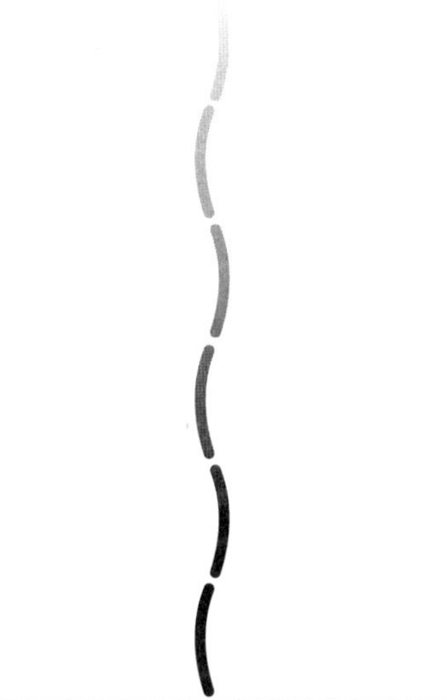

Figure 8.13
An infinite tower of moves for Black

A very popular game among young children is the game

$\omega - \omega$

If Left goes first, she will pick a number from ω. Then Right will pick a larger-sized number from –ω, and the sum of those two will be less than 0—that is, a win for Right. Similarly Left will win if Right picks first, so ω – ω = 0 (a second-player win). This game is more commonly known as "my dad makes more money than yours."

You can think of ω as "infinity," but normally it's hard to make sense of concepts like "infinity plus one" or "infinity minus three." However, ω + 1 and ω – 3 make perfect sense in this theory.[10]

10. Being able to talk sensibly about ω + 1 and so on predates combinatorial game theory, though. It goes back to the late nineteenth century and Georg Cantor's theory of transfinite ordinals.

Note that $* = \{ 0 \mid 0 \}$ is not a number according to our definition. And a good thing too, because $* > 0$, $* < 0$, and $* = 0$ are all false, and we'd want *one* of those three things to be true for any respectable number! (Which in fact is true, and it's another of the things one would prove when developing this theory carefully.)

Before leaving the world of theory and looking at another specific game, we'll quote a result that really shows off the power of the theory. It does require you to know about Nim, which fortunately is easy to describe. Nim is a two-player game played with piles of pebbles or other objects. On your turn, you can take any number of pebbles from any one of the piles. If there are no pebbles left for you to take, you lose. (You might try playing a few games . . . it's not too hard to figure out the strategy if the starting position has one or two piles, but it's quite hard to figure out how to play if there are three or more piles.)

Call a game G *impartial* if L and R have the same options at every step. So Nim is impartial (anyone is allowed to take any pebble they want), but Hackenbush isn't because Black can only take black edges.

Lastly, let's write $*n$ for the very simple game that's a Nim heap of n pebbles (note $*n$ is a first-player win, i.e., $*n \parallel 0$, i.e., $*n$ is fuzzy). The games $*1 = *$, $*2$, $*3$, . . . are sometimes called "nimbers" (note that they are *not* numbers in the sense that we defined them above, but they are still games).

Exercise 8.2: How do you write $*n$ in the $\{ \mid \mid \}$ notation?

Theorem (Sprague-Grundy): If G is any impartial game, $G = *n$ for some integer n.

This is quite remarkable. If you see any game, no matter how complex, that's impartial, then you know it's really a pile of pebbles in disguise. (In particular, any collection of pebble piles is equal to a single pebble pile of some size, although not in the way you might think, e.g., it turns out $*3 + *2 = *1$, not $*5$!)

Exercise 8.3:

1. Show $*n + *n = 0$, i.e., $-(*n) = *n$.
2. Verify $*3 + *2 = *1$. (*Hint*: Using (a), it's enough to show $*3 + *2 + *1$ is a second-player win.)
3. (Hard) Figure out how to add $*m$ and $*n$ for any two whole numbers m and n. (*Hint*: Try writing out the addition table for small values of m and n, say 1–10 or 1–20. Look for patterns involving powers of 2.)

IV. Domineering

Hackenbush was a nice game to start with because it was simple, and because the values of the positions turned out to be numbers we are already knew. Domineering is a nice game to look at now because it's still simple, but lots of nonnumerical values arise very naturally.

We won't try to do anything like a complete analysis of Domineering. Instead, we'll just show a few positions and what values arise from them.

The game is played with dominoes on a grid (say a chessboard). Players take turns placing dominoes so that they cover two squares. Left places her dominoes vertically, and Right places his dominoes horizontally. As usual, if someone is unable to move, that player loses.

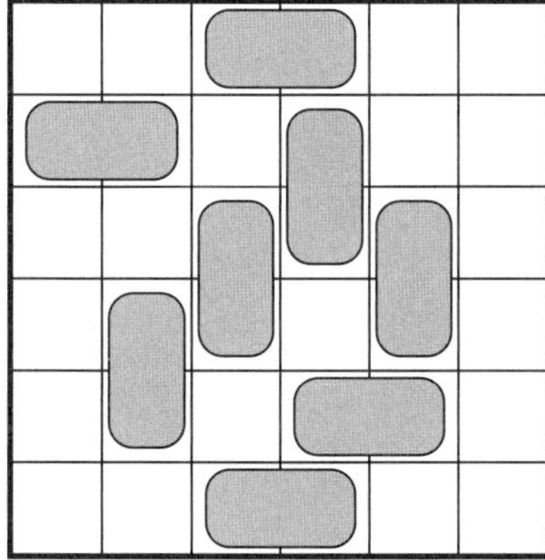

Figure 8.14
A 6 x ×6 Domineering game in midstream

Once a few moves have been played, the Domineering game breaks up naturally into a sum of games (the various still-empty regions that are left on the board). So we can hope to understand Domineering better by evaluating the various shapes that empty regions might have and understanding how to add them (if shapes correspond to numbers, of course, it will be very easy to add them).

This is a pretty big project, but let's do just a little to see how it would go.

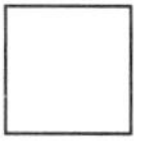

Figure 8.15

Here's a single empty square. Nobody can place a domino here—that is, nobody can move here—so this is the game 0 = { | }.

Figure 8.16

Left can place a domino here (after which nobody can move), and Right can't move at all. So this game is 1 = { 0 | }.

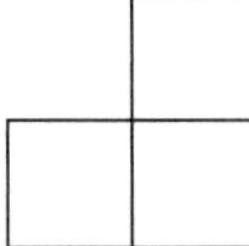

Figure 8.17

Either player can move to 0 from this position. So this is * = { 0 | 0 }.

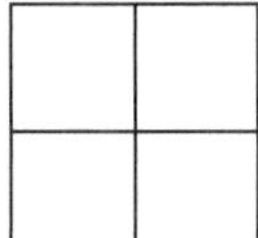

Figure 8.18

Left can move to 1, and Right can move to –1, so this is the game { 1 | –1 }. This is a game we haven't met before. Let's call it ±1. It's very good to grab this position quickly, because if you do it gives you yet another move, and if your opponent grabs it, it gives him another move. Such positions are called "hot," and there's a whole "temperature theory" within combinatorial game theory that tells you about hot positions, how to evaluate them, how to play in them, and so on.

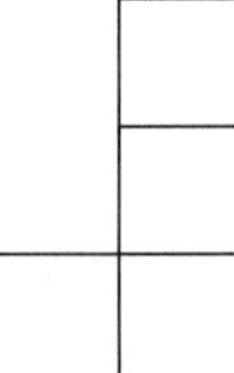

Figure 8.19

Left can move to either 0 or –1. Of course, 0 is better—why give Right a free move? Since we are assuming everyone plays perfectly, we should just say Left moves to 0. Meanwhile Right can move only to 1. That makes this game { 0 | 1 }, which is our old friend 1/2.

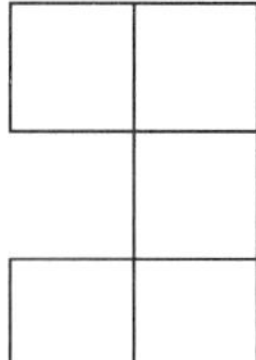

Figure 8.20

Left can move to –1, and Right can move to *. So this is { –1 | * }, which looks confusing at first, until we realize that it's just a game where whoever moves first loses (Left moves to –1, Right takes the –1, and then Left has no move, or Right moves to *, Left takes the *, and then Right loses). So this game is in fact just 0!

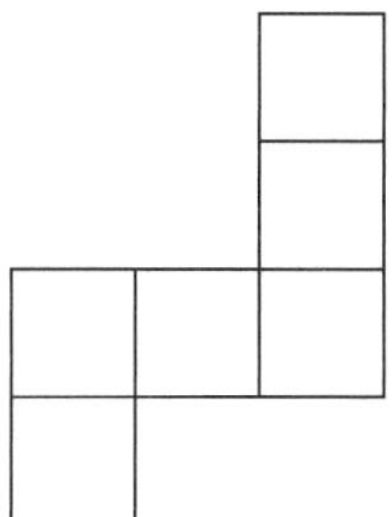

Figure 8.21

Here Left can move to 1/2, *, or –1/2, and 1/2 is clearly Left's best move. Meanwhile Right can move to either 1 or 2, and 1 is the best choice. So this is the game { 1/2 | 1 }, which you can show (using Hackenbush pictures, or doing the same trick but with Domineering pictures if you prefer) is 3/4.

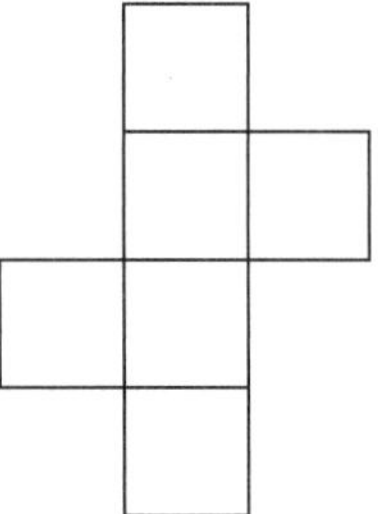

Figure 8.22

Here Left can move to 0 or * (0 is better for Left), and Right can move only to *. So this is the game { 0 | * }. This is a game we haven't seen before; it's called ↑ (pronounced "up"). No matter who goes first, this game is a win for Left, so ↑ > 0. But ↑ is smaller than *any* positive number. In other words, ↑ + ↑ + ↑ + ··· + ↑ + (–1) < 0 (the game is a win for Right) no matter how many ups you add. So our system has infinitesimals built right in, and they aren't even that complicated (we've made one out of 0 and *, two very simple games).

Exercise 8.4: Show ↑ + ↑ + ↑ + ··· + ↑ + (–1) < 0 for any number of ups. (*Hint*: If you're having trouble, try playing the game with just two or three ups first.)

V. Concluding Remarks

This survey has only scratched the surface of combinatorial game theory. It's a big field, and still fairly young, so it's still growing at a good rate.

The theory only helps you analyze certain types of games, so its usefulness is somewhat limited (but then, if you are looking for direct usefulness, games might be the wrong place to be looking!). But it's a very beautiful theory that combines games and numbers in an elegant way. And it certainly stretches your brain in the way abstract math does.

It's perhaps ironic that although the von Neumann theory doesn't actually let you analyze any real-life games, it can be useful in thinking about more complex games (e.g., in looking at the abstract rock-paper-scissors relationships in an RTS), whereas Conway's theory actually lets you do a good bit of serious analysis on real games like go, but isn't terribly useful for thinking about complex games outside of its tightly defined domain of applicability.

References

Again arranged roughly in increasing order of difficulty—very roughly indeed this time, because the books vary so much in tone. Some may find the chattiness and casual approach of *Winning*

Ways to be the most accessible; other readers may find the more structured approach of *Lessons in Play* more to their taste.

Winning Ways for Your Mathematical Plays (4 vols.), by Elwyn R. Berlekamp, John H. Conway, and Richard K. Guy. Introduces the theory using lots and lots of example games. If you are wondering how the theory might apply to some particular game you like, this is the place to look.

The Dots & Boxes Game: Sophisticated Child's Play, by Elwyn Berlekamp. In-depth application of the theory to the classic childhood game of dots & boxes. Read this book and be an unstoppable dots & boxes force!

Surreal Numbers, by Donald E. Knuth. An odd but fun little book about two people stranded on a desert island who decide to pass the time by constructing the surreal number system. Good if you are a Knuth fan, or like the Socratic style of presentation.

Luck, Logic, and White Lies: The Mathematics of Games, Part II, by Jörg Bewersdorff. Part II of Bewersdorff's three-part survey of the math of games (mentioned in the previous appendix) is on combinatorial game theory; it also covers some other topics like computer chess.

Lessons in Play: An Introduction to Combinatorial Game Theory, by Michael H. Albert, Richard J. Nowakowski, and David Wolfe. A textbook (complete with exercises and answers in the back) at an undergraduate level. Good for those who found the casual approach of *Winning Ways* more confusing than friendly.

On Numbers and Games, by John H. Conway. A more formal treatment of the subject. Good for those who want precise definitions, statements and proofs of theorems, and a generally mathematical approach. More abstract and more advanced than *Lessons in Play*.

Mathematical Go: Chilling Gets the Last Point, by Elwyn Berlekamp and David Wolfe. A fairly involved application of the theory to a very complicated game. Good if you want to see the theory applied in a big way to a hard problem.

Games of No Chance, *More Games of No Chance*, and *Games of No Chance 3*, edited by Richard J. Nowakowski. Separate collections of papers on combinatorial game theory. Good if you want to see a broad scope of applications of the theory and if you want to get an idea of the state of (relatively) current research. Most areas of math are so dense and complex that it's basically impossible for a layperson to get to current research, but combinatorial game theory is young enough that it's almost approachable for a smart and hard-working amateur.

C. List of Games

This appendix lists most of the games referenced in the text (we occasionally omit games that receive extremely brief mentions). In most cases, a nodding familiarity with the game will be enough to understand these references.

We often use specific games as stand-ins for others in their genre—for example, we might give *Starcraft* as an example game to illustrate some point, but almost any other real-time strategy game could serve as an example as well. Context should make our usage clear, and in doubtful cases we say something like "unlike other RTS games, *Starcraft* . . ." Games we use especially often in this synecdochic fashion we mark below by putting their genre after them. For these games we list similar games after the entry; our hope is that a reader who has not played the game we mention has played one of the others. Substituting one for the other in the reader's mind should do no harm.

Underlined games are ones that have an entry elsewhere in this appendix.

Our descriptions of the games are necessarily brief, and tend to focus on the features relevant for our discussion in the main text. Many games have variant ways of playing them, or are actually part of a series of closely related games; we do not mention such details unless we have a particular need to make distinctions.

Discussion of a game in the main text, and the corresponding inclusion in this list, should not be taken as a measure of the quality or the importance of the game. We often reference lesser-known games to make some particular point. Many very important and well-known games are not included in this list.

Games are marked with one to four asterisks based on how often we use them as examples. A game marked **** is one readers should be familiar with or they'll miss a lot of what we're trying to say. Games marked * are only mentioned once or twice and little harm will be done if readers don't know them. This is *not* in any way a rating of the quality of the game in question.

BOARDGAMES, CLASSIC

Backgammon**

A two-player race game in which players move their pieces in opposite directions around a track according to the throw of a pair of dice. There is interaction between the pieces in both capturing and blocking. The winner is the first player to remove all his pieces from the board. When played as a gambling game, players may use the *doubling cube*, a device that allows them to alter the stakes in a controlled way as the game progresses (typically a player who feels he's winning offers to double the stakes, and the other player may either concede immediately for the original stakes or play on for the doubled amount).

Checkers**

A two-player game with no overt random elements played on an 8×8 grid. Players alternate, moving their pieces with the goal of capturing all the enemy pieces.

Chess****

A two-player game with no overt random elements. Players take turns moving a variety of pieces with different movement and capture rules on an 8×8 grid. The game is won by *checkmating* the opponent's king: putting it in a position where it would be captured with certainty on the next turn.

Not part of the game rules, but still familiar to most players, is a point-value system for the pieces: 1 point for a pawn, 3 points for a knight, 5 points for a castle, and so on. Players can get a rough idea of how far ahead or behind they are by comparing the total point values of captured pieces on each side.

Chinese Checkers*

A race game for two to six players with no overt random elements. Players alternate moving their pieces across a star-shaped board with 6 points and 121 holes, often by leapfrogging enemy and friendly pieces. The goal is to be the first to move one's pieces across the board.

Chinese Chess (Xianqi)*

A Chinese two-player game in the same family as chess. Interesting features of Chinese chess include a river and castle on the board, which restrict piece movement.

Chutes and Ladders*, Snakes & Ladders (race game)**

A children's race game for two or more players in which a player's single piece is moved according to the roll of a die, with the goal being to reach the end of the track first. There are many spaces that advance a piece further along the track (ladders), and many spaces force a piece to fall back to a previous square (chutes or snakes).

Similar games: *Candyland*, Game of Goose, *Game of Life*, *Parcheesi*.

Fox & Geese (Fox and Hounds, Wolf and Sheep)*

A family of two-player games with no overt random elements, characterized by the asymmetry between the two sides' pieces and goals. The fox player has a single piece and is attempting to capture or bypass the geese; the geese player has several pieces and is attempting to immobilize the fox.

The (Royal) Game of Goose*

A race game for two or more players played on a spiral track with movement being determined by a die roll and board spaces often having a reward or penalty. This game is one of the first examples of the commercialization of proprietary boardgames.

Go (Wei-chi, Weiqi, Igo, Baduk)***

A two-player game with no overt random elements. Players alternate placing pieces on the intersections of a 19 × 19 grid with the goal being to surround the most territory (vacant intersections). While not well known in the West, it is extremely popular in East Asia, with a history stretching back over 2,000 years.

Mancala*

A family of two-player games with no overt random elements, generally played in Africa and the Middle East. The games are played on a board with a track of pits. The pieces in these pits are moved by "sowing" them around the track, and the game is generally won by capturing all the pieces on the opponent's side.

Monster Chess*

A highly asymmetric variation of chess in which one player has far fewer pieces but can make two moves each turn.

Parcheesi/Pachisi*

A race game for two to four players where moves are determined by dice. Players move around a cross-shaped track and interact via capture and blocking.

Reversi/*Othello**

A two-player game with no overt random elements. The pieces are white on one side and black on the other and when captured are flipped to join the capturer's team. Players alternate placing pieces on the board, with the goal being to have the most pieces at the end.

Senet*

Perhaps the oldest known boardgame, dating back to at least 3500 BC. It is presumed to be a racing game, although all rules used today are educated guesses as to the actual rules.

Shogi (Japanese chess)*

A Japanese two-player game in the same family as chess. One interesting feature of shogi is its "drop" rule, where captured pieces can be placed on the board so as to join the capturer's side.

CARD GAMES, CLASSIC

Asshole/President/Dai Hin Min*

A family of games for four or more players, in which the goal is to get rid of your hand. Each player can only play higher-ranked combinations of cards in the same category as the previously played combination. The last player to play leads to the next trick. These games often give significant advantages to particular seats and disadvantages to others, and players switch seats to more favorable ones if they do well in a hand, leading to a "king of the hill" feel to the game.

Barbu*

A game for four players. Similar to hearts, but the scoring rules vary (in accordance with a standard sequence) every deal—for example, in one round every trick taken might lose points, and in another round only tricks with queens in them carry a penalty.

Blackjack**

A gambling game for one or more players against a house. Each player is dealt as many cards as they want, one at a time after an initial pair, with the goal of getting a sum as close as possible to, but not exceeding, 21. Among gambling games played against the house, blackjack is distinctive in the amount of skill (typically involving card counting and probability calculation) that can be applied. Even more unusually, when played optimally the game is generally in the player's favor—the house relying on the difficulty in playing optimally.

Bridge***

A trick-taking game for two teams of two. Players receive a hand of thirteen cards and bid for the right to name trump based on the number of tricks they can take. One of the distinctive features of bridge is the elaborate bidding systems that have been created, and that are designed to communicate to the partner the nature of the hand and obfuscate the ability of the opponents to bid effectively. Another interesting feature of bridge is that the team that wins the bid plays with one open hand, known as the "dummy," reducing the amount of hidden information (especially for the bidding team, which will know all the cards its partnership has).

Cribbage*

A game for two players. Players alternately deal six cards and each casts off two cards and plays out the remaining four, scoring points for a variety of plays, which include matching the previous play and bringing the total to 15 points. After the hand is played it is scored on its own, and the dealer scores the discarded crib cards. The game involves lots of scoring and so is traditionally played with a pegboard, which easily keeps a running score for all the players.

Gin*

A game for two in which players alternately draw cards from the deck or from the opponent's discards in an attempt to make a hand that scores. There are many games for a wide number of different players using the basic gin mechanics, including Mah Jong and *Phase 10*.

Go Fish*

A children's game in which players attempt to get the most sets of four of the same rank. On a turn a player can ask another player for their cards of a particular rank and that player must give them those cards. Any sets of four can be immediately scored. If a player fails to name a card that the chosen opponent has then her turn is over.

Hearts**

A game generally for three to five. All the cards are dealt out and played and captured in tricks. Taking hearts and the queen of spades is bad for your score, but getting them all is called *shooting the moon*, and is very good for your score, which allows for some big comebacks at a risk.

Oh Hell*

A family of trick-taking games for two or more players, in which players receive a hand and a random trump is selected. Each player must bid exactly how many tricks he will take (in contrast to most trick-taking games, where making extra tricks is not penalized). Often the number of cards dealt in each hand varies.

Old Maid*

A children's game. The deck is stripped of three of the four queens, dealt out, and players take turns drawing cards from their neighbor's hands. Whenever a player has a pair the cards are discarded. Since the queen has no mate, it will be in the game until all other cards are discarded. At that point the player with the queen is the loser.

Pinochle*

A game for two to four, which involves both melding (laying down certain combinations of cards from the hand) and trick taking. Each hand has three stages: bidding, melding, and trick taking.

Poker****

Poker is a family of card games for two or more players. Poker involves players receiving cards and betting. The player with the best five-card hand (based on an established hand ranking) wins the *pot* (all the money bet during the hand). Usually there are several rounds of betting each hand, with players receiving additional cards between rounds.

Often players have more than five cards and choose which of the five cards to use. Some of the cards may be public (everyone can see them), and some may be communal (all players can use them to make their final five-card hand). During a round of betting, each player in turn will either *call* (pay the round's current wager), *raise* (increase the round's current wager), or *fold* (drop out of the hand). Versions of poker include:

Stud Poker. Players have some hidden cards and some public cards. The hand has several rounds of betting where players receive more cards.
Draw Poker. Players receive five cards, have a round of betting, and then can exchange some of their cards for new cards, followed by a final round of betting.
Texas Hold 'Em. The currently most popular form of poker, in which players receive only two secret cards and share five communal cards, which are progressively revealed in rounds of betting.
Dealer's Choice. Each round, the deal rotates, with the dealer choosing which poker variant to play for that round.

Skitgubbe*
A game for three to five players. The object of the game is to avoid being the *goat*: the last person to get rid of his cards. The game is played in stages. In the first stage players accumulate a hand, and in the second they get rid of that hand. The two stages work completely differently from one another.

Solitaire (Patience)**
A large family of single-player card games (or, more generally, any single-player card game). The rules vary widely, as does the skill required to win: some variants are completely mechanical, with no player choice at all, and others are quite complex. Most solitaire games involve laying the cards out in some specified pattern (the *tableau*) and then attempting to clear the laid-out cards according to various allowable pattern-matching rules. Some popular variants include Canfield, Clock, FreeCell, Klondike, Pyramid, and Spider. The term *solitaire* is also sometimes used to refer to Klondike in particular.

Spit*
A speed game for two. The cards are divided equally between the players and players make a tableau of cards that can be played from onto a central pair of cards, a legal play being up or down one rank with suit being irrelevant (this play is essentially a two-player form of solitaire). The play is simultaneous and as fast as the players want. The first player to exhaust her tableau wins the hand and will have fewer cards in the subsequent round. Rounds are played until one player has all the cards, at which point that player loses.

Tarock*
A trick-taking game played with tarot cards. Contrary to common belief, tarot cards were developed for gaming, not divination.

War*

A children's game for two or more players. A deck is divided randomly among the players. Every round, each player simultaneously exposes a single card. The highest exposed card captures the trick, and the game continues with players shuffling all their captured cards into a fresh pile when the old one is exhausted. When a player loses all her cards she is out of the game.

BOARDGAMES, MODERN

Acquire*

An abstract game for three to six players in which players invest in hotel chains that grow and merge over the course of play. The hotel growth is based on the play of tiles from a hand that players are randomly dealt.

Axis & Allies*

A mass-market strategy game that is a global World War II simulation for two to five players. Combat is resolved by dice.

Battleship*

A two-player game of guessing hidden information—the location of the opponent's ships. Each player hides his ships on his own 10×10 grid.

Candy Land**

A children's race game similar to <u>*Chutes and Ladders*</u> using cards instead of dice, and with a delicious candy motif.

Can't Stop** (press-your-luck game)

A board-and-dice game in which players attempt to be the first to advance three of eleven pieces to the end of a track. Each turn a player can roll the dice as many times as desired, but if a bad roll is made all progress for the turn is lost.

Similar games: <u>*Yahtzee*</u>.

Clue**

A three- to six-player game of guessing hidden information with a whodunit theme. Three cards are hidden from all players and the rest are divided between them. Players move around the board using dice, asking questions about the other players' cards until someone guesses the hidden cards' identity.

Cosmic Encounter*

A game for three to five players characterized by each player having a different "alien power" that allows them to break or modify the rules in a prescribed manner. Each turn players attack a random opponent, which makes long-term alliances difficult to maintain. A player that accumulates five foreign bases wins. More than one player can win at a time, leading to shared victories.

*Cranium**

A party boardgame in which players must perform various tasks to advance along the track. Tasks include drawing pictures, doing charades, unscrambling words, and answering trivia. Since many of these tasks appear as the sole tasks of other games, *Cranium* has the feel of a combination of several different games.

*Diplomacy**

A strategic political game for six or seven players (rules exist for fewer players but the game changes radically). The game is about the creation, maintenance, and breaking of alliances in an attempt to take over pre–World War I Europe. Each turn is in three phases: a negotiation period, writing down of orders, and simultaneous execution of all players' orders. Success in the game is only possible through cooperation (and eventual betrayal) with other players.

Dune (Avalon Hill boardgame)*

A strategy boardgame based on Frank Herbert's series of *Dune* science fiction books. Players represent one of the powerful factions from the Dune universe and attempt to control the resources of a fictional planet. A notable feature of the game is a complex set of victory conditions that can allow groups of players to share a win in various ways.

*The Game of Life**

A race game for two or more players played on a spiral track, with movement being determined by a die roll. There are squares with penalties and squares with rewards. Not to be confused with the abstract game Life.

*Kingmaker***

A strategy simulation for two to seven players set during the War of the Roses. Each player builds and controls a faction of nobles and attempts to eliminate the other players' factions.

(Reiner Knizia's) *Lord of the Rings**

A cooperative game for two to five players. Players as a group advance through several scenarios corresponding to situations in the books. Players win or lose as a group. A later expansion puts one player in the role of Sauron, who plays against all the other players.

*Mastermind**

A two-person game of deduction. One player secretly chooses four pegs of different colors. The other tries to guess the color combination in the fewest guesses possible, while being told after each guess the number of pegs that are correct.

*Monopoly****

A family game for two or more players in which players move around a circular track, accumulating property and paying penalties to other players when landing on their property. The goal is to bankrupt your opponents.

*Pandemic**

A cooperative game for two to four players. Four diseases have broken out and the players represent specialists attempting to discover cures before too much damage is done. Players win or lose as a team.

*Pictionary***

A party game for two to four teams in which the goal is to communicate words to teammates using only drawing. It is a race game, in which teams advance by rolling a die after successfully communicating a word.

Pinko Pallino (*Quoridor*)*

An abstract strategy game for two players with no overt random elements. Players attempt to be the first to move their pawn to the opposite side of the board while placing walls to block the pawns' progress (walls block both pawns, but players try to place them so as to cause more problems for their opponent's pawn than for their own). *Quoridor* is a slightly different version of the game for two to four players.

*Risk***

A dice-based global conquest strategy game for two to six players. Broadly similar to *Axis & Allies* but more abstract.

*RoboRally**

A boardgame for two to eight players with a comical robot theme. The robots race across the board, avoiding various obstacles while frequently shooting at or otherwise interfering with each other. Occasionally a robot can find an "option"—piece of special equipment—that gives it additional new powers.

*Scrabble***

A game for two to four players in which players create words from hands of random letter tiles on a board in a crossword fashion.

Settlers of Catan (European-style boardgame)**

A game of resource accumulation and building with a medieval motif, for two to four players. Like many European boardgames, it has a light theme (rather than being a detailed simulation), considerable random elements, and victory points that are different from the resources one uses to make in-game actions. It differs from many European boardgames in that it has a random board setup and multiple paths to victory.

Similar games: *Agricola, Carcassonne, Puerto Rico, Tigris and Euphrates.*

Stratego*

A boardgame with two-sided pieces. Each player sets up his pieces with the blank side facing his opponent. The true nature of a piece is only revealed when an enemy piece tries to capture it; at that point values are compared to see which piece wins the battle.

(Rise and Decline of the) Third Reich (hex-based wargame)**

A strategic hex-map-based World War II simulation wargame. Combat is resolved by dice and table lookup (the so-called combat results table). Games in this genre tend to have extremely long and complex rules.

Similar games: *PanzerBlitz, Squad Leader, Tactics II.*

Titan*

A fantasy-themed strategy game in which players muster and battle armies of creatures. Each battle takes place on a tactical map that is distinct from the strategic map. Strategic movement and combat are resolved with dice.

Trivial Pursuit**

A party trivia race game for two to six sides. Sides advance by answering questions correctly. There are many different versions of the game that focus on different areas of knowledge.

Trouble*

A boardgame similar to <u>*Parcheesi*</u>, notable for its "Pop-o-matic" dice roller. Rather than rolling dice in the normal fashion, players press a transparent bubble on the board that contains the dice; on release, the bubble pops back up, rolling the dice automatically.

OTHER NONDIGITAL GAMES, MODERN

Apples to Apples*

A party game for three or more players. A rotating moderator exposes an adjective card and each player secretly picks a noun card from her hand that she believes the moderator will choose as most representative of that adjective.

Dungeons & Dragons* (paper role-playing game, RPG)**

A cooperative fantasy role-playing game, with a referee (the Dungeon Master) that handles hidden information and rules adjudication. The first paper-based role-playing game. In role-playing games, each player plays a single character with specialized attributes and abilities, and gains more power and equipment (enabling her to face greater challenges) as the game progresses. Computer RPGs (both single-player and massively multiplayer) evolved from paper RPGs, but are different in many ways, primarily due to the differences in having a computer adjudicating the game rather than a human being.

Similar games: *Vampire: The Masquerade, GURPS, Traveller, Champions, Shadowrun.*

Eleusis*

A card game in which one player making up the rules is part of the game. One player creates the rules without telling the others, and then the other players must attempt to guess them based only on being told that various attempted actions are legal or illegal.

Similar games: Mao, *Zendo (Icehouse), Fluxx,* <u>Calvinball</u>.

Magic: The Gathering* (trading card game/collectable card game)**

A fantasy card game generally for two players, and the first trading card game. Trading card games are characterized by players assembling their own decks of cards and competing with them against their opponents. There are different rules on how a player may construct a deck, corresponding to different play formats, some of which are

Constructed Players may use any cards they own that are in a predefined subset of cards (e.g., all cards printed in the last two years).
Sealed Players choose a subset from a small number of randomized cards (e.g., each player receives five packs of fifteen random cards each).
Draft Players draft cards from a small common pool (e.g., all cards found in eight packs of fifteen random cards each).

Similar games: *Pokémon* trading card game, *Digimon* card game, *Yu-gi-oh.*

Nuclear War* (card game)

A game for two to six players in which players combine warhead cards with booster cards to deliver damage to opponents of their choice. Fast paced and humorous.

Uno**

A card game with mechanics similar to the classic card game Crazy Eights. Players attempt to play all their cards, but the only legal plays are playing the same rank or suit as the preceding card. *Uno* adds many special cards to liven things up, which do things like reverse the direction of play or skip players.

*Warhammer 40K*** (miniatures game, minis game)

A tactical miniatures wargame for two or more players set in a futuristic fantasy world. In a wargame of this nature there are no spaces on a board—units move a measured physical distance that is determined by the unit, its condition, and the terrain it is moving over. Similarly, when units attack one another the physical distance between them is measured to determine the range. An important part of the game for many players is the collection and elaborate painting of the miniatures.

Similar games: *Chainmail*, *Warhammer Fantasy Battles*, countless historical rulesets (Napoleonics, Roman, U.S. Civil War, etc.).

*Yahtzee***

A dice game for two or more players in which players are scored based on specific die combinations. Each turn a player is allowed to reroll some dice up to two times.

ABSTRACT GAMES

Also see the list "'Toy' Games Created for the Text" below, and the various example games discussed in appendixes A and B above.

Dots & Boxes***

A game for two played with pencil and paper on a grid of dots. Each turn a player connects two adjacent dots. If that completes a square, the player scores that square and takes another turn. At the end of the game the player who has scored the most squares wins.

(Conway's) Life**

This is sometimes described as a game for zero players. A rectangular array has some cells that are alive and others that are not. Each generation a cell will become alive or dead according to a simple set of rules. The behavior of the cells can be quite complex considering how simple the starting rules are. Not to be confused with the modern boardgame *The Game of Life*.

Nim****

The game starts with several piles of chips. Each player's turn consists of taking as many chips as he wants from a single pile. The player who takes the last chip wins (or, depending on the rules used, loses—the two versions turn out to be more or less equivalent). The game is essentially impossible to decipher for a new player until the last few steps, but is completely solved for the expert. All moves except the exactly correct one are essentially equivalent, so a beginner has no better or worse move, and is effectively playing randomly until close to the end of the game.

Rock-Paper-Scissors****

A simple two-player game played using hand shapes. Each player simultaneously chooses one of three options: rock (fist), paper (flat hand), or scissors (two fingers held out). Rock beats scissors, scissors beats paper, and paper beats rock. If the players choose the same option the game is a draw (and is typically immediately replayed).

Tic-Tac-Toe (Noughts and Crosses)****

A two-player game played on a 3 × 3 grid. Players alternate taking one of the nine cells. The winner is whoever first captures three cells in a row. Tic-tac-toe is typically regarded as a child's game, because it is easy to win or force a draw as the first player.

DIGITAL GAMES (COMPUTER, CONSOLE, HANDHELD, ARCADE)

Age of Empires*

A real-time strategy game with a flavor of historical empire building and warring. Players collect resources, build bases and an army, advance in technology from Stone Age to Iron Age, and battle their opponents. Originally players could play nine different cultures, and many more were introduced with expansions and sequels.

Asteroids*

An arcade game from the late 1970s in which a player uses a spaceship to shoot at a set of asteroids moving around the screen. Each time an asteroid is shot it is replaced with two smaller asteroids, except for the smallest asteroids, which disappear. A player progresses through levels by destroying all the asteroids and surviving the occasional alien ships.

Bejeweled*

A single-player game in which the player swaps pairs of jewels in an 8 × 8 grid, attempting to line up jewels of the same color.

Civilization**

A turn-based strategy game of exploration, development, and conquest set over the course of human history—beginning in the Stone Age all the way through the exploration of Alpha Centauri. Randomized setup helps makes the game highly replayable.

Civilization has multiplayer versions, but it's mostly played as a single-player game, in large part because multiplayer play can involve a great deal of downtime.

*Command & Conquer**
A real-time strategy game set in an alternate history.

*Counter-Strike**
This was originally a mod (game variant) for *Half-Life*, and is strictly a team game with one side being terrorists and the other counterterrorists. Unlike most multiplayer first-person shooters, if a player is killed he does not respawn. Instead, he must watch his team struggle on without him. Each game is quite short, so the time you spend watching is not too onerous.

*Crystal Quest**
A single-player computer game in which a player attempts to collect crystals while being harassed by enemies. If all crystals are collected the player moves on to the next level.

*Dance Dance Revolution**
A series of arcade and console games using a special controller: a pad placed on the floor. Players step on the pad in various locations, as directed by the screen instructions and in time with the music.

*Dark Age of Camelot**
A fantasy-themed massively multiplayer online role-playing game. *Dark Age of Camelot* was distinctive for its large-scale player-versus-player combat.

*Defense of the Ancients**
A mod (game variant) built from the *Warcraft III* engine. The game is for two teams of five, with each player controlling only one unit. The object is for each team to wipe out its opponents' base. During the game, players will go up levels and purchase new equipment while fighting the opponents and their computer-controlled units. One of the attractions of the game is the wide variety of heroes each player can control, each with mechanically distinct spells and skills. Another is the packaging of the leveling-up RPG process into a thirty- to sixty-minute game (RPGs typically take tens or hundreds of hours to complete).

*Diablo/Diablo II****
A computer action role-playing game. Players choose from several character classes and fight monsters, collect loot, and become more powerful. Action role-playing games involve some degree of coordination and fast button clicking.

*Donkey Kong***

One of the first examples of a platformer—a single-player game where the player must navigate a map, jumping, climbing, and avoiding obstacles. It is also one of the first (if not the first) example of a complete narrative in an arcade game, complete with cut scenes. The characters and world have been developed over time to be one of the most popular computer game franchises today—Mario.

*Dune II**

A real-time strategy game that became the design template for real-time strategy games that followed. Other RTS-style games existed before *Dune II*, but *Dune II* marked the point where the RTS game was recognized as a genre and the design standards were all in place—collecting resources, building bases and technology, and ultimately battling the opponents' units and bases.

*Everquest***

A fantasy-themed massively multiplayer online role-playing game. Players have characters in a variety of races and specialties that fight against computer-generated monsters (and sometimes other characters). Over time players gain power and resources, which allows them to handle larger challenges.

Final Fantasy** (computer role-playing game, or RPG)

A series of computer role-playing games known for their elaborate stories. In computer role-playing games, players have one or more characters in a variety of races and specialties that fight against computer-generated monsters. Over time characters gain power and resources, which allows the player to handle larger challenges. In many computer role-playing games the story is secondary to the mechanical trappings of a role-playing game—such as combat and equipment choice—but not in the *Final Fantasy* games.

Similar games: *Baldur's Gate, Fallout, Knights of the Old Republic.*

*Gauntlet**

A cooperative arcade game for one to four players with a fantasy RPG theme. Each player maneuvered a single character (Warrior, Wizard, Valkyrie, or Elf) through a maze, fighting monsters and grabbing treasure and useful items.

*Guitar Hero**

A console game with a special controller: a guitar-shaped object with buttons on the guitar's neck. Players press the buttons and "strum" the guitar in a manner reminiscent of playing a real guitar, in time with music and images played on-screen.

Similar games: *Rock Band.*

*Half-Life***
A first-person shooter that was highly acclaimed for its integration of story into the solo game.

*Ico**
A third-person action game—that is, a game where you see your own character over the shoulder. The gameplay includes both solving puzzles and fighting enemies. *Ico* had a story that was acclaimed for its elegant integration into the gameplay.

*Impossible Creatures**
A real-time strategy game with a mad scientist theme, in which players create their own unique units by combining animals (unlike a normal RTS game, where the unit types are fixed).

*Karate Champ**
An early arcade fighting game; widely seen as the precursor to later fighting games such as *Street Fighter*.

King Kong: see under Peter Jackson's King Kong

*Lunar Lander** (physics game)
An arcade game from 1979 in which a player attempts to land a lunar module on the moon. The player has control of the direction and of the thrust and must touch down on a flat surface with a low velocity. Since then, a number of other games revolving around physics simulations, albeit more complex ones, have been created, mostly by independent game designers.

Similar games: *Armadillo Run, Bridge Builder, Tower of Goo, Triptych, Crayon Physics.*

*Mario Kart****
A computer racing game with a Mario theme. *Mario Kart* is distinctive for the wacky power-ups that spawn during the course of play, allowing for players who are behind to make spectacular comebacks.

*Mario Party**
A party game in the Mario franchise. Players move on a board (as in a traditional boardgame, using dice) with the goal of collecting stars and coins. After all players have moved, there is a random minigame in which players compete, and that can reward players with coins or cost them coins. The minigames are sometimes cooperative, sometimes free-for-all, and sometimes played in teams.

Masters of Orion II*

A turn-based strategy game of exploration, development, and conquest set in space among several alien races. The randomized setup helps make this game highly replayable.

Minesweeper*

A single-player computer game in which a grid is randomly seeded with hidden mines. The player must reveal all the mines without detonating any of them.

MUDs (Multiple-User Dungeons)*

An early form of online multiplayer game, often text-based. MUDs were the forerunners of MMORPGs (and indeed the first MMOs were sometimes referred to as "graphical MUDs").

Myst** **(puzzle-solving game)**

A game in which the player explores and solves puzzles that are naturally integrated into the world.

Similar games: Adventure (Colossal Cave Adventure), *The Longest Journey*, *The Secret of Monkey Island*, *Zork*.

Myth*

A real-time strategy game distinct for its lack of in-game resource gathering and base and technology building. It is, instead, entirely about the battle between the units that each side brings to the fight. For this reason the *Myth* series is sometimes referred to as a real-time tactics game (the games in the *Total War* series are similar in this respect).

Pac-Man*

An arcade game where the player navigates a puck-shaped character through a maze, eating "dots" that are spread throughout the maze and avoiding ghosts that will destroy the player on contact. Certain dots when eaten briefly reverse the roles of hunter and hunted, allowing the player temporarily to destroy the ghosts on contact.

Peter Jackson's King Kong*

The adventure fighting game based on Peter Jackson's movie *King Kong*. The game was somewhat unusual in having a minimalist user interface.

Pokémon*

A handheld game that spawned a whole series of other games and merchandise. In the original game, the player controlled a character in an RPG world. Unusually, the player did not fight and level up with that character, but instead collected creatures (called Pokémon) and "trained" them (leveled them up) to fight for him.

Progress Quest*

A satirical computer role-playing game in which all decision making has been removed and a player's character plays automatically. A player simply watches as her character fights monsters, loots enemies, levels up, and even completes quests.

Quake** **(first-person shooter, or FPS)**

In first-person shooters players move around a virtual world in first person—that is, the screen shows you the view you would see if you were in the world yourself, rather than showing you a view that includes your character. Typically players can equip a number of different weapons, mostly projectile weapons. They seek to destroy other players or computer-generated monsters in a solo or cooperative campaign.

Similar games: *Doom*, *Half-Life*, *Halo*, *Wolfenstein 3D*.

Q*Bert*

A single-player game in which a player hops around a lattice of cubes avoiding enemies. When a cube is visited the color of the cube changes, and the next level is reached when the entire lattice is changed to a particular color.

Rogue/NetHack/Angband**

Among the very earliest computer role-playing games. They are all single-player, and the graphics were originally ASCII based—all elements of the game world, from the map to the monsters to the characters and treasure were all letters and symbols (nowadays there are often overlays for the games that substitute simple graphics for the ASCII characters). These games tend to be highly replayable, since the dungeons are randomly generated.

Shadow of the Colossus*

A third-person action game—that is, a game where you see your own character over the shoulder. *Shadow of the Colossus* featured only boss fights—fights against the game's gigantic colossi—rather than the mix of boss fights and fights against many smaller enemies common to most such games.

Sid Meier's Alpha Centauri*

A turn-based strategy game very similar to *Civilization* in game mechanics, but with a far-future science fiction theme instead of a historical theme.

SimCity*

A game in which the player manages a virtual city, zoning various areas, building infrastructure and public buildings, setting tax rates, and the like. Although there were also scenarios with specific objectives, SimCity was noted for its "sandbox" play: gameplay modes with no specified objectives, where the player could instead simply try different gameplay actions and observe the consequences.

Similar games: *The Sims*, *Roller Coaster Tycoon*.

The Sims*

A sandbox-style game in the manner of *SimCity*. Players had partial control of a small number of simulated humans, called sims, who had basic needs (Hunger, Hygiene, Comfort, etc.) that could be fulfilled by means of various objects and people in their environment. The player would set up the environment and instruct/encourage her sims to do things to fulfill their needs. *The Sims* is the best-selling PC game of all time, and has spawned numerous sequels.

Starcraft** **(real-time strategy, or RTS)**

A real-time strategy PC game for two to eight. Players collect resources, build bases, and have their armies fight other players' armies and bases. The game is won by destroying all opposing base buildings. *Starcraft* has a science fiction theme and three races that can be played, each of which has distinct game mechanics.

Similar games: *Age of Empires*, *Command and Conquer*, *Dune II*, *Impossible Creatures*, *Total Annihilation*, *Warcraft I*, *II*, and *III*.

Street Fighter**

An arcade fighting game. In a fighting game, players choose a character that has its own set of combat moves, strengths, and weaknesses and battle it against another (player-controlled or computer-controlled) character. For beginning players, the combat itself is one of speed and reflex; for expert players, predicting and countering the opponent's moves become increasingly important. Additionally, in many fighting games, characters have secret moves that need to be discovered.

Similar games: *Karate Champ*, *Marvel vs. Capcom*, *Mortal Kombat*, *Tekken*, *Virtua Fighter*.

Super Mario Brothers**

A platform game where players jump, climb, and dodge obstacles and enemies. This is one of the many games in the popular Mario series.

Team Fortress*

A two-sided team shooter, notable for its character classes (Medic, Sniper, Scout, etc.).

*Tetris**

A single-player game in which random shapes are dropping in a grid at a faster and faster rate. The player can rotate each piece as it drops and choose which column it will land in. If a row is completely filled the row disappears. Eliminating rows is necessary for the player to continue playing, because the game is lost when the grid fills up to the top. The player can never win (a feature also seen in many arcade games), but instead tries to get the highest possible score before finally losing.

*Tomb Raider**

A third-person action game—that is, a game where you see your own character over the shoulder. The game includes both solving puzzles and fighting enemies. *Tomb Raider* featured the archeologist adventurer Lara Croft and was the basis for many games and a movie.

*Tribes**

A first-person shooter designed entirely for team play.

Warcraft I, II, and *III***

A series of real-time strategy games that take place in a fantasy world. Players collect resources, build bases and an army, advance in technology, and battle opponents. Multiple races can be played—two in *Warcraft I* and *II*, four in *Warcraft III*. *Warcraft III* is notable for its hero system, which evolved into the very different game *Defense of the Ancients*.

*Wario Ware**

A single-player game in the Mario series that is composed of a series of simple fast minigames. Each minigame takes only a few seconds to play, so the play is fast and frenetic. Quickly understanding how to play the next (randomly selected) minigame is a big part of the overall game.

*World of Warcraft***** (MMO, MMORPG)

A fantasy-themed massively multiplayer online role-playing game. Players have characters in a variety of races and specialties that fight against computer-generated monsters as well as (sometimes) other characters. Over time players gain power and resources, which allow the player to handle larger challenges. There are many "games" within *World of Warcraft*, some cooperative, some competitive, some of short duration, some open-ended.

Similar games: *City of Heroes*, *Dark Age of Camelot*, *Eve Online*, *Everquest*, *Lineage*, *Maple Story*, *Puzzle Pirates*, *Runescape*, *Ultima Online*.

*Zork**

A text-based adventure game in which players could type what their character was going to do and the program would describe the results. Part of the charm (and, for some players, the frustration) was that the words the game understood were not known and had to be discovered by the player.

SPORTS

Auto racing *(Formula 1, NASCAR)**

Similar to footraces, but cars are used instead of feet. There are many different formats and rules. Due to the expense involved, high levels of sponsorship are generally a requirement. Some formats (e.g., stock-car racing) emphasize limits on the kinds of cars that may be used, so that all participants begin with a more or less even chance; other formats (e.g., Formula 1) emphasize custom cars, with each entrant attempting to build a superior car. Auto racing is one of the most popular spectator sports in the world.

Baseball***

A two-sided bat-and-ball team sport where one team plays defense on a large field with nine players on the field while the other team plays offense with one to four players on the field. Teams alternate offense and defense at least nine times during the game. Teams have specialized roles for their players, some of which are supported by the rules.

Basketball****

A team game where two teams compete against each other trying to put the ball through the opponent's hoop on opposite ends of a long court. Each team fields five players at a time. There are restrictions on movement while handling the ball. Teams often have specialized roles for their players, but these roles are not supported by the rules. Games are played for a fixed amount of time and won on points.

Bicycle Racing**

Similar to footraces, but bicycles are used instead of feet. There are many forms of bicycle racing, but due to the speeds involved drafting is much more important than in footraces. Consequently many bicycle races are either team races or *time trials* (individual races where each cyclist races separately against the clock, with times compared at the end). Distances commonly range from 750 meters to hundreds of miles.

Bowling*

An indoor sport in which players roll a heavy ball down a lane, attempting to knock over the pins at the end of the lane. Although bowling is frequently played in teams or leagues, the players do not interact directly, but instead compare scores at the end of a fixed number of rounds.

Boxing*

A one-on-one sport of physical combat using fists covered with gloves. Rules vary, but generally points are awarded for performing strikes on the opponent within certain limitations. Victory can alternatively be achieved by knocking out the opponent, regardless of points scored.

Calvinball*

A fictional sport from the cartoon strip *Calvin & Hobbes*. In Calvinball, rules may be invented spontaneously by the players, but the same rule cannot be used twice.

Darts*

A team or individual game where players attempt accurate throwing of darts into a board with different target zones. There are many rule variants, which detail different objectives on the board.

Fencing*

A one-on-one sport of physical combat using swords. Rules vary, but generally points are awarded for performing strikes on the opponent within certain limitations.

Football (American)***

A team game where two teams compete trying to get the ball across each other's goal line, or through their goalposts, both sets located at opposite ends of a large field from each other. Each team may field only eleven players at a time. At any given moment, one team is in possession of the ball and attempting to advance it, while the other team plays defense. Teams have highly specialized roles (or *positions*) for their players, some of which have special standing under the rules. Games are played for a fixed amount of time and won on points.

Footrace****

A multisided game where individuals attempt to be the fastest to get from the starting line to the finish line by running. Race length varies widely, from sprints of a few dozen yards to marathons of twenty-six miles or even longer.

Golf*

An individual sport played with a set of clubs used to strike a small hard ball across long distances outdoors. The object is to get the ball into a small specified hole in the least number of attempts while avoiding various natural hazards. The game is commonly played in a series of eighteen of these holes.

*Hacky Sack**

Hacky Sack is a trademark for a game more properly known as footbag. Players stand in a circle and cooperate in attempting to keep a small beanbag-like object from touching the ground by kicking it repeatedly up into the air with their feet.

Hockey*

A team game where two teams of six players on skates attempt to put a puck through the opposing team's goal using sticks. Each goal is located at the opposite end of a large field of ice. Teams have specialized roles for the players, one of which in particular (the goalie) is supported by the rules. Games are played for a fixed amount of time and won on points.

HORSE*

A game for two or more players using a standard basketball and hoop. Players attempt to match difficult shots made by the others. Those who miss shots are assigned letters from the word *horse*, losing when they spell out the entire word.

Horse Racing*

Similar to footraces but with horses instead of feet. Horse racing is an ancient sport with a wide range of rules, but it commonly consists of one to two dozen horses running on a circular track. The distances vary widely across the world but are usually between 1/2 mile and 3 miles, with 1 1/4 miles being most common. The sport is inextricably associated with spectation and gambling.

Pool*

A table game involving balls and sticks. The object is to use a stick to strike one ball, thereby striking others and knocking them into pockets. Pool can be an individual or team sport and in some variants is three or more sided.

Similar games: Billiards, Snooker.

Pro Wrestling*

A highly stylized and theatrical form of staged combat based on wrestling. Spectacular violations of the rules (e.g., hitting opponents with folding chairs found near the ring) are a common occurrence, all in the service of heightening the over-the-top drama.

Regatta*

A boat race (compare footrace). Widely varying in rules and can involve oar-, sail-, or motor-powered boats.

Roman Gladiatorial Combat*

A varied series of physical combats, both lethal and nonlethal. There were many different styles of combat falling under this heading. Combats could involve teams or individuals, weapons of many different sorts, and even animals. Primarily fought using slaves and primarily played as a spectator sport with gambling.

Rugby*

A physical team game played on a large field sharing common ancestry with American football. Two teams of fifteen (or, in some versions, thirteen) players attempt to score by moving a ball across their opponent's goal line by running with the ball or kicking it.

Soccer (Football)**

A team game where two teams of eleven players attempt to put a ball through the opposing team's goal. Each goal is located at the opposite end of a large field. For the most part players are only allowed to advance the ball without the use of their hands. Teams have specialized roles for the players, one of which in particular is supported by the rules (the goalie, who can use her hands). Games are played for a fixed amount of time and won on points. Generally considered the most popular sport in the world.

Stickball*

A version of baseball adapted to fit local, generally urban environments. A broom handle or stick is used in place of a bat, and the general rules of baseball are roughly adhered to with exceptions made as needed.

Target Shooting*

A team or individual sport where participants attempt to shoot targets accurately. There are many forms of this sport involving different types of weapons and targets.

Tennis*

A racket sport with two sides of either one or two players each, played on a court with a net and a ball that can bounce. Players hit the ball back and forth across the net. Points are scored when the opponent fails legally to get the ball across the net. Games are played until a certain score is reached by one player or team, which is then the winner.

Ultimate/Ultimate Frisbee[11]*
A team sport roughly similar to football or soccer, but where a Frisbee is used instead of a ball.

Wrestling*
A one-on-one sport of physical combat. Rules vary greatly, but generally points are awarded for performing maneuvers on the opponent. Maneuvers may involve throwing, tripping, or immobilizing the opponent, with striking being illegal.

"TOY" GAMES CREATED FOR THE TEXT

Listed here are references to model games created specifically as examples for the text. In general, they are more thought experiments than games of the sort one would actually play for fun.

Balloon-Popping Game (p. 55)
Chip-Taking Chess (p. 48)
Chip-Taking Game (p. 48)
Die-Rolling Chess (p. 152)
Guess the Digit (of Pi) (p. 29–30)
Money in the Bag (p. 31)
Money on the Table (p. 31)
Resource Commitment Game (p. 104)
Truel (p. 50–51)
Voting Game (p. 50)

MISCELLANEOUS

Charades*
A common party game where teams compete at guessing a word or phrase, with clues given solely through pantomime performed by one participant (verbal or written cues are forbidden).

Chocolate Russian Roulette*
A game in which a number of identical-appearing candies, one of which has something nasty inside, are presented to the players. Each player eats one. The object is to avoid eating the bad-tasting one.

11. Although it's commonly called "Ultimate Frisbee," the official name for the sport is "Ultimate," because "Frisbee" is a trademark of the Wham-O toy company.

Crossword Puzzles*

An individual puzzle where the player attempts to fill in a grid of blank boxes with words derived from information given in the form of indirect clue phrases.

Drawing Straws*

A traditional method for choosing a single individual from a group, for the purpose of performing an unpleasant task. A number of long thin objects (e.g., pieces of straw), all of the same length except for one shorter object, would be held in someone's fist, concealing their length. Each person would take an object; the person who "drew the short straw" was the loser.

Drinking Games*

A large and varied family of games that revolve around drinking alcohol. Typically some task is presented to the players in turn, and failure requires a player to drink.

Fantasy Sports (Rotisserie)*

Multiplayer games in which each player takes on the role of manager for a sports team. A player selects the players for his team from a list, and games are resolved automatically according to some statistical rules (typically using data from real-world sports matches involving the selected players). Most often the fantasy sport is played in a season paralleling the real-world sports season. Originally a somewhat esoteric paper-and-pencil pursuit, fantasy sports have reached enormous levels of popularity online.

Fear Factor*

A television game show in which contests are challenged to do things that many people would find frightening or repulsive (eating insects, walking a tightrope, etc.).

Ghost*

A word game for two or more players. One player chooses the first letter. Each player in turn chooses another letter until a player forms a word and loses, or forms a string of letters from which no word can be made and is challenged (losing if she cannot give a word beginning with that string).

Killer/Assassin*

A live-action game for many players usually played over the course of days or weeks. Each player is given a target that she must eliminate from the game, typically by shooting him with a squirt gun or similar toy weapon. A player may only shoot her target or shoot in self-defense. If a player knocks another player out of the game she inherits her victim's target. The winner is the last player remaining.

Pari-mutuel Betting*

A form of betting commonly used for sports such as horse racing. All bets are pooled, and payouts are determined by how much was bet on each racer. In other words, the odds are not fixed at the beginning, but are determined by how the bets are placed—the fewer people who bet on a given racer, the more that racer will pay out. It can be thought of as a game that each bettor plays against all the other bettors.

Qualifier*

A tournament or race where the main purpose is not to pick a single winner, but rather to pick a subgroup of players who will then go on to another tournament or race. Participants typically only care about whether they make it into this subgroup (who can be thought of as all equally "winning"), not how they place overall.

Raindrop Races*

A "zero-player game": two raindrops roll down a windowpane. The first to reach the bottom is declared the winner by the onlooker(s).

Rating Systems**

If a game has an organization devoted to furthering its play, that organization may attempt to maintain *ratings* for the game: a system of numerical values, one for each player (or team), that represent that player's skill at the game.

The simplest form of rating system is *point accumulation*: each player receives a certain number of points for a win (and sometimes some smaller number for a loss), and the point totals accumulate. The disadvantage of such a system is that high player ratings will tend to be due as much or more to frequency of play as to player skill.

More complex rating systems involve giving players points when they win, but subtracting points when they lose. Such systems will produce more accurate measures of player skill, but the occasional loss of rating points may discourage some players. The best-known such rating system is the *Elo system*, invented by Arpad Elo for rating chess players. In the Elo system, at the end of a match the winning player adds to her rating the same number of points that the losing player subtracts from his. Additionally, this point amount is larger or smaller based on the expected outcome of the matchup: beating a highly rated opponent will gain a player more points than beating a low-ranked opponent. The Elo system is designed to be statistically predictive: given any two player ratings, one may calculate the odds that the first player will beat the second.

Slot Machines*

Single-player gambling games in which a player puts money into a machine, pulls a lever or pushes a button, and several random symbols are generated. Different combinations of symbols have different payouts. Usually a player can choose to play different amounts in the same machine, and the larger amounts have a larger payout and may open more combinations for payout. Some slot machines may be *progressive*: having larger and larger payouts the more they are played without a payout, until finally someone wins.

*Survivor***

A television reality game show for sixteen to twenty players with a wilderness survival theme, in which contestants undergo a series of challenges. After each round of challenges, one contestant is voted out of the game ("voted off the island"). Once there are two contestants left, the vote is decided by previously eliminated players. The object is to be the last person left.

Tournament Types*

For almost any game, one can hold a *tournament*: a series of matches of that game, with one player (or team) declared the overall winner at the end. Individual matches may be assigned by random pairings, on the basis of preexisting rankings (also called *seedings*), or by some other system. There are many different styles, or *formats*, of tournaments, among them:

Single elimination As soon as a player loses a match, he is out of the tournament. The last player left is the overall winner.
Double elimination As soon as a player loses two matches, she is out of the tournament. The last player left is the overall winner.
Round robin All players play all others, with the player having the best record being declared the winner (ties are broken by looking at the matchup results of the tying players). Round robin tournaments work best with a small number of players.
Swiss After each round of matchups, players with the same record play each other (e.g., players who have won four and lost one are matched against other 4–1 players). The player(s) with the best overall record is/are declared the winner(s). Depending on the details, Swiss may be equivalent to single or double elimination in terms of determining the overall winner.

Many tournaments are organized in a hybrid form—for example, Swiss or round robin to determine a subset of eight, followed by single elimination among the top eight. For some games, tournaments may happen over the course of one or two days; for other games (particularly team sports), a tournament may take place over the course of months (a *season*).

TV Game Shows*

A broad category of games designed specifically for spectation through television broadcast. Contests can be individual or team-based, and contestants compete publicly for prizes through a wide variety of physical and mental means. Particularly common are trivia contests packaged in varying rule sets and themes.

Twenty Questions*

One player thinks of something and the others try to guess what it is using twenty yes-or-no questions.

Werewolf (Mafia)*

A game for a large group, typically eight or more. The two teams—werewolves and townsfolk—are randomly determined ahead of time, with each player knowing only his own designation. Every turn, the werewolves secretly choose a townsfolk to kill, and then all the players (werewolves and townsfolk together) decide on one player to kill. Killed players' identities are revealed. The game ends when either all the werewolves or all the townsfolk are eliminated. Play revolves around the townsfolk figuring out who the werewolves are, with the werewolves trying to conceal their identity. A moderator is required (for coordinating the secret decisions), and generally there are some players with special powers as well. Mafia is a version of the game with the same rules but with an organized crime motif.

Bibliography

Websites

The study of games in general, and computer games in particular, is a rapidly evolving field. Thus much of the most current information is to be found on the Internet. Some general sites worth looking at include:

www.boardgamegeek.com (for boardgames)
www.gamasutra.com (for computer games)

A few individual designer blogs:

www.eldergame.com (Eric Heimburg and Sandra Powers, MMOs)
www.raphkoster.com (Raph Koster)
www.zenofdesign.com (Damion Schubert)
www.sirlin.net (David Sirlin, fighting games and game balance)

Of course, the blog world changes all the time, and doing a search for "game design blog" is probably the best way to see what's current.

Books and Articles

Albert, Michael H., and Richard J. Nowakowski, eds. *Games of No Chance 3*. Mathematical Sciences Research Institute Publications 56. Cambridge: Cambridge University Press, 2009.

Albert, Michael H., Richard J. Nowakowski, and David Wolfe. *Lessons in Play: An Introduction to Combinatorial Game Theory*. Wellesley, MA: A K Peters, 2007.

Alexander, Christopher. *Notes on the Synthesis of Form*. Cambridge, MA: Harvard University Press, 1964.

Avedon, Elliott M., and Brian Sutton-Smith. *The Study of Games*. New York: Wiley, 1971.

Bell, R. C. *Board and Table Games from Many Civilizations*. New York: Dover, [1960] 1979.

Berlekamp, Elwyn. *The Dots and Boxes Game: Sophisticated Child's Play*. Wellesley, MA: A K Peters, 2000.

Berlekamp, Elwyn R., John H. Conway, and Richard K. Guy. *Winning Ways for Your Mathematical Plays*. 2nd ed. 4 vols. Wellesley, MA: A K Peters, 2001.

Berlekamp, Elwyn, and David Wolfe. *Mathematical Go: Chilling Gets the Last Point*. Wellesley, MA: A K Peters, 1994.

Bewersdorff, Jörg. *Luck, Logic, and White Lies: The Mathematics of Games*. Wellesley, MA: A K Peters, 2005.

Binmore, Ken. *Game Theory: A Very Short Introduction*. Oxford: Oxford University Press, 2007.

Caillois, Roger. *Man, Play, and Games*. Urbana: University of Illinois Press, [1958] 2001.

Cassell, Justine, and Henry Jenkins, eds. *From Barbie to Mortal Kombat: Gender and Computer Games*. Cambridge, MA: MIT Press, 1998.

Conway, John H. *On Numbers and Games*. 2nd ed. Wellesley, MA: A K Peters, 2000.

Crawford, Chris. *The Art of Computer Game Design*. Berkeley: Osborne/McGraw Hill, 1984. http://www.vancouver.wsu.edu/fac/peabody/game-book/Coverpage.html.

Crawford, Chris. *On Game Design*. Indianapolis: New Riders, 2003.

Crawford, Chris. *On Interactive Storytelling*. Indianapolis: New Riders, 2004.

Eatwell, John, Murray Milgate, and Peter Newman, eds. *The New Palgrave Game Theory*. New York: Norton, 1989.

Elo, Arpad E. *The Rating of Chess Players Past and Present*. Bronx, NY: Ishi Press International, [1978] 2008.

Friedman, David D. *Law's Order: What Economics Has to Do with Law and Why It Matters*. Princeton, NJ: Princeton University Press, 2000.

Fudenberg, Drew, and Jean Tirole. *Game Theory*. Cambridge, MA: MIT Press, 1991.

Garfield, Richard. Getting lucky. *Game Developer* 13 (10) (2006): 11–19.

Gibbons, Robert. *Game Theory for Applied Economists*. Princeton, NJ: Princeton University Press, 1992.

Gilovich, Thomas, Robert Vallone, and Amos Tversky. The hot hand in basketball: On the misperception of random sequences. *Cognitive Psychology* 17 (1985): 295–314.

Gutschera, Robert. Costing and balancing game objects. White paper for talk "Magic Lessons: Designing and Balancing Game Objects," given at Game Developers Conference, March 5–9, San Francisco. 2007. http://www.gdcvault.com/play/519.

Huizinga, Johan. *Homo Ludens: A Study of the Play Element in Culture*. Boston: Beacon Press, 1950.

Jacoby, Oswald, and John R. Crawford. *The Backgammon Book*. New York: Bantam Books, 1970.

Johnson, Steven. *Everything Bad Is Good for You*. New York: Riverhead Books, 2005.

Kahneman, Daniel, Paul Slovic, and Amos Tversky, eds. *Judgment under Uncertainty: Heuristics and Biases*. Cambridge: Cambridge University Press, 1982.

Knuth, Donald E. *The Art of Computer Programming*. 2nd ed. 3 vols. Reading, MA: Addison-Wesley, 1981.

Knuth, Donald E. *Surreal Numbers*. Reading, MA: Addison-Wesley, 1974.

Kreps, David M. *Game Theory and Economic Modelling*. Oxford: Oxford University Press, 1990.

Kushner, David. *Jonny Magic and the Cardshark Kids: How a Gang of Geeks Beat the Odds and Stormed Las Vegas*. New York: Random House, 2005.

Kushner, David. *Masters of Doom*. New York: Random House, 2003.

Lakoff, George. *Women, Fire, and Dangerous Things: What Categories Reveal about the Mind*. Chicago: University of Chicago Press, 1987.

Levine, David. *Do Baseball Players Have Hot Streaks?* 2007. http://www.retrosheet.org/Research/LevineD/HotStreaks.pdf.

Milne, A. A. *When We Were Very Young*. New York: Dutton, 1924.

Murray, H. J. R. *A History of Board-Games Other Than Chess*. Oxford: Oxford University Press, 1951.

Norvig, Peter. *Paradigms of Artificial Intelligence Programming: Case Studies in Common Lisp*. San Francisco: Morgan Kaufmann, 1992.

Nowakowski, Richard J., ed. *Games of No Chance*. Mathematical Sciences Research Institute Publications 29. Cambridge: Cambridge University Press, 1998.

Nowakowski, Richard J., ed. *More Games of No Chance*. Mathematical Sciences Research Institute Publications 42. Cambridge: Cambridge University Press, 2002.

Ohira, Shuzo. *Appreciating Famous Games*. Tokyo: Ishi Press, 1977.

Orbanes, Philip E. *The Game Makers: The Story of Parker Brothers from Tiddledy Winks to Trivial Pursuit*. Boston: Harvard Business School Publishing, 2004.

Parlett, David. *A History of Card Games*. Oxford: Oxford University Press, 1991.

Parlett, David. *The Oxford History of Board Games*. Oxford: Oxford University Press, 1999.

Power, John. *Invincible: The Games of Shusaku*. Tokyo: Kiseido, 1982.

Rollings, Andrew, and Dave Morris. *Game Architecture and Design: A New Edition*. Indianapolis: New Riders, 2004.

Salen, Katie, and Eric Zimmerman, eds. *The Game Design Reader: A Rules of Play Anthology*. Cambridge, MA: MIT Press, 2006.

Salen, Katie, and Eric Zimmerman. *Rules of Play: Game Design Fundamentals*. Cambridge, MA: MIT Press, 2004.

Schell, Jesse. *The Art of Game Design: A Book of Lenses*. Morgan Kaufmann, 2008.

Smith, John Maynard. *Evolution and the Theory of Games*. Cambridge: Cambridge University Press, 1982.

Von Neumann, John, and Oskar Morgenstern. *Theory of Games and Economic Behavior*. Princeton, NJ: Princeton University Press, 1944.

Wittgenstein, Ludwig. *The Blue and Brown Books*. New York: Harper and Row, 1958.

Wittgenstein, Ludwig. *Philosophical Investigations*. Malden, MA: Blackwell, [1953] 2001.

Wolf, Mark J. P., and Bernard Perron, eds. *The Video Game Theory Reader*. New York: Routledge, 2003.

Index